LOST WORLDS

For Isha
and a world of new possibilities

Anthem South Asian Studies
Series Editor: Crispin Bates

LOST WORLDS

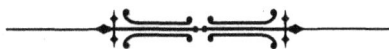

Indian Labour
and its Forgotten Histories

CHITRA JOSHI

Anthem Press

Anthem Press
An imprint of Wimbledon Publishing Company
75-76 Blackfriars Road, London SE1 8HA
or
PO Box 9779, London SW19 7QA
www .anthempress.com

This edition first published by Anthem Press 2005

British Library Cataloguing in Publication Data
A catalogue record for this book is available from the British Library .

Library of Congress Cataloging in Publication Data
A catalog record for this book has been requested.

1 3 5 7 9 10 8 6 4 2

ISBN 1 84331 128 3 (Hbk)
ISBN 1 84331 129 1 (Pbk)

Typeset by Footprint Labs Ltd, London
www .footprintlabs.com

Printed in India

Contents

Part II

Part III

List of Figures

Acknowledgements

—⊹⇌·⇌⊹—

Over the years many friends and institutions have been important to the making of this book. At the Centre for Historical Studies (CHS) in Jawaharlal Nehru University (JNU), Sabyasachi Bhattacharya, who supervised my initial research into labour history, has always been a demanding critic and continues to be a source of support. The interest shown by Bipan Chandra, Satish Saberwal and Ravinder Kumar, and the encouragement from P.C. Joshi and K. Damodaran in my initial years of research, were important for me.

This work owes a lot to the times in which my initial engagement with labour history began. Not only were the worlds of labour different but the vibrant mid-1970s in JNU were times when working class history was the subject of discussion, inside and outside the classroom. Rana (Sen), among others those days, made labour history meaningful. In subsequent years friends have helped to keep my project going. Prabhu commented on countless drafts, helped untangle knots and pulled the manuscript through its despairing moments. Interacting with Bappa, Dilip, Indu, Janaki, Rana and Marcel in the Association of Indian Labour Historians made writing labour history a more exciting collective enterprise. Dipesh Chakrabarty, Robi Chatterjee, Sumit Sarkar and Tanika Sarkar, and Sumit Guha have read and offered valuable comments on earlier fragments of my work.

Vrinda and Jugal willingly took over the burden of helping with the graphs and illustrations. Others provided stimulus and support: Anomita, Ben, Bhaity, Madhu, Nilofer, Pankaj, Pragati, Radha, Radhika, Rajeev, Rashmi, Ravi, Shalini, Sikha, Shobha, Sunita, Suvritta, Tani, Vasudha, Virginie. My family in Lucknow made my research trips always pleasurable, and my father, who took a keen interest in my work, made access to government record rooms an easier process.

Isha's anxieties and curiosity about my manuscript were more important than she imagines. Mukul opened up possibilities, helping me find new ways of looking at issues. Neel has nurtured many different versions of this book, ripping it apart at various points of time, throwing all my deadlines to the wind. In retrospect I am glad he did, and if the finished work does not match up to his standards of empirical depth and conceptual rigour, he is equally responsible.

Finally I must thank the staff in different libraries where I have worked: Nagari Pracharini Sabha, Benares; Kanpur Collectorate; Kanpur Municipality; Upper India Chamber of Commerce; Labour Commissioner's Office; Citizen Office; UP State Archives, Lucknow; Secretariat Record Room, Lucknow; Police Commissioner's Office, Lucknow; National Archives; Nehru Memorial Museum and Library; the Central Secretariat Library, Delhi; and the India Office Library, London. The co-operation of many in Kanpur, Ganesh Pandey, Munishwar Nigam, Neelam Chaturvedi, Sudarshan Chakr, M. Khaitan, and S.P. Mehra was invaluable. In recent years, the friendship and hospitality of Laxmi Sehgal and Subhasini Ali has made research trips to Kanpur enriching for me.

A special thanks to Rukun for the care with which he edited the manuscript, and to Shyama Warner for the proof-reading.

Abbreviations

AILH	Association of Indian Labour Historians
BIC	British India Corporation
EPW	*Economic and Political Weekly*
ERR	English Records Room
FR	Fortnightly Report
GOI	Government of India
HPD	Home Political Department
IESHR	*Indian Economic and Social History Review*
IFC	Indian Factory Commission
IFLC	Indian Factory Labour Commission
IHR	*Indian Historical Review*
IOL	India Office Library
KLIC	Kanpur Labour Inquiry Committee
KMS	Kanpur Mazdur Sabha
LIC	Labour Inquiry Committee
MAS	*Modern Asian Studies*
NAI	National Archives of India
NMML	Nehru Memorial Museum and Library
NWP	North West Provinces
RCL	Royal Commission of Labour
RNP	Report on Native Newspapers
SAID	Secret Abstract of the Intelligence Department
UICC	Upper India Chamber of Commerce
UPCC	United Provinces Chamber of Commerce
UPGAD	Uttar Pradesh General Administration Department
UPLEC	Uttar Pradesh Labour Enquiry Committee
UPSA	Uttar Pradesh State Archives

Glossary

—⊹⸺⸺⊹—

Achut	untouchable
Adda	meeting place
Akhara	a space for exercise and wrestling
Ata	flour
Badmaash	literally a person with a bad (bad) livelihood (mash)
Bandi	vest
Basti	settlement
Begar	in the pre-British period: certain forms of labour for the community. During the colonial period: unpaid labour
Beizzati	insult
Berozgar	unemployed, a person without earning
Chabena	dry roasted grain
Charpoy	a rope mesh cot used for sleeping and as a couch in the day
Chela	disciple
Chhut-pat	touch pollution
Churri	knife
Dada–chela	gang leader and disciple
Dhoti	loincloth
Gaikhana	place for keeping cows
Gali	lanes
Ganj	market
Gaon bhai	fraternal association between people of the same village
Ghat	quay, bank, wharf

Goonda	hooligan
Gur	jaggery
Hakim	a physician (trained in the Unani system)
Hata	lit. an enclosed compound. Here it refers to a compound inside which are enclosed hundreds of small huts
Havan	a fire sacrifice
Hookah	hubble-bubble
Inquilab Zindabad	long live revolution
Jamadar	a head of a group
Jutha	defiled by eating, drinking
Katha	religious discourse
Khomcha	a vendor's selling basket
Lathi	a big stick
Lehenga	long loose skirt
Lungi	a dress consisting of a single piece of unstitched cloth to cover the lower half of the male body
Mastaan	a neighbourhood leader with influence and physical prowess
Matka	earthen pitcher
Maulud sharif	a gathering in celebration of the Prophet Mohammad
Mela	fair
Mofussil	suburb of a town
Nala	big drain
Nazul	royal estate, escheated property
Pachisi	a game of dice
Pahalwan	a wrestler
Pakki naukari	permanent job
Pan supari	betel-nut
Panchayat	an assembly of elected representatives
Prasad	offerings made to an idol and distributed amongst devotees
Rashtra	nation

Rashtriyata	nationalism
Sarkar	government
Sharif	gentlemanly
Shuddhi	lit. purification. In the context used here it refers to a movement for conversion of Muslims and others to Hinduism
Tabligh	a movement for the propagation of Islam and for conversion
Tanzim	a movement to propagate Islam and forge unity within the community
Updeshak	preacher
Yagya	sacrifice
Zamana	age

Introduction
Labour and Its Historiography

This book has a long and fractured history. The assumptions of the 1970s that underlined my original interest in labour history have changed. For many young scholars twenty-five years ago, a concern with labour was inspired by socialist dreams and visions of social transformation. Studying labour, in that context seemed more than an academic project. Hopes of social transformation, in radical history writing, were tied up with faith in the emancipatory power of the working class and working class movements. Reworked through the 1990s, this book bears traces of the changed times: not only have the frameworks of labour history altered, the worlds that I set out to explore are crumbling.

Two important trends influenced my initial interest in labour. One, vestiges of euphoria of student and workers' movements of May 1968, which influenced radical intellectuals in India and outside; two, the post-Emergency context of a resurgence of strikes and democratic movements all over India in the hope of a sympathetic labour policy under the newly elected government.[1] These were times when many on the left expressed their opposition to Stalinist orthodoxy by celebrating the self-activity of workers outside the framework of established trade unions. Spontaneous action by workers, as opposed to actions organised by parties, was seen as vindicating a critique of Stalinism and party bureaucracies.

It was against this background that reports of militant action by workers in late 1977, in industrial areas around Delhi and other cities, seemed momentous. In December 1977, workers of the Swadeshi Cotton Mills in Kanpur went on strike and virtually

[1] This refers to the period 1975–7, when Prime Minister Indira Gandhi declared Emergency Rule, abrogating all democratic rights.

besieged the factory. The strike was repressed through brutal police action, killing several workers. Repression created a wave of sympathy for the strikers through the city, and organisations in support of the Swadeshi workers came up in neighbourhoods and factories. The context was one in which the meanings of such events were amplified, their significance overstated. As a researcher exploring labour history, happenings like this left deep impressions; and along with others from Delhi and Bombay I collected oral testimonies on the events in the city. My focus on Kanpur had also something to do with its proximity to Lucknow, where I spent my childhood. Memories of tannery smells and factory smoke each time I passed through the city on journeys from Lucknow made its industrial character very palpable for me. As I proceeded with my research, my interest in Kanpur was livened by old communists for whom the city was associated with a vibrant trade union past. In returning to the momentous strikes of the 1930s, I began tracing a teleology of workers' power, discovering the roots of the present struggle in those of the past.

By the late 1980s things had changed. Visions of socialism seemed to be in crisis, labour movements the world over were in decline, narratives of emancipation and the certainties of earlier frameworks were under question. The celebration of spontaneity and of the rank-and-file militancy that characterised the writings of the 1970s was increasingly criticised. In India the failure of the eighteen-month long strike of the Bombay textile workers was symptomatic of a deeper crisis and of the retreat of labour. In Kanpur a powerful protest against the restructuring of workload in February 1989 was virtually the last of such movements in the city.[2] The very future of the textile working class seemed threatened.

By the 1990s there was a growing crisis in the textile industry, with a large-scale closure of mills and retrenchment of workers. The worlds that I had set out to reconstruct seemed to be fading. Statements by workers captured this sense of loss.

Pahle Gwaltoli me chalna mushkil tha itne mazdur sarak par hote the. Pahle yahan rat me admi soya nahin dikhta tha. Ab yahan cheh baje tak chiriya nahin bolti.

[2] The strike was against the implementation of the K.K. Pandey Award of 1989 on rationalisation and intensification of workload.

(Earlier it was impossible to walk in Gwaltoli, with workers crowding the streets. Earlier the streets were awake with people at night. Today not even a bird chirps before six in the morning.)

Gwaltoli in Kanpur was famous among workers as a *mazduron ka garh* (fortress of workers). It was from here that the first strikes began. Now Gwaltoli sleeps. Statements like this are witness to the times that the labouring population in industrial cities like Kanpur has seen.

Descriptions of Kanpur as one of the most important industrial centres in North India, as the Manchester of the East, seem misplaced today. Sprawling mill compounds—noiseless and deserted—majestic buildings worn down and crumbling, tall and smokeless mill chimneys stand as silent reminders of the past. In the bastis and hatas men, young and old, the unemployed waiting for jobs or for mills to reopen, sit around vacantly; others push carts, ply rickshaws, or work in cottage industries in alleys and bylanes. Women in the bastis roll bidis and toil at other small jobs, their work invisible. A city that provided hope and opportunity to migrants from the neighbouring districts and villages is now pervaded with a sense of weariness and hopelessness for the poor and unemployed. The trajectory of the industrial city traced here is not peculiar to Kanpur. Large industries in other old centres—Bombay, Ahmedabad, Calcutta—have undergone a similar process of decline.

Workers in fact are faced with a double death. Decimated by economic transitions, they are at the same time being effaced from the pages of history. Just as there is a crisis of industry today, there is a crisis in the old frameworks of labour history. The declining employment in large industries, the trend towards the casualisation of labour and weakening of trade union movements—phenomena that have increasingly global dimensions—have been paralleled with a crisis of socialism, a breakdown of earlier certainties, visions of the future, optimisms. If the mid-twentieth century was still a time of hope and dreams of socialism, now a feeling of despair and hopelessness seems all-pervasive among workers. This change in mood has also created a crisis in labour history. A study of labour appears a project of little relevance today. Historians seem complicit in denying to workers their right to be the subjects of history, their claim to be represented. To write labour history today, then, is to flow against the tide.

Labour history in India emerged in the post-colonial period, when questions of economic growth were of central concern for most historians. A study of the characteristics of the workforce in India formed part of a larger agenda towards understanding the constraints to industrialisation. Writings in the 1950s and 1960s shared many of the assumptions that underlined colonial discourse on labour. Stereotypes about the lack of commitment to work and irregular work rhythms continued to haunt these discussions. While Morris David Morris critiqued old colonial and sociological frames that saw caste and other social institutions as impediments to labour supply, he did not fundamentally challenge their assumptions. By asserting that industrialisation was dissolving earlier forms of social relations, Morris only reaffirmed the old paradigm. By arguing that traditional social ties did not hinder industrialisation, he denied the significance of these characteristics in the processes of workforce formation.

Social history writing from the late 1970s onwards grappled more seriously with these issues. Two important trends were important in the labour history of the period. First, there was a shift away from arguments which framed the discussion of modernisation theorists like Morris. Instead of looking at caste and village ties through the prism of labour commitment and supply, labour historians now re-examined the significance of these ties in understanding working class formation.[3] Second, there was also an attempt to develop a critique of the economistic assumptions dominant in writings on working class protests. E.P. Thompson's

[3] One of the earliest such pieces was P.S. Gupta, 'Notes on the Origin and Structuring of the Industrial Labour Force in India 1880–1920', in R.S. Sharma, ed., Indian Society: Historical Probings (New Delhi 1974); Ranajit Das Gupta, 'Factory Labour in Eastern India: Sources of Supply 1855–1946: Some Preliminary Findings', IESHR, 13:3, 1976; C.P. Simmons, 'Recruiting and Organizing an Industrial Labour Force in Colonial India', R. Newman, 'Social Factors in the Recruitment of Bombay Millhands', in K.N. Chaudhuri and C.J. Dewey, eds, Economy and Society: Essays in Indian Economic and Social History (Delhi 1979); D. Mazumdar, 'Labour Supply in Early Industrialization: The Case of the Bombay Textile Industry', English Historical Review, 26:3, 1973.

critique of economism had a powerful impact on historians, making them more sensitive to the need to study the power of cultural traditions in understanding crowd behaviour.[4]

While labour historians expressed an increasing discomfort with the teleological and deterministic assumptions implicit in the Marxist social histories, the struggle against the burden of past assumptions was not easy.[5] Historians did shift away from conventional trade union histories, in which workers as human subjects were absent, to histories that explored the social and cultural worlds of workers.[6] But linear notions of class consciousness—suggesting that a mature class consciousness would gradually displace community consciousness—continued to underline the narratives of the labour movement.[7] Determinist assumptions drawing causal connections between economic contexts and cultural characteristics underpinned a lot of writing, especially when historians tackled questions of religion and community.[8] Besides,

[4] E.P. Thompson, *The Making of the English Working Class* (Harmondsworth 1968); *idem*, 'Eighteenth-Century English Society: Class Struggle Without Class?', *Social History*, 3: 2, May 1978; *idem*, 'The Moral Economy of the English Crowd in the Eighteenth Century', *Past and Present*, 50, 1971; *idem*, 'Time, Work-Discipline and Industrial Capitalism', *Past and Present*, 38, December 1967.

[5] See, for instance, the debate between Dipesh Chakrabarty and Ranajit Das Gupta, 'Some Aspects of Labour History of Bengal in the Nineteenth Century: Two Views', Occasional Paper No. 40, 1981, Calcutta, Centre for Studies in Social Sciences.

[6] For trade union histories, see V.B. Karnik, *Strikes in India* (Bombay 1967); Karnik, *Indian Trade Unions: A Survey* (Bombay 1960); A.S. Mathur and J.S. Mathur, *Trade Union Movement in India* (Allahabad 1957); G.K. Sharma, *Labour Movement in India* (Delhi 1963); S.D. Punekar, *Trade Unionism in India: A Study of Industrial Democracy* (Bombay 1948); S. Sen, *Working Class of India: History of Emergence and Movement, 1830–1970* (Calcutta 1975).

[7] Ranajit Das Gupta, 'Poverty and Protest: A Study of Calcutta's Industrial Workers and Labouring Poor, 1875–1899', in R. Das Gupta, *Labour and Working Class in Eastern India: Studies in Colonial History* (Calcutta 1994).

[8] Community consciousness and communal conflicts among workers appeared somewhat of an aberration. Strikes over festival holidays, for instance, were explained by Ranajit Das Gupta as a form of resistance to the conditions of oppression and exploitation workers faced in the city. 'Poverty and Protest'.

culture tended to be compartmentalised: slotted into the space of the community and neighbourhood. It did not touch lives in the sphere of production, within the factory, nor did it mediate political spaces. Family, gender and other issues concerning working class lives were not subjects of serious inquiry.[9]

In writings over the last decade and a half we can see the emergence of a new labour history in India.[10] Even as scholars predict the end of labour as a subject of historical inquiry, there seems to be a renewal of labour history and a widening of perspectives with the exploration of new themes and issues.[11] Not only have questions of culture, community, family and gender become more important, the boundaries of labour history have opened up to incorporate 'unorganised' home-based workers, casual labourers, self-employed artisans and others who existed on the fringes of academic writing.[12]

A major break in the writing of labour history in India came with Dipesh Chakrabarty's pioneering work, *Rethinking Working-Class History*, based on a study of jute workers in Bengal. Examining the dynamics of power at the workplace, Chakrabarty shows how the relationships between workers, managers and mistris, and between union babus and workers, were embedded

[9] There were some exceptions. Among the earliest to appear was Radha Kumar's 'Family and Factory: Women in the Bombay Textile Industry 1919–1939', *IESHR*, 20:1,1983.

[10] Among the new writings were Dipesh Chakrabarty, *Rethinking Working Class History* (New Delhi 1989); Rajnarayan Chandavarkar, *The Origins of Industrial Capitalism in India: Business Strategies and Working Classes in Bombay, 1900–1940* (Cambridge 1994); Janaki Nair, *Miners and Millhands: Work, Culture and Politics in Princely Mysore* (New Delhi 1998); Samita Sen, *Women and Labour in Late Colonial India: The Bengal Jute Industry* (Cambridge 1999); Dilip Simeon, *The Politics of Labour Under Late Colonialism: Workers Unions and the State in Chotanagpur* (New Delhi 1995).

[11] Verity Burgmann, 'The Strange Death of Labour History', cited in *International Review of Social History (IRSH)*, 38, Editorial, Supplement 1, 1993.

[12] See, for instance, Jan Breman, *Footloose Labour: Working in India's Informal Economy* (Cambridge 1995); Peter Knorriga, 'Artisan Labour in the Agra Footwear Industry: Continued Informality and Changing Threats', in Jonathan P. Parry, Jan Breman and Karin Kapadia, eds, *The Worlds of Indian Industrial Labour* (New Delhi 1999).

in a pre-bourgeois hierarchical culture. The identities of workers were defined by primordial ties of religion and community; they were never politically emancipated from religion; not even in moments of confrontation between labour and capital. While Chakrabarty provides illuminating insights into the specific cultural peculiarities of the Bengal jute mill workers, he essentialises certain given features within this culture, seeing these as constant and unaffected by historical mediations. In contrast to Marxist histories in the past that valorised processes of economic transformation in the making of class, Chakrabarty tends to reify culture. A framework that homogenises culture in terms of certain determinate categories does not allow space for practice in the production, reproduction and transformation of culture. The subjects of an inquiry framed in these terms appear eternally entrapped in culturally given relationships of power; they show no capacity to reconstitute these relations.

Although not framed within a similar culturalist paradigm, other studies on labour in India over the last decade and a half have explored issues concerning culture. Raj Chandavarkar's important study of the Bombay working class looks at the formation of the working class in terms of the nature of the labour market and the fluctuating labour demands of the cotton textile industry. Business strategies at the workplace and the volatility of the labour market, Chandavarkar argues, created a labour force that was deeply sectionalised.[13] Through a rich description of working class neighbourhoods in Bombay, he shows how culture was actively constituted through everyday relationships and networks forged within the mohalla and the factory. Ties formed in the neighbourhood intruded into the workplace and relationships at work widened and created new networks in the neighbourhood, not determined by earlier separations. Breaking away from totalising narratives of class that have been dominant in labour history writing in India, Chandavarkar suggests that fractures within the workers, their sectionalism and inner divisions, endure: unities

[13] Chandavarkar argues how 'The labour-intensive strategies of the mill-owners served to encourage rivalries within the workforce . . . The diversity of conditions within the industry, accentuated by these strategies of production, informed competition and conflicts within the workforce.' *The Origins of Industrial Capitalism*, p. 332.

across these lines are conjunctural and momentary. There is, how-ever, a tension within Chandavarkar's narrative between on the one hand his recognition that heterogeneity was not an aberration but an intrinsic characteristic of the working class, and on the other his defensive use of class as merely a 'descriptive category'. Underlying such a usage is the assumption that class in the real sense can exist only if there is greater homogeneity. Chandavarkar seems to share the assumptions he sets out to criticise.

Certain shared assumptions about labour history seem to un-derline Chandavarkar's and Chakrabarty's writings. In contrast to radical histories on labour that glorified working class action, politics has a marginal role in their frameworks. Worker protest in Bengal is spasmodic, ephemeral—it has no lasting impact on working class culture. In Bombay, class solidarities are contin-gent: forged at one moment, they could disappear at another. In both cases, at an everyday level, in day-to-day relationships at the workplace, workers have no agency. In Chandavarkar's framework, business decisions crucially affect strategies of labour deployment and relationships at the workplace, while for Chakra-barty the pre-modern outlook of the workers and traditional relationships of hierarchy shape the culture of work. As opposed to linear conceptions of change in conventional Marxist writings, many recent writings deny possibilities of change and allow workers no agency in shaping their culture.[14]

The focus on essentialised notions of workers' unity seem to be replaced today by frameworks valorising fragmentation and con-flict. If earlier Marxists searched in vain for 'class for itself', today there is a defensiveness in relation to using categories like class. This shift is not peculiar to the Indian context. The linguistic turn has unsettled earlier conceptions within labour history in Europe. We can see two significant shifts since the early 1980s. First, there

[14] Samita Sen's *Women and Labour in Colonial India,* while filling im-portant lacunae in Indian labour history—in which women had a marginal place—shares some of these problems. Locating the marginalisation of women in the context of patriarchal notions of seclusion and domesticity, Sen widens the terrain of discussion by shifting the focus from economic stra-tegies of employers to issues of culture and ideology. In her argument, the lives of women are determined by patriarchal structures which are closed and not open to negotiation. A conception of patriarchy that is closed, undif-ferentiated and unmediated can be problematic.

was a move to an understanding of class as a discursive structure. Stedman Jones critiqued the direct relationship between experience and consciousness posited by Thompson and other social historians, emphasising instead the linguistic ordering of experience.[15] Second, the shift to discursivity also meant a questioning of earlier notions of class and class consciousness. Deconstructing the language of Chartism, Jones argued that the unity, homogeneity and class specificity that is attributed to the Chartists is missing in their discourse; and the radicalism of their language in fact draws upon an older tradition of political radicalism pre-dating the entry of artisans and factory proletariat into politics. Similarly, Sewell's work on the discourse of labour in nineteenth-century France emphasises that working class consciousness in 1848 was 'universalist' and inclusive in character, and class conflict in mid-nineteenth-century France was not necessarily articulated in terms of a confrontation between employers and workers.[16] While Thompson's writings stretched the boundaries of class by incorporating pre-industrial traditions in the making of working class culture, Jones and Sewell questioned the 'working classness' of workers' culture. Through an exploration of vocabulary and rhetoric, they emphasised the ambiguities within their political culture and consciousness. This argument in a sense prepared the ground for a shift from holistic and totalising conceptions of class to narratives of fragmentation and disunity. Moving away from homogenised and unified notions of class interest, Somers argued for a notion of narrative identity. She suggested that social beings are constituted through a plurality of narrative identities and social actions have to be understood within these narrative structures.[17] Writings on everyday life fed into the discourse of fragmentation, by shifting focus from organised political actions to

[15] Gareth Stedman Jones, *Languages of Class: Studies in English Working Class History, 1832–1982* (Cambridge, 1983).

[16] William Sewell, *Work and Revolution in France: The Language of Labour from the Old Regime to 1848* (Cambridge, 1980).

[17] Margaret R Somers, 'Deconstructing and Reconstructing Class Formation Theory: Narrativity, Relational Analysis, and Social Theory', in John R. Hall, ed., *Reworking Class* (Cornell 1997), pp. 73–105. In a somewhat similar way, Katznelson distinguishes between different spaces—the workplace, community and home—arguing against class discourse that unifies these disparate spaces. Ira Katznelson, *City Trenches: Urban Politics and the*

the individualised acts through which workers tried to redefine notions of work and leisure. In reading political meanings into everyday practices of the workplace, Ludtke and other theorists of *altagsgeschichte* have redefined and extended the space of the political.[18]

In the present context there seems to be a reluctance to use categories like class, and an attempt to reinterpret class in a more fluid and open-ended way. In a context where working classes everywhere are fractured along race, ethnic and religious lines, and large numbers are increasingly pushed into the margins—into the ranks of the unorganised, informal labour—new conceptions of class and politics need to be explored for a renewal of labour history.[19] But any such exploration has to grapple with the problems of these conceptions.

In this book I engage with some of these issues. Identities of class and community, I argue, were continuously negotiated within changing historical situations. Categories of community with which workers identified were not pre-given and primordial, they were actively created and given new meanings. A worker had different identities and some of these were in conflict with each other. The assertion of any one identity at a particular moment

---

Patterning of Class in the United States (Chicago 1981). See also I. Katznelson and A. Zolberg, ed., *Working Class Formation: Nineteenth-Century Patterns in Western Europe and the United States* (Princeton 1986).

[18] *Altagsgeschichte* = history of everyday life. Alf Ludtke, 'The Historiography of Everyday Life: The Personal and the Political', in Raphael Samuel and Gareth Stedman Jones, eds, *Culture, Ideology and Politics: Essays for Eric Hobsbawm,* History Workshop Series (Routledge 1982); Alf Ludtke, 'Cash, Coffee Breaks, Horseplay: Eigensinn and Politics Among Factory Workers in Germany, *circa* 1900', in Michael Hanagan and Charles Stephenson, eds, *Confrontation, Class Consciousness and the Labour Process* (New York 1986).

[19] Jan Pakulski, 'The Dying of Class or of Marxist Theory?', *International Sociology*, 8:1993; Ellen Meiksins, *The Retreat from Class* (London 1986). For an extremely rich exploration of the ways in which class can be reinterpreted, see Frederick Cooper, 'Back to Work: Categories, Boundaries and Connections in the Study of Labour', in P. Alexander and Rick Halpern, eds, *Racializing Class, Classifying Race: Labour and Difference in Britain, the USA and Africa* (London 2000).

meant a 'misrecognition' of other identities.[20] Such conflicts and misrecognition were part of the process of identity formation. If the culture of community left its traces on workers' lives, moments of solidarity cutting across community lines also marked and shaped the lives and consciousness of workers. Experiences of solidarity during moments of mass upsurge become sedimented as part of working class memory, recalled and celebrated in subsequent periods of struggle. Experiences of defeat and repression nurtured an amnesia in which stories of past solidarities faded from consciousness.[21]

I emphasise also the significance of work in the constitution of identities. The shift away from conventional Marxist arguments about the homogenising impact of work and workplace collectivity has often meant a marginalisation of the workplace as a site where identities are formed. The significance of work to a sense of self is best discovered in its absence, through voices of despair. The culture of worklessness in the present, I suggest, gives insights into the meanings of work. Work meant a forging of relationships, bonds between wage earners, a sense of power of their collectivity in the city, a sense of pride and dignity. While their daily lives in the city, their hata existence, strengthened ties of caste and community, it created at the same time a sense of 'oneness' against the world outside, the kothiwalas. The characterisation of mazdur bastis as slums within élite discourse sharpened these polarities and deepened self-perceptions of collectivity amongst workers. It was these oppositions that came into play when entire neighbourhoods joined in workers' struggles. In tracing workers' pasts we need to look at both linkages which tied workers together, as well as those that fractured these unities. The breakdown of earlier ideas of collectivity does not mean that we dispense with a notion of unity altogether.

---

[20] The term 'misrecognition' is used by Michel Pecheux to analyse the process through which a subject recognises or identifies himself/herself, forgetting and misrecognising other determinations constituting the subject. Pecheux, *Language, Semantics and Ideology* (Macmillan 1982). The term 'misrecognition' has also been used by Stuart Hall in 'Introduction: Who needs Identity?', in his *Questions of Cultural Identity* (Sage 1996).

[21] See ch. 9.

In restoring agency to workers our focus cannot be fixed just on times of mass upsurge when existing hierarchies and structures of power are turned upside down. Workers act in their daily life in small ways, resisting pressures as well as submitting to demands, being silent at times and vocal at others, conforming to rules as well as negotiating them, and through small acts of self-assertion seeking to retain a sense of dignity.[22] I explore how work norms within the factory were continuously negotiated and the culture of work actively shaped by workers. Everyday practices are not always acts of resistance: they reproduced and reaffirmed, just as much as they resisted, dominant structures of power and authority. Yet public gestures of submission could coexist with private and 'hidden transcripts' of resistance. Historians need to understand both transcripts.[23]

In a sense the central story in the book—of lost worlds—is one that could be written only in the present context. The loss of factory jobs in today's context, however, is only one part of a recurring theme of lost worlds, with workers struggling to retain their pasts. The loss of factory work, the theme of rupture, of distancing from the familial world, was a theme that appeared in narratives of earlier times too. In the early twentieth century peasants and artisans looking for jobs in the city had to negotiate a new life within a new milieu, grappling with the worlds they lost. But in many ways the past still lived, inscribed in their present. This book looks at the way workers struggled to retain their pasts— their worlds of work and life as peasants in rural households, their ties with the village, the family and community. Moving to the city meant both a fracturing of cultural worlds and an attempt to retain and create a new familial world. Migrants coming in often tried to straddle both worlds—returning to the village for work and retaining and re-creating kin and family networks in the city

---

[22] Here, the category of *eigensinn* used by Ludtke to define the everyday acts through which workers tried to appropriate time and space for themselves is important in understanding the complex processes through which working class culture is constituted. By focusing on the day-to-day processes of negotiation and resistance at the workplace and outside, Ludtke politicises the sphere of the everyday.

[23] The idea of 'hidden transcripts' has been developed by James Scott in *Domination and the Arts of Resistance: Hidden Transcripts* (Yale 1990).

in various ways. Work in the factory involved negotiation and conflict as workers attempted to create space and time for themselves, making seasonal visits to the village a part of the factory rhythm. The feeling of loss today, however, is fundamentally different from the experience of loss earlier. Today it is difficult to sustain any sense of link with the past, or hold on to cherished worlds. The loss now seems to have a brutal finality. With a whole way of life annihilated, the search is for new alternatives.

The book is divided into three parts. I begin Part I by examining the links between workers and the space they inhabit and how the presence of a working class population reshapes the landscape of the city. In Chapter 1, which explores the history of that space, I try to understand how it was shaped through the politics of merchants, the East India Company military and civil establishment, the industrialists and the labouring poor. In Chapter 2 I show that the lives of workers in the city was constituted through a complex intertwining between the past and the present, the world of the city, the village, caste and community. For migrants the move to the city was always torn by conflicting pressures, and for many the city never became a home. How did families deal with migration? This is investigated in Chapter 3. How did family strategies work out in the city and how did workers deal with everyday life? In investigating these questions, Chapter 3 moves from individual stories to wider experiences of living in the city, exploring how work in the factory was important to a sense of self and identity. Chapter 4 examines the experiences of work and authority in the factory: the relationship between the strategies of managers, the power of mistris, everyday practices at the shopfloor, and the role of trade unions in defining and legitimising specific norms of work. Notions of work within the factory were imbued with cultural meanings and work norms were continuously negotiated. There were silent and hidden acts of resistance and spectacular and demonstrative ones, all of which were important in defining the culture of work.

Part II focuses on two important conjunctures of strikes: the

post-war upsurge in 1919 and 1937–8, when the Congress ministry was in power in the province. I elaborate, in Chapter 5, the
links between informal networks and formal structures of organisation in 1919, the relationship between the state, managers and
workers and the rituals through which power was exercised. The
next chapter looks at 1937–8, when the spectre of 'Lal Kanpur'
worked up capitalist anxieties. The imagery of radicalism, the
inversion of notions of order, the representations of the strike in
official and non-official discourse are evocative of the mood of
the period.

From moments of collective action and class solidarities, the
last part of the book shifts focus to other forms of identities, be-
longings and consciousness: ties of community and visions of the
nation. In Chapter 7 I try to see how community ties were reproduced in the urban milieu in the neighbourhood and the factory,
and the ways in which these ties are redefined and boundaries
between communities pushed and redrawn. How did everyday
practices and events like communal riots reaffirm or deepen the
lines of difference? How did caste identities cross-cut, merge or
conflict with class identities? I go on in Chapter 8 to examine the
relationship between nationalism and labour movement and the
significance of nationalist imaginings to working class consciousness. How did workers' visions of the nation conflict with dominant discourses on nationalism? I explore how nationalists tried
to grapple with their own inner contradictions and with the pressures from a working class city in a period when the Congress
came to power in the province.

In the end I come back to the theme I began with—the theme
of lost worlds—the changed landscape of the city and the politics
of despair and worklessness in the present. Today, the worlds of
labour that this book set out to explore are not only physically
annihilated, but are in the process of being erased from working
class memory altogether.

CHAPTER 1

Barracks, Bazaars and Bastis

———————

The history of every working class is tied up with the history of its location. Workers reconstitute the spaces they inhabit, they reinscribe them with their actions, they reshape them with the rhythms of their everyday lives. But their spaces also bear the traces of earlier histories, other lives. They have histories which prefigure the birth of the industrial city.

Settlements of artisanal and labouring population had come up in Kanpur long before factory industries. By the 1840s, there were more than 16,000 artisans, leather workers, weavers, tailors and other miscellaneous labourers in the city and cantonment.[1] Large numbers came in with the influx from the countryside during the famine years in the 1830s, working in relief works.[2] The migrants moving in these times in waves, from Bundelkhand and the neighbouring regions, stayed on in Kanpur, providing artisanal labour in the Company establishments or as coolie labour, loading, unloading, carting goods coming up and down the river through Kanpur. While other urban centres in North India declined, Kanpur became commercially more important, drawing merchants, gentry and labour from other areas. With the growth of commerce and establishment of a cantonment, labouring settlements expanded and a range of small enterprises mushroomed to service the cantonment and the new merchant gentry. Montgomery's list of 1849 shows 113 haberdashers, 401 barbers, 353 butchers, 91 dyers, 175 hackerymen, 21 hatmakers,

[1] R. Montgomery, *Statistical Report of the District of Cawnpore* (Calcutta 1849), App. xxvii. The figures in this para are based on his data.

[2] Surya Kant Tripathi and Narayan Prasad Arora, Kanpur kaa Itihaas (Kanpur 1940), p. 75. On the famine of 1830s, see also Sanjay Sharma, *Famine, Philanthropy and the Colonial State: North India in the Early Nineteenth Century* (New Delhi 2001), pp. 63–4, 75–7, 144–5.

320 palkibearers, 420 prostitutes, 474 tailors working in Kanpur. Gradually the old settlement of 'Kanhpur' with its bathing ghats, temples and a palace dating back to the early eighteenth century, became the 'Kanpur kona', a small corner at the western margin.

The history of 'Campoo Kanpur' was linked to bazaars in the region. In 1778, when Company troops were transferred from Bilgram in Hardoi district and encamped in Kanpur, the plan was to set up a Company trading factory along with the military camp. By the turn of the century, merchants of varied origin congregated here. Greek, French, Portuguese and Swiss traders could be seen doing business in the cantonment–bazaar nexus, alongside their English counterparts.[3]

The growth of this European population created new consumption demands. Amongst India's European inhabitants Kanpur soon acquired a reputation for its rich supplies of a wide range of foreign goods. An inventory of the goods marketed by John Price, a trader from Kanpur who died in 1801, included cocked hats, ladies' garters, men's black silk gloves, Smythe's lavender water, gilt chit-paper, black ink powder, violet hair powder, silver tongue-scrapers, souchong tea, and mounted pistols.[4] A trading body, Peake Allen and Company, specialised in English tooth powder and later diversified into other products, bringing in medicines, surgical instruments, veterinary stores and implements, aerated waters and perfumes.[5] The desire for familiar English goods among Kanpur's European inhabitants seemed insatiable. Wives of European families waited anxiously for the arrival of their boxes from England and exchanged excited letters with friends about the goods coming in.[6]

[3] R. Montgomery, *Statistical Report of the District of Cawnpore* (Calcutta 1849), p. 94.

[4] Zoe Yalland, *A Guide to the Kacheri Cemetery and the Early History of Kanpur* (London 1983), p. 38.

[5] Yalland, *Boxwallahs*, p. 220.

[6] 'My box which Bob . . . so kindly brought out for me arrived some time ago, with some very nice things, a pretty bonnet and two nice cold weather dresses besides frocks and hats for Willie. Have you got your box yet? Who is getting your things for you?' Yalland, *Boxwallahs*, p. 112.

The consumption demands of the growing European community reshaped the nature of local production. By the 1830s Kanpur's milliners, dressmakers and glovemakers were famous. In fact the story ran that, in the mid-nineteenth century, a young bride no longer had to wait for her bridal trousseau to arrive from England: she could buy almost everything locally.[7]

Perishable goods not brought upriver were produced locally. English farmers settled in the cantonment, reared poultry, game and pigs, cured ham and bacon. With the exception of English broad beans, almost all European vegetables and fruits were grown on local farms.[8] Pre-industrial artisanal manufacture in Kanpur also developed in response to European consumption demands. Much before the setting up of large-scale industries, leather was prepared locally to meet the military demand for carriage, harness and saddlery. Some of these products were then exported out of Kanpur. Cured meat was sent to distant places; carriage, harness and saddlery from Kanpur were sold in all parts of India; furniture was supplied to neighbouring districts, especially Lucknow.[9]

The trade in European goods next touched local village markets. Reports from the nineteenth century refer to the extensive sale of English cloth in Akbarpur, Shahpur, Bithur. At the bi-weekly village markets of Baripal were sold cloth and other goods from England.[10] Although common coarse cloth was manufactured locally by Julahas and Koris, the 'better classes' in the Akbarpur and Shahpur parganas of Kanpur district preferred cloth imported from other regions, and English cloth. [11]

Trade in consumption goods for cantonment inhabitants was linked closely with trade in raw materials produced or marketed in Kanpur. Boats coming up with soda water and other items of general merchandise travelled back towards Calcutta with indigo

[7] Yalland, *Traders and Nabobs*, p. 223.

[8] Emma Roberts, *Hindostan: The Shores of the Red Sea and the Mountains*, vol. 11 (London n.d.), p. 44.

[9] Montgomery, *Statistical Report*, p. 110.

[10] E.T. Atkinson, *Statistical and Descriptive Account of the North-West Provinces*, vol. VI (Allahabad 1881).

[11] Montgomery, *Statistical Report*. p. 91.

seed and valuable cash crops.[12]Indigo cultivation was introduced in Najafgarh, in the neighbourhood of Kanpur, by Claude Martin, an officer in the service of the Awadh government who built numerous vats and a large processing factory towards the last decades of the eighteenth century.[13]Subsequently, indigo was cultivated in Narwal tahsil by one Adam Maxwell, son of John Maxwell by an Indian mother. John Maxwell, who left his indigo estates in Tanda and settled in Kanpur in 1806 as an agent to army contractors, set up a rum distillery at Jajmau to supply the troops. But indigo remained a major concern of the Maxwells. Their extensive estates in the Kanpur region were acquired by John Maxwell, who evaded restrictions on property rights for Europeans by using the legal title of his Indian-born son Adam. The Maxwell legacy in Kanpur, controlled by Burnett and Company after John Maxwell's death, was almost wiped out in the speculation boom of the 1820s, and it took almost two decades to revive the family concerns. After 1857 the Maxwell enterprises were re-established in partnership with a Dr Begg,[14] as Begg Maxwell and Company. Leather entrepreneurs like William Cooper started work in India on indigo estates in Bihar and later moved to the Maxwell estates at Etah, and from there further west to Kanpur. The Gavin Jones family came originally from Wales, settled in Calcutta, from where the *pater familias* moved westwards to the Jaunpur region and acquired a vast indigo estate. The Jones's fortunes fell with the Union Bank collapse of 1847. In the mid-1820s Kanpur was second only to Farukhabad in indigo production in the Ceded Provinces.[15] But with the collapse of the indigo boom in the 1830s, the business contracted drastically, being now limited primarily to the supply of seed rather than finished produce. After

[12] Nevill, *Gazetteer*, p. 82.

[13] Atkinson, *Statistical Account of NWP*, p. 107. See also Rosie Llewellyn-Jones, *A Very Ingenious Man: Claude Martin in Early Colonial India* (Delhi 1992), pp. 163–7.

[14] Dr Begg came originally as a planter's doctor in the 1830s. Like many other Europeans in India, he took advantage of the Company's lucrative trade to build up a vast trading network for himself.

[15] Asiya Siddiqi, *Agrarian Change in a North Indian State* (Oxford 1973), p. 142.

a brief revival of some factories in the 1860s indigo was displaced by cheap synthetic dyes around the turn of the century.

Another cash crop on which many Kanpur merchants made their fortune was raw cotton, this being both cultivated and mar-keted here before the textile mills came up. The years following the Napoleonic wars were particularly prosperous for the cotton trade, and parganas like Ghatampur, Akbarpur, Bhognipur and Derapur came to specialise in the crop.[16] It was bulk-sold in the cotton mandis of Kanpur, together with cotton from Bundelkhand, and sent on to Mirzapur. However, cotton like indigo suffered the vicissitudes of the export market in the 1830s, and it was only in the second half of the century, especially after rail links, that the trade was rejuvenated. Indigenous merchants controlled important networks in the trade, but in the late nineteenth century their inte-rests were threatened by the aggressive expansion of European merchants in the field. Cooper Allen and Company, who later became leather magnates, displaced indigenous control over the cotton trade in important ways. In later years, Cooper Allen and Company obtained a contract for the entire cotton supply to the Muir Mills, displacing the indigenous earlier supplier.[17]

The traders who dealt in indigo and cotton were often connected with the opium trade of Kanpur. The period of decline of indigo and cotton were periods when the Company started business in opium. Opium cultivation was introduced under official super-vision. The collector, E.A. Reade, directed the setting up of opium kothis in Kanpur, Bilhaur and Akbarpur. P. Maxwell, another of the ubiquitous Maxwells of Kanpur, acted as sub-deputy agent of the Company.[18] Large tracts were brought under poppy cultiva-tion despite resistance from local peasants and zamindars and, in 1877, 14,877 maunds of opium were exported from Kanpur.[19]

In value terms, grain constituted 43 per cent of the goods im-ported into Kanpur in 1846–7, the cantonment and city population providing a large urban market. Kanpur was also a bulking centre importing grain and sending it upriver to up-country districts and

[16] Siddiqi, *Agrarian Change*, p. 64.
[17] Yalland, *Boxwallahs*, fn. 11, p. 461.
[18] Montgomery, *Statistical Report*, App. ii, pp. viii–xiii.
[19] Atkinson, *Statistical Account*, p. 147.

sending it downriver to other stations. Grain was brought into Kanpur by bullock cart.

As Kanpur grew into a trading centre, indigenous traders flocked to the area.[20] Merchants from declining centres of trade were drawn towards Kanpur, building up trading networks around the camp–bazaar establishment. During the Depression of the 1830s, old centres of trade were more severely affected; Kanpur offered relatively promising prospects. Even after the cotton boom of the 1820s was over, there were around fifty banking houses in Kanpur (1848), many of them drawn from declining centres like Farukhabad.[21] Among them was the Marwari banking family of Baijnath Ramnath which, like many such families settled in Chatai Mohal in Kanpur, traded in cotton, grain and flour, apart from being bankers and general merchants. They also dealt in imported goods, chiefly yarn and piece-goods, and were commission agents. Offshoots of the Baijnath Ramnath group were involved in setting up flour mills, sugar works, cotton ginning factories, oil mills and later the famous Juggilal Kamlapat enterprises in Kanpur.[22] Other indigenous banking families of Kanpur—Tulsi Ram Jia Lal, Nihal Chand Baldeo Sahai, Janki Das Jagannath—combined grain trade with the banking business.[23]

In the 1830s certain wealthy and notable families, prominent among them Nawab Mutumad-ud-Daulah (ex-minister of Awadh), moved to Kanpur, followed by a large number of wealthy Lucknow families. Neighbourhoods came to be named after such migrant

[20] For a richly textured account of the changes in North Indian urban society and its implications for Kanpur and other new cities, see C.A. Bayly, *Rulers, Townsmen and Bazaars: North Indian Society in the Age of British Expansion, 1770–1870* (Cambridge 1988), especially chs 6–8.

[21] Montgomery, *Statistical Report*, p. 110, *Annual Report of the Sanitary Commissioner*, NWP, 1868. With the construction of the East Indian Railway this process was accelerated. Gavin Jones graphically recounted how: 'Faruckhabad, through which the trade of Rohilkhand passed down the Ganges, likewise yielded to the superior advantages of Cawnpore and Oudh, the "garden of India", abandoned the waterway of the Ghagra for the ironway of Cawnpore'. 'Rise and Progress of Cawnpore', in S. Playne and A. Wright, *The Bombay Presidency, the UP and the Punjab: Their History, People, Commerce and Natural Resources* (London 1920).

[22] Playne and Wright, *The Bombay Presidency, the UP and the Punjab*, p. 422, Nevill, *Gazetteer*, p. 73.

[23] Nevill, *Gazetteer*, pp. 73, 269.

elite families. Thus, Nawabganj was named after Nawab Mutu-mad-ud-daulah, Etawah Bazaar had a clustering of merchants from Etawah.[24]

Along with the migrant gentry came a large body of artisans and retainers who settled in neighbourhoods like Gwaltoli and Khalasi Lines.[25] When attempts were made to clear out working-class settlements in the Gwaltoli area more than a century later, the inhabitants protested and asserted their links with the royalty of old times. There was also a large demand for both coolie and artisanal labour from the growing cantonment establishment by the end of the eighteenth century. Many were engaged in producing tents, ropes, leather pouches, saddles, and bung leather for barrels for the army establishment. Others served as menials in the cant-onment. By the 1840s there were around 308 households engaged in leather production and trade.[26] Contemporary European ac-counts depict the great demand for leather making travellers on horseback wary: it was widely believed that horses were poisoned for leather.[27] The inflow of coolie labour into Kanpur fluctuated. In some months, like November, the number of coolies coming in from the Pandu bridge numbered over a thousand, while in June and July the numbers went down by more than half.

By the 1870s we see evidence of increasing competition for control over the Kanpur landscape. Banking families were now making large investments in land. They acquired substantial pro-perty in the villages in and around Kanpur district. By the 1870s there were reports of rapid and extensive changes in land-owner-ship in Kanpur, partly through purchase and partly through re-sumption of mortgages, by new groups. Hindu bankers and 'wealthy Muhamadans' were said to have acquired one-third of the district by the 1880s.[28]

Within the older centres business declined. Kanpur's trade

---

[24] Tripathi, *Kanpur ka Itihaas,* pp. 172, 176.

[25] Cawnpore expansion committee, UP Mun. Progs., Dec. 1918, no. 1 (a).

[26] Montgomery, *Statistical Report,* p. 110.

[27] 'The first stage out of Kanpur is famous as a place where horses die on their march, and hides are there procurable for tanning.' Fanny Parks, *Wand-erings of a Pilgrim in Search of the Picturesque* (London 1850; Karachi 1975).

[28] See statement showing mutations in property since cession, Montgomery, *Statistical Report,* App. xii, p. 103; Atkinson, *Statistical Account,* p. 115.

grew at the expense of Fategarh and Mirzapur, and it drew away a substantial part of wholesale business from Lucknow.[29] Merchants retailing imported goods in Lucknow bought their supplies from the Kanpur market. Railways accelerated the process of change, bypassing old centres of trade and connecting others with ports and their hinterlands. Kanpur was already connected by metalled roads to Bundelkhand, Lucknow and Rae Bareilly before the 1850s. The East Indian Railway linking Kanpur with Calcutta, and the Oudh and Rohilkhand railway connection with Lucknow gave Kanpur an edge over other North Indian towns.[30] As old river routes lost their significance, port towns on rivers were marginalised. Kalpi, which lay on the Jumna and received the trade in cotton, grain and oil-seeds from the Bundelkhand region, was now deserted. Farukhabad on the Ganges, through which the trade from Rohilkhand had passed, now 'yielded to the superior advantages of Cawnpore'.[31] By the 1870s Kanpur had become possibly the most important centre of trade in the North West Provinces. 'The roads leading to it from all sides,' reported Fuller, 'are lined with what often appears to be unending streams of carts, and its market-place Collectorganj, exhibits a scene of bustle and commercial activity not often seen in Indian cities.'[32]

The increasing commercial importance of the centre was recognised in administrative changes. The consolidation of the fourteen parganas around Kanpur into a district of Kanpur by the mid-nineteenth century formalised a process of change already

---

[29] W. Hoey, *Trade and Manufactures in North India* (Lucknow 1880), p. 30. Sanitary Commissioners annually reported on the changing fortunes of different market towns. See *Annual Report of the Sanitary Commissioner, NWP*, 1868, 1869, 1870, 1873. See also D.A. Thomes, 'Lucknow and Kanpur, 1880–1920: Stagnation and Development Under the Raj', *South Asia* 5:2 (New Series) 1982, pp. 68–80; R.G. Varady, 'The Diary of a Road: A Sequential Narration of the Origins of the Lucknow–Kanpur Road, *IESHR* 15: 2, 1978.

[30] 'In the vicissitudes which befell the towns of North India, Kanpur was a considerable gainer. It became the emporium where the grain of Awadh, Bundelkhand and Agra was collected for exportation by rail', Atkinson, *Statistical Account*, p. 224.

[31] Jones, 'Rise and Progress of Cawnpore', in Playne and Wright, *The Bombay Presidency, the UP and the Punjab*, p. 496.

[32] Note by C.S. Fuller, cited in Atkinson, *Statistical Account*, p. 147.

under way. While earlier Kanpur had been a part of Jajmau tahsil, by the turn of the nineteenth century Jajmau was a moribund town in Kanpur tahsil. New names and new boundaries were recording some of the changes in the life of the region.

Campoo Kanpur

In 1778, when the Company's troops first moved to Kanpur, they were granted twelve villages stretching along the riverfront from old Kanpur on the west to Jajmau on the east.[33] The settlement of old Kanpur, to which the city's origins are traced in local folklore, was overshadowed by the sheer physical spread of the cantonment territory. It was referred to as Kanpur kona (Kanpur corner)—differentiating it from Campoo (camp) Kanpur or cantonment. The changing profile of the riverfront and the shifting boundaries of the cantonment expressed larger conflicts over space.

Travel accounts of the 1780s describe Kanpur as 'a large military station on the Ganges . . . a cantonment for a brigade, amounting, on the war establishment to 10000 men'.[34] By 1803 it was 'the largest upcountry Cantonment in India'.[35] Substantial military presence here was felt necessary, for Kanpur in the late eighteenth and early nineteenth century was seen as a dangerous frontier zone, vulnerable to attacks from Maratha territories. Till the early nineteenth century the growing cantonment continued to be housed in tents. So strong in fact was the association of cantonment with camp that the term campoo came to be permanently associated with Kanpur in the nineteenth century, even after the camp colony had become a cantonment town.

Early travellers found the region desolate and dreary. Emma Roberts described the landscape around Kanpur as 'one wide waste of sand'.[36] Fanny Eden loathed Kanpur. It appeared to her as the 'ugliest' of all Indian stations: 'dead flat of course but not

---

[33] This was in accordance with the treaty of Faizabad signed after the Rohilla wars in 1773, by which the Company agreed to provide a brigade for the protection of Awadh. The troops were paid for by the Nawab and were initially stationed at Bilgram from where they were transferred to Kanpur in 1778. Montgomery, *Statistical Report*, p. 1.

[34] William Hodges, *Travels in India, 1780–83* (London 1793), p. 100.

[35] Yalland, *A Guide to the Kacheri Cemetery* (London 1983), p. 7.

[36] Roberts, *Hindustan*, vol. II, p. 44

one single blade of even brown grass to be seen—nothing but loose brown dust which rises in clouds upon the slightest provocation.'[37] To European travellers in the 1830s Kanpur did not convey the impression of a town: it appeared no more than an army encampment. Emily Eden, describing her first entry into Kanpur, wrote: 'This morning we made one of our grand entries into Kanpur, or rather *on* to it; for there is no particular Kanpur visible. But we drove over a miniature plain to our tents.'[38]

By the first few decades of the nineteenth century the Company position in the region became militarily and commercially secure. Kanpur was no longer considered a dangerous frontier zone, and from a temporary camp the cantonment came to acquire the character of a permanent station. Within the bleak landscape the company officials sought to re-create the images in their minds (see Fig. 1). By the 1840s the cantonment filled out with large bungalows, with 'splendid suites of apartments', 'well-fitted interiors' and 'well-kept gardens'.[39] Emma Roberts describes how 'all the English vegetables, with the exception of broad or Windsor beans, come to great perfection in the cold season'.[40] This English garden imagery in descriptions of Kanpur is laced with lush images of abundant oriental fruits, large bungalows with shady trees, and circular driveways which allowed vehicles to enter by one gate and leave by another.[41] Visual representations of Kanpur are coloured by notions of the picturesque that influenced European art of the period (see Fig. 2). By the 1870s thatched roofs were prohibited.[42] In Cantonment houses thatch was replaced by tiles

---

[37] Janet Dunbar, *Tigers, Durbars and Kings: Fanny Eden's Indian Journals, 1837–38* (London 1988), p. 98. Similarly, Emily Eden wrote how 'The dust at Cawnpore has been quite dreadful . . . People lose their way on the plains and everything is full of dust—books, dinner, clothes everything. We all detest Cawnpore.' *Up the Country*, p. 64.

[38] Eden, *Up the Country*, p. 52.

[39] Emma Roberts, *Hindostan: The Shores of the Red Sea and the Mountains*, vol. II (London n.d.), p. 44.

[40] Ibid.

[41] Ibid.

[42] Orders prohibiting thatched roofs were in response to frequent cases of fire in thatched encampments. In 1869, for instance, there was a discussion on providing tiled roofs for married barracks in the cantonment because of a serious case of fire. Mil. Progs., Feb. 1869, nos 736–8.

Fig. 1: Sketch by Robert Smith, 1828

Fig. 2: Trading activity within a rural idyll

and, by the late nineteenth century, with brick roofs.[43] The stability of Company power was, at this point, being celebrated by permanent and aesthetically pleasing structures.

By this time the town, to many officials, merchants and their families, seemed attractive for its theatricals, suppers and balls. The influx of women and families was a sign of changed times. A young official posted in Kanpur wrote home almost wearily: 'Ball after ball, dinner after dinner is all the go here. Late hours and fearfully hot weather begin to tell on our complexions and sickly faces in the morning appear on parade.'[44] Armymen composed ditties; a popular one went:

Civil servants who've come [from] all parts of the country
Boldly avow, indeed one of them swore,
For dancing, and dressing, for sky, and caressing,
No Indian station can vie with Cawnpore. [45]

In the winter months, the racecourse drew crowds of Europeans. Spectators tried to recreate images of the English countryside by dressing up as country gentlemen, farmers, rustics.[46] In the evenings the gentry from the cantonment and Nawabganj went on pleasure drives down the racecourse road, and once a week carriages congregated at the bandstand to hear the King's Dragoon Regiment play. Letters from the 1860s note how women chose to stay on in Kanpur even in the summer months, and theatricals, musical evenings, parties continued into May.[47]

Up to the mid-nineteenth century Kanpur was still largely a cantonment town. The cantonment occupied the best stretches of land on the riverfront, and over 90 per cent of the space: in contrast to the 6477 acres of cantonment area in 1848, only 690 acres were under civilian control. The civil area was hemmed in by the

---

[43] Wright, the settlement official narrated how: 'The oldest inhabitant is fond of relating how such and such a Collector Sahib converted thatched into tiled roof, ending with a description of *pukka* roofs under the vigorous administration of W Halsey.' Atkinson, *Statistical Account*, p. 75.

[44] Cited in Yalland, *Traders and Nabobs*, p. 167.

[45] Ibid., p. 171.

[46] Ibid., pp. 168–9.

[47] Millie Stewart to Tina, her sister-in-law, 28 Mar. 1864, reproduced in Yalland, *Boxwallahs*, pp. 120–1.

military on three sides. The cantonment grew by displacing the old residents who had inhabited the riverfront in the Jajmau area; these were now pushed back, further away from the river, to Patkapur, Kursawan, Sisamau, or westwards towards old Kanpur and Nawabganj.[48]

District courts and civil offices were located within the cantonment premises. Growing disputes between civil and military authorities led to their relocation in Bithur in 1811, and then at Nawabganj in 1819. After 1857 conflicts between civil and military authorities took a new turn. Many within officialdom were convinced of the need to strengthen imperial power by extending the bounds of civil authority. Ultimately, these pressures were important in redefining the powers and functions of civil authority as well as its territorial jurisdiction. Civil jurisdiction was extended by adding two tracts from the western portion of the cantonment: one along the riverbank (extending from old Kanpur on the west to the Harness and Saddlery Factory, and southwards to the canal on the east), and the other an inland tract consisting of Sadr Bazar and some mohallas adjoining it on the east, and the brick-kiln area on the west.

The expanded frontiers of civilian Kanpur and the shrunken cantonment encompassed within it the complexities of the changing relationships of power between civil and military authorities. Changes in boundaries involved processes fraught with conflict. The inclusion of areas like 'Sudder Bazar', Faithfulganj and Harrisganj within the boundaries of the cantonment was considered by some officials 'an anomaly': these were seen as 'portions of the mercantile city of Cawnpore'.[49] Military authorities strove to preserve the purity of the cantonment, untainted by the polluting city, yet they were resistent to proposals excluding bazaar areas from their control. Markets like Harrisganj were important centres for salt, grain and cotton and brought in substantial revenues for the cantonment. Besides, bazaars occupied a liminal zone where soldiers could seek pleasure within the boundaries of the cantonment: among the bazaar dwellers were prostitutes. Military authorities were concerned about the incidence of venereal disease,

[48] Tripathi and Arora, *Kanpur ka Itihas*, pp. 164–8
[49] From J. Simson to Secy, NWP and Awadh, 27.2.1880, in Mil. Progs. A, no. 2077.

yet emphasised that sexual relations with registered prostitutes were important for the health and virility of European soldiers. Prostitutes in the cantonment bazaars were within easy access of the barracks and could be brought under surveillance and control.[50] In the summer months soldiers tended to confine their liaisons to the vicinity of their barracks. In pleasanter winter days they often ventured out of the bounds of the cantonment to solicit women in the villages around.[51]

By the late nineteenth century the civil areas with 'fine houses' clearly overshadowed the cantonment, which looked dilapidated and forsaken in contrast.[52] Harrisganj, a bazaar, which serviced the cantonment was, in comparison with Collectorgunj, decaying. By the 1880s only salt traders operated from Harrisganj; the grain and cotton trade had shifted to markets like Collectorganj and Couperganj, more conveniently located near the East Indian Railway station.[53]

These changes in Kanpur were linked to broader processes within North Indian economy and society. What other towns were losing by the late nineteenth century—with the decline of old regional chieftains, shifts in centres of local power, changes in routes, patterns and composition of commerce—Kanpur was gaining. From a cantonment it became a big ganj and trading mart, and later an important industrial city with a substantial labouring population.

[50] For a detailed discussion on the contagious diseases and cantonment acts, see Kenneth Ballhatchet, *Race, Sex and Class Under the Raj: Imperial Attitudes and Policies and their Critics, 1793–1905* (London 1980); Judy Whitehead, 'Bodies Clean and Unclean Prostitution, Sanitary Legislation and Respectable Femininity in Colonial North India', *Gender and History*, 7:1, 1995.

[51] The average daily number of soldiers afflicted by venereal disease went up to 56 in November and 65 in December, and fell to 18.86 in May and 5.75 in July. The report on lock hospitals explains this fluctuation by the seasonal preferences of the soldiers: 'During the cold months of the year the men give up frequenting the regimental bazaars and take to roaming over the country in search of fresh women.' Home Public Progs. A, May 1870, no. 77.

[52] Gavin Jones on his return to Kanpur in 1896, cited in Yalland, *Boxwallahs*, p. 352.

[53] F.N. Wright, Offg Mag., Kanpur, to Commsr, Allahabad, Mil. Progs. A, July 1881, no. 2077.

The Brutal City

The events of 1857 marked the city with a new significance. The chief event by which Kanpur was remembered in the annals of the Mutiny was the brutal massacre of European civilians on the banks of the Ganga, just when they were about to board boats to flee the city besieged by rebels. Before retreating from Kanpur in July 1857, Nana Fadnavis, an important Maratha chieftain and leader of the rebel forces in Kanpur, reportedly ordered the massacre of civilian hostages. This became emblematic of the barbarity of the rebels and provided the point of reference for subsequent stories of massacre. Rumours now multiplied with amazing speed and every embroidered detail of rebel brutality now appeared believable.[54]

Official descriptions of Kanpur and travel accounts of the late nineteenth century dwell almost entirely on the happenings of 1857. It was as if this event had repressed all other histories, all other memories and associations of the place. A handbook on Bengal and the North West Provinces stated: 'The sole interest attaching to the place being from the frightful massacres which took place.' *The Story of the Cawnpore Mission*, published in 1923, begins dramatically:

> CAWNPORE! More than sixty years have passed since the name sent a thrill through the heart of every man and woman of English race. Only those that were alive then can imagine the shock and the sense of horror and astonishment that fell upon England when the tidings came of the surrender of the beleagured [*sic*] British garrison and the treacherous, cold-blooded massacre of over 1000 of our countrymen, including women and children.[55]

Cawnpore had become a metaphor expressing many new meanings. The name chilled English hearts, fusing a sense of fear with the experience of humiliation and shame: the surrender was imperial disgrace. The 'Cawnpore Massacre', as the event was designated, reconfirmed imperial visions of oriental barbarism and

---

[54] See Rudrangshu Mukherjee, *The Spectre of Violence* (Viking 1998). On the symbolic significance of the massacre, see Jenny Sharpe, *Allegories of Empire* (Minneapolis 1993).

[55] Society for the Propagation of the Gospel, *The Story of the Cawnpore Mission* (Aberdeen 1923), p. 1.

debauchery. Images of violated women and murdered children were tirelessly recreated in emotive narratives and romanticised art. Drummer John Fitchett of the 6th Native Infantry, for instance, gave a graphic account of what he claimed to have seen at Bebee Ghar, where 206 European women and children were reported to have been imprisoned and killed:

> Five men then entered, they had swords, it was about sunset. The lady who spoke to the jamadar was first cut down. I saw her fall . . . I heard fearful shrieks. This lasted half an hour or more. I did not see any of the women or children try to escape. . . . The groans lasted all night. I was only fifteen or sixteen paces from the house . . . At about 8 o'clock the next morning, the sweepers living in the compound were ordered to throw the bodies into a dry well, near the house. The bodies were dragged out, most of them by the hair of the head, those whose clothes were worth taking were stripped. Some of the women were alive, I cannot say how many, but three could speak; . . . Three children were also alive. I do not know what orders came, but I saw one of the children thrown in alive. I believe the other children and women who were alive were then thrown in. There was a great crowd looking on; they were standing along the walls of the compound. They were principally city people and villagers. The children were running round the well, where else could they go? And there was no one to save them. No, none said a word, or tried to save them.[56]

The helplessness of innocents is contrasted with the villainy of all natives. The people of the city are implicated in the murder: the act of being mute witnesses becomes an act of complicity.

Soon after the event, on 27 October 1857, Major Anson returned to Bebee Ghar, as if to relive the experience: 'We saw lots of remnants of gowns, shoes, and garments dyed in blood, and blood upon the walls in different places. Outside in the compound there was a skull of a woman, and hair about on the bushes. Oh! what tearful eyes and aching breasts must there have throbbed!'[57]

Places and monuments in the city came to be seen through the lens of 1857. After standard descriptions of Benares, Jaunpur, Brindaban, Agra, Lucknow, etc., G.W. Forrest's account of Kanpur is emotionally charged: 'Seated on the steps of the temple of Siva

[56] Cited in Yalland, *Traders and Nabobs*, pp. 271–2.
[57] St G. Anson, *With JM 9th Lancers during the Indian Mutiny* (London n.d.), cited in Yalland, *Boxwallahs*, p. 42.

it is hard to realise *that*historical tragedy . . .'(emphasis added).[58]
The roots of evil are now traced to the pre-British period: 'The
town bore an evil reputation. During the lately suppressed rule of
the King of Oude it had become a city of refuge for bad characters
flying across the Ganges from the not too exacting justice of that
monarch. It had also become the depot from which criminals,
urged by pressing reasons to quit the British territories, had em-
barked for Oudh. Cawnpore had indeed become the Alsatia of the
middle Doab.'[59] It was as if evil had become an innate, a permanent, characteristic of the town: this was repeatedly expressed
even in the 1920s and 1930s. In the official imagination, 1857
signified the desolation of the town, a savage assault on civility,
order and reason, the end of an era:

> I took a walk in the morning to view the second desolation of he
> Cantonment. You have no idea what a waste the poor unfortunate
> station is—compounds eaten up, trees all cut down, walls broken
> down—it is quite difficult to find one's way about so utterly changed
> is the whole aspect of the place. . . . the assembly room is roofless,
> and one vast mass of bricks and rubbish inside, with huge beams,
> charred all over lying about. Huge shot-holes are visible in nearly
> every large house.[60]

The fate of a community is presented in such accounts as the
fate of the town as a whole. The Indian traders and gomasthas, the
shopkeepers and bazaar dwellers disappear in such representations.
A new town had to be built on the ruins of the old.

Industrial Kanpur

On the ruins of the old cantonment emerged the first industrial
concerns in Kanpur. The bungalows that lined the riverfront were
destroyed during the Mutiny and the western portion of the cantonment was added to the civil area. It was at the site of these
broken-down bungalows that the first factories were built. Now
the landscape of the riverfront changed dramatically. Factory
chimneys dotted what had been picturesque; earlier, all that was

---

[58] G.W. Forrest, *Cities of India* (London 1905), p. 244.
[59] Atkinson, *Statistical Account*, p. 163.
[60] Anson's description, in Yalland, *Boxwallahs*, p. 78.

visible beyond the bathing ghats and temples was the outline of bungalows behind rows of trees.[61] Sailboats on the river dwindled as railways replaced much of the river traffic.

Tall, impressive looking Lancashire-style factory buildings came up in a cityscape which nineteenth-century travel accounts described as architecturally barren. Travellers looking for the novelty of Indo-European architecture in nawabi Lucknow, or those admiring the grandeur of gothic Bombay and neo-classical Calcutta, found nothing of comparison in Kanpur.[62] A description from the 1880s notes:

> few buildings of any architectural pretensions and none of any antiquity. The Jami Masjid is a commonplace unadorned structure, Prayag Narayan and Guru Parshsad's new temples are the costliest buildings of their kind . . . The houses of Diwan Nasir Ali and Aga Mir's sons are the only dwellings of any importance. The former has tanks, fountains and an audience hall of some beauty, but all these are falling into slow decay from the increasing embarrassments of their owners. The kotwali or chief police station is an unpretending building . . .[63]

In nawabi Lucknow monuments were part of a culture of power: the nawabs were responding to Company presence through their own imaginative mixture of European and Indian architectural styles. Kanpur, never such an administrative centre, lacked the architectural legacy of power. Here pious, parsimonious Vaishnava merchants built ghats and temples along the Ganges while the European army built its barracks and bungalows.

Kanpur's military past remained inscribed within the new industrial city. Many areas retained names they had acquired when they serviced the cantonment. Filkhana, for instance, was the place where elephants were tied; Roti Godown was the storehouse for bread supplied to the army; Parade was an area where soldiers paraded. Sadr Bazaar (the main market), Gora Bazaar (a bazaar where natives were excluded), Bhusa Toli (where hay was sold), Garariya Mohal (locality of ironsmiths), Danakhori (where grain

[61] See description in Yalland, *Traders and Nabobs*, p. 107.

[62] There were of course many travellers who abhorred the 'decadence' of Indo-European architecture. See Rosie Llewellyn-Jones, *A Fatal Friendship: The Nawabs, the British and the City of Lucknow* (Delhi 1985).

[63] Atkinson, *Statistical Account*, p. 220.

for military cavalry was sold), Butcherkhana (which supplied meat to the cantonment) and Coolie Bazaar (where a coolie market was held), were all connected with the daily life of the cantonment.[64]

Workers continued to identify factories through indigenous categories that had associations with the past. The Harness and Saddlery factory, for instance, was locally referred to as the kila (fort). It was located in the now-broken-down Cawnpore Magazine which had served as a fort and store for ammunition and equipment since the 1780s. The Cooper Allen works was familiarly known as Hazari Bangla or a military bungalow, hazari connoting a military chief of a thousand troops. Other factories that came up in subsequent years had names which were meaningful in terms of the prefigurative structures of those who worked in them. Elgin Mills was for generations of workers Purana Putlighar. It was the oldest cotton mill in the city, and purana evoked this significance for workers. Cawnpore Cotton Mills was Couperganj-ka-putlighar, Woollen Mills was Kambal Putlighar.[65] The term putlighar derived from a rural, artisanal context where machines for weaving cotton were called putli, ghar being the space where these were housed. The terms had no necessary precision: the Kambal Putlighar did not produce only blankets (kambal). But these descriptive categories conveyed to workers a sense of what the factory produced or when and where it was set up.

In the years to come the Gwaltoli and Khalasi Lines area, in the neighbourhood of some of the old mills, became a nucleus of militant working class activity. The office of the first trade union, the Kanpur Mazdur Sabha, was established here. A large number workers lived in the Gwaltoli, Khalasi Lines and Parmat area,[66] in bastis which date back to times before the factories, when the labouring population serviced the cantonment.[67] In later years,

[64] Tripathi and Arora, *Kanpur ka Itihaas*, p. 172.

[65] The Woollen Mills also came to be known popularly as 'Lalimli' from its trademark—a tamarind tree in the compound.

[66] Parmat derives its name from 'permit' or the passes issued by the Customs House located on the banks of the river. To obtain a pass, duty had to be paid on goods going down the river, and for products coming for sale in Kanpur, town dues had to be cleared.

[67] Report of the Cawnpore Expansion Committee, UP Mun. Progs., Dec. 1918, no. 1(a).

when factories came up in the Juhi area to the south, new settlements of workers came up at the far end of the city in Lachmipurwa
and Darshanpurwa (see Fig. 3).

Kanpur's emergence as an industrial centre is linked closely
with its trading and military past. The early entrepreneurs in
Kanpur were those like the Maxwells, Jones and Coopers who
had made their fortunes on indigo estates; or men who served in
the Company army and moved to industrial entrepreneurship.
The old industry, and the Cawnpore Magazine where it was located, were wiped out in 1857, and it was a decade after the Mutiny
that leather was revived. Military needs for leather lay behind the
efforts to revive and modernise production in the 1860s. The
expertise of European soldiers who had worked in tanyards in
England was utilised to introduce improved methods of tanning.[68]
Abundant supplies of bark from babul trees was available locally;
and raw hide was supplied largely by butchers who provided meat
to Company troops. Many big merchants dealt exclusively in raw
hide at Delhi, Meerut, Mathura, Etawah, Jhansi and Moradabad.[69]
From the very beginning the quality of harness and saddlery
produced by Kanpur was considered of very high quality, even
better than the English products it was replacing.[70]

The growing military demand provided the context in which a
leather factory, manufacturing boots and shoes for the army,
Cooper Allen and Company, was set up by William Cooper and
George Allen, both of whom started out on indigo estates. Cooper
Allen and Company initially traded in raw cotton and moved
later to the manufacture of leather goods. Allen's connections
with influential military and viceregal circles helped his company
secure a renewable seven-year contract with the government for
the supply of 25,000 pairs of boots.[71]

The first textile mills in Kanpur came up in the1860s, when
Lancashire cotton faced a crisis because of a shortage in the supply of American long-stapled cotton. There was a spurt in the

[68] Jones, 'Rise and Progress of Cawnpore', in Playne and Wright, *The
Bombay Presidency, the UP and the Punjab.*

[69] Ahmad Mukhtar, *Report on Labour Conditions in Tanneries and
Leather Goods Factories* (Simla 1946).

[70] Col. Lewis, Offg Inspector, General Ordnance and Magazines, to the
Secy, Mil. Dep. 7 Mar. 1872, Mil. Progs. A, Apr. 1872, no. 849.

[71] Yalland, *Boxwallahs*, p. 223.

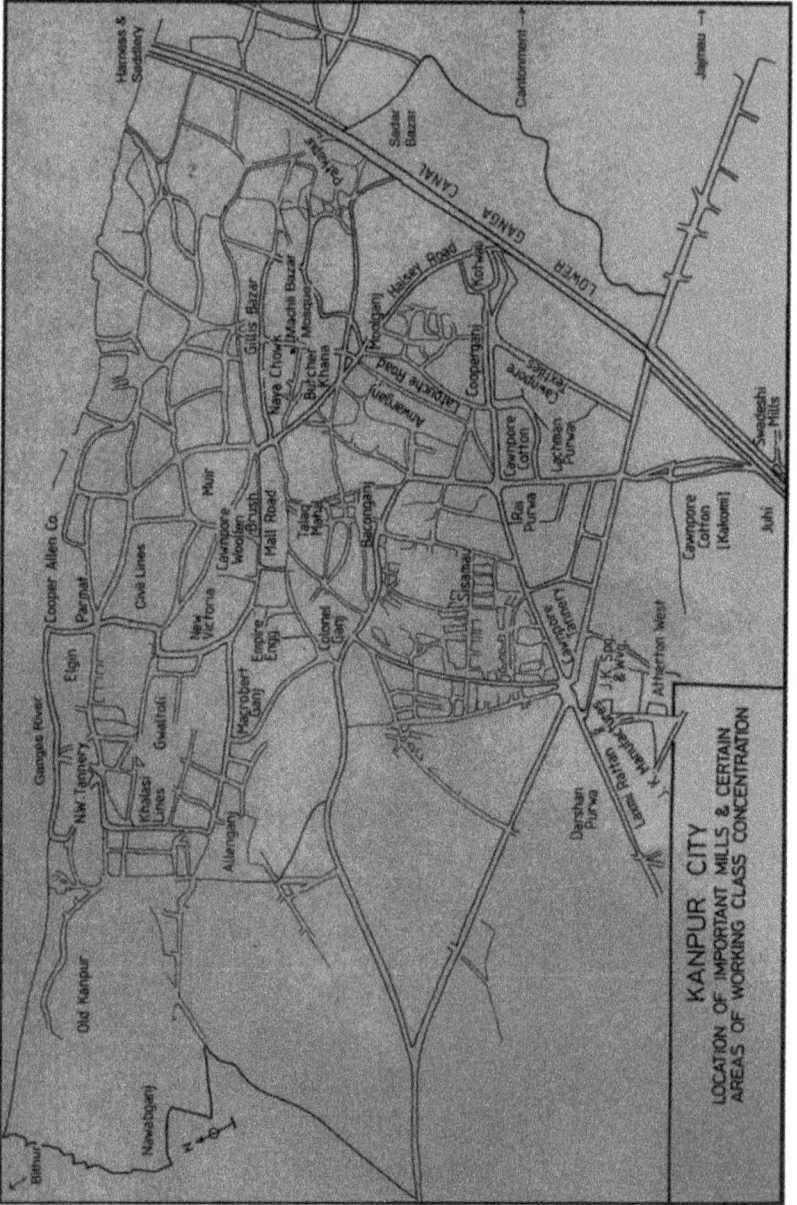

Fig. 3: Location of important mills and areas of working class concentration

demand for Indian cotton. Kanpur, which had been a trading centre for cotton since the eighteenth century, suddenly had more raw cotton flowing in than it could handle.[72] The glut in raw cotton and the need to meet the army requirements for tents and uniforms provided the context within which plans to produce textiles locally were floated. Officials from the army commissariat tried to give shape to a scheme, and Elgin Mills, named after the ruling viceroy, was set up. Eventually this company had to be auctioned because it ran out of credit and Hugh Maxwell, from the same family that had long business links with Kanpur, the only bidder, became a proprietor. Indian merchants and bankers played an important role in financing Elgin Mills. The names of Lala Ishaq Lal and Lala Guneshee Lal figure among the directors of the company, although as a proportion of the total shareholders Indians constituted only around 12 per cent. Technical expertise was provided by Europeans, leading among whom was Gavin Jones, celebrated as a hero of 1857 in contemporary European accounts. He had trained as an engineer after the decline in the indigo fortunes of the family. His shift to the textile industry, as manager of Elgin Mills, was related partly to his family ties with the Maxwells. Elgin Mills made successful inroads into markets supplied formerly by imported products and towels, drills, tents, and dhotis, and the Elgin trademark became famed for quality and durability.[73]

The mills that came up in subsequent years were largely initiated by a different kind of entrepreneur. Skilled workers, technicians, fitters, weaving masters and chemists, had sailed out from England to explore job openings in the new textile mills of India.[74] The quick success of Elgin Mills and the expanding demand created by the Afghan campaigns provided an opportunity for new

---

[72] 'Cawnpore was flooded with countless bales of cotton that poured from Bundelkhand, Rohilkhand, Awadh and the Doab in huge streams, beyond the carrying capacity of the railway . The roads in the city were piled high above the house-tops, completely blocking the way.' Gavin Jones, 'Rise and Progress of Cawnpore', in Playne and Wright, *The Bombay Presidency, the UP and the Punjab*, p. 496.

[73] Yalland, *Boxwallahs*, p. 184

[74] Most jute mill managers in Calcutta, similarly, were from a working class background. Chakrabarty, *Rethinking Working Class History*, p. 168.

enterprises to come up in Kanpur. Two entrepreneurs, John Harwood and Atherton West, were both from a working class background in Lancashire. Harwood worked briefly in a Bombay mill, from where he was drawn upcountry to Kanpur by the hope of better terms. After a stint as weaving master in Elgin Mills, he set up the Cawnpore Cotton Mills. West joined Elgin as weaving master in place of Harwood after initial training at Burnley. Later, in 1886, he started Victoria Mills with financial help from Juggilal. Francis Horsman was a Yorkshireman. After working in mills in Bombay and Indore, he joined Elgin Mills as a fitter, and many years later set up Swadeshi Cotton Mills (1911).

Till the 1920s, there were no Indian-owned textile mills in Kanpur. Unlike jute in Bengal, trade in raw cotton and ginning and pressing was largely in the hands of Marwari trading families.[75] Indian traders and bankers were, however, closely involved in financing European-owned enterprises. Bankers like Juggilal advanced loans to Elgin Mills, Atherton West Mills, Victoria Mills; Lalmun Mishra, Shiv Prased Baldeo Choudhary and Harnandrai Ram provided credit to Muir Mills. The possibilities for expansion of indigenous industry during the post-war period, and a more favourable tariff policy, provided the context in which Marwari trading families invested in textiles. The Singhanias, descendants of a Farukhabad merchant family—Baijnath Ramnath—settled in Kanpur for many decades, set up JK Cotton Spinning and Weaving Mills (1921), JK Cotton Manufactures (1933), and JK Jute Mills (1931) and the JK. Iron and Steel Company (1934), and collaborated with Ram Ratan Gupta in setting up Laxmi Ratan Cotton Mills (1934). Mangtu Ram Jaipuria, a trading agent for Horsman, the proprietor, purchased Swadeshi Cotton Mills in in 1946. By the 1930s, many indigenous merchants who had financed European concerns were industrial entrepreneurs.

The racial and economic divide between European and Indian capitalists was evident in the organisation of separate chambers of commerce by them. European capitalists in Kanpur organised the Upper India Chamber of Commerce in 1888, partly to take concerted measures to regulate the increasing competition for labour within industry and to articulate their unified voice against

[75] Nevill, *Gazetteer*, p. 3.

proposed factory laws. The chamber came into conflict with the colonial state over various issues. It opposed restrictive factory legislation in India, seeing it as an effort by Lancashire interests to hamper the growth of the mill industry in India;[76] it criticised state policy on cotton duties—the exemption of handlooms, it argued, would threaten the interests of the mill industry.[77] Indian merchants like Juggilal, major financiers of the early European mills, were included, but on the whole their representation was marginal.

In 1914 an organisation of Indians traders and industrialists, the UP Chamber of Commerce was set up in the changed context of pressures generated by the swadeshi movement. This criticised the fiscal policy of the colonial state and urged the government to help industry through measures like financial aid, encouragement to commercial and technical education, and representation of non-officials on the Fiscal Commission. The two chambers, shared many concerns, a fact publicly acknowledged by the representatives of the UICC.[78] There were also important differences. Till the early 1920s the majority of members of the UP Chamber were connected with trade and banking and not manufacture.[79] Many were involved in the import and sale of piece-goods from Europe, and it was only during the non-cooperation movement that several switched to trade in indigenous manufactures.[80] Various

[76] *UICC Report*, 1890, p. 22.

[77] The president of the chamber pointed out that the large extensions in the spinning department of the mills and the absence of any extensions in the weaving department was related directly to the impositions of excise duty on cotton. *UICC Report*, 1896, p. iv.

[78] Welcoming the formation of the UP Chamber, the President of the UICC noted: 'There has been room for this Chamber and its establishment is a welcome sign of our times. Its creation can be of valuable assistance to our common purposes . . .' *UICC Report*, 1914, p. ii.

[79] There were however those like Shriram Mahadeo Prasad who owned flour mills and cotton ginning and pressing factories, or Seth Nanak Chand Shadiram who owned flour mills and an iron foundry. *Silver Jubilee Souvenir 1914–31, UP Chamber of Commerce* (Kanpur n.d.), p. 110.

[80] Seth Lakshmi Narayan Girdharilal, an importer of printed and coloured cloth from Europe, stopped trade in imported goods and became a sole selling agent for Cawnpore Cotton Mills and later for Victoria Mills. *UPCC Silver Jubilee Souvenir*, p. 100.

Fig. 4: Cawnpore Woollen Mills, 1938

Fig. 5: Cooper Allen and Co., Kanpur, 1938

constraints inhibited Indian enterprise. The close racial ties with the military commissariat gave European entrepreneurs a large captive market—the army being a major consumer of Kanpur production. Discriminatory credit policies of European banks towards Indian merchants created other problems.[81] One of the issues that the UPCC pressed for was the appointment of Indians to the Directorate of Presidency Banks. In the 1930s, however, European and Indian industrialists drew together in the Employers' Association of North India, which was set up to deal collectively with labour upsurge.[82]

The world that European members of the UICC shared was culturally distinct from that of Marwari entrepreneurs. The difference was affirmed through their exclusive social and sports clubs. Within the UICC there were, obviously, lines of difference between the indigo gentry turned capitalist and those from humbler, artisanal backgrounds. George Allen, for instance, ran his boot and shoe company like an absentee owner, dividing his time between his home in Allahabad and his summer retreat in Mashobra, Simla. The Maxwells became patrons of the Cawnpore Tent Club and made pigsticking an important part of the sporting activity of the Kanpur elite.[83] Those from artisanal backgrounds like Atherton West, or Horsman, were not so used to the leisurely ways of the gentry. They set up their own mills, setting aside savings by parsimony and thrift. The punctiliousness with which Atherton West supervised each detail of the mills earned him the reputation of a 'white Marwari'.[84] Beyond this divide there was a racial unity forged against the colonised, a unity that appeared particularly important in the post-Mutiny conjuncture. The upper crust came together with the lower in associations like the Cawnpore Volunteers Club. Among the leading members were John

[81] See A.K. Bagchi, *The Evolution of the State Bank of India, vol. 2: The Era of Presidency Banks, 1876–1920* (Delhi 1997), p. 190.

[82] In a vote of thanks, at a meeting of the Employers' Association, Singhania commended the services of Gavin Jones: 'You have done a great service to the employers of North India by combining them and by organising them into such an institution as this from which they can see the great benefits of unity.' *National Herald*, 6.4.1939.

[83] Yalland, *Boxwallahs*, p. 194.

[84] See ibid. on the careful management of mill production by West and Horsman, pp. 253–7, 259–62.

Harwood, Alfred Butterworth and Atherton West. The association, open only to Europeans and Anglo-Indians, was formed to train volunteers in military combat and prepare for emergency situations. Among its important activities was the staging of mock battles at Jajmau, an important site of the Mutiny.

The social world of the indigenous merchant community in Kanpur was fractured along religious lines. The cultural divide between Muslim merchants and tannery owners from the Marwari–bania trading community often made debate over local economic issues very acrimonious. Muslim traders saw the politics of the Hindu-dominated Municipal Board as clearly discriminating against them.[85] This upper-caste Hindu bias of the municipality also drew the attention of European entrepreneurs, who were critical of the municipality's lack of support to the leather industry.[86]

Rhythms of Industrial Expansion

The initial expansion of the textile industry took place in the context of imperial campaigns in the north-west frontier and Africa. Kanpur was an important supplier of tents and warm clothing to Company troops in China and South Africa in the late nineteenth century. The UICC noted in a self-congratulatory tone how Kanpur was becoming a major resource centre which could meet sudden demands on the frontier or at sea: 'There can be no doubt that Kanpur is prepared to cooperate both heartily and effectively in the propagation of that spirit of imperialism which

[85] See ch. 7.

[86] In a letter to the DM, the Cooper Allen managers attributed the municipal octroi policy and the unreasonably high octroi duty on babul bark, a tanning agent, to the Hindu majority in the municipality: 'We beg to remind you that the majority of your municipality is composed of Hindu gentlemen of more or less high caste. These gentlemen have . . . their prejudices and among them [the prejudices] a very pronounced contempt and dislike for anything connected with the manufacture of leather. . .' Letter, 21.1.1893, NWP and Awadh Mun. Progs., Jan. 1893, no.15. On another occasion, the members of the chamber were critical of the Municipal Board for giving time and money to sentimental matters like the maintenance of a gaikhana and on a bathing ghat instead of improving sanitation in the city. W.B. Wishart on behalf of UICC to Municipal Board, Kanpur, 16.7.1890, NWP and Awadh Mun. Progs., Oct. 1890, no. 82.

the recent difficulties of the Empire have awakened in so remarkable a manner throughout all colonies and dependencies.'[87] In the domestic market the industry faced serious competition from the handloom industry in the 1890s. In 1896, the UICC complained how one of the local mills had accumulated stocks amounting to around 600,000 lbs, and nearly 1000 looms in Kanpur were silent.[88] The 'brisk demand for yarn of low counts for the handloom industry', the chamber argued, was evidence of this competition.[89] Apart from yarn, which was woven into cloth, the Kanpur mills produced a vast quantity of bundled yarn supplied to handloom weavers.[90] However, unlike the Bombay industry, which was a major supplier of yarn to the China market, Kanpur's mills always had a strong weaving component and supplied large orders for tents, sacking, drills, sheets and bandages to the army.[91] In fact, what gave the Kanpur mills special significance was the

[87] Presidential address, *UICC Report*, 1897, p. vii. The President added that in the face of growing threats to the Suez Canal route and the realisation that India had to become self-sufficient, Kanpur came to be seen as a storehouse and manufactory which could supply stores if communications were disrupted.

[88] *UICC Report*, 1896, p. iv.

[89] 'The experience of the [cotton] trade in Bombay, Bengal and Upper Provinces is that the handloom industry can and does compete successfully as a commercial rival, with the mills . . .' *UICC Report*, 1896, p. iii. Earlier too, W.E. Cooper of the UICC pointed to the threat to the mill industry in the coarse goods trade, because of the exemption of the handloom industry from the Amended Cotton Duties Act. *UICC Report*, 1895, App. xi.

[90] UP Ind. Progs. A, no. 11(a), File 533, 1919 (UPSA).

[91] Elgin Mills, for instance, manufactured the following goods for government consumption: tents, sacking, jhools, cordage for the ordnance department; white drill, khaki drill, silesia, lining cloths, webbing, grey shirting, foot bandage material, cotton putties for the army clothing dept; hospital sheets, barrack sheets, followers, turbans, pillow-case material, towels, tablecloths, dusters for the commissariat dept; wax drammer, kharwa, sewing thread, doosootee for the supdt of stationery; drill uniforms, printed turban cloths, purdahs, durries, floor cloth for the state railway dept. Source: Letter, 31.7.1895 from UICC to Secy, Bengal Chamber in App. K, p. 147, *UICC Report*, 1895. On Bombay, see Raj Chandavarkar, *The Origins of Industrial Capitalism in India: Business Strategies and the Working Classes in Bombay, 1900–1940* (Cambridge 1994), pp. 244–51.

large scale on which they were organised. As early as 1905, none of the mills had less than 40,000 spindles and 500 looms.[92]

A dramatic spurt in textile production took place during the First World War period, when most of the mills were busy supplying government contracts in yarn and cloth.[93] By 1917 more than 50,000 tents had been supplied and an outturn of 17,850,000 yards of cotton material was recorded.[94] The total production of woven goods increased from an index figure of 100 in 1908–10 to 135 in 1915–16, and yarn production increased from an index figure of 100 to 134 in the same period (Fig. 6). Figures for the production of tents, drills and jeans supplied to the army showed a more substantial increase (Fig. 7).

The woollen mills also had huge orders for army supplies, some of the work being subcontracted to village weavers. The supply and distribution of yarn to weavers and the collection of woven blankets from them was organised through syndicates, which were also responsible for finishing them according to army specifications.[95] To meet increased production targets the mills worked longer hours and tightened labour discipline.[96] The profits of the textile industry went up sharply, despite the steep rise in raw cotton prices.[97] The hike in yarn and cloth prices more than made up for the increased costs of raw cotton; in fact the mills made huge profits by selling large stocks which they had produced out of cheap cotton purchased early in the year[98] (Figs 9 and 10).[98] In New Victoria Mills profits peaked to an index of 1117 from a base of 100 in 1911 (see Fig. 11). The heavy army orders led to a de-

[92] See M.M. Mehta, *Structure of Cotton Mill Industry of India* (Allahabad 1949), pp. 270–2.

[93] Com. and Ind. Dept, GOI, Dec. 1917, Files 20–1.

[94] *UICC Report,* 1917, p. x.

[95] Com. and Ind., Dec. 1917, nos 20–1 (NAI).

[96] C. Joshi, 'The Formation of Work Culture: Industrial Labour in a North Indian City (1890s–1940s)', *Purusartha,* 14, 1991.

[97] 'The year 1916–17 witnessed a sensational rise in the price of cotton, but the year under report (1917–18) has witnessed a rise in prices to levels never previouly recorded.' UP Ind. Progs. A, no. 11(a), File 24,1919, Bundle 45 (UPSA).

[98] Com. and Ind. Progs., Dec. 1917, nos 20–1.

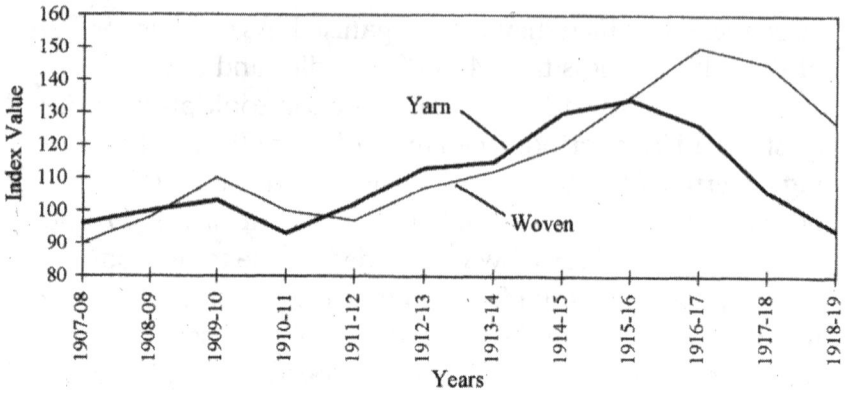

Fig. 6: Mill production of yarn and woven goods in UP (1907–1919)

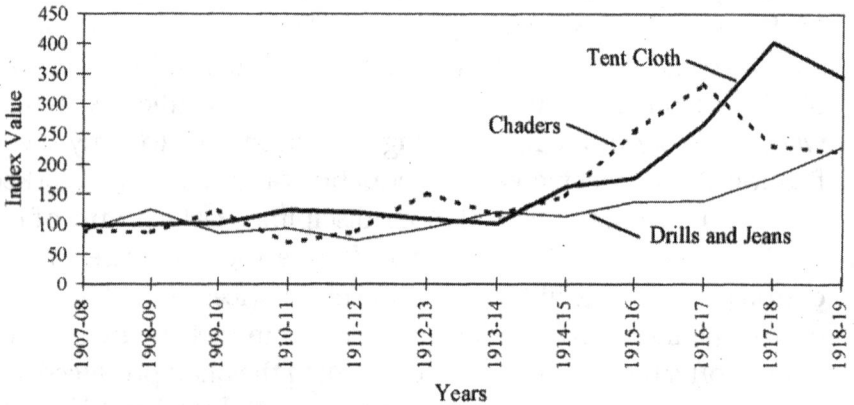

Fig. 7: Mill production of chadars, drills, and tent cloth in UP (1907–1919)

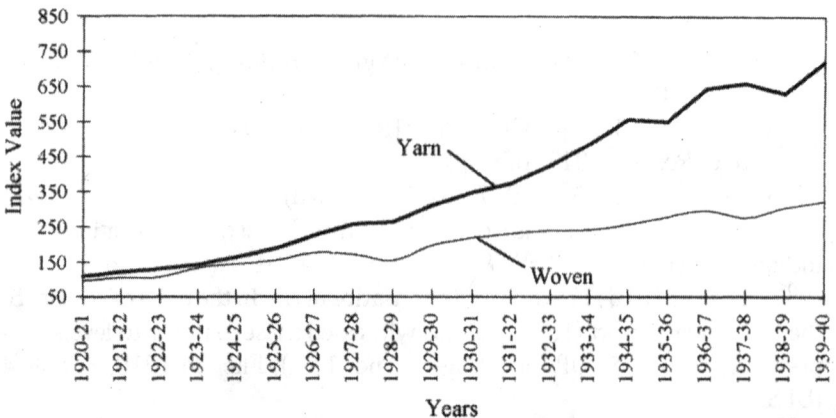

Fig. 8: Mill production of yarn and woven goods in UP (1920–1938)

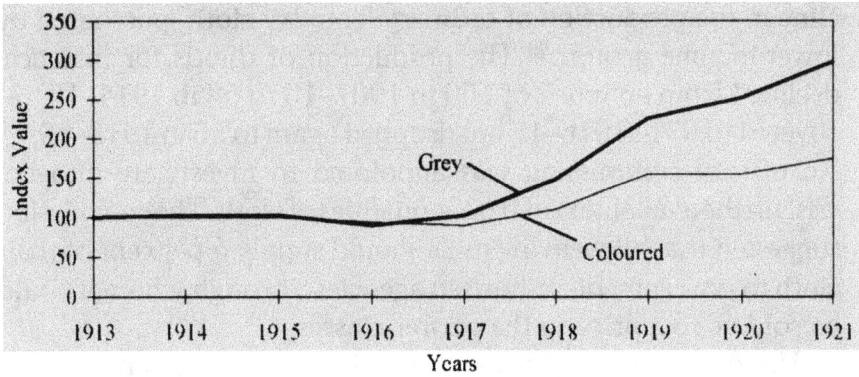

Fig. 9: Prices of exported cotton goods (All India: 1913–1921)

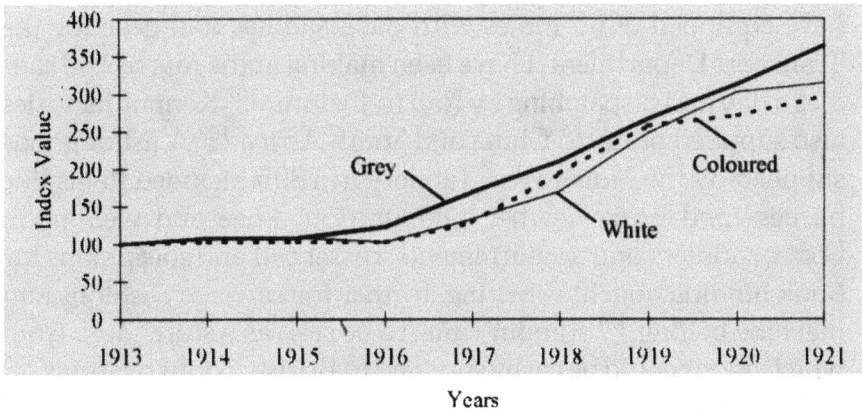

Fig. 10: Prices of imported cotton goods (All India: 1913–1921)

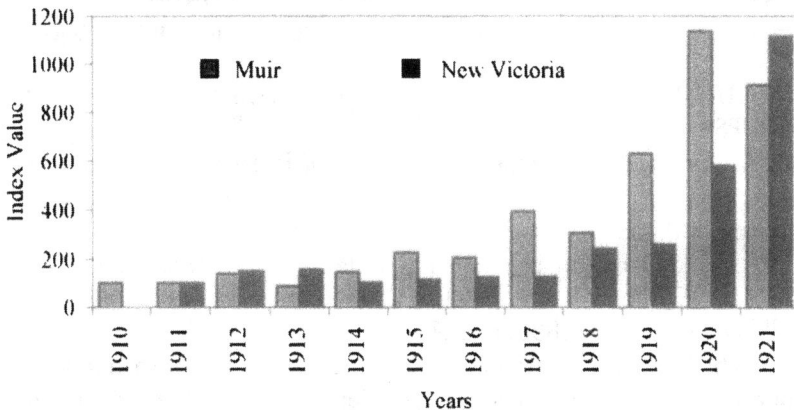

Fig. 11: Profit of selected mills (Kanpur: 1910–1921)

cline in the production of ordinary 'country cloth' purchased by lower-income groups.[99] The production of dhotis for instance, declined from an index of 100 in 1907–10 to 58 in 1914–15, recovered to 97 in 1916–17 but dropped again to 56 in 1918–19.[100] An official commission was appointed to investigate into the crisis in the availability of bazaar qualities of cloth. The commission suggested that all weaving mills should supply 5 per cent of their cloth to government authorised agencies, through whom it could be sold at cost price to the poorer classes. [101]

The Afghan campaigns and the First World War encouraged the expansion of other industries. The Harness and Saddlery worked overtime to meet the demand for military supplies. Stewart of the Saddlery works claimed: 'Within the last six weeks I have equipped 3000 mules with pack saddles and gear for the Transport Department. I have been making at the rate of 100 saddles a day and dispatching by Rail to Jhelum.'[102] Kanpur factories also supplied boots to China and South Africa.[103] A list of goods supplied by the North West Tannery in 1895 included items like harness and bridle leather, ammunition, knee and wellington boots, saddlery and accoutrements, rosset calf and sheep skins for book binding, machine belting, leather for carriage cushions and machine belting.[104] Kanpur came to be seen as a storehouse from which goods could be easily supplied to British troops overseas.[105]

The expansion of the textile industry during the war period gave the Kanpur mills an opportunity to reach out to markets that had earlier been supplied by Lancashire. There was now a growing domestic market for mill-made shirtings and dhotis. By 1918–19, some mills had placed orders for new machinery, though the

[99] *ARI*, 1916–17 and 1917–18, UP Industries Dept, 1919, File 24, Bundle 45 (UPSA).

[100] *Financial and Commercial Statistics of British India* for the relevant years.

[101] UP Ind. Progs. A, no. 11(a), File 533, 1919 (UPSA).

[102] Stewart family papers, cited in Yalland, *Boxwallahs,* p. 225.

[103] *UICC Report*, 1897, p. viii.

[104] *UICC Report*, 1895, p. 147.

[105] The UICC President noted: 'The authorities have learned to look with confidence to Kanpur when emergent demands arise either for the frontier or over the sea.' *UICC Report*, 1897, p. viii. One firm alone was manufacturing 5750 boots a day, *ARI*, 1916–17.

constraints of the war period on getting delivery for machinery orders continued.[106] The 1920s saw a steady growth of the cotton industry in UP, interrupted only by a slight dip between 1919 and 1923 (Fig. 8). Official surveys for the early 1920s emphasised the 'undeniable' improvement in the industry pointing towards its increasing ability to withstand foreign competition and supply the domestic market.[107] Production and export of cotton textiles showed a continuous increase after 1925, with exports matching up to the War levels in 1930. The Depression years were marked by a decline in mill profits and wage cuts and retrenchment, yet production figures do not indicate any decrease. On the contrary, evidence on textile production in UP and the amount of cotton consumed by the Kanpur mills shows a continuous increase.

Millowners complained about contraction in the market; there were reports of accumulating stocks in the mills. Outside managerial circles, however, many believed the millowners were deliberately controlling supply in order to push up prices.[108] The fall in mill profits was related partly to the decline in prices of cotton manufactures and increasing competition from cheaper Japanese cotton manufactures.[109] Managements tried to protect their profits by lowering production costs through direct and indirect cuts in workers' wages—mills worked fewer days and fewer hours in the week, and there were periods of 'forced idleness' when several categories of workers received no wages.[110] The overall position of the industry in terms of the amount of reserve funds did not show a significant deterioration, and mills like Muir and Swadeshi continued to pay high dividends, 40 per cent and 15 per cent per annum, even during the Depression years.[111]

[106] UP Ind. A Progs., nos 91–4, File 584,1920. See also Comm. and Ind. Progs. GOI, Dec. 1917, File 20–1.

[107] *ARI*, UP, 1922–3, p. xiii, *ARI*, UP, 1923–4, p. xx.

[108] The Kanpur Labour Inquiry Committee noted: '. . . The mills tried to push up prices by controlling supply even at the cost of higher overhead charges per piece of woven cloth'. KLIC Report, 1938, p. 34.

[109] *UICC Report, 1932*, p. 3; *UICC Report*, 1934, p. 4.

[110] KMS Memo, KLIC Progs., UP Ind. Dept, File 1145, 1937, Bundle 110 (UPSA).

[111] The position of reserve funds improved in several mills by 1933. For example, in the New Victoria Mills reserves amounted to Rs 912,533 around 17 per cent over the 1926 level; and those of Elgin Mills were 24 per cent

With the revival of trade after the Depression three new mills came up, all owned by Indian capital.[112] There were also extensions to old plants and additions to spindles and looms. Between 1929 and 1937 the average daily number of looms and spindles at work increased by 35 per cent and 17.7 per cent respectively, and the average daily employment of workers increased by 31.2 per cent. Some mills invested in new improved machinery, such as high-speed winding and warping machines, and new humidification plants. According to estimates drawn up by the Elgin and Muir mills' management, the total investment in new machinery in the two mills was estimated to be around Rs 1,100,000 to Rs 12,500,000 each.[113]

Additions to machinery were related partly to shifts in the range of products produced since the 1920s. As the mills made inroads into markets supplied earlier by imports, the production of cloth of finer counts increased. Over 1929–37 the production of yarn of counts between 20 and 30 increased by 152 per cent and that of counts between 30 and 40 by 117 per cent. By 1936–7 yarn of counts over 20 constituted 70 per cent of the total production, as against 20 per cent in 1928–9 and a mere 5 per cent in 1918–19.[114] There was a shift away from the domestic market during the Second World War period, when the production of war goods showed a phenomenal increase.

The expansion of industries transformed the demography and urban landscape of Kanpur, leading to new concerns and problems.

The Politics of Space and Sanitation

Divisions and boundaries between different areas of the city began to crystallise. Official language drew a distinction between

---

higher than the 1926 level. *Investor's India Yearbook* (Calcutta) for the relevant years.

[112] The JK group, which financed many European concerns and established the JK Spinning and Weaving Company in the 1920s, set up the JK Jute Mill, and JK Cotton manufactures. Ram Ratan Gupta, in collaboration with the JK group, set up Laxmi Ratan Mills (1934).

[113] KLIC Progs., UP Ind. Progs., File 1145, 1937, Bundle 110 (UPSA).

[114] *Statistical Abstract of British India* (Calcutta) for the relevant years.

the 'city proper' and the 'civil station': the latter with its parks, theatres, bungalows, the Mall, banks and offices was quite different from the 'city proper', described as an 'agglomeration of crowded brick-built mohallas separated by narrow lanes and a few wider thoroughfares.' Commerce and shops in the Mall had a respectability that local bazaars in the city lacked. Moreover, bazaar signified not just a commercial area but a broader category with obvious pejorative connotations for the quality of indigenous habitations: thus the frequent references to the insanitary state of 'bazaar dwellings'. Similarly, hata (enclosed space) became synonymous with 'slum' and the terms were used interchangeably in official and managerial discourse.

Attempts to regulate and reorder spaces in the city were related to an urban ideological climate similar to that of nineteenth-century Europe. Middle-class fears of respectable quarters being swamped with 'dangerous' and 'degenerate' classes determined the social landscape of the city. The mills and leather works that came up in the nineteenth century were located primarily on the riverfront or on lands in its immediate hinterland—territory earlier occupied by military bungalows destroyed during the Mutiny. A municipal regulation passed in 1905 disallowed the construction of industrial works in the neighbourhood of the Mall.[115]

Two kinds of industrial settlements came up in Kanpur: bastis (settlements) and hatas. Artisanal and coolie labour providing various services to merchants on the river front and the cantonment created their own bastis around Gwaltoli, Khalasi Lines and Parmat area. Gwaltoli and Khalasi Lines lay on the ravines in the cantonment, while Parmat (from permit) housed the famous Customs House that issued permits to merchants. In this area one could see blacksmiths and carpenters working on chests, in which goods were carried on boats downriver; and coolies loading and unloading goods. Leather workers, scavengers and porters performed services for the cantonment. Initially, small settlements of these labouring poor were tolerated, even encouraged, near the cantonment bungalows. When these areas passed from the

[115] H.Z. Darzah, Commsr, Allahabad Div., to Secy, NWP, UP Mun. Progs., June 1905, no. 18.

cantonment to the civil authorities and mills came up in the vicinity, workers continued to live here. It became customary for labouring families to settle on nazul land near the mills by paying a small fixed rent to the municipality for the ground that they occupied.[116] Worker families settled on habitations here helped to attract a continuing supply of labour through wide networks of kin, caste and region.

In later years the municipal strategy of shifting settlements to the outlying areas of the city seemed to work. The borders of the city moved southwards as factories and working class settlements came up at the southern end by the early 1920s. Here, landowners and men with capital enclosed spaces, paying a small rental to the municipality. Many acquired authority and prestige through their control over workers' housing: among them were proprietors like Chote Mian, Farhad Mian and Mangli Prasad. Enclosed compounds or hatas, each with 10–12 tenements or more, became part of the cityscape. Small mud huts with bamboo and tile roofs were constructed by tenants or by hata owners. There were no sanitary facilities in the hatas. In the absence of drains in the hatas, the water used for bathing and washing flowed into pits dug outside the huts, collecting and putrefying. Vessels were washed in this water.[117] The dominance of hatas in the urban landscape captures the politics of urban space. The continuous pressure to move outwards created new pockets where a lack of sanitary arrangements was taken for granted.

Around the turn of the nineteenth century, especially after the plague epidemic and riots of 1900, there was great concern over lower-class settlements in the heart of the city. They were seen as 'blots', sources of 'danger' and 'disfigurement'. The warnings and advice of the first decade gave way to stronger and sharper tones evident in the Ledgard Committee Report of 1918: 'To allow these bastis to remain in the middle of the extended Civil Lines is out of question.'[118] Not only were the settlements constructed in an insanitary way, the nature of the terrain made proper drainage

---

[116] Report of the Cawnpore Expansion Committee, UP Mun. Progs., Dec. 1918, no. 1(a).

[117] *BSER: Wages and Labour Conditions*, p. 89.

[118] UP Mun. Progs., Dec. 1918, no. 1(a).

almost impossible. However, the objections of the committee were not entirely related to hygiene. It ruled out alternative proposals for levelling and draining the land and constructing a cleaner workers' settlement. The overriding concern being with the class of people living in the Civil Lines, even a model workers' village was an anathema: 'We consider it highly inconvenient to have a large labouring establishment in the middle of the civil lines ... we therefore strongly recommend that these abadis should be completely wiped out.'[119] Although the rhetoric of sanitation and cleanliness constantly reappears in official discussions on urban space and housing, it is overwritten by arguments of class. The presence of working-class-tainted space lowered its social value and 'letting' power.[120]

The aesthetic and moral objections of the Civil Lines and bungalow inhabitants acquired greater force with pressures from European property speculators. Messrs Stromeyer, Mayer and others appealed to the Lieutenant-Governor to prohibit 'native habitations' near their building sites.[121] Anxious about estate value and its impact on their business, they emphasised that the construction of a settlement for workers of Cooper Allen and Company would adversely affect the market for the bungalows they had erected: 'Few people would care to live on the Nawabganj road in such close proximity to a noisy and at best of times, dirty habitation of low-caste natives.'[122] Municipal and provincial officials echoed these arguments. More than a decade later the Ledgard Committee pointed out that the Cooper Allen settlement would permanently disfigure the new bungalow area. It was convinced that even if a sum of two and three-fourth lakhs had to be paid as compensation to the company and a new site provided by the river, free of charge, the Improvement Trust would more

[119] Ibid.

[120] 'There can be no matter of question that the presence of a native village, no matter how sanitary the general arrangement may be, in the close vicinity of European house will be a very serious nuisance and must affect its letting value.' H.Z. Darzah, Commsr, Allahabad Div. to Secy, NWP, 30.1.1904. UP Mun. Progs., 1905, no. 18.

[121] UP Mun. Progs., June 1905, no. 9(b).

[122] UP Mun. Progs., June 1905, no. 9(b).

than make up the loss by a substantial enhancement in the selling value of all the land and its neighbourhood.[123]

Naturally, this politics of class had racial undertones: frequent references to 'native reserves', to the separation between the native bazaar and the bungalow areas, the Bithur road forming the rough boundary line between the two, make clear the interplay between race and class in shaping the social urban landscape. The bungalow area in the Civil Lines was initially inhabited primarily by Europeans, ties amongst whom were affirmed through the city's famed social life, the parties and dancing and sports. This racial segregation was, however, persistently breaking down, threatened forever by the politics of class. Within European inhabitants of the bungalow area distinctions were drawn. Europeans employed in the factories and working closely with native workers while earning between Rs 300 and Rs 800 per month, it was held, were less likely to object to living near lower-class habitation than those drawing over Rs 2000: 'They are accustomed to noise, dirt and other unpleasant accompaniments inseparable from native labour.'[124] The white elite pushed the white underclass to the margins of their white space even as wealthy Indians were keen on crossing the racial boundaries from the other side. After the turn of the century, wealthy Indians queued up for bungalows in the Civil Lines area. India's anglicised urban middle classes were influenced by nineteenth-century European ideas on disease that drew connections between epidemics and overcrowded urban spaces. New ideas about sanitation and the fear of epidemics after the plague outbreak of 1900 accounted for the growing demand for bungalows in the sanitised Western enclaves. Bazaar dwellings now came to be identified with disease and mortality. This reordering of spaces meant a broader cultural conflict within the middle classes. Indigenous traders moored to more traditional ways continued to live in the crowded bazaar areas. For upper-class Indians appropriating Westernised lifestyles, a shift to the Civil Lines symbolised their distance from the bazaar.

The organisation of the urban landscape remained a problem. The need to satisfy the labour requirements of an industrial city

[123] UP Mun. Progs., Dec. 1918, no. 9(b).
[124] UP Mun. Progs., June 1905, no. 18.

conflicted with the desire for an 'invisible' working population. Each scheme had its contradictions: there was the option of housing workers on the Unnao side of the river, but it was abandoned because of the Civil Lines being 'shut in' by a new native city across the river, and a 'daily overrun' by labourers going to and from work. The acquisition of new lands from the cantonment did not ease the congestion. The bulk of the labouring poor were squeezed into a small area, with little possibility of extension: there were the old brick kilns and ravines in the west, Civil Lines in the north, the cantonment on the east, and the railway line on the south. Areas like Butcherkhana had a population of 578 per square mile and Coolie Bazaar 562 per square mile in 1918. Ambitious paper plans were made for shifting workers out of the city limits onto the Hamirpur road that was to be linked by a tramway.[125]

Although the municipal authorities were categorically against any intrusion of lower-class dwellings into the bungalow area, they were worried about a rigid separation between different classes of housing. These apparently contradictory considerations continued to plague the municipal administration: upper-class fears of being swamped by lower-class habitations had to be placated, yet there was danger in oversegregation: municipal authorities believed it was easier to administer and control plebeians if they were in proximity of the enlightened:

> if a large area is given over entirely to lower-class dwellings there is no enlightened opinion on the spot to maintain a decent standard of municipal administration . . . . What we want to avoid is the fate of West Ham and such parts of London, where you will find hardly a decent house in a square mile; owing to the desertion of the locality by all the better classes . . .[126]

The sanitation and drainage schemes for the city sharpened variations in the quality of physical life between different areas. Dirty and overcrowded bastis, and the grossly inadequate drainage system were subjects of concern for both managers and officials. Ideas on sanitation drew on wider European discourses on health

[125] UP Mun. Progs., Dec. 1918, no. 1(a).
[126] Interim Report of the Cawnpore Improvement Trust Committee, UP Mun. Progs., no. 9(b).

and hygiene. The terms in which the sanitary commissioner, NWP and Oudh, describes the system of drainage in the city is similar to descriptions of nineteenth-century Paris, when the very existence of the city seemed threatened by the accumulation of excrement.[127]

> Public and private latrine drains and urinals have their outfall into the street drains; and thus at Cawnpore a system obtains which admits of at least a portion of the sewerage being conveyed in open channels along streets and lanes to decompose and undergo foetid fermentation throughout at least 3/4 ths of the area of the city . . . it has been observed that the latrine stuff has been used as a semi-fluid flushing agent to scour the foetid drains leading from the latrine to the street drain. House and latrine drains are not properly piped and permit the percolation of sullage and filthy water into the walls of the houses and basement of the dwellings, so that a certain proportion of the sewerage of city percolates into and around almost every inhabited site in Kanpur. The result is an almost inconceivable insanitary condition of polluted dwellings and excessively contaminated sub-soil from which potable water is taken . . .[128]

Images of putrefaction, of excrement and effluvia seeping into the soil, recur in writings on urban sanitation in Europe. Before

[127] Descriptions of Montfauçon (an area commonly associated in literary and other representations with prostitution, criminality and the lower classes) for instance: 'The place was horrible because of the charnel house on permanent display. The offal rotted on the spot in heaps 4 or 5 feet high until the plowing season . . . gut-dressing works and chemical factories were established nearby, and the discharge from them ran through the marshes and flowed in the open beside the rue Grange-aux-Belles to the city sewer in the rue des Marais near the rue de Lancry. Around the charnel house were the rats, in such swarms that if carcasses of quartered horses were left in any corner of a yard during the day, they were completely stripped by the next. . . . The place was horrible, too, for the stench it spread over the neighbourhood and, when the wind was in the right quarter, to the furthest confines of the city.' Louis Chevalier, *Laboring Classes and Dangerous Classes in Paris During the First Half of the Nineteenth Century*, pp. 210–21. Two important works, also on France Alain, Corbin, *The Foul and the Fragrant* (Harvard 1986) and Georges Vigarello, *Concepts of Cleanliness: Changing Attitudes in France since the Middle Ages* (Cambridge 1988) offer lively and penetrating analyses on social attitudes to odours, excrement and cleanliness. On the significance of the discourse on health and hygiene in India, see Mark Harrison, *Climates and Constitutions: Health, Race, Environment and British Imperialism in India, 1600–1850* (New Delhi 1999).

[128] NWP and Awadh, Mun. Progs., Oct. 1890, no. 52.

Pasteurian theories on germs and disease became known, it was widely believed that foul smelling exhalations, the odour from excrement and carcasses, and vapours released by a mass of human bodies living together—all kinds of miasma in fact—were disease. Foul odour in this discourse was synonymous with disease. Efforts to cleanse and eradicate disease focused on protecting aerial space from the emanations of the earth by paving and draining the soil. This explains the concern among Kanpur's sanitary officials, about seepage from cesspools penetrating into the subsoil, thus contaminating wells, and refuse and excreta providing material for decomposition.[129]

Concern for disease and dirt translated into action in a halting and discriminatory way. Sanitation within the 'city proper' drew attention when it was threatened by disease: the cholera epidemic of the 1890s and the plague in 1900 created alarm. The Chamber of Commerce was anxious about the effect of epidemics on the supply of labour to the mills and tried to put pressure on the municipal authorities to improve sanitation.[130] But schemes for sanitation were contentious and sanitary standards uneven. In a city that initially acquired significance as a cantonment, the health and well-being of British troops was important in determining sanitary provisions. Baldwin Latham, President of the Royal Meteorological Society, who drew up ambitious sanitary schemes for the city, stressed this:

> In dealing with the municipal area of Cawnpore, it is imperative that the sanitary requirements of the adjoining Cantonment be considered and provided for. The Cantonment in Cawnpore, in respect to the city, is situated in a very bad position, both as regards the movement of wind and more especially that of underground water. The wells within the Cantonment of Cawnpore are very liable to be polluted from the municipal area, as they are located on the lower side of the city on the direct line of the underground flow. It is important for the Cantonment, having regard to its position with respect to the city, that the city should be freed from impurities which, if not removed, are very liable to affect the health of the Cantonment.[131]

[129] NWP and Awadh, Mun. Progs., Oct. 1890, no. 52.

[130] Chamber to Chief Secy, NWP and Awadh, 5.9.1895, *UICC Report,* 1895, App. x, p. 233.

[131] Baldwin Latham to Secy, NWP, 5.2.1891. NWP and Awadh, Mun. Progs., Apr. 1892, no. 30.

Prolonged debate and official correspondence followed his proposals. The point of contention was the construction of a main
intercepting sewer with its outfall into the Ganges near the eastern
boundary of the cantonment. The military authorities were convinced it would leak: 'Leaky sewers were a matter of common experience.'[132] A masonry drain running through the cantonment
would tend to absorb sewage unless it was continuously flushed
by water. And even flushing was not an adequate solution: fecal
matter would still collect at intervals within the drain. The alternative of sewage pipes was too expensive, and in any case military
officials asserted that it would not prevent effluvia escaping
through manholes and polluting the cantonment air. They suggested an alternative: removing and transporting excreta and
other filth by pails and tramways to a sewage farm outside the
cantonment, where it could be used by cultivators to fertilise the
soil.[133]

Civil officials ridiculed the exaggerated fears of the military
authorities. Since the the drainage line was to run parallel to and
in close proximity of the river, the northward tendency in wind
direction would carry any escaped effluvia towards the river. Even
if the wind blew in the opposite direction, the distance of the drain
from the barracks would dissipate its effect.[134] The proposal for
removal of excreta by pails and tramways was criticised by the
civil authorities as 'clumsy' and 'unscientific'. Engineers in the
civil administration pointed out that around 912,500 cubic feet
of sewage was already carried manually to the trenching grounds
by 4000–5000 sweepers; a complete system of hand removal
would cost ten times more. Besides, almost all available land near
the cantonment had already been trenched and it would be impossible to find more land for sewage disposal.[135]

A committee on Kanpur sewage, consisting of civil and military
representatives, reaffirmed proposals for a sewer through the

[132] NWP and Awadh, Mun. Progs., Apr. 1892, no. 82.

[133] Major Gen. E.H.H. Collen, Secy, GOI, Mil. Dept to Secy, NWP,
15.7.1892, NWP and Awadh, Dec. 1892, no. 43.

[134] Remarks by Civil Surgeon , Kanpur, 3.10.1892, NWP and Awadh,
Mun. Progs., Dec. 1892, no. 49(a).

[135] Note on city sewerage by Lt. Col. G. Hutcheson, Sanitary Commsr,
NWP and Awadh, and A.J. Hughes, Supervisory Engineer, Mun. Works,
NWP, 24.11.1892, NWP and Awadh, Mun. Progs., no. 50(a), Dec. 1892.

cantonment. Accepting the likelihood of leakage from sewers, it suggested that sewage could be diluted with 20–40 gallons of water per head of sewage, and government grass farms near the cantonment could be irrigated with it. The committee imagined possibilities of the sewage farm in Kanpur turning into a green and pleasant meadow, like certain Craigantinny meadows near Edinburgh.[136] It proposed the setting up of a sewage farm to the east of the cantonment, which was less saturated than land to the west or south-west.[137]

These issues continued to trouble municipal officials, caught between conflicting pressures: between the demands of the cantonment and civil areas, and between the Civil Lines and the inner city. There were times when the Government of India overruled the objections of the cantonment to sanitary schemes; at other times it refused to concede to the demands of Civil Lines inhabitants. In periods of urban crisis, like the plague of 1900, when representatives of industry in Kanpur panicked about the decimation of the mill population, initiatives on implementing sanitary and housing schemes had to be undertaken. A main sewer was now taken out through the cantonment, ignoring the protests of the cantonment authorities. At other times the 'salubrity' and 'comfort' of the cantonment were considered inviolable. When merchants connected with the cantonment trade for generations pleaded against the destruction of their homes by the proposed canal route through their areas, their protests were dismissed. 'When it is considered that Tradesmen and others only live there by sufferance, with a primary regard to the wants and necessities of the Cantonments, the Governor-General considers that there seems to be no reason for remonstrance.'[138]

As conflicts between the Civil Lines and the inner city intensified, municipal officials wavered, trying to placate pressures from different quarters. Despite strong representations from Civil

[136] Sanitary Commsr, to Secy, GOI, Home Dept, 4.12.1893, NWP and Oudh, Mun. Progs., June 1894, no. 10(a).

[137] Report of Committee on Sewage and Conservancy, NWP and Oudh, Mun. Progs., June 1894, no. 10(b).

[138] H.M. Elliot, Secy, GOI, 22.3.1851, Home Public, Apr. 1851. Cited in Yalland, *Traders and Nabobs*, App. II, p. 355. The petitioners numbering over five hundred were based in Generalganj and Brigadier Ghat, important grain marts in the city, through which the canal was to pass.

Lines inhabitants to wipe out the old working class settlements of Gwaltoli, Khalasi Lines and Parmat, this did not prove possible. The Gwaltoli residents organised meetings and refused to shift to alternative areas in Juhi or Nawabganj. In their appeals to the state against eviction, the residents asserted their claims to the area on the basis of a long past: '*Yeh abadi shahi zamane ki hai*...'[139] This was a time when workers from these areas were busy with war work in the mills. The uprooting of entire working class neighbourhoods would have endangered industry. Similarly, despite the angry protests of Civil Lines residents against dhobis washing in the backwaters of their vicinity, and their fear that sickness and disease might force them to abandon their bungalows, their pleas were ignored by the municipality.[140]

Sanitation policies were further complicated by the politics of the Municipal Board. The majority of the board members were high-caste Hindus preoccupied with notions of ritual cleanliness.[141] The board was attacked by members of the UICC for its obsession with 'sentimental' matters. The chamber criticised the board for not sanctioning grants to improve sanitation while spending large amounts to protect cows from desecration by Chamars by setting up a gaikhana and for constructing bathing ghats off the Ganges.[142] The board went to the ridiculous length of attributing high infant and female mortality to the lack of milch animals. The provincial governor was told to protect cows to save the humans: 'If your Excellency be pleased to prohibit the slaughter of milk cows and take steps for their growth by providing pasturage ground at every place, the scarcity will be removed ... and thus thousands of infants saved.'[143] The preoccupation of the board with such sectarian matters became an issue of intense conflict in the communalised context of the late 1920s.[144]

---

[139] This settlement dates back to imperial times (i.e. Mughal times): '*Yahan ke nivasi raj bhakt hain ... vahan der so varsh se muharram, chehalum, ka mela hota hai aur vahin tazia dafan hoten hain.*' *Pratap*, 22.2.1914

[140] *UICC Report*, 1916.

[141] See also fn 86.

[142] Address by W.B. Wishart , UICC, 16.7.1890, NWP and Oudh, Mun. Progs., Oct. 1890, no. 82.

[143] Progs. of Municipal Board meeting, 16.7.1923, records of the Kanpur Municipality, Kanpur.

[144] See ch. 7.

Glaring disparities in the sanitary state of different localities became a structured part of the cityscape. While efforts were made to cover sewers in close proximity of the Civil Lines and cantonment, other areas remained thoroughfares for open sewers with no connecting pipelines. Reflecting on the filth and muck, the stinking sewers and swampy roads, inhabitants of the city wondered (as they do even today): '*Yeh shahr hai ya narak?*'[145] The municipality, they complained, earned lakhs through taxes but cared little for the health of the city. Hatas that came up in the outlying areas became synonymous with slums, and 'slum clearance' became a major object of municipal policy in the 1950s. But then Kanpur was for the municipality a working class city. It was as if the association of the working class with filth and disease could not be broken: they could either be cleared out altogether or allowed to wallow.[146] To leaders of independent India such as Nehru, the state of hatas in Kanpur seemed antithetical to all dreams of an ideal future for modern India's cities. After a tour of the 'slums' in 1952, Nehru could not restrain his sense of outrage and anger. 'Hang the Development Board President', he said, 'burn down these hatas.' [147]

---

[145] *Pratap*, 11.6.1917.

[146] 'So hopeless has the insanitary condition of Cawnpore appeared, that even the heroic remedy of abandonment has been suggested, and the building of a new city seriously advocated.' *UICC Report*, 1903, p. 17.

[147] Nehru categorically told industrialists that the hovels he had seen in Kanpur were 'a disgrace . . . It would be better if the workers had no place to live than these hovels. It would be better if the pace of industrialization slowed down than workers should be made to live in these shocking and humiliating conditions.' Address to FICCI, cited in S.P. Mehra, *Cawnpore Civic Problems* (Kanpur 1952).

CHAPTER 2

Between Two Worlds

The Village and the City

By the early years of the twentieth century, factory chimneys dominated the city and the politics of sanitation shaped a landscape in which squalor and working class bastis became synonymous. The city's population grew by 140 per cent between 1901 and 1941, from 202,971 to 487,324. There was a continuous inflow from the countryside of people in search of jobs in the mills and elsewhere. To migrants from the villages around, Kanpur was a city that could change their lives and open up a new world. But survival in the city became tied up with the vicissitudes of factory employment. The life of the city was thus defined by a continuous coming and going, with people moving between the city and country, between the factory and the street, between jobs and joblessness. Apart from those employed, there was always a large floating population living on the margins—a class which colonial officials saw as potentially dangerous.[1] The boundaries between those in the city and the village, those in factories and outside, those between castes and communities, were never rigidly demarcated. People moved between these spaces, the boundaries stayed fuzzy and fluid, the imprint of one area was carried into another. These links between village and city, between work in cotton mills and outside, between castes and communities, defined the ways in which the factory workforce was structured.

In the last few decades, writings on labour in India have moved away from the old supply-centric frameworks concerned primarily with industrialisation and the problems of labour supply. Indigenous social institutions, caste and community ties, rural links

---

[1] See ch. 7.

and kin networks, were all seen as holding back and restricting the flow of labour to industries. The critique of the supply-cons-traint argument by Morris David Morris—his assertion that lab-our was mobile, that it was not bounded by social values and institutions—did not fundamentally question the old framework. By demonstrating the abundance of labour supply, Morris in fact reaffirmed the focus on the issue of supply. The shift away from a supply-centred frame towards a demand-centred frame has other problems. Within this frame, working class formation is conditioned by the nature of demand for labour, which in turn is shaped by the structure of industry and the business strategies of managers. The structure of the workforce, relationships of power and authority, patterns of labour deployment, the nature of disci-pline, are seen as crucially determined by managerial strategies.[2] It is as if the forms of discipline and authority were not shaped in any way by the actions of workers and their modes of resistance. In looking at fluctuations of demand, we need to see how workers experience these conditions and devise strategies to confront them. To understand the working class we need to look at the stra-tegies of both managers and workers, at the imperatives of the textile industry, at the calculations of millhands.

Workers in Kanpur: Numbers

In the 1990s, when the mills of Kanpur stand like ghosts, it is dif-ficult to imagine that a general strike by the city's workers in the 1930s could threaten the industrial life of the entire province. However, the sheer visibility of the working class in Kanpur at that time, and its powerful political presence, can distort our view of the structure of the labour force. If we consider the total indus-trial labour force in UP, a large proportion appear to have been working outside Kanpur: about 71 per cent in 1921 and 63 per cent in 1931. Most worked in small-scale industries (see Fig. 13). Sugar mills dotted the countryside in the sugarcane zone, employing

[2] In Raj Chandavarkar's finely crafted study of labour in Bombay, busi-ness decisions are crucial determinants of working class formation. Although at the outset Chandavarkar begins with a critique of such histories, his fram-ing argument remains firmly demand-centric. Chandavarkar, *The Origins of Industrial Capitalism*. See, in particular, pp. 295, 326, 334.

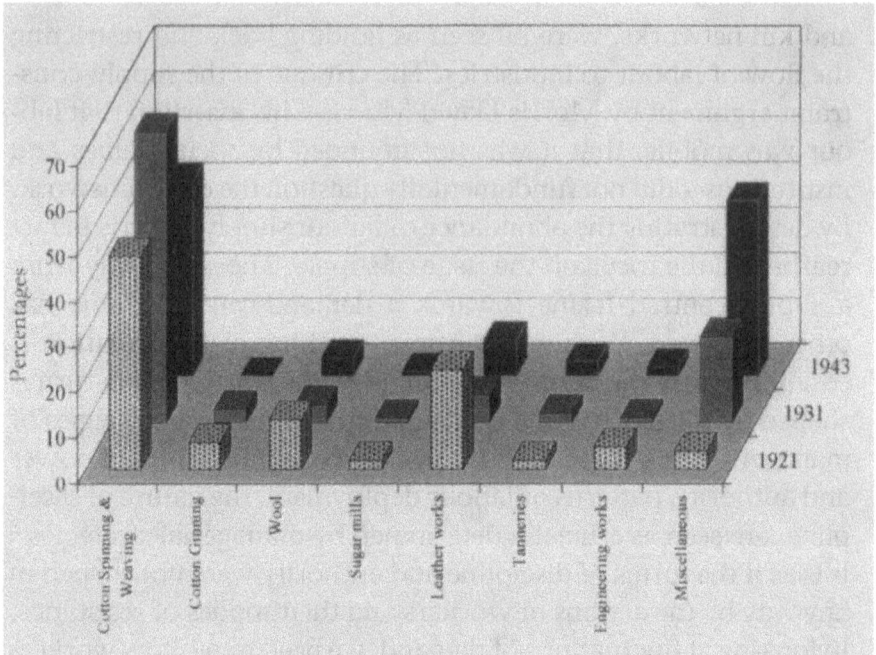

Fig. 12: Workers in different industries of Kanpur
(per cent of total industrial workforce)

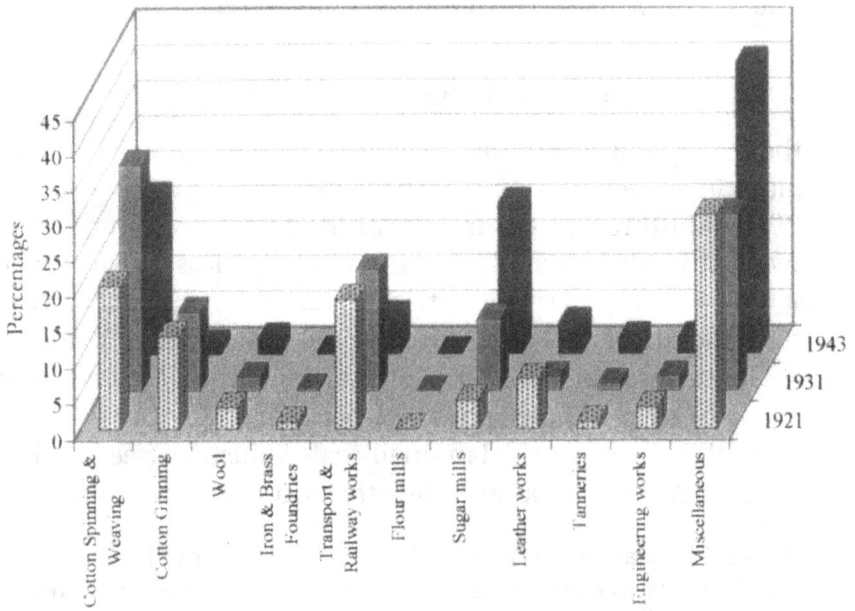

Fig. 13: Workers in different industries of UP
(per cent of total industrial workforce)

3348 workers in 1921 and 9555 in 1931. Over 11,000 workers, about 13 per cent of the total labour force, worked in 138 ginning and pressing mills dispersed over UP, each employing not more than an average of 85 to 95 workers. The Depression hit cotton ginning, but sugar factories mushroomed under tariff protection: the workforce jumping to 52,000 by 1943.[3] Apart from these industries workers were employed in a whole range of other small industries, such as brick and tile works, lime works and printing presses.[4]

Yet Kanpur was seen by workers as a 'dehat ka kendra', a centre to which they would flow in search of jobs. Here they were visible everywhere, on streets, in teashops, in market-places, on riverbanks. They stamped the city with their presence and defined its character. The textile and leather factories of UP were almost all located in Kanpur. In 1921 Kanpur employed 70 per cent of the cotton and spinning workers of UP, all its woollen textile workers, 90 per cent of its leather workers, and 92 per cent of its tannery workers. Cotton textile was the single largest employer (see Figs 12 and 13): textile labour constituted 32 per cent of the labour force in UP in 1931, and by 1941 about 80 per cent of them were in Kanpur. Between 1921 and 1941 their number more than trebled: from 12,802 in 1921 to 44,480 in 1943 (see Table 1).

The concentration of labour in Kanpur, and the scale on which the mills were organised, accounted for the greater visibility and cumulative power of the textile labour force in the city. In 1905 none of the mills had less than 40,000 spindles and 500 looms, and in 1944, five out of the eleven major units were equipped with more than 50,000 spindles and 1000 looms; one of these, Swadeshi Cotton Mills, had a capacity of over 100,000 spindles and 2000 looms. Six out of ten units employed over 4000 workers each.[5]

[3] *Statistics of Large Industrial Establishments* (Calcutta, relevant years). With tariff protection the number of cane crushing sugar mills shot up from 29 in 1931 to 137 in 1936–7. On this, see Shahid Amin, *Sugarcane and Sugar in Gorakhpur: An Inquiry into Peasant Production for Capitalist Enterprise in Colonial India* (Delhi 1984).

[4] With changes in the Factories Act in 1934, workers employed in a range of small industries were included in the figures for industrial workers. As a result the numbers went up.

[5] The Indian-owned mills which came up after 1905 were relatively

Table 1. Growth of Cotton Textile Workforce in Kanpur

Year	Number of Mills	Workers
1906	4	7781
1913	6	10,469
1918	7	10,971
1921	7	12,802
1929	9	18,491
1933	10	23,191
1935	14	30,118
1937	14	34,636
1940	15	35,108
1943	17	44,480

Source: *Financial and Commercial Statistics of British India*, 1906 to 1918 (annual); *Statistics of Large Industrial Establishments*, 1921,1931, 1933; *LIC: Labour in Cotton Mills.*

Other textile mills in Uttar Pradesh—in Agra, Aligarh, Morada-bad—were mostly spinning units catering to the local demands of handloom weavers.[6]

The numbers employed in the textile industry in Kanpur show a continuous increase from 1906 to 1943 (Table 1). The post-Depression years between 1933 and 1937 were marked by a sharp increase in workforce (49 per cent).[7] Tariff protection and a consequent decline in British imports allowed mills in Ahmeda-bad, Kanpur and other upcountry centres to make inroads into the domestic market. Three new mills were set up in Kanpur and the workforce in the existing mills increased, with many of them running multiple shifts.[8] The demand for military supplies in the war years led to the setting up of three new weaving units and an increase in the workforce in the existing mills (Table 1).

---

smaller in size, with approximately 2000–4000 spindles and 500–1000 looms. M.M. Mehta, *Structure of the Cotton Mill Industry in India* (Allahabad 1949), p. 135.

[6] Mehta, *Structure of the Cotton Mill Industry*, p. 131.

[7] According to the figures supplied in the KLIC Report the increase is only 16 per cent.

[8] See also ch. 1.

The figures on the numbers employed, however, do not tell us about the fluidities of industrial employment, the movement between jobs, the shifts between city and country that often mark-d workers' lives. During the Depression years, for instance, when mills ran fewer days and fewer hours in the week and there was no continuous work for many, the actual numbers employed daily were lower than the numbers on the rolls. The numbers on the rolls do not reveal changes and fluctuations in figures, hidden employment and unemployment.

Average figures for employment do not tell us anything about badlis or substitutes employed in most establishments. Informally, the practice of employing substitutes to fill in for absentees always existed. In the 1930s this practice was institutionalised, with the system of maintaining regular 'substitute lists' from which permanent vacancies were filled. Workers employed as substitutes were given cards with which they had to present themselves at the mill gate every morning. Around 30 to 35 per cent of those on the rolls were unemployed most of the time.[9] Long periods could elapse with no work for the badli. The wait for a regular job could be anything from two years to ten years.[10] For employers, the badli system ensured continuity of production at lower costs and provided a mechanism for training labour without any additional expense. Casualisation of the workforce was also a strategy managements increasingly employed to deal with the labour movement. Substitutes had no striking power and often provided mill managements trained hands to replace striking workers. When mills went in for drastic rationalisation in the 1950s, the retinue of badlis became much larger: they provided a labour force that could be more easily retrenched. In the 1940s, badlis in some mills constituted 19 per cent of the workforce, in others between 5 and 7 per cent.[11] By 1955, badlis constituted almost a quarter of the total workforce in the mills: 17 per cent of piecers, 41 per cent of doffers, 24 per cent of weavers were badlis; the proportion of

[9] *Report of the Kanpur Textile Mills Rationalisation Enquiry Committee, 1955–56* (Lucknow 1956), p. 191.

[10] Ev. Zawar Husain, KMS witness, KLIC Progs. UP Ind. Progs., File 1145, 1937, Bundle 110 (UPSA).

[11] *LIC: Labour in Cotton Mills*, App. XIII, p. 167. Not all mills provided figures on the number of badlis.

badlis being in inverse proportion to the skill requirements of a job.[12] By the 1980s there were many who spent their entire working life as substitutes. When such casualisation of the workforce became dominant, the past took on a golden glow as the time when jobs could be passed on as an inheritance to children.[13]

Many who worked regularly were often not shown on the mill registers at all. Musahib Ali of Laxmi Ratan Cotton Mills reported that 'one operative looked after two machines but in the registers four machines were shown against him. The extra man working the two machines was not shown in the registers. There were one hundred 60" machines in the shed on which 50 men were working but the names of 25 men only were entered in the register. This was a general practice.'[14] Musahib Ali himself worked without his name being entered in the register. He tended four looms and repaired others. Factory inspectors were lax, and in any case extra people around the compound were not unusual. Workers testified that managers explained away the presence of extra hands to inspectors by saying they had come with food or for other work.

Apart from regular workers, most mills employed a large number of casual workers hired on a daily basis. Many were engaged in jobs such as loading and unloading goods. They formed part of a mobile workforce moving between different industries, and at other times as coolies in the local bazaar. Formally, employers recognised only four categories of non-permanent workers: probationers, substitutes, temporaries and apprentices. Others employed as casuals, relievers or extras were not always shown on the rolls.[15]

Statistics on the number of women and children in factories are problematic. Official investigators of 'large industrial establishments' were not seriously interested in figures on women: their numbers were considered too insignificant. They enumerate details on average daily employment in factories without indicating

---

[12] *Rationalisation Enquiry Comm.*, p. 191.

[13] See ch. 9.

[14] Ev. Musahib Ali, KMS witness, KLIC Progs., UP Ind. Progs., File 1145, 1937, Bundle 110 (UPSA).

[15] In 1944, for instance, only five out of 15 textile mills at Kanpur provided figures on the number of casual workers. *LIC: Labour in Cotton Mills*, App. XIII, p. 167.

the number of women. With the introduction of factory legislation, managers employed women and children without formally enrolling them as workers. This was common not just in textile factories. The Labour Investigation Committee reported in 1944 that a large number of women were employed in tanneries to bring in bark for tanning. Ahmad Mukhtar, a member of the committee reported that: 'When my investigating staff paid surprise visits to two tanneries, about 6 to 7 women were being rushed out from the back door to escape detection. The object of this practice is to pay them low wages (6 to 7 annas per day) without dearness allowance and to avoid the liability of payment of maternity benefits.'[16] The poor were ready to work without being on the rolls, and managers could escape factory regulations by refusing to classify workers as workers. In ginning factories, similarly, managers pleaded that workers engaged in picking and cleaning damaged and discoloured cotton in the compounds of factories ought not to come under the Factories Act since they were not classed as workers. In the case of children, apart from those actually employed, many accompanied parents and relatives to the factory from a very young age. For workers, this was a way of claiming an inheritable right over a job. For mill managers, children provided extra hands at no cost.

Considering the nature of enumeration, it would appear that the overall figures for workers in big industries were seriously understated, except in periods like the Depression when factories did not work to capacity. The extent of underestimation would be at least 20 per cent by the 1940s. The proportion appears to have increased over the decades with the increasing significance of badlis, the growth of trade unionism, and a stricter enforcement of wage regulations.

The Question of Supply

Over the years Kanpur became a centre with a continuous inflow of migrants from the countryside, the influx peaking during the Depression and post-Depression years and in the 1940s. The supply to the city was linked with the seasonality of rural employment,

[16] *Labour Investigation Committee: Report on Labour Conditions in Tanneries and Leather Goods Factories* (Simla 1946).

increasing in certain periods, ebbing in others, with a flow back to the countryside from the city during sowing and harvest time.

Recruitment of labour to the mills was through mistris (jobbers). Community and regional ties between workers and mistris were important in getting jobs. All the same, the notion of a market completely segmented by 'primordial' ties of community is as problematic as managerial assertions, in the 1930s, that there was a free market for labour. The fact of the matter was that access to jobs was through a patronage network of mistris but the codes regulating entry were neither fixed nor impenetrable. Workers could sometimes rework networks or create alternative networks and thus gain entry into jobs. Besides, links with mistris were not *always* based on traditional kin networks: workers often forged new relationships in the mohalla and outside, and these helped them access jobs.[17] There were also instances of workers manipulating the ticket system that regulated entry into the factory. In the 1930s managers complained about mill tickets—or cards issued to bona fide employees—being traded in the bazaar. One worker, Raghubir, for instance, recounted how he got his first job through a worker in Kanpur Textiles who offered him his ticket. Raghubir worked under the name of Ramgopal. He changed his name and his caste as well: he was registered as a Brahman and not as a lower-caste Kachi.[18]

Most workers did not work continuously in one mill, they moved between mills, sometimes across cities.[19] These movements between mills were not under conditions of a free market, with workers moving from lower-to-higher paid jobs.[20] If this was the case, a greater equalisation of wages between mills was likely.[21]

---

[17] After a quarrel with the supervisor, Chakr left the job he got through his father's friend and moved to another mill where his brother knew a mistri who was in the same Ramlila mandali (team) as him. Chakr, *Jay Janta*, pp. 20–1.

[18] Interview, Raghubir.

[19] See also ch. 3 for more on individual life histories.

[20] Morris analyses the interchange between mills primarily as a result of a competition between mills in a more or less free labour market. See, for instance, Morris, *Emergence*, p. 161. Similar assumptions seem to underline the statements of Kanpur industrialists who attributed the movement between mills to 'the insatiable craving for novelty' of workers. *UICC Report*, 1900, p. 5.

[21] On wage differentials, see ch. 3.

The shift was in very insecure market conditions: workers were never sure of the terms of their employment. They moved because they were arbitrarily dismissed or because conditions were harsh and oppressive.

Millowners often drew on the floating labour in the city to fill in for absentees.[22] In fact managers tended to argue that most jobs other than weaving could be done by almost anyone: 'A bag carrier might, for example, be put to work as a piecer. If a weaver fell sick his loom had to lie vacant.'[23] Such pronouncements tend to exaggerate the extent of mobility within the labour market and understate the requirements of experience and skill. The job of a piecer, for instance—of piecing broken ends of yarn—was a delicate one, requiring care and deftness.

Statements like this by managers were more characteristic of the 1930s, when they were trying to resist schemes for regulating recruitment through an official bureau. In the late nineteenth century there was general panic about trained spinners and weavers moving from Kanpur to other centres. In devising strategies to prevent an exodus, official and non-official discourse on labour supply valorises notions of skill in relation to textile workers. Around the same period, employers deployed arguments about skill and training to press for the continuation of child labour. They argued that child workers 'are a necessity because it is from them that spinners are recruited, and if children were not taught when young the supply of spinners would be precarious indeed'.[24]

For unskilled work the mills drew on a pool of labour that moved between different occupations, often blurring the distinctions between different forms of work. While cotton textile was the single largest industry in Kanpur, about 60 per cent of the labour force worked in a range of small industries—tanneries, engineering works, woollen mills, cotton ginning, flour, oil and sugar mills (Fig. 12). In UP as a whole cotton textile industries provided work to no more than 20 per cent of the workforce;

[22] Leather works, for instance, employed a large number of casual workers to load and unload goods, many of whom worked in the local bazaar at other times of the year. Ev. Larmour, Harness and Saddlery Factory, *RCL III (ii)*, p.125.

[23] Ev. of Watt and Bancroft of the Cawnpore Woollen Mills, 25.1.1938, KLIC Progs., UP Ind. Progs., File 1145, 1937, Bundle 110 (UPSA).

[24] Ev. Muir Mills, *IFLC*, p. 205.

almost an equal proportion worked in the railways and sugar mills (Fig. 13).

Within Kanpur, large numbers were employed as porters and pushers of hand-carts handling goods coming into the city or on roads and building construction sites. A regular coolie market was held at a central spot in the city where contractors sought out their labour. Even in times of exceptional pressure, employers said, 'The first flow to the mills is from the city. Any replenishments of the city's requirements, is from the country, and when that pressure ceases that flow goes back into the city and is reabsorbed in its previous employment.'[25] Settlements of artisanal labourers had grown around the military establishments in Kanpur since the eighteenth century, many of these artisans were now absorbed in the mills. There was also a regular flow from the countryside. In certain seasons, at harvest time for instance, the inflow declined, but at other times, especially during periods of famine and crisis in the rural areas, supplies increased sharply.[26]

In the 1890s, millowners in Kanpur, like jute managers in Calcutta, talked of a crisis in labour supply. Was this real or imagined? Anxieties about labour shortage often characterise early periods of industrial expansion when rural–urban migration flows are not well established, and industrialists fear that unlimited industrial expansion may be constrained by supply shortages and consequent high wages. But around the turn of the century, and later at the end of the war period (1918–19), there were strong reasons for such fears. The plague of 1900, like the influenza epidemic of 1918, took a heavy toll in urban areas. Official reports suggest that notoriously insanitary cities like Kanpur suffered more than others and 'many of the trained hands died and many others went away to other towns, which had a better reputation for health'.[27] Disease and mortality magnified fears of a labour

[25] Oral ev. UICC, *RCL III (ii)*, p. 164.

[26] Pointing to these seasonal fluctuations, Freemantle wrote: 'At certain seasons, when the crops are being harvested or the export business is particularly brisk or a plague scare empties the city, there is a great scarcity of workmen, wages mount up rapidly, and all employers have difficulty in retaining their regular hands.' Freemantle, 'Report on the Supply of Labour' to UP and Bengal. UP Rev. Progs. B, May 1906, no. 91. I have throughout used this unpublished version of the report.

[27] Ibid.; see also Home Pub. Progs. A, June 1900, no. 298.

shortage. Riots against the imposition of plague regulations added to the crisis, leading to a large exodus from the city.[28] The Chamber of Commerce panicked over an imminent decimation of the labouring population: 'The effect on trade was disastrous. During October, November and December the supply of labour was less than half, in some cases only a third, of the requirements. Workpeople seized with panic left the town.'[29] During the influenza epidemic in 1918, Kanpur municipality reported the highest death rate. More than 50 per cent of mill workers were affected, about 50 to 60 per cent being absent for over two months.[30]

Managerial apprehensions were articulated against a background of growing competition for labour. During the 1880s and 1890s the demand for labour had increased because of huge military orders for imperial troops in South Africa and the Far East. This was also a time when new mills in Delhi, Agra, Hathras and Mirzapur were competing for skilled labour.[31] All the new mills initially imported skilled labour from Kanpur. Inquiries in Delhi in 1906, for instance, revealed that two-thirds of the spinners in one mill had worked earlier in Kanpur.[32] Over the war period there was again a heavy demand for labour to service the manufacture of military supplies. There was alarm among managers: 'The class of unskilled labour which used formerly to flow so freely into Kanpur from the Unnao district across the Ganges in Awadh and which was broadly known as *Gangapari* labour has now entirely ceased to come into Cawnpore.'[33] Mill managers saw military recruitment in the neighbouring districts as competition for their labour needs. The Chamber of Commerce appealed to the government to give millowners powers under the Defence of India Rules to prevent workers engaged in war work from

[28] On the plague riots, see ch. 7.

[29] *UICC Report*, 1902, p. iv.

[30] The ratio of deaths from influenza per 1000 per annum (between Aug. and Nov. 1918) in Kanpur municipality was 115.39 followed by 106.98 in Agra and 102.47 in Mathura. In other municipalities the figures were below 100 per mille. UP San. Dep. Progs., Feb. 1919, no. 3.

[31] Freemantle, 'Report on the Supply of Labour', UP Rev. Progs. B, May 1906, no. 91.

[32] Ibid.

[33] Letter, 18.6.1918, from Chamber to Dir., Industries, UP, *UICC Report* 1918, App. P, p. 208.

withdrawing from their contract. The War Board gave orders stopping the recruitment of soldiers from the ranks of workers.[34] Managers sought to preserve certain territories as secure catchment areas. Proposals for recruitment to the tea gardens from Unnao, Rae Bareli, and Lucknow were firmly ruled out on the grounds that: 'These are industrial districts, and, further are recruiting grounds for the supply of labour to the large industrial centres of Cawnpore and Agra which obtain therefrom large numbers of weavers and spinners and tent and durrie makers.'[35]

Disease, mortality, and the growing competition for labour all fed into the managerial rhetoric of labour crisis: 'There is so much competition and the supply is so uncertain that it is feared a perilously high scale of wages will be established. Many of us, in fact, believe that this stage has already been reached, and that a permanent increase in the wages of certain classes of operatives has been conceded.'[36] At other times the argument was reversed by capitalist logic and high wages identified as the cause of short-age:

> In the opinion of all those best qualified to judge both officials and non-officials—the principal cause of the scarcity of labour in these provinces is the high standard of wages. The standard of comfort, the social condition of mill-hands in the mofussil is very low: their needs are few, and such as they are, of the simplest. They have no use for money beyond that for actual present wants, and, being as a class improvident in the extreme, when they find themselves in possession of more money than they can spend, they stay away from work until it is all gone, and then, and then only, return to work. If a man finds he can earn in twenty days what will keep him for thirty days he will only work twenty days and idle the remainder.[37]

Mill managers tried to devise strategies to regulate competition and reduce labour costs: the organisation of a chamber of commerce in 1888 was part of this effort. Members of the association

[34] Initially the orders prohibiting recruitment in Kanpur and Unnao were limited only to the recruitment of non-combatants. It was after a great deal of pressure from industrial interests that the President, War Board, agreed to stop recruitment of combatants. *UICC Report*, 1918, p. 19.

[35] Letter, 28.4.1916, Chamber to UP Govt, *UICC Report*, 1916, p. 215.

[36] *UICC Report*, 1902, p. iv.

[37] *Pioneer*, 24.8.1905.

agreed that no employer would take on a person from another concern without a certificate of discharge from the old employer.[38] In practice the principle never became operative. The majority of managers were convinced that recruitment from distant sources, along the lines of plantations in Assam and the colonies, was the only solution to problems of supply: 'I consider we ought to follow more or less closely the system under which foreign emigration is conducted. We can have our own recruiting agents and Government can assist by pointing out where recruitment can be carried on, but the name and address of every recruit should be registered by Government officials at the place where recruited . . . . should any of these recruits abscond within the limits of their agreements, Government should assist by helping to trace each one and have him sent back to his employer.'[39] Recruitment of cheap labour from communities declared 'habitually criminal' under the Criminal Tribes Act of 1871 was another strategy.[40]Employers seriously considered this alternative in a period when the state was devising ways of reforming and rehabilitating such communities. Their focus turned to the Barwars from Gonda district who were declared to be 'a caste of professional thieves' under the act of 1871. Provincial officials expressed concern about the fate of Barwar children whose parents were in jail or absconding, and proposed their employment in Kanpur factories.[41] Employing workers from criminal tribes was seen as beneficial both for employers and the state. The factory was seen as a reformatory, a disciplinary institution carrying through moral reform, reintegrating the deviant into society. It also provided an enclosed space for easier surveillance. The Barwar recruits who worked in Cooper Allen and Company were given lodging in the mill premises. 'The compound

[38] Freemantle, 'Report on the Supply of Labour', UP Rev. Progs. B, May 1906, no. 91.

[39] Letter from a manager in *Pioneer*, 24.8.1905.

[40] For a discussion on strategies of employing and disciplining criminal tribes as factory workers' see Meena Radhakrishna, 'Colonial Construction of a " Criminal Tribe" : The Itinerant Trading Communities of Madras Presidency', in N. Chandoke, ed., *Mapping Histories: Essays Presented to Ravinder Kumar* (New Delhi 2000).

[41] GO, 8.6.1891, from Commsr, Faizabad to DC, Gonda, Home Police Progs., April 1896, File 473A, List 57 (UPSA.)

is surrounded by a high wall,' reported the Deputy Commissioner of Gonda, 'and has, I understand, only one exit at which there is always a gatekeeper on duty.'[42] Schooling the children in an industrial school was difficult: their number—125—was considered too large for any single school. In the factory the children would learn productive work, become normative citizens, and produce profits for their employers. Industrialists could reduce their expenditure on wages while helping the state to cut its costs on disciplining society.

Mill managers believed that state intervention was necessary for recruitment strategies to be successful. The state could help identify potential 'catchment' areas and prevent absconding by new recruits. In the past, they argued, attempts to recruit outside labour had failed because of the hostility of old hands towards new recruits. The problem, then, was twofold, 'how to get labour from outside and keep it'. They suggested that the 'Government should assist by helping to trace each one [absconders] and have him sent back to his employer . . . if a recruit found he would have to stay and the local man found his efforts to dislodge newcomers were futile, we would have a steady influx of surplus labour from other districts, emigrants would get to like the work . . . while local labour would have to be less intermittent or it would be displaced altogether.'[43]

Schemes for recruiting cheap labour from criminal tribes constantly came up against the problem of absconding. Employers complained that Barwars had a 'tendency to suddenly throw up their employment and return to their village or seek work in the bazaar'.[44] Six Barwars employed by Muir Mills left work, saying the climate did not suit them.[45] The manager of Cooper Allen and Company demanded additional disciplinary powers: only corporal punishment could control the Barwar worker. Some managers congratulated themselves for doing social service by employing Barwars.

[42] DC, Gonda to Auckland, 29.6.1892. Home Police Progs., File 473A, List 57(UPSA).

[43] *Pioneer*, 24.8.1905.

[44] DC, Gonda to Commsr Faizabad Div., 5.5.1906. Home Police Progs., File 473A, List 57(UPSA).

[45] Letter, 23.3.1895, from NW Tannery to Chamber, *UICC Report*, 1895.

Legally, managers had powers under the Breach of Contract Act (Act xiii of 1859) to compel workers to abide by the terms of their contract. In actual practice, prosecutions for a breach of contract were rare. Mill managers complained that it was virtually impossible to get new recruits to keep to the terms of their agreements, even when they were formally made on stamped paper. Skilled workers, in particular, were wilful and irreverent. All efforts to enforce terms of contract on shoemakers in the North-West Tannery were futile. The manager admitted helplessness: 'they [shoemakers] come to work and stay away as it pleases them' and when threatened with penal action against absenteeism 'they simply stay away in a body for a few days, till we are forced to send for them and practically agree to the aforesaid clause not being enforced'.[46] Warnings of dismissal for breach of contract were treated with complete indifference. This was the judgement in the *Queen Empress* versus *Indarjit* case: 'Indarjit a carding *mistri* had entered into a contract for three years on 22 March 1888. He gave a 24 hour notice quitting the job on 1 November 1888. This notice was not accepted. He applied for leave which was refused. He therefore threw down his keys and left service. The employers filed a case against him. He was convicted under the Breach of Contract Act xiii of 1859. His petition against the application was rejected.'[46]

Signed contracts between employers and workers were in fact rare. Factory officials were categorical that while superior supervising staff in factories was employed under a written contract, 'in a large majority of cases there is nothing more than a verbal agreement between master and man'.[47] Despite claims of ineffective laws pertaining to master and servant, managers in Kanpur were unanimously opposed to proposals for the repeal of the Breach of Contract Act (1859) in 1921, and were anxious that alternative provincial statutes should be enacted giving them similar powers over employees.[48]

[46] *UICC Report*, 1895, p. 106.

[47] Mackay, the Chief Inspector of Factories, clarified: 'Some of the larger organised concerns have rules and terms of employment which are shown to workmen, or read to them if illiterate, when first employed, and they are required to agree to accept and abide by them.' *RCL III (i)*, p. 232.

[48] *UICC Report*, 1921, p. 8; *UICC Report*, 1923, p. 6 and App. J, p. 116.

In contrast to plantations in the West Indies, where the colonial state intervened actively to enforce penal provisions under the Breach of Contract Act, in India the state did not respond enthusiastically to managerial pleas for intervention.[49] On the contrary, officials investigating the condition of labour supply to UP and Bengal were sceptical about state-aided recruitment schemes. Working conditions, Freemantle felt, had to be more attractive to induce workers to stay, and would be more effective than state legislation to check desertion.[50] An improvement in wage levels, more frequent payment, fewer fines, and the provision of housing were among the measures he considered essential. Although representatives of the state did not necessarily share Freemantle's vision of labour welfare, they endorsed his opinion that 'there should be no direct interference by the Government in the actual supply of labour'. On measures to ensure the stability of the labour force, the state was explicit that they 'can best be left to individual employers to adopt'.[51]

By the late 1920s the panic about labour shortages seemed well past. Representatives of industry were quite complacent that a second generation of workers had come into being.[52]

Caste and Community

How did caste and community ties define the structure of the workforce? What were the ways in which colonial discourse, managerial strategies, and worker practice transform workplaces into community spaces? How did work itself redefine given notions of community?

Till the early decades of the twentieth century, workers from

---

At the same time, industrialists admitted that the repeal of the act did not affect all employers.

[49] On West Indies and Assam, see Prabhu Mohapatra, 'Immobilising Labour: Indenture Laws and Enforcement in Assam and the West Indies 1860–1920', paper presented at the First Annual Conference of AILH, New Delhi 1998.

[50] Freemantle, 'Report on the Supply of Labour', UP Rev. Progs. B, May 1906, no. 91.

[51] Letter, 26.3.1907, from Secy. Dep. of Com. and Ind., GOI to Chief Secy, UP, UP Rev. Progs., June 1907, no. 58.

[52] Ev. UICC, *RCL III (ii)*, p. 169.

artisanal castes were predominant among factory workers in Kanpur. In 1906, for instance, Koris constituted 21 per cent, and Muslims 33 per cent of the total workforce in two textile mills. Koris were traditional weavers, and about a third of the total number of Muslims in the mills were Julahas or handloom weavers (Table 2).[53] Many of the Shaikhs among the Muslims employed were also handloom weavers.[54] In later years, as the table shows, the proportion of Koris declined, though Muslims continued to form a large proportion of the cotton textile workforce. The decline in the relative proportion of Koris continued into the 1940s. Only 43 out of the 648 muster rolls of Elgin Mills (7 per cent) and 69 out of the musters in JK Mills (14 per cent) indicated a Kori background. The proportion of Julahas is not shown. However, Muslims as a whole comprised 25 per cent of the workforce in Elgin Mills and 14 per cent in JK Mills.

Chamars, traditionally associated with leather work, were dominant in tanneries and leather factories. Chamar leather workers had been involved in the manufacture of leather goods for the Company troops since the eighteenth century.[55] By the 1940s the prejudices against leather work amongst upper castes were no longer as rigid, yet Chamars constituted 65 per cent of the workforce in leather factories.[56] By the 1930s and 1940s a large

[53] This is based on Freemantle's survey of five industrial units in Kanpur, which included Cawnpore Cotton Mills, Elgin Mills, Muir Mills, Woollen Mills, and the Empire Engineering Company. I have not included Muir Mills because the figures for this mill do not give a detailed breakdown of the caste composition provided for the Cawnpore Cotton and Elgin Mills. The proportion of Koris and Muslims in the mills was higher than their relative weight within the population of Kanpur (4.5 and 9 per cent).

[54] *RCL XI (i)*, p. 68. The Superintendent, Census Operations in Bengal, made a similar suggestion. See R. Das Gupta, 'Factory Labour in Eastern India', *IESHR* 12:3, Sept. 1976, pp. 313–14.

[55] In 1906 Freemantle reported: 'The rough work in the tanning and currying shops is done entirely by this caste while leather stitching and finishing is done either by Chamars or by Musalmans . . .' Freemantle, 'Report on the Supply of Labour, UP Rev. Progs. B, May 1906, no. 91.

[56] The predominance of Chamars in the tannery, curriery and saddlery department continued later, although in other departments their dominance was displaced by migrants from upper castes. *LIC: Report on Labour Conditions in Tanneries and Leather Goods Factories*, p. 29. For a contemporary

Table 2: Caste Background
(per cent of total labour force)

	1906 Kanpur	1921 UP	1921 Kanpur	1940s Kanpur
Koris	21.0	7.1	7.8	9.8
Mussalmans (includiing Julahas)	33.0	18.6	19.2	20.4
Chamars	3.6	14.3	7.3	19.1
Brahmans	7.1	15.5	9.6	15.1
Thakurs	1.5	5.6	12.7	12.8
Ahirs	5.6	9.9	5.9	5.8
Lodh	3.9	0.9	2.9	7.5
Kurmis	1.2	0.01	NA	0.4
Lohars	0.8	1.03	1.4	3.1
Kachis & Muraons	1.4	3	3.8	0.6
Barhais	0.5	5.5	6.4	2.4
Pasis	4.9	3.6	4.9	2.6
Others	15.5	14.6	29.5	19.5

Source: Figures for 1906 are based on Freemantle's data for the Elgin and Cawnpore Cotton Mills. Freemantle, 'Report on the Supply of Labour', UP Rev. Progs. B, May 1906, App. A; for 1921 they are compiled from Census, UP, 1921, Part 2, Table xxii, Parts iv &v; for the 1940s from the muster rolls of the JK and Elgin Mills.

Note: The category 'skilled' according to the census classification includes weavers and spinners, 'unskilled' includes others. The statistics of 'skilled' workers relate to UP as a whole and not Kanpur.

number of Chamars also worked in the cotton mills. In Elgin Mills, for instance, their proportion within the total labour force went up from 4.5 in 1906 to 20 per cent in the 1940s.

The Koris and Chamars employed in the factories were largely from Kanpur district. Around 30 per cent of the Chamars were 'gangaparis' (from across the river) who travelled to Kanpur for work in the day. Julahas were usually immigrants from distant regions like Fyzabad, Benares, Hardoi, Fatehpur and Farukha-

---

ethnographic account on Chamars, see G.W. Briggs, *The Chamars* (Calcutta 1920).

bad.[57] Large number of Koris, Julahas and Chamars were settled in Kanpur for generations. Many lived in mohallas with a long association of work in the manufacture of military goods at the Cawnpore Magazine. Besides, managers preferred workers from an artisanal background because of their traditional skills: Koris and Julahas with cotton, Chamars with leather. In Bombay some of the early mills recruited weaving castes from as far away as Madras, UP and Bengal.[58]

In the 1930s and 1940s the caste composition of the workforce grew diverse. During the Depression and post-Depression period there was an increased influx of migrants from rural areas. A series of bad harvests and a general decline in the prices of agricultural commodities in the Depression years affected the fate of small tenants in the province. Ejectment suits against occupancy tenants showed an increase, leading to a decline in the area held by occupancy tenants. Agricultural labourers were adversely affected both by the fall in rural wages and by the decline in rural employment.[59] Workers from an agricultural background and from upper castes—Brahmans, Rajputs—were now more visible in factory jobs.

In 1906 Brahmans employed in the Elgin and Cawnpore Cotton Mills constituted 7 per cent of the total workforce. In 1921 they comprised 9.6 per cent of the 'unskilled' workers in Kanpur

[57] Freemantle, 'Report on the Supply of Labour', UP Rev. Progs. B, May 1906, no. 91. On the decline of traditional industries and displacement of Julahas in UP, see G. Pandey, 'Economic Dislocation in Nineteenth Century Eastern Uttar Pradesh: Some Implications of the Decline of Artisanal Industry in Colonial India', in P. Robb, ed., *Rural South Asia: Linkages, Changes and Development* (London 1983); P.C. Joshi, 'The Decline of Indigenous Handicrafts in Uttar Pradesh', *IESHR* 1:1, 1963-4.

[58] Morris, *Emergence*, p. 81. In other regions too, workers from traditional weaving castes like Julahas, Tantis, Mahars were sought out. R. Das Gupta, 'Factory Labour in Eastern India—Sources of Supply, 1885-1946', *IESHR*, 12: 3, Sept. 1976, pp. 310-14.

[59] Applications for ejectment increased by 34 per cent between 1929 and 1931. *AR*, UP, 1931, p. 19. On the decline in position of occupancy tenants, see *AR*, UP, 1931, p. 3, *AR*, UP, 1932, p. 12, *AR*, UP, 1933, p. 2. See also 'Note on the Agrarian Situation in UP', AICC Papers, File 14, 1931 (NMML). On the decline and rural wages, see also *Rural and Urban Wages in the United Provinces* (Lucknow 1956), pp. 341, 343 and *Census UP*, 1931, Part 1, p. 40.

and 15.5 per cent of the 'skilled' workers. The percentage of Brahmans in factories increased with the expansion of employment during the 1940s. A sample of 272 musters of JK Mills showed that 22 per cent of the workers recruited in this period were Brahmans and 10 per cent Thakurs. Niehoff's sample similarly suggests that workers from an upper-caste rural background formed a majority among those migrating to the city in the 1940s.

The distribution of particular castes within mill departments shows both continuity and change. Koris and Julahas were dominant in the weaving sheds in most mills. In 1906 Koris constituted 38 per cent of the workforce in the weaving department of Elgin Mills, Ahirs formed the largest proportion in carding, and Brahmans were dominant in the weaving preparation department.[60] Assertions by officials like Freemantle that 'Brahmans and Chhatris work cheek by jowl with the Chamars and do not find their touch polluting as they would in their villages', obviously cannot be fully substantiated.[61] Although norms of purity and pollution were never practised in the same form as in the rural areas, lines between the 'pure' and 'impure' castes were maintained at the workplace in other ways. The ritually 'impure' Koris and Muslim Julahas tended to cluster in the weaving sheds, and Brahmans in the warehouse and miscellaneous departments, even in later years. In 1929 the Factory Inspector noted how 'a good sprinkling' of the weavers were Muslims.[62] Evidence from the 1940s shows that 70 per cent of the total number of Muslims employed in JK and Elgin Mills, were concentrated in the weaving department.[63]

[60] Freemantle, 'Report on the Supply of Labour', UP Rev. Progs. B, May 1906, App. B.

[61] Freemantle, 'Report on the Supply of Labour'. Freemantle pointed out that it was 'probably accidental that there are, for instance, more Ahirs or Brahmans in the carding than in the spinning, the case of the Chamars and others being exactly the opposite'. In more recent times Morris makes a similar suggestion. He sees caste ties in the urban context as 'institutional carryovers' from the rural sector. Morris, *Emergence*, p. 82. R. K. Newman, in contrast, overstresses the resilience of tradition. 'Social Factors in the Recruitment of Bombay Millhands', in C. Dewey and K.N. Chaudhuri, eds, *Economy and Society* (Delhi 1979), pp. 288–9.

[62] Ev. Mackay, Inspector of Factories, *RCL III (ii)*, p. 111.

[63] In the JK Mills 49 out of the 68 Muslims and in Elgin Mills 120 out of

The concentration of certain castes within departments did not imply the total exclusion of other castes. In the 1940s, a large number of Brahmans were to be found in the weaving department in JK Mills. The migration of upper castes into the city, in fact, threatened the dominance of weaving castes in the weaving departments of certain mills.

Caste distribution within the workplace was related both to managerial preferences and to worker practices. The dominance of particular castes in certain departments, Koris and Julahas in weaving for instance, represented an effort by weaving castes to preserve their space within a higher paid category. The preponderance of particular groups within industries was sustained by the system of chain migration through which workers from villages came to work in the mills. A practice that started in the early years of the industry gradually developed into an accepted tradition. Molund's study of the 1970s reveals interesting evidence on the working of the system of serial migration, although it relates to a period when Koris were no longer dominant in the mills. He shows how a single Kori mistri of the Ahirwar jati brought in a chain of around 27 kinspeople, men and women. Kallo, who came with two brothers to the city, brought in his son-in-law, his son's brother-in-law. Kallo's son-in-law brought in his daughter and son-in-law and so the chain continued.[64] Powerful mistris who held on to their job for long years were able to bring a retinue of kinsfolk. Baldeo Master who was a head jobber in Laxmi Ratan Mills for three decades, fixed jobs for many of his relatives in the weaving department. Some of his recruits were promoted to positions of power as line jobbers and supervisors, thus delegating authority down the line.[65] However, such evidence needs to be treated carefully. Mistri power was subject to contestation, both by those in authority and by workers from other castes and communities. Managements tried to displace dominant groups when they posed a threat. In the 1940s, for instance, there was an

---

164 Muslims were concentrated in the weaving department. Evidence from muster rolls of the 1940s.

[64] Stefan Molund, *First We are People . . . the Koris of Kanpur between Caste and Class* (Stockholm 1988), p. 183.

[65] Molund, *First We are People*, p. 189.

effort to undermine the dominance of Koris in JK Mills and Julahas in Cawnpore Cotton Mills.[66] But these efforts were not always successful. In this period, managements could more successfully displace dominant and militant groups because the expansion of production and increased jobs coincided with wartime restrictions on strikes.[67]

Mistri control and serial migration ensured caste clusterings within mills and reproduced community bonds within the industrial space. But there was no simple continuity with the community past. As we shall see, community rituals, practices, norms and values were refigured in various ways.

Of Women and Children

The proportion of women in the textile workforce in Kanpur was never large: it declined from 5 per cent in 1906 to 2 per cent in 1921 and 1 per cent by 1944.[68] These are definitely underestimates and the downward bias must have increased with the stricter enforcement of factory legislation restricting the hours of women's labour. But there is no doubt that the overall proportion was very small, and it declined over time. The lower proportion of women in relation to men was not peculiar to Kanpur. The proportion of women fluctuated between 20 and 25 per cent in the cotton

[66] See also ch. 7.

[67] A communiqué from the Dept of Labour (GOI) to all provincial governments stated: 'In order that industrial production may not suffer in wartime the machinery of DIR 81 A and orders thereunder have been devised to deal expeditiously with strikes and lockouts. By the general order made under DIR, 81A; 14 days notice is required to be given of intended strike.' HPD, File 42/9/1942. In relation to the general strike in Kanpur in July 1941, the UP government noted: 'No government can tolerate interference with the supply of essential articles to troops in the field in time of war and so [the] Governor intends to use his powers under the defense of India Rules to the full to restore normal working in Cawnpore.' Telegram, 7.7.1941, from UP Govt to Home Secy (GOI), HPD, File 12/5/1941.

[68] *Financial and Commercial Statistics of British India* 1906–7, and 1913–14, *Census UP*, 1921, Part 11, Table XXII, parts, iv and v, *LIC: Labour in Cotton Mills*. The UICC, estimated: 'In 1921 in 4 cotton mills, 1 woollen mill, 1 leather work, there were 1041 women employed in all. Now in cotton mills and others there are just a little over 600 employed.' *RCL III (ii)*, p. 170.

industry in Bombay and around 12 to 15 per cent in the jute industry in Calcutta. What strikes one about Kanpur is the hugely smaller proportion of women.

A simple argument in terms of the abundance of male labour does not explain this. The question is: in a situation of abundant labour supply why were men preferred over women? The preference can be understood in terms of a masculinist ideology that devalues women's labour. Employers and colonial officials saw women as less productive and efficient than men. The premise was that, given the same wages, men would produce more. They had greater energy and could work with greater intensity of labour per unit of time. Linked to such assumptions were notions about the fragility of women, their delicate constitution, their tender health. Women were more prone to diseases like tuberculosis, the incidence of death being higher for women than men.[69] Maternal duties constrained them further and blurred the distinction between domestic space and the factory. Women moving in and out of the gate, carrying infants into the workplace, feeding and nursing them[70]—such images displeased managers.

Yet, confronted with the possibility of legislation restricting the hours of work in the late nineteenth century, there were apprehensions about the deterrent effect of such legislation on women's employment. Worried by fears of labour shortage, masculinist ideology was turned on its head. Some officials argued that protective legislation was unnecessary since lower-caste coolie women were actually used to long and strenuous hours.[71] It was as if lower-caste women, untouched by civilisation, had not acquired femininity. But with an increasing number of women vanishing, this argument lost its force.[72]

[69] Ev. UP Govt, *RCL III (i)*, p. 154.

[70] In cotton ginning factories, officials reported: 'Many a time babies have been found concealed in a heap of cotton at odd times of day to keep them warm.' Note by Director Industries, UP Ind. Progs., Dec. 1921, no. 7(a).

[71] Ev. Baker, *IFLC*, p. 208. Ginning factory owners were anxious about getting alternative supplies of labour if night work for women was prohibited: 'It is doubtful if an efficient substitute for women would be forthcoming, as men who are physically fit for work at a gin can earn good wages during the day, and will not work at night.' Ev. Meti, Volkart Brother, Kanpur, *IFLC*, p. 212.

[72] When proposals for maternity benefit schemes were put forward in the

In regions where the pace and scale of industrialisation created pressures, opportunities for women's employment were likely to open up more than in regions where industrial expansion was limited. In 1913 there were six otton mills employing a total of 10,971 workers in Kanpur, in contrast to 90 cotton mills employing 110,033 workers in Bombay and 64 jute mills employing 216,377 workers in Bengal. In fact, the number of women workers in Bombay at this time was 22,402, more than double the total workforce in Kanpur. The increase in employment of women workers in Bombay and Calcutta in the 1890s and the first decade of the twentieth century took place in a context when fears of labour shortages were widespread and the effectiveness of factory legislation limited.[73] Given the more limited scale of industrialisation in Kanpur, pressures to employ women workers were weaker. When the Kanpur industry expanded in the post-war decades, restrictive factory legislation gave greater strength to masculinist arguments against women's employment in factories.[74] The introduction of the Maternity Benefit Act in most states by the late 1930s, similarly, made it easier for mill managements to justify a reduction in women workers, although a downward trend in the employment of women had set in before the introduction of these acts.[75]

----

post-war period, many officials tried to oppose them: 'Women who work in factories are of a low caste and are not bound hard and fast by caste rules. They generally work up to a few days before delivery and return to work as soon as they feel fit, usually 10–12 days.' Letter, 15.6.1921, Inspector Factories to Director Industries, UP Ind. Progs., Dec. 1921, no. 7(b).

[73] In the jute mills in Calcutta, for instance, managers devised ways of evading restrictive laws. Sen, *Women and Labour,* p. 115. In Bombay, Morris points out that there was a rise in the proportion of women workers despite the introduction of the Factories Act of 1891. *Emergence,* p. 67.

[74] The Factory Act of 1891 restricted the hours of work for women to 11 per day and the Act of 1911 prohibited night work for women. However, during the war, factories were allowed exemption from these rules. Employers in Kanpur pointed to a distinct reduction in the numbers of women and children employed because of Factory Act regulations. *RCL III (ii),* p. 160.

[75] The Maternity Benefit Act did not dramatically affect employment. In Kanpur, women in regular factories were a minuscule number, and in Bombay and Calcutta the decline in women's employment had set in before the legislation. In 1929, the UP government in its evidence to the RCL noted: 'the

Masculinist notions about women's work were reaffirmed by an ideology of domesticity and seclusion that influenced the discourse of managers and colonial officials in the 1920s and 1930s: women were valorised as mothers and homemakers rather than as workers.[76] The emphasis on family ideas tended to legitimise the marginalisation of women from the workforce and the politics of trade unions validated such an ideology. For Bengal, it has been argued that these ideas were appropriated by working class families who tended to associate seclusion with a higher social status. In such families, especially in those with higher incomes, women tended to withdraw from work: seclusion became a marker of status.[77]

The decline in the number of women employed after the 1920s did not, however, necessarily mean seclusion and domesticity and withdrawal from work. The domestic became an arena of wage employment.[78] Women, especially those from lower castes, continued to work in cottage industries at home and outside. The notion of a male breadwinner, never an adequate category for working class families, had little meaning in a context where women's earnings from making bidis or brushes, and other kinds of work was what pulled families out of crisis.[79]

---

number of women operatives in regulated factories is very small, both absolutely and as a proportion.' *RCL III (i)*, p. 159. See also, Sen, *Women and Labour*, p. 175; R. Kumar, 'Family and Factory: Women in the Bombay Cotton Textile Industry, 1919–1939', in J. Krishnamurthy, ed., *Women in Colonial India* (Delhi 1989), p. 151.

[76] Colonial officials made statements like: 'New-born babies are our national assets and it is our duty to see that mothers live lives conducive to the welfare of their babies as well as their own.' Note by Director Industries, UP Ind. Progs., Dec. 1921, no. 7 (a). Sen powerfully argues that the influence of the ideology of domesticity was crucial in shaping the gendered pattern of working class formation in Bengal. *Women and Labour*, ch. 3. See also Catherine Hall, 'The Early Formation of Victorian Domestic Ideology', *White, Male and Middle-Class: Explorations in Feminism and History* (Oxford 1992).

[77] Sen, *Women and Labour*, pp.133–41.

[78] See Joshi, 'Making Spaces: Questions of Gender and Domesticity', paper presented at the Second International Conference of the AILH, V.V. Giri Institute of Labour, March 2000.

[79] See ch. 4. On the male breadwinner debate, see Colin Creighton, 'The

The proportion of children employed in Kanpur's industries was never large and dropped further after the amendments to the Factories Act in 1922. By the 1940s the number of children formally employed in textile factories was negligible: 0.26 per cent in 1944, most of them doffer boys.[80] But the anxiety about labour supply led to a vociferous defence of child labour in the early years of the industry. Managers marshalled a variety of justifications. Early employment allowed training for the future worker, provided a livelihood to the poor, and ensured a regular supply of labour for the industry: 'Children are almost entirely employed in spinning, and unless they commence early they can never become spinners, so that if they have been employed for 4 or 5 or maybe 6 years in carrying bricks for instance, their hands will certainly be unfit for employment in piecing up delicate yarns, and meanwhile they have been deprived of a better means of earning their livelihood than they can have possibly obtained elsewhere.'[81]

Within managerial discourse the child worker was an adult for whom long and arduous work was not unnatural. Contrary to colonial conceptions, in which the colony was a child who had to be tutored and guided by imperial power, the child worker in managerial eyes did not need protective care. Respect for custom, in fact, demanded that a child be treated as an adult: 'I consider that in India as a male child of over 12 is in his manner, customs and privileges treated almost as an adult, he should at this age be

---

Rise of the Male Breadwinner Family: A Reappraisal', *Comparative Studies in Society and History*, 38:2, 1996; Sylvia Walby, *Patriarchy at Work: Patriarchal and Capitalist Relations in Employment* (Oxford 1986), Wally Secombe, 'Patriarchy Stabilized: The Construction of the Male Breadwinner Wage Norm in Nineteenth Century Britain', *Social History*, 11:1, 1986; Sonya Rose, 'Gender at Work: Sex, Class and Industrial Capitalism',*History Workshop*, 21,1986.

[80] Definitions of who constituted a child or an adult vis-à-vis factory work changed over time. The prescribed age for working children changed from 7 to 11 in the 1880s, to 9 to 13 in the 1890s, to 12 to 15 after 1922.

[81] Ev. Muir Mills,*IFLC*, p. 205. Although the children were meant to work half time, it was customary to employ half-time children for full time in the Kanpur mills. Ev. Lt. Col. Baker, Civil Surgeon, Kanpur, *IFLC*, p. 210; see also ev. Bevis of Elgin Mills, *IFLC*, p. 216.

permitted the freedom of working full time as an adult.'[82] It would 'be grossly inconsistent' to introduce restrictive legislation 'for one who is permitted by law, and by the popular voice, and even coercion of his own class to be himself the father of an infant.'[83] If in other contexts the reforming voice of colonial officialdom stigmatised child marriage, here marriage became a passport to manhood: 'If the state is not prepared to legislate as to the physical fitness of youths to exercise paternity it would seem to us to be improper to interfere with their desire to maintain their offspring by working as adults in mills.'[84] Protective legislation, moreover, seemed unnecessary to them when 'native' children working in the factories looked 'extremely healthy' and 'well cared for'. Conditions in the mills, they asserted, were safer and more sanitary than in workers' homes. In fact, if children were not employed in the mills they would be forced to work for petty employers in the bazaar who used sweated labour. In the nineteenth and early twentieth century, mill managers saw all attempts to introduce protective legislation as attempts by the state to push the interests of the English textile industry. The UICC warned the government against being swayed by Lancashire and Manchester interests in the English Parliament. Their object, the chamber cautioned, 'appears to be to reduce, or at all events, to check the cotton manufacturing industry in this country, and it signifies nothing to them if this means want of employment and misery to thousands of natives whose condition they affect to commiserate'.[85]

The imperatives of the labour demand, in the context of a feared shortage in the early twentieth century, led to convoluted reasoning. The logic of humanitarianism was turned on its head. Managerial practices were justified as paternalist projects: employment in the factory provided women and children with a home and sanitary spaces they otherwise lacked. But as the supply of labour eased and male migrants flooded the labour market after the 1920s, women labour came to be seen as superfluous. When low-waged male workers are in abundant supply, women tend to become dispensable within capitalist logic.

[82] Ev. Allen, *IFLC*, p. 188
[83] Ibid., p. 187.
[84] Ev. Woollen Mills, *IFLC*, p. 192.
[85] UICC Report, 1890, p. 23.

Linkages

Writings on labour look at the question of linkages from an industry-centric perspective. The rural link was initially seen as a problem for industry, accounting for irregular work habits, high rates of absenteeism, and a lack of work ethic.[86] Morris countered the argument and questioned the reliability of the statistical data but left unquestioned the frame of reference.[87] Others asserted that absenteeism could coexist with commitment and industrial growth.[88] The question of rural links, in this argument, became unimportant since it had no bearing on the phenomenon of industrialisation. In this frame, industrialisation was the measure of all value. Recent studies re-establish the importance of the rural connection, but the industry-centric perspective survives. The social identity of those who work in the mills is taken for granted: they are classed as industrial workers and their rural ties are seen as residual. This teleology of industrialisation and modernisation— the assumption of a unilinear process of transition to a modern industrial system—is flawed. We need to displace the terms of the discussion and consider what absenteeism and ties with the

[86] See, for instance, W.E. Moore, *The Impact of Industry* (New Delhi 1969); Charles A. Myers, *Labour Problems in the Industrialization of India* (Cambridge 1958); Clark Kerr, J. Dunlop et al. eds, *Industrialism and Industrial Man* (London 1973).

[87] Morris argues that available estimates were highly inflated and the seasonal cycle of absenteeism does not indicate the rural links of workers. *Emergence*, pp. 92–6.

[88] See also Angus Hone, 'High Absenteeism and High Commitment', *EPW*, 3: 21–2, May 1968, pp. M31–2; Baldev R. Sharma, 'The Industrial Worker: Some Myths and Realities', *EPW*, 5: 22, 30 May 1970, pp. 875–8. A typical argument is that 'commitment' increases progressively as industrialisation advances: 'Supply and demand thus progressively interact to produce a given level of commitment. At early stages of industrialisation supply is likely to be fairly steep, but flatten out progressively . . . Thus at the early stages of development the wage-earning group and the level of commitment attained are likely to be low, with employers who desire higher levels of commitment paying sharp premiums. Progressively, the proportion of wage earners will increase, but the relative premium paid for securing commitment as well as their degree of commitment decline.' Subbiah Kannappan, 'Labour Force Commitment in the Early Stages of Industrialization', *Indian Journal of Industrial Relations*, 5:3, 1970, pp. 290–349.

village really meant—not only for the industry but also for the workers. The question of a rural link remains important even when we shift discussion away from the question of commitment. So we need to consider two issues: one, the strength of rural ties; and two, the meaning of these ties. We need to examine more closely the space of the rural in the world of those working in the mills. Did they see themselves as peasants temporarily employed in urban work, or as workers residually connected to the village?

Most workers in the Kanpur industries came from neighbouring districts. Unlike the jute mills of Bengal, where migrants from UP, Bihar and Orissa increasingly replaced local labour, strategies for distant recruitment never worked in Kanpur.[89] As we saw, labour flowed in from the countryside through kin networks. In the first decade of the twentieth century, labour from within Kanpur district comprised 41 per cent of the total workforce in Muir Mills, 44 per cent, in the Cawnpore Cotton Mills, and 26 per cent in the Woollen Mills (Fig. 14). The rest came largely from contiguous districts. In the 1930s, similarly, workers from Kanpur district comprised 51 per cent of the total workforce in all industries (Fig. 15).

A common measure of the strength of rural ties is the data on absenteeism: the higher the rate, the stronger the ties. But figures on absenteeism have always been a problem. Accepting the limitations of standard musters kept by mills, the general trend in Kanpur seems one of increase, not decline, in absenteeism over the years.[90] In 1929 the average monthly absenteeism was highest among 'skilled' and 'semi-skilled' workers in the tanneries (9.3 per cent), followed by textile factories (6 per cent).[91] Figures for

[89] Ranajit Das Gupta, 'Factory Labour in Eastern India: Source of Supply, 1885–1946', *IESHR*, 12:3, Sept. 1976; Lalitha Chakravarty, 'Emergence of an Industrial Labour-Force in a Dual Economy-British India, 1880–1920'. *IESHR*, 15:3, July 1978. In Bombay too the number of migrants drawn from distant regions like UP rose in the 1880s and became more significant in the early twentieth century. See Chandavarkar, *The Origins of Industrial Capitalism*, pp. 129–30; Morris, *Emergence*, p. 64.

[90] This is elaborated by Morris in the case of Bombay. The standard muster roll of the daily number of employees tended to overestimate the average daily number of workers required, thus resulting in inflated absenteeism statistics. Morris, *Emergence*, pp. 92–6.

[91] *RCL III (i)*, App. 1, p. 237.

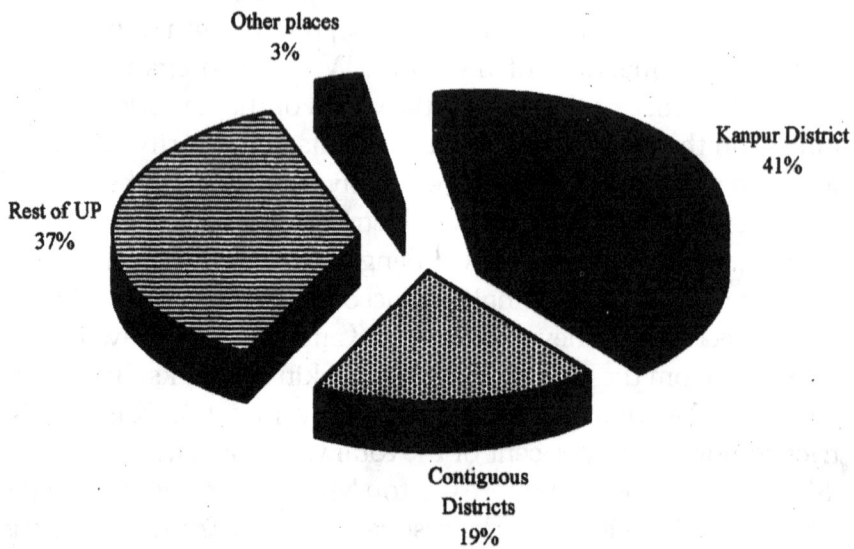

Fig. 14: Where did the workers come from in 1906?

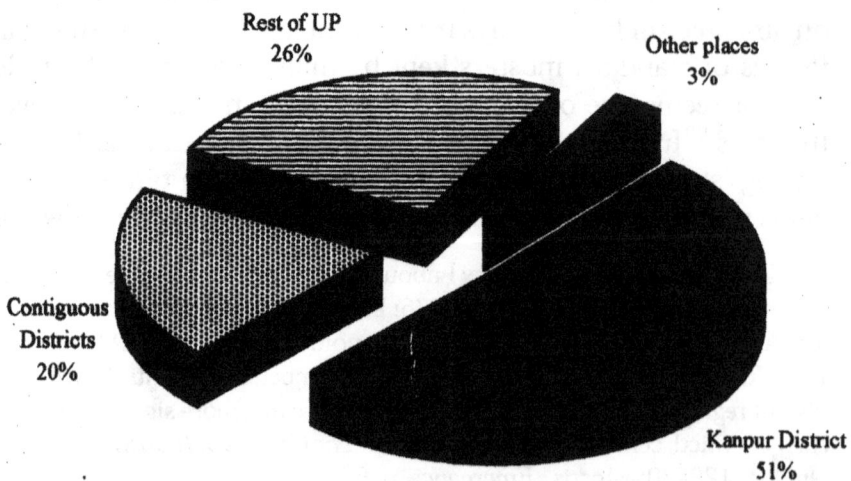

Fig. 15: Where did the workers come from in 1931?

the 1940s show an annual average rate of 10.6 per cent in 1944 and 13 per cent in 1946.[92] It is not clear whether these figures show any definite trend of increase in absenteeism. It is possible that the contraction of income and employment opportunities in the countryside accounted for the reduced absenteeism figures in 1929. In the 1940s, although there was an expansion of employment in the city, the sharp rise in the cost of living created the need for supplementary income: thus the greater absenteeism for harvest and other work in the villages. However, the 1929 figures give the monthly average rates and those for the 1940s give annual rates.

Average figures on absenteeism conceal fluctuations in monthly rates. In the Cawnpore Cotton Mills, absenteeism in the spinning department varied from 4.6 per cent in January to 17.5 per cent in September and 25.4 per cent in October; in the carding department from 5.5 per cent in January to 11 per cent in October. In weaving, absenteeism was highest in July, though it remained higher than the average monthly absenteeism in other departments throughout the year.[93] Monthly fluctuations in the figures for 1906 show a marked increase in the harvest months (Fig. 16). This was when many worked as agricultural labourers or on family farms; it was also a time of festivals and rituals. The monthly fluctuations in absenteeism in the 1940s show a certain change in the pattern of variation during the year (Fig. 17). The peak in May was not paralleled by a similar one in October. The commercialisation of agriculture and production of higher-value labour-intensive rabi crops meant a heightened labour demand in May—the time of rabi harvest.

Another index commonly used to show the rural connections of workers is the evidence on the proportion of family members in villages, and the remittances sent by those employed in factories. In 1929 the ratio of family members of workers living in the village to the city was 1:3 (Table 3). Significantly, the figures show that the proportion of family members remaining in the village was higher in lower-income groups. The average expenditure on

[92] *Labour Bulletin*, UP for the relevant years.

[93] In other years the harvest-time exodus was likely to be greater, since 1906–7 was a period in which the famine in the countryside reduced the demand for agricultural labour.

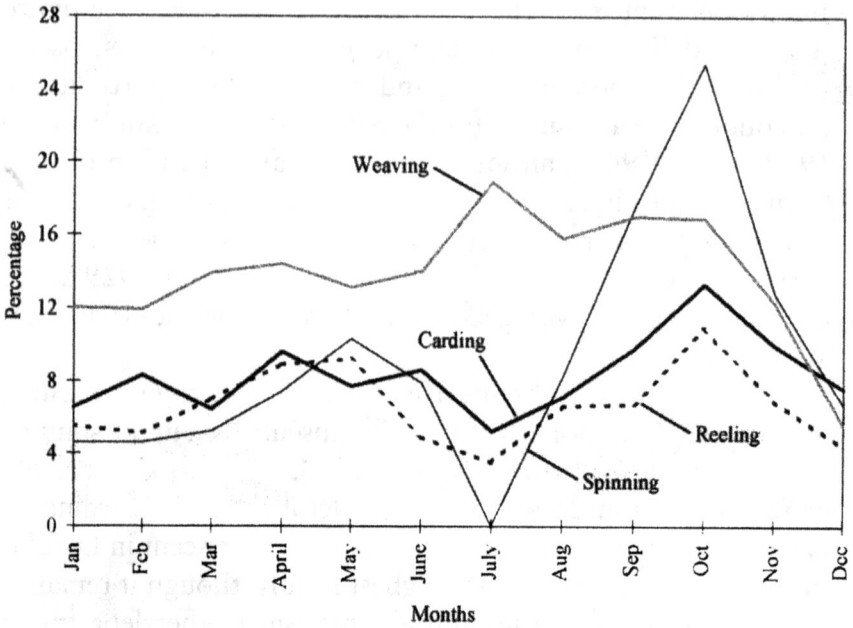

Fig. 16: Seasonal fluctuation of absenteeism in 1906

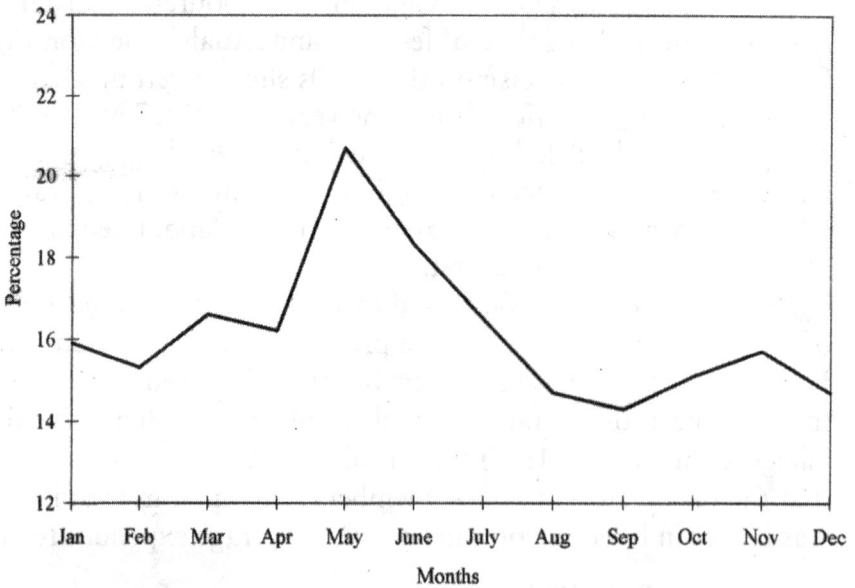

Fig. 17: Seasonal variations in absenteeism in cotton mills of Kanpur in 1948

Table 3: Ratio of Persons per Family Living in the City
to Those Away

Group	No. of families	Men	Women	Children	Ratio of those in the city to those away
I	35	11.7:1	4.7:1	4.6:1	4.8:1
II	95	9.6:1	4.7:1	4.7:1	5.9:1
III	231	5.3:1	1.3:1	2.6:1	2.8:1
IV	581	3.8:1	1:01	1.3:1	1.8:1
All groups	419	6.2:1	2.1:1	2.1:1	3.3:1

Source: RCL, Supp. vol. xi (i), Table 4, p. 88.

monthly remittances shows a similar pattern. In proportion to
their total income, the remittances of those earning less than
Rs 15 was higher than those who earned more.[94] Those with a
higher income could bring a larger number of dependants into the
city. However, village connections remained strong even for those
who migrated with their families. A large number of workers
from the Jalaun and Jhansi region of south-west UP, who came
with their families returned to their villages more than once a
year.[95]

[94] Remittances sent to the village:

Group	Monthly remittance (in Rs)	Remittance % of monthly income
1	1.66	3.68
11	1.64	4.68
111	1.36	6.18
1V	1.26	8.53
Average	1.43	4.76

Source: Calculated from RCL XI (i), Table xi, p. 92.
Note: Income Group I = Rs 40–50; Group II =Rs 30–40; Group III=Rs 15–
30; Group IV=Rs 15 and below.

[95] See details on 'Recruitment, Service and Contact with Villages of
"Typical" Kanpur Mill', RCL III (i), App. J, p. 236. Over 80 per cent of the
immigrants from Jalaun and Jhansi had their families with them in the city.

Members on official commissions, such as the Royal Commission, informed by liberal ideas, assume that with increasing industrialisation there was a decline in contact with the villages. The Director of Public Health, queried about workers' visits to their villages, asserted: 'I am informed by millowners in Cawnpore that the habit used to be, when the industrial centre here was first formed and mills began to spring up, that they drew practically all their labour from the agricultural tracts. The labourers came for a period and went back home. They were in no sense an industrial population. This phase has been gradually passing away and there is now an established industrial population which forms a very large percentage of the general labourers.'[96] Statistical details on absenteeism in the Royal Commission are accompanied by figures on the duration of employment, showing that the length of service of workers was increasing over time, and that a 'stable', 'committed' labour force was emerging.[97]

In reality the picture was not as clear-cut as colonial officials suggest. As late as the 1960s the proportion of workers drawn from rural areas was high.[98] Besides, a large number of workers continued to move between city and village in a circular way. In areas just bordering the city, such movements were more apparent. In the Gangaghat area near the Ganges Bridge, for instance, there

[96] Ev. Lt. Col. C.L. Dunn, Director, Public Health, *RCL III (ii)*, p. 147.

[97] According to estimates of the Factory Inspector, the average duration of employment of textile workers in the industry as a whole varied from 6.5 years for 'skilled' and 'semi-skilled' workers, and 3.75 for 'unskilled' workers. The higher income groups, i.e., those earning Rs 40–50 had a larger number of workers residing in the city for over 20 years and those earning Rs 15 and below had a larger number resident in the city for 1–5 years. *RCL XI (i)*, table 3, p. 86. By the 1940s, surveys point out that a large proportion of workers had become permanent residents in the city: 'The Cawnpore mill-worker began learning to settle at Cawnpore about 10 years back.' J.K. Pande, 'The Cawnpore Mill-worker, His Family and Expenditure', *Sankhya: Indian Journal of Statistics*, 7:2, Nov. 1945, p.185.

[98] Even in older established mills like Muir and New Victoria, the proportion of workers drawn from rural areas was high: of the total workers, 67 per cent in Muir Mills and 80 per cent in New Victoria were from rural areas. In the JK Cotton Manufactures and Laxmi Ratan Mills established in the 1930s the proportion of workers from a rural background was 87 and 86 per cent respectively. V.B. Singh, *Wage Patterns, Mobility and Savings of Workers in India* (Bombay 1973).

was often a dearth of field labourers: villagers moved to the city whenever they were out of employment. Rates of wages here were higher than in other areas.[99] The final destination could not always be anticipated. Sometimes a temporary search for work ended up in a long-term shift to the city.[100] Simple assertions about workers becoming permanent residents of the city do not capture the fluidity of links, the tensions between contrary pulls, the ambiguities of contrary identities. Even for those who eventually settled in the city, the process of becoming 'permanent residents' was torn by conflicts. Living in the city entailed a constant longing, waiting for home. As one old worker remembered: '*Mil mein kam karne ki ek bari samasya lagti thi, vah thi ghar ki yad: ghar kab ja payenge.*'[101] Times in the city seemed transitional even to workers who had lived there for years. For others, the rupture with the village became final: family trajectories, the timing of migration, the nature of work, the dynamics of city life, all made it so. But remembrances of the past in oral or written recollection are always mediated by other times and experiences. For those to whom the city became a home, the moment of rupture seems easier and more final when it is refigured in the present. Or conversely, the despair of the present and worklessness re-evokes a desire for a return to the home and the village.

Writing his life-story sometime in the 1970s, Shriram recounts how he never looked back once he came to the city. Orphaned when he was an infant and left in the care of his paternal aunt, he inherited his parents' home, one and a half bighas of cultivable

[99] 'Generally male labourers get around 3 to 6 annas per day. The labourers in fields near the banks of the Ganges get 7 to 8 annas when labour is insufficient.' R.K. Mukerjee points out that 'whenever rains are deficient, labourers in view of the approaching calamity leave their homes to seek employment in Cawnpore'. *Fields and Farms in Oudh* (Calcutta 1929), p. 245.

[100] Ramdai, who worked in the Woollen Mills, came looking for work during the famine of the 1880s but she stayed on and as the Factory Commission recorded: 'She does not know when she will go home again as she is in debt to the mahajan now.' *IFC*, p. 72.

[101] One major problem of working in the mills was the constant yearning for home. 'When can we go home' was the constant worry. Interview, Shiv Ratan (known familiarly as Daddu). Daddu was almost 90 when I met him in the early 1980s. Even after living for years in the city, he remembered the pain and anguish of leaving home.

land and seven bighas in another village. His recollections of childhood create images of plenty, of riches and land: '*Ghar mein rupya paisa jewar adi kafi tha jisse main achi tarah khana kha sakta tha kapre pahan sakta tha aur parhai kar sakta tha.*'[102] Yet they had no bullocks to plough with, so they had to lease their land to sharecroppers. He feels a sense of anguish about the absence of bullocks, almost as though they lost control over their property for lack of them: '*Itna sab hote hue bhi kami thi to kewal do bailon ki, jinke dwara kheti ki ja sakti thi. Bas vahi nahin the.*'[103] They had already lost control over their seven bighas in the neighbouring village.

When Sriram was about twelve he left for Kanpur. His story moves by constructing a series of contrasts between city and country. In contrast to the stereotypical images of simple countryfolk and wily, deceitful townspeople, his images are the reverse. His relatives in the village were greedy for money: '*Jaise ki mare janvar ki khal nochne ke liye gidh baithe the . . . vaise vah kar rahe the.*' (They were like vultures waiting to feed on a carcass).[104] In the city, in contrast, he finds caring relatives. His brother-in-law was a mistri in the Woollen Mills and helped him get work there as a half-timer. Times were good then—one earning member could support a whole family on factory wages. What he earned, even as a half-timer, was enough for him to save and send money to his aunt in the village.

Sriram was writing about the 1930s and 1940s, when factory jobs gave a sense of security. Ramcharan, who worked in more recent times, tells a different story. He resigned from his job and went back to his village after being a permanent worker in Muir Mills for 11 years. He spent six to seven years in the village before coming back to the city again: '*Jab bahut vakt ho gayo tab lagat hai zamin batai phir Muir Mill's se certifcate nikalwa kar Laxmi Ratan mein bharti ho gaye.*'[105] He worked as a badli for two to

[102] I was well provided with wealth and riches. I could dress and eat well and be educated.

[103] Yet we had no bullocks to cultivate the land with. That was all we lacked.

[104] Shriram, *Ek Sarvahara ka Jivan Vritanta* (Kanpur n.d.), p. 5.

[105] After I had been in the village for a long time, I gave my land on sharecropping and I took my certificate out from Muir Mills and got a job in Laxmi Ratan Mills.

three years and then became permanent. He worked for around 25 years, after which '*Phir permanint hamne chorkar jab zamin ka jhagra par gaya tab ganv chale gaye, istifa laga kar.*'[106] His repeated emphasis on the permanence of the job suggests that leaving was not an easy decision. Conflicts over land in the village made it imperative for him to go back. He explained: '*Is liye istifa lagaya. Jab zamin pari hai vah zindage bhar khilayegi bal bachan ko.*'[107] Eventually he lost all his property, although he spent over a lakh and a half trying to recover it. With a sense of bitterness and envy he added: '*Zamin hamari chale gayi chamar ke hath mein. Us jagah chamar 50,000 ki phasal kamata hai.*'[108] There is a constant play between 'naukri' and 'zamin' in Ramcharan's narrative of his past. In the distant past, in his father's days, a factory job could give the kind of security which only land can provide.[109] Sriram had broken off all ties, yet in his old age it was the village that gave him comfort and security. The story is one of continuous conflict between living in the city and in the village.

Stories like this raise important questions about the formation of identities. How does one straitjacket people like Ramcharan? It would be simplistic to categorise them as either workers or peasants. In a sense they were labourers-in-between, living partially in both worlds and fully in neither. Just as the lines between city and village blurred, so did boundaries between the employed and unemployed, between substitutes and regulars, between factory jobs and other work. Divisions between castes seemed diluted: workers from upper castes not only joined factory work, many worked at 'unclean' jobs involving leather.

How did these movements across spaces, across categories, influence the ways in which workers grappled with life in the city? What were the kinds of family strategies and experiences of mohalla life in the city?

[106] I left a permanent job. There were quarrels over land. I went back to the village, giving in my resignation.

[107] This is why I resigned. If there is land it will feed the children through their lifetime.

[108] I lost my land to a Chamar. In that area Chamars harvest over Rs 50,000 worth of crops.

[109] See ch. 3.

CHAPTER 3

Family Strategies and Everyday Life

—+⸻⸻+—

As peasants moved to the city to work, or in search of work, their family lives were reordered: the meaning of family and household, the boundaries of inside and outside, were stretched and altered. Ties with the village and social lives in the city were sustained and reproduced through specific family strategies. These strategies reveal the various processes of social confrontation and adjustment in the everyday lives of workers.

Families: Structures and Strategies

If the old argument about the decline of the family and community with the rise of the factory system has been disproved, an overemphasis on the tenaciousness of such ties can be equally misleading. Appropriation of tradition in the urban context meant significant changes. Family and rural links continued, but in different forms.[1]

Official investigations into working class families were informed by a framework that accepts the transition from a joint to a

---

[1] For a discussion on family and industrialisation, see Michael Anderson, *Family Structure in Nineteenth Century Lancashire* (Cambridge 1971); Anderson, 'Household Structure and the Industrial Revolution: Mid Nineteenth Century Preston in Comparative Perspective', in Peter Laslett, ed., *Household and Family in Past Time* (Cambridge 1972); Martine Segalen, 'The Industrial Revolution: From Proletariat to Bourgeoisie', in Andre Burguiere and Christiane Klapisch-Zuber, eds, *A History of the Family, Vol. II: The Impact of Modernity*; Louise A. Tilly, 'Individual Lives and Family Strategies in French Proletariat', *Journal of Family History*, 4:1979.

nuclear family as a universally valid phenomenon. The joint family represents the past, the nuclear family the present—towards which the history of the family naturally moves. Nuclear and 'natural' families were considered synonymous in official categorisation.[2] Official investigators attempting to evolve a neat categorisation had to confront informants who were unable to comprehend their categories. The Royal Commission surveyors were perplexed by 'the tendency of the average labourer to include all relations as members of his family'.[3] The commission preferred to include only co-resident kin as part of the family, excluding family members who lived in the village, despite the evidence of remittances to the villages, the inflow of food 'supplements' into the city, and the seasonal visits of workers to their village homes.[4] A family defined in these terms thus excludes members closely tied through emotional and material interests but residentially separated.[5] There is a likelihood of under-representation of joint families in official representations that implicitly accept such a definition.

Despite this problem the RCL figures show a preponderance of joint families among workers in Kanpur. The proportional distribution (based on a sample of 729 families) in 1929–30 shows 44 per cent 'natural' and 56 per cent joint families.[6] A natural family, according to the commission, consisted of a father, mother and their unmarried children; a joint family included other relations as well.

This seems to have been the pattern in the 1950s too. The conjugal family unit was not a dominant feature in the 1950s. Of the103 family groups surveyed by Niehoff, 58 per cent were joint.

[2] *RCL XI (i)*, pp. 70–1.

[3] Ibid., p. 70.

[4] Food items received from the village were accounted for in the worker budgets computed by the Royal Commission. Ibid., p. 73.

[5] Goody includes members linked by material and emotional ties within his definition of family, distinguishing it from the household or a kin group sharing a common residential space. Jack Goody, 'The Evolution of the Family', in Peter Laslett, ed., *Household and Family in Past Time*. The Royal Commission uses the two terms, family and household, interchangeably: it refers to 'natural' families and joint households. *RCL XI (i)*, p. 71.

[6] *RCL XI (i)*, p. 71.

Out of this, in 13 per cent of cases there was an upward extension of the family. The parents of the male member of the unit formed a part of the household. In 45 per cent of the households studied by Niehoff there was a lateral and a downward extension. Lateral extension accounted for 33 per cent of joint households. These included families of siblings and more distant relatives.[7] The proportional distribution of joint and nuclear families thus shows a relative stability over time. There is no unilinear shift from extended to nucleated households. The 'joint' remained as much 'natural' as the nuclear.

The Royal Commission evidence shows a variation in the relative distribution of joint and nuclear families according to income groups. In the higher-income groups, those earning Rs 40–50 per month, 71 per cent of the families were joint, while in the lower-income groups, those earning Rs 30 and below, the percentage fell to 50 per cent. Higher-income groups, according to the Royal Commission, could afford to maintain larger households. Workers in the lower-income groups, the commission reported, 'keep a larger number of family members away at home'.

Economic conditions thus had an obvious bearing on household strategies, poorer working class families finding it prudent to keep most family members in the village. But this was not the general pattern. Income categories in family surveys done by the Royal Commission were based on the earnings of male heads of households; they did not take into account the earnings of other family members. Family strategies were not always determined by the income levels of males. For many families, the earnings of women were crucial to survival strategies in the city. In the case of impoverished landless rural families who migrated to the city, women's earnings made it possible for the family to survive. Kassia and her husband (Koris) both worked as reelers in textile mills. Her household consisted of her mother-in-law, father-in-law, her eight-year-old brother, and herself. Reelers were within the lower-income category, but the joint earning of two members enabled them to support the family. When her brother was eleven or twelve, she expected him to work in the mill. Although women

[7] Niehoff, *Factory Workers*, p. 77. In Molund's study of Koris the proportion of extended households is smaller at 37 per cent. However, Koris were an artisanal caste with longer links with the city. Molund, *First We are People*, p. 179.

employed in factories constituted a minuscule proportion, other forms of their waged work influenced family survival strategies. The functions performed by womenfolk in the villages were significant here. Wives of worker migrants worked in the fields and looked after older members and infants in the household. These roles sustained the rural links of worker migrants. Sometimes women reluctantly stayed on in the village to labour in the fields: to them life in the city seemed more attractive and pleasurable.

The composition of joint households in the city varied. Multiple family households (two or more conjugal units residing together) were difficult in the one-room huts in which many workers of the low-income groups lived. But there were instances in which two conjugal units, married father and married son, lived in the same room. Sometimes a dhoti would be hung across the room to provide a shred of privacy to the two units.[8]

Matrilineal kin sometimes co-resided and formed part of one domestic group. Male migrants would stay with their female cognates while they were single or till they made alternative arrangements. Shriram, a worker in a cotton mill, stayed for several years with his sister's conjugal family in Kanpur. Later he moved in with his father's sister. Distant kin or sometimes kin of kin from the same or another village moved into a household and became permanently a part of it. Away from the village the notion of 'gaon bhai' was important in forming relationships. Migrant workers stayed for long periods with gaon bhais or neighbours and friends from the village, usually belonging to the same sub-caste.[9] After moving out from his aunt's house Shriram lived with a friend of his brother-in-law. In this household, as in those of his previous hosts, he was treated as a family member, free to stay as long as he pleased.

Thus, joint households in the city involved both a creation of new ties and a reaffirmation of relationships which existed in the village. An important feature was also the fluidity and openness in the composition of these households. Kin and other migrant connections from the village formed an accepted part of these households. Segmentation was accompanied by integration, a

[8] *BSER: Wages and Labour Conditions*, p. 90.

[9] This was unlike the male co-residential households discussed later, where workers residing together were not necessarily from the same commensal group.

broadening out of the notion of family to include all village residents—as distinct from those of other villages.

Which households do we classify under the category 'nuclear'? Can worker households with family members in the village be categorised as nuclear? Many such households still saw themselves as part of the larger family in the village. It is a problem to see them as natural nuclear units. Migration to the city involved a spatial separation from the parent household in the village but was not always perceived by family members as a break-up of the larger family. Migration in such cases was a survival strategy, a separation necessitated by contingency; but a strategy that could be reversed when circumstances altered. A conjugal unit in the city could rejoin the larger family. Many households, as we saw, had close economic ties with their families in the village. Remittances were regularly sent from the city to the village.[10] There was a reverse flow too: grain, ghee and other items of consumption were brought in from the village home. This reverse flow is taken into account in the family budgets computed by the Royal Commission. A large proportion of workers employed in the Kanpur mills continued to return to their villages during harvest time, the income from harvesting providing a supplement to their meagre earnings. These seasonal visits reconfirmed a sense of belonging and responsibility to the family; they sustained the unity of the family despite the division of households. Workers saw it as their duty to share the burden of work in a busy season, even if it meant a spell of unemployment when they returned to the city.

Ties with the family in the village were not affirmed through economic linkages alone. Some saw themselves as part of their parent household despite the absence of any direct economic bonds. Bhola, a weaver in the Cawnpore Woollen Mills, took a train to his village in Bithoor every Saturday and returned on Sunday evenings. Bithoor, of course, is close enough to Kanpur for weekend sojourns. Unlike Doorga, the gunny weaver referred to earlier, Bhola does not assert that he is a resident of the city. Migration, clearly, was seen as a survival strategy: 'He is the younger son, and there not being sufficient work for him at home he came here for work,' recorded the Factory Commission of 1890. Most others who still had a village home preferred to

[10] See ch. 2.

perform birth, death and marriage rituals among their rural kinfolk. Out of 140 marriages recorded by Niehoff in the 1950s, 107 were performed in the village.[11] Those who had land and a home in the village often went back there in old age. Most workers relied on traditional medicine and preferred to go to their villages during convalescence. This, together with the forcible segregation of workers, contributed towards the mass exodus of workers from Kanpur during the plague epidemic in 1900.[12]

It seems clear that not all conjugal units in the city constituted nuclear households. Both interest and emotion made for close ties between the conjugal unit in the city and the household in the village. Members of the urban unit participated in important production tasks like sowing, hoeing and harvesting. Remittances to the village contributed towards the household budget, while food articles from the village supplemented the urban budget.

It is difficult to statistically separate out real conjugal family units from conjugal households that were extensions of the farm family in the village. There is indirect evidence of conjugal family units that were independent from their family of origin (natal family). Workers from artisanal castes like Chamars, Koris and Julahas had been in the city for a longer period.[13] Their links with the village were often more tenuous than those of other workers. My evidence suggests that workers in leather factories had weaker links with the village. Leather workers were drawn mostly from the Chamar caste (traditionally engaged in leather work). Their expenditure on remittances to dependants was smaller than other workers.[14] The closer ties of artisanal castes—Julahas, Koris, Chamars—with the city is evident from the fact that around 37 per cent of marriages among them took place in the city as against 7 per cent among the higher-caste workers.[15]

[11] Niehoff, *Factory Workers*, p. 81.

[12] See ch. 7.

[13] Niehoff, *Factory Workers*, p. 33.

[14] '. . . leather workers are mostly Chamars and they said that their income in the village was very low and therefore they found it cheaper to bring their family members with them instead of keeping them in the village for agriculture.' *RCL XI (i)*, p. 74.

[15] Niehoff, *Factory Workers*, p. 81. Niehoff tries to substantiate this argument by pointing to an instance when a worker from a Kureel caste married a village woman but the ceremony was performed in Kanpur city.

Longer urban residence and weak rural ties, it seems, had some effect on family strategy. Given the lack of dwelling space and resources, nucleation was part of a survival strategy for many families. Niehoff points out that amongst workers from lower castes, for instance Chamars, the conjugal family was more common. Many of them came from families in which the process of nucleation had already started in the village.[16]

But income levels or caste did not produce any single strategy. Relatively better-off working class families could also form nuclear households. Doorga, the gunny weaver of the Kanpur Jute Mills, had his natal family and property in the village—the land in the village (not named) was cultivated by his father and brother. Doorga, who was from the Ahir caste, lived with his wife and daughter in Kanpur. He considered himself a 'resident' of Kanpur city. 'He has no other home' was the statement recorded by an official inquiry.[17] Doorga was probably better off than many other workers. The fact that the house in which he lived was his own is testimony of this.

A new form of household in urban Kanpur was the male co-residential unit. Unmarried men or those who left their families in the village would often share a common dwelling unit in the city. In some units the co-sharers were linked through ties of kin and caste. But this was not characteristic of all such households. In most cases ties of the village—the notion of gaon bhai—provided a basis for the formation of a mixed male household. Workers drawn from the same or neighbouring village would live together. Single male migrants from the Benares region (Banarsis) for instance, commonly shared a room. A shared dwelling place allowed a pooling of financial and energy resources. Rules of purity and pollution were important in the constitution of these households. Workers from the Chamar or other castes low down in the ritual hierarchy never formed a part of the mixed households.[18] The ties

[16] Bernard Cohn, 'Chamar Family in a North Indian Village', *An Anthropologist Amongst the Historians and Other Essays* (Delhi 1987).

[17] *IFC*, p. 75.

[18] Mixed households were rare among lower castes. This, according to Niehoff, was related to the fact that single migrants were not as common among them. A larger proportion among them was settled in the city with their families. Niehoff, *Factory Workers*, p. 78.

between gaon bhais allowed a sharing of space but did not necessarily create commensal bonds between workers from different
castes. A common hearth was rare. Those from a higher ritual
status, Brahmans, for instance, did not eat food cooked by men
from other castes. Usually, each member would cook for himself.
In contingencies, when a worker was ill, for instance, norms
might be broken. In some units, a Brahman member would serve
as a cook.[19]

The male co-residential household, however, did not represent
an absolute continuation or reaffirmation of ties that had existed
in the worker's natal village. Village brotherhood or unity between
gaon bhais acquired meaning only in alien surroundings, outside
the village. Everyday acts of sharing created new ties outside kin
and family networks. Young male immigrants, in particular, enjoyed the relationship of camaraderie with other mates. The to-
getherness was cherished later—a joke or a story would rekindle
old memories.

Identities, Images, Experiences

In what ways did everyday life define identities and shape the self-
perceptions of workers? In Dipesh Chakrabarty's portrayal of
jute mill labour, primordial loyalties and categories imposed by
those in authority structure the way in which identities are shaped. Their perceptions are defined by ties of religion and region—
they are Muslims, Hindus, Bengalis, Oriyas. Elsewhere he argues
that the worker is a child vis-à-vis the ma-baap—the managers, or
as an ordinary coolie vis-à-vis the trade union babu. There are
moments of transgression when the worker tries to overcome the
boundaries of such a relationship, but these are sporadic and
ephemeral and have no lasting impact on structured relationships
and pre-given categories. The coolie sees himself as a coolie. The
question of identity, in such an analysis, seems to me somewhat
unproblematic because certain given structures of ideas remain
constant and unaffected by everyday events, by location and cultural context, by changing relations between the self and world.

[19] For instance, Niehoff pointed to a household consisting of workers
from the Lohar (ironsmith) caste where the Brahman did the cooking.
Niehoff, *Factory Workers*, p. 78.

Identities were, rather, formed through contestation—a worker could have different identities, real and imagined, in conflict with each other, and it was through such conflicts that a dominant identity could emerge. The self-perception of workers is important to an understanding of identity formation. While he was a coolie in the eyes of the babu, he could see himself as a mastaan, a dada. At home he was a patriarch, exercising power over women and others in the family. The unemployed vagrant harassed constantly by the police, implicated in crimes not necessarily committed by him, tried in his own way to maintain a sense of dignity and respect. Going out to look for work was important to maintain dignity with children and the family. Many vagrants in the city, or mere badlis, maintained self-respect in their village homes by claiming to be employed in a factory. Coolies at the workplace also had the pride of a pakki naukari with their kinsfolk, which a badli or an unemployed worker did not. Also, while managers often saw them as 'ignorant' and 'peasant-like' in their attitude to the machine, workers with skill and experience had a sense of work pride. Workers from the Julaha caste, many of whom had been weavers for generations, had a pride in their skills, which distinguished them from other workers. This difference was important to their self-perception and the way they acted in everyday life. Besides, identities are continuously constituted and reconstituted. Categories of community, with which workers identified, were not pre-given, primordial categories defining the mental outlook of the workers, but were re-created and given new meanings in the context in which they lived and worked. Identities of religion and community were not pre-bourgeois carryovers but were constructed in the context of urban industrialisation.[20]

To immigrants, the city meant trauma, hardship, a yearning to go back to their familial roots. Statements expressing a longing for home, a nagging anxiety about when they could go home find resonances in many lives. This would appear to reconfirm the stereotype of the peasant rooted to the village, the conventional notions of the 'reluctant peasant-worker' being 'pushed' to the city. Romanticised representations of rural life tend to gloss over hardships in their past. Besides, a nostalgia for the village coexisted with an attraction towards the city. For many, these contradictory

[20] For an elaboration of this argument, see ch. 7.

pressures expressed themselves through movements back and forth between the village and the city. The city was thus a transitional moment in their lives. Times of crisis in the city were periods when they sought refuge in the village. Others had to seek resolutions within the world of the city.

Everyday life for workers was thus characterised by conflicts between their city of dreams and the 'real' world, between the distant and the immediate world. These experiences mediated their perception of themselves and the realm outside. For young migrants like Shriram the first experience of the city was not an easy one. He moved to Kanpur because of bitter conflicts with relatives over a property dispute. In Kanpur Shriram was unemployed for a year and a half. Relatives in the city did not readily help. They felt it was his moral duty to go back and look after his ancestral land. He was eventually taken in as a doffer boy in the Woollen Mills on a half-time (*adh pahra*) basis. Shriram enjoyed the *yaraana dosti* (camaraderie) with other workers in the factory, but after two years of work in Kanpur he yearned for a different experience. Images of new cities, new places, appeared more beautiful. Stories were brought in by labour recruiters and others from distant places and these fed the fantasies of workers. Experience for migrants like Shriram alternated constantly between his lived and imagined world. When Shriram and his friends heard of the arrival of a recruiter from Delhi they went to him willingly. They needed little persuasion. They were excited about travelling to Delhi—and that too at the expense of the recruiter.

But new and distant cities could be disillusioning. After a few months in a textile factory in Delhi Shriram and his companions were disappointed ('*Ab hamara dil yahan Dilli se bhi uchta*'). They moved to Hathras. Here Shriram was employed as a machine man in the spinning department. Work in new cities allowed him quicker vertical mobility—he was pleased to be promoted from a doffer to a machine man. Yet Shriram and his companions felt cheated and underpaid in Hathras, so they travel further—to Amritsar. But Amritsar proved equally frustrating.

The imagined world now becomes evil. Fraud, cunning, deceit is what they find here. Recruiters appear as fraudulent people who 'enticed' them with false promises. What is the point in travelling to new places, Shriram now asks himself.

If the outside was disillusioning, there was the home—the real world to come back to (*Ab punah apne shahar Kanpur laut aaye*). The home world now acquires a new meaning and there is a new fondness and sense of identity with it. From being a helpless immigrant in strange, unfriendly cities, Shriram feels a new sense of power on returning to Kanpur. 'Here there was no question of being cheated,' Shriram declares with supreme confidence. It was as if nobody could dare them in their own city. Home was the space over which one had control.

Yet Shriram longs to travel more. He and his friends set off on their small savings, to look for work in distant Bombay.[21] The journey ends again with a return to Kanpur.[22] There is a constant mobility between the inhabited space and another space, an imaginary world towards which people move only to refigure their imagination, return to the place of origin, and move again. Distant cities—Delhi, Bombay—play on their imagination. The immediate appears mundane, the distant fascinating. The perception of one defines the meaning of the other, and in the process perceptions and experiences themselves are transformed. After the experience of Delhi and Hathras, Kanpur appears more appealing. The mundane itself becomes romanticised: Kanpur becomes good and clean; there is no treachery or fraud here.

Workers trained in skilled jobs had greater possibilities and more leverage in finding better-paid jobs in new cities. Reports for the turn of the twentieth century refer frequently to skilled workers moving out from Kanpur to other centres.[23] Even in later years workers like Devi Datt, trained as a fancy jobber,[24] worked in many cities, leaving and moving elsewhere when he got into a fight. Looking back on his past he admits that he was careless and shirked work and thus got drawn into conflicts at work. But Devi Datt also gives a political meaning to his travels. His first stint in

[21] In my interview with him the chronology of events is a little different. He travels to Bombay first and then to other cities in the north.

[22] The desire to come back and work in a place near home was common. Zawar Husain left work in Bombay and came to Kanpur because it was 'nearer home'. Ev. Zawar Husain, KLIC Progs., UP Ind. Progs., File 1145, 1937, Bundle 110 (UPSA).

[23] See ch. 2.

[24] A fancy jobber supervised patterned weaving on looms with a jacquard attachment.

Gujarat and the Central India region, he points out, was related to the jungle satyagraha going on. He then joined work in Nagpur and moved on to Bombay, Indore and Ujjain before coming to Kanpur.[25]

This mobile world of travel and freedom was not open to all. Young, male, single, migrants not burdened with family responsibilities could explore new places. The kind of mobility and freedom that the city gave to single men was obviously not accessible to women cloistered in hatas. Yet the experiences of women cannot be homogenised: there were differences in the way in which women negotiated life in the city. For most women, even for those dependent on male earnings, living in the city often helped to ease the pressures of patriarchal structures. Many women preferred the seclusion of the hata to being in the village. In the city they felt they could do what they pleased: they did not have to obey the dictates of an oppressive, patriarchal father-in-law.[26]

Those not moving outside often carved out their own female spaces within the precincts of the hata. In the daytime, when the men were at work, the hata courtyard was a space of female communion, where jokes were shared, sometimes with strongly sexual undercurrents. In hatas inhabited by working class families from a lower-caste background, where women not working in the mills or outside were involved in a range of domestic industries, work and social communion went alongside. Women rolled bidis and chatted to female companions. Women integrated into hata life in the city were reluctant to go back and work in the fields. Not only did they find rural work more arduous than what they did in the city, going back to the patriarchal household in the village denied them many of the pleasures and freedoms of the city.

Work away from home allowed women to know about spaces that other women did not.[27] It gave them a sense of identity and self-pride. Women who worked in factories earlier found it hard to reconcile themselves to the loss. Stories from more recent times

---

[25] Interview, Devi Datt Agnihotri.

[26] See Joshi, 'Making Spaces'.

[27] These differences seemed more apparent while talking to women in recent times. Krishna, a widowed worker in a parachute factory, for instance, talked about travelling to distant places in the city and of bazaars far away with a sense of confidence and self-assurance. See Joshi, 'Making Spaces'.

tell us something about the anguish and pain women experience when they are suddenly turned out. Munni Devi, who lost her job many years ago, continues to talk nostalgically of her past. She repeatedly came back to the refrain: '*Kya karen baithe hain, koyi kam nahin mil raha hai. Ham log kahin bhi jaten hain . . . kahan jayen?*'[28] Like many other women she used to empty out bobbins from reeling machines. She contrasts her work in the factory, standing all day at the machines, with the present: 'sitting' all day: '*Reeling chalate the khare khare, ab ham logon ko baithal diya.*' The play on *khara hona* and *baithna* in her account expresses her transition from work to non-work. Work gave her everyday existence a sense of meaningfulness that worklessness denied her.

Yet life and work in the city, for women, had its own problems. Widowed women, living on their own and without the usual familial restrictions, faced the constraints of patriarchal ideology in other ways. A large proportion of women employed in the mills were widows.[29] Yet in their everyday life in the mohalla or the factory they had to tread on precarious ground. Patriarchal society, anxious to preserve its own norms, often termed such women as 'loose' and 'licentious'. Women living in these circumstances were in constant fear of being violated, physically and verbally. Women workers moving out of the mohalla had to face taunts by leering men. Many women admitted they would rather not step outside to work if they were not forced to.[30] There was always a nervous fear of molestation and abuse, by those in power at their place of work or by others outside. In the mill settlements, widows were constantly under watch. Any perceived transgression of moral codes invited censure. In the Allenganj settlement in the 1950s, widows had to stay in a separate corner created for them so that they could be under watch. But the 'widow lines' were soon maligned and labelled as immoral. Managers saw these as areas where men solicited women. So the widows were moved

[28] What can we do, we sit idle. There is no work for us. Where can we go? Interview with Munni Devi who worked in Swadeshi Cotton Mills for over twenty-five years, from 1964 till 1990.

[29] In the late 1930s, for instance, 39 per cent of the women workers in Kanpur factories were widows. 'Report on the Earnings of Women Mill-Workers in Cawnpore', *Labour Bulletin*, 1:4.

[30] Interview, Shyama, Mathiya Vala Hata, Kanpur.

close to other family settlements, in the belief that proximity to families would help preserve their moral character. It was only with time and age that an older generation of women could laugh at past experiences and make jibes at the men in their hata or other widow companions. Life in the same hata for years helped nurture a friendly, teasing relationship. Shanti, a widow living with her brother, was the object of such affectionate taunts. 'He is her lover,' they quipped, 'she cannot live without him.'[31] Shanti took up waged work while her husband was alive because his earnings went into gambling.

Underlying the attempts to regulate the lives of widows were certain stereotypes about widows and lower-class women in general. In official eyes the morals and social practices of women who worked in the mills were different from those of other classes. Women who worked in the mills, they argue, could easily remarry if they were widowed. After the Cawnpore Cotton Mills riot the state abdicated responsibility to provide for widows of injured workers, arguing: 'In the case of widows, I have already mentioned to you there is little reason to doubt that they will all marry again as they belong to castes in which this is permitted and in any case they are accustomed to earn their living by daily labour.'[32] To colonial officials the absence of a stigma against remarriage symbolised an alternative morality characteristic of working class bastis.

In official and managerial representations, widows were considered promiscuous and immoral and working class bastis were characterised by 'unseemly squabbles about women and litigation . . .'[33] The imbalance in the sex ratio in the city added to their fears. In Kanpur, as in many other industrial cities, men were more numerous. In 1921 the sex ratio in the city was ten men for every six women. Out of the total number of 106,810 immigrants in Kanpur city in 1921, 35 per cent were female.[34] A more detailed survey suggests that in Gwaltoli, a predominantly working class

[31] Interviews, Krishna and Shanti in Mathiya Vala Hata, Kanpur.

[32] Clay to A.W. Lilley, Jt. Manager, BIC, File 94/1924, Dep. xviii (Jud Cr.) (ERR, Kanpur). The DM suggests that all that was needed was a lump sum of Rs 200 to Rs 250 to give them a fresh start.

[33] Ev. UP Govt, *RCL III (i)*, p. 156.

[34] *Census UP,* 1921, p. 191.

area, the ratio was around 67 females to every 100 males.[35] In the 1950s, roughly a third of the workers had their wives and children living in the village.[36]

Official concern over the skewed sex ratio is in many ways similar to their worries over venereal disease in the bastis. Official witnesses acknowledged the problems of verifying the sociological background of patients from hospital records since there was no data on the spatial distribution of the disease; yet they confidently asserted that 'venereal diseases are very prevalent in the bastis'.[37] The assertion was premised on a series of official prejudices. The practice of cohabitation of two families in a single room and the accretion of distant adult kin, it was assumed, must lead to sexual immorality, promiscuity, and venereal disease.[38] Nucleated households were normal and moral; they alone could be the basis of a 'natural', healthy sex life. One of the reasons for the large number of leprosy cases in Kanpur, some accounts argue, was the prevalence of venereal disease in the city.[39] Venereal disease, in these accounts, is symptomatic of promiscuity and sexual immorality in the bastis. It was a part of the basti landscape in the same way as dirt, stinking drains and filth. Everything about such surroundings was ugly: 'Fighting involving the use of physical force and other crime are a characteristic feature of basti life.'[40] Life itself was ugly.

In the mill settlements the lives of workers were more closely regulated. The Allenganj settlement, for instance, was a walled settlement, with Company guards inspecting all incoming strangers. Despite these restrictions some workers managed to smuggle in women in purdah rickshaws and ekkas. There were also instances of single migrants having relationships with widowed women workers living in the settlement.[41]

---

[35] *BSER: Wages and Labour Conditions*, p. 101. Disaggregated figures for all areas with a large industrial population are not available.

[36] Niehoff, *Factory Workers*, p. 46.

[37] Ev. Dir. Public Health, UP Govt, *RCL III (i)*, p. 156.

[38] Ibid.

[39] A report in a local paper argued that sexual promiscuity and congestion in Kanpur accounted for the large number of cases of venereal disease and consequently leprosy in the city. *Citizen*, 4.12.41.

[40] Ev. UP Govt, *RCL III (i)*, p. 156.

[41] Niehoff, *Factory Workers*, 88.

Official discourse on the moral conduct of workers presents an interesting contrast to their notions of morality and health in the cantonments. A power that celebrated masculinity was keen on preserving the virility of its soldiers; and for this it was necessary to arrange the services of healthy prostitutes.[42] Similarly, drink was an essential component of the male culture of barracks and supplies of liquor to soldiers were arranged for. What was a sign of immorality among one class was considered essential for the moral upkeep of another.

Recollections of the past in accounts of male migrants often erase the fears and hardship which travel entailed. New immigrants to the city experienced insecurity and uncertainty in a variety of ways, and this crucially shaped their images of themselves and the world in which they lived. Many workers had to wait years before they found regular work in the factory. Some worked as coolies; others tried to survive through vending and petty trading, making a small margin sometimes, often none at all after paying off their advance. They lived in perpetual uncertainty, presenting themselves at the Coolie Bazaar every morning, coming back with nothing on some days, sweating out the loading and unloading of goods in the bazaars and factories other days. Added to the economic insecurity and hardship, male workers often lived in fear of a loss of patriarchal authority within the household. A head of the household bringing in no money did not enjoy the usual respect at home. To many, going out for a 'fictive' job which gave virtually no income, seemed preferable to facing humiliation at home.

In periods of heavy migration into the city, like the Depression years (1929–31), conditions for immigrants were worse. This was clearly not a period when the large immigrant population could hope to find regular jobs. Hundreds were out on the streets, sleeping the nights on canal banks or on any other available space. Life for them was precarious. In the eyes of officialdom such people 'with no fixed abode' were always suspect. Moreover, this was a period when the crime rate in the city was rising.[43] And it was these homeless vagrants with an anonymous status to whom the rising crime rate is attributed in many official reports.

[42] See ch. 1.
[43] Over 1929–30, the figures for cases run under Sec. 109 Criminal Procedure Code in Kanpur were the highest for any city in UP. See ch. 7

The world of these unemployed migrants and casual labourers was in certain ways closely connected with that of factory workers. Not all factory workers were regularly employed. Workers in seasonal industries like cotton ginning, sugar, and oil were periodically unemployed. Others had long spells of no work, and uncertainty between their occasional stints as badlis. However the difference between factory workers, and casuals and others, cannot be ignored. Badlis, and others only temporarily employed in factories, considered themselves as distinct from ordinary coolies and casual workers in the city. Similarly, regular workers perceived their status as quite different from badlis. And the coolies and homeless vagrants who constituted in official descriptions the 'floating population' of 'lawless folk', cannot be lumped with goondas and badmashes.[44] They often had their own codes of dignity and censure and would try to maintain a moral distance from goonda activities. Nor were those labelled as goondas a homogeneous lot. Their experiences and identities varied. They made their own separations and differences between the good and the bad. Those whom the state called goondas were often dadas in particular localities. And the term dada did not have the pejorative connotation of goonda. It is with a great sense of achievement that Shriram tells us: 'Ab mere sar par Colonelganj vale Shriram dada ka taj baith gaya' (Now I was crowned as Dada of Colonelganj).[45]

By becoming part of a dada–chela network a young worker to the city could hope to transcend the helplessness and insecurity he experienced as a new immigrant. He could invert the world in which mistris and older workers bullied the young. A dada commanded both respect and fear in the neighbourhood. He wore fashionable clothes and moved around with a band of followers. Dadagiri involved a display of physical prowess, of masculinity. Recognition as a dada gave a sense of power and confidence. It is with the supreme confidence of a dada that Shriram asserts: nobody could dare cheat workers in Kanpur. This contrasts with his position as a worker in other cities like Delhi and Amritsar where he was a new and vulnerable immigrant. Looking back on his past

---

[44] See also ch. 7.

[45] Shriram, *Ek Sarvahara ka Jivan Vritanta,* p. 12.

after he had already been 'crowned' as a dada, Shriram extends his personal experience in Kanpur to workers in that city as a whole.

The world of the dada had its own structures of hierarchy, its power relations and codes of conduct. Entry into a dada following was through personal association. The akhara, for instance, was one such place where workers and others could come in touch with dadas. Shriram would start the day with a trip to the akhara, and after the day's work at the factory come back to it in the evening. His friends at the akhara were a group of dadas whose favourite pastimes were *mar-pit* (beating up) and drinking. Close association, encouragement and acclaim by veteran dadas could initiate new entrants into dadagiri. Shriram began by helping out his dada associates at the akhara in their exploits; their approval made him bolder and he soon became a dada in his own right, with a following of fifty to a hundred chelas.

The authority of the dada was a visible one: few in a neighbourhood could afford to ignore it. Dadas had a style and appearance that marked them off. They were particular about their dress, their hair was well oiled, their swagger and their whole bearing smacked of self-confidence. It was an assertion of their power as well as their difference from others. The maintenance of this visual façade was expensive. And it was often through financial demands on chelas that this image could be maintained.

A dada was recognised also by his actions. They acted as protectors of the community in their neighbourhood, avenging any threat to their honour and authority. Each neighbourhood had its own dadas. Their spheres were clearly demarcated and transgressions by outsiders were punished. They had their own notions of order and they performed policing functions in the neighbourhood to preserve an order that maintained their power and supremacy in the area.

There was often conflict and tension between norms defined by dadas and norms of the community. Dadas defied norms as well as accepted them; they resisted social codes as well as reaffirmed them. Shriram, in his dada days, fell in love with a jeweller's daughter and wanted to marry her. His relatives disapproved and scuttled his marriage plans. But Shriram remained intractable and refused to conform to their terms. He pledged to remain unmarried all his life. He expressed his non-conformity through this act of conformity: the renouncer both resists and accepts the normative world. The event, in fact, marked a deeper move towards conformity. Hereafter Shriram renounced his identity as a dada, though traces of his dada life remained etched in his identity.

Identities and self-images were, as we noted earlier, often fluid. A dada at one time, Shriram becomes a militant communist trade unionist in the 1930s. The identity of a trade union militant conflicted as well as replicated some of the attributes of a dada in a new context.[46] In contrast to a dada who was distinguished by his capacity to 'consume' and 'indulge', a communist militant of that period was recognised by his austerity and renunciation. Shriram's conception of dadas changed once he became a trade union activist. Dadas now appear goondas to him: '*Ab maine goonda line chor di*' (Now I was no longer a goonda). He renounces the drinking and extravagance of his dada days and takes a vow of celibacy.

His style changes but his function as a trade unionist is in many ways similar to his role as a mohalla leader. Earlier he would avenge predators in his domain in the mohalla, now he speaks in the same tone about predators violating communist authority in the mill: '*Hamara ek hi kaam tha—jo strike torega uski ham tang torengen.*' As a communist his goonda past is censured; but the attributes of his goonda days are important in the present. Communists needed 'muscle men' like Shriram to establish their authority in the mills.

The visible hyper-masculinity of the dada world was in subtler ways characteristic of the city culture as a whole. Male workers, specially single migrants, spent a large part of their time after work outside their homes: wandering around the bazaar, wrestling at the akhara, playing games like pachisi, or sitting outside in the gali, smoking and chatting with friends. The akhara provided more than just the facilities for wrestling and bodybuilding. Regular akhara-goers had a certain image by which they were recognised

[46] Recognition as a trade union leader was an identity many workers dreamt about. Moolchand and Raghubir both claimed that this was their fantasy from the time they joined factory work. Moolchand proudly recounted how he was a member of the first committee of the Mazdur Sabha in 1919. Even at the age of 90 Moolchand saw himself as a militant and wore a red shirt. He sat on a dharna to demand a public latrine in the Lachmipurwa area.

and this defined their own perception of themselves. They had their own addas where they gathered. Boastful talks about pugilistic exploits, one-upmanship, were an essential part of such addas. The favourite pastime of Shriram's friends at the akhara was drinking and engaging in brawls. Once he associated with them he also tried to identify with the image of an akhara pahalwan. He displayed his muscle power in a way that made him an object of envy among neighbourhood dadas and pahalwans: '*Mujh se ache mane jane wale dada log kanni katne lage . . . ache nami badmaash mere naam se hi darne lage.*' Similarly, partridge fighting, a sport popular among some workers, was more than a source of entertainment.[47] Bets were placed on the birds, which had been fed and trained to fight. Sports like wrestling and partridge fighting were both expressing as well as creating a culture of masculinity—of violence and aggression.[48]

There was an aggressive effort on the part of many male migrants to distance themselves from their village 'innocence' and internalise a new urban male morality in which tabooed practices found a new practical sanction, despite moralists and reformers.[49] But we need to be cautious in generalising about this morality, for our evidence is tainted by official and unofficial prejudices.

In official eyes single male migrants were 'wayward' and 'immoral'. Without the restraining influence of the family and with no fixed home, young men in the city sought diversion in drinks, drugs and the bazaar.[50] The bazaar in many writings is virtually

[47] Niehoff, *Factory Workers,* p. 95.

[48] When the hours of work were long, and in the winter months when daylight hours were short, the time for such recreation was very limited. Besides, single men needed time for domestic jobs like shopping and cooking. Sheo Audhar, a boy of eleven working in the Kanpur Cotton Mills, had no time to play even on Sundays. He had to help his father with shopping and household chores. *IFC,* p. 71.

[49] Newspapers like *Pratap* reflect such moralising concerns in making repeated attacks on prostitution in the city and outside.

[50] The consumption of liquor and narcotics was not peculiar to single migrants, but was common among other workers too. Country liquor and narcotics, e.g., charas, ganja, bhang, figure in the items of expenditure in working class family budgets. *RCL XI (i),* table XI, p. 92. A study in the 1960s shows that liquor consumption was more common in industrial towns like Kanpur. About 70 per cent of the workers in Kanpur were believed to be 'occasional drinkers' and 30–50 per cent 'regular drinkers' who spent on an

synonymous with evil. The main centre for prostitutes was located in the central bazaar of the city—Moolganj.[51] Men visiting
prostitutes in this area were considered not only immoral but also
a 'turbulent' and 'riotous' lot. After the riots of 1931 there was a
proposal to remove prostitutes from this area; this might help
preserve peace in the area: 'If the prostitutes were removed much
of this turbulent element would disappear from Moolganj.'[52]

Bazaars were also depicted as places where homosexuals
courted prospective partners. A poem on homosexuality and
prostitution in Kanpur talks about the increase in *londabaji*
(homosexuality) in the city. Prostitutes were woebegone; their
clientele was on the decline while londas were thriving ('*Duniya
mein londebaji ka hai jor aajkal . . . . london se aajkal hui mat
randiyan/baithi hain dhare hath pai ab hath randiyan*'). Londas
dressed in fashionable clothes roamed the bazaar and lured men
with pan and cigarettes ('*Kamseen haseen londa agar dekh pate
hain/kahten hain pan khayen cigarette pilate hain / phir mithi
mithi baton se pahlu main late hain*').[53] The poem suggests a
breakdown of the normative world in the city—homosexuality it
assumes was displacing heterosexuality—a rise in one phenomenon
was causing a decline in the other. Going to prostitutes was not
above moral censure, but to many it was the lesser evil: as opposed
to masturbation and homosexuality, it preserved male virility.

---

average around 20–25 per cent of their wages on liquor, the amount going
up to 50 per cent in the case of single men. *Report of the Study Team on
Prohibition, Vol. II*, 1964, p. 227. See also report on goondas and gambling
in Kanpur, *Vartman*, 12.11.1928.

[51] Men visiting prostitutes spent anything from Re 1 to Rs 12 for their
services. Niehoff, *Factory Workers*, p. 88.

[52] 'Removal of prostitutes from the Central Localities of Cawnpore City',
File 43,1931, Imp. Trust, Mun. Progs., Box 51 (UPSA). Residents living in
the vicinity of Moolganj continued to complain that despite measures to
remove prostitutes from the area: '*Raat ko do do baje tak gundon ke samuh
raha karte hain aur veh sharab ityadi modak vastuen pi pi kar yahan ke
nivasiyon ki raat ki nidra mein khalal pahunchate hain*' (Gangs of hoodlums
under the influence of alcohol and other intoxicants gather here till two in
the night and cause us much disturbance). *Pratap*, 11.2.1924.

[53] Maggulal Rathor, 'Mitr', *Chu Chu ka Murabba*, PP, HIN B177, pros.
pub. (IOL). The date is not specified but it was probably written around the
1920s or 1930s.

Cruel Habitations

To migrants coming in, the city always offered dreams of a better life—of things and ways that the village denied. Workers, especially young single migrants visiting home, carried tales of the good life and freedom in the city, stories that lured others to follow. But there was always another story—of penury and hardship, of homelessness and squalid miserable homes—themes which contemporary descriptions of working class life tend to dwell on.

Descriptions of working class life seem tediously repetitive and cliché ridden. Images similar to that of working class neighbourhoods in Kanpur—the dirt, the squalor, the overcrowding—could be found in descriptions of other cities, Bombay, Calcutta or even nineteenth-century Paris. The Royal Commission on Labour in 1929 describes the 'deplorable' conditions in the bastis: 'A bad odour permeates the whole place, due to dirt, stinking drains and filth and the conditions after the rains is even worse.' When it rained heavily the galis and hatas flooded and hundreds of mud houses collapsed and submerged under water.[54] More than 75 per cent of the workers lived in hatas owned by private landlords: among the well-known ones were Chote Mian ka Hata, Farhad Mian ka Hata, Mangali Prasad ka Hata. This is what a typical hata looked like:

> huts in hundreds, and sometimes in thousands . . . each enclosing a space about 10 ft by 8 ft. There are no verandahs attached to these huts and no drain in the whole compound. Latrines are nowhere to be seen and the occupants ease themselves in adjoining fields or municipal drains . . . Because of the absence of the drains in the compounds the occupants dig a pit in front of their dwellings and the water is left to accumulate there. Sometimes water overflows out of the pits and gives out bad smell. It is near these pits that the workers wash their vessels morning and evening . . . In the hata near the Swadeshi Mills there was a big pit adjoining the well. Water constantly fell into the pit because of the nearness to the well and putrefied the heap of refuse.

Mud houses in bastis like Khalasi Lines, Raipurwa, Gwaltoli, Colonelganj, Sisamau, Lachmanpurwa and Begamganj were also

---

[54] See, for instance, a report in *Pratap*, 6.9.1915.

owned by private landlords. The huts were small, poorly ventilated, 10 ft x 10 ft structures, with tiny window-like openings that could only be entered bent down. The hut roofs were too low for a person to stand upright: the usual practice was to lower the ground level by digging the earth to a depth of two feet.[55] This made the huts extremely damp. Rents ranging from Re 1 to Rs 2 absorbed on an average around 9–10 per cent of a worker's income. They often pooled in resources with others and shared rooms. There were instances where seven single men shared a hut, staying huddled inside in winter and in the rains; sleeping out on the street the rest of the year. In areas like Lachmipurwa, with a large working class component, around 31 per cent of the total population lived four–six persons to a room and 15 per cent six–eight to a room.[56] Members of official inquiries were outraged that more than one conjugal family not only shared a room but gave shelter to other adult relations, a practice that was seen as a sign of promiscuity and venereal disease in working class bastis: the fact that two conjugal units had nothing but a thin dhoti slung across a room separating them seemed almost symptomatic of promiscuity.

The death rate in areas inhabited by the labouring population was higher than in other areas and in times of epidemics these were the areas worst hit.[57] The highest rate of mortality, over 1921–8 was recorded in the Gwaltoli area, followed by Khalasi Lines and Raipurwa, all of which had a substantial population of

[55] Describing the conditions in the hatas, a Kanpur resident writes how the dwellings in which workers and other low-income groups lived were unfit even for animals. The bastis behind the Kanpur Cotton Mills overflowed with effluents from the sugar mills and in the neighbourhood a pond from old times had turned into a virtual bog. This, the author adds, was located immediately behind the municipality office. The letter ends with a rhetorical question: *'Kanpur shahar hai ya narak?'* (Is Kanpur a city or is it hell?). *Pratap*, 11.6.1917.

[56] *UP Census*, 1931, part II, Sub Table V, pp. 172–83.

[57] Freemantle observed how 'the epidemic was particularly fatal to boys and young men employed in the mills', 'Report on Supply of Labour', UP Rev. Prog. B, May 1906, no. 91.

industrial workers.[58] The precariousness of life in these areas is evident from the rate of infant mortality in areas like Raipurwa this was as high as 727 per mille in 1921.[59] The UP government, in its evidence to the Royal Commission in 1929, attributed the high rate of infant mortality in Kanpur partly 'to the necessity felt by expectant women workers to remain at work as late and return to it as early as possible'.[60]

Working class localities were crowded areas, with 71 per cent of the families living in one-room dwellings.[61] Tuberculosis was common. But there was a gendered pattern in the way the disease attacked men and women: in Hiraman Purwa, for instance, where many of the neighbouring Juggi Lal Kamlapat Mill workers lived, the rate of tuberculosis mortality among men and women was 2.9 and 8.8 per mille, respectively, in 1925.[62] Women, who usually had to survive on poorer diets and spent longer periods inside in damp, ill-lit homes, were worst hit by tuberculosis. In general the labouring poor in the city were the victims in times of an epidemic, like the plague of 1900. Diseases like malaria and cholera were recurring seasonal features.

[58] Average Morality Rate in Some Settlements in Kanpur 1921–28 (per mille)

	City as a whole	Gwaltoli	Khalasi Lines	Rai-purwa	Colonel-ganj	BIC settle-ment
Per cent of factory pop.	40	60	90	70	50	90–5
Av. mortality	46.32	75.3	66	54.4	46.4	34–58

Source: Ev. UP Govt, RCL III (i), p. 153.

[59] The proportion of working class population to the total in Raipurwa was 70 per cent. For figures on infant mortality, see BSER: Wages and Labour Conditions, p. 95.

[60] RCL III (i), p. 159.

[61] UP Census, 1931, Subsidiary Table v, Tenement Census, p. 178.

[62] In Gwaltoli the mortality rate for men and women was 3.4 and 5.5, Anwarganj 1.1 and 5.9, and Colonelganj 1.6 and 4.5 per cent respectively. BSER: Wages and Labour Conditions, p. 95.

Settlements provided by the mills, with better sanitation and water supply arrangements, were relatively less disease prone, but they catered to a small fraction of the working class population.[63] The first settlements came up during the panic about labour supply in the period following the plague riots of 1900.[64] Managers claimed that attendance improved with the provision of housing facilities.[65] Managements quite clearly saw the provision of workers' settlements as a strategy of control.[66] Workers living in the mill settlements were subjected to various kinds of regulations. In the Elgin Mills settlement, for instance, only one conjugal family unit was allowed to stay in one tenement. With the exception of widowed mothers and sisters, relatives were not allowed to join the unit. Single men were allowed to live in groups of three and four.[67] Sanitary restrictions like the prohibition on keeping cattle and goats were unpopular among many who preferred to keep their own milch animals.

Housing of the poor allowed control over their bodies; sanitisation of the environment went along with the disciplining of labour. The settlements had company guards posted at the entrance to keep a check on incoming strangers. Such policing arrangements were intensified during periods of crisis.[68] Managements always

[63] They catered to 9.4 per cent of the rural population in 1935. *BSER: Wages and Living Conditions*, p. 84. Some companies like the Cawnpore Woollen Mills, Cawnpore Cotton Mills, and Cooper Allen and Company provided accommodation for a larger proportion of its employees (57%, 66% and 38% respectively), but others provided hardly any housing facilities. Housing schemes started by public bodies like the Improvement Trust brought little benefit for workers. Large areas of trust land located near the mills that was to be sold to workers was actually bought off by private landlords to build hatas. *BSER: Wages and Labour Conditions*, pp. 88–9. On land and the workings of the land mafia in Bombay, see Prashant Kidambe, 'Housing the Poor in Colonial Bombay: The City Improvement Trust, 1898–1918', *Studies in History*, 17:1, Jan.–June 2001.

[64] See ch. 7.

[65] Ev. Cawnpore Woollen Mills, *IFLC*, p. 194.

[66] Freemantle pointed out how the settlements had 'given the management better control over the hands'. 'Report on the Supply of Labour', UP Rev. Progs. B, no. 90 (UPSA).

[67] *LIC: Labour in Cotton Mills*, p. 82.

[68] This figured among the grievances of the KMS in 1945: '6465 families live in quarters built by employers where civil liberties are so much crushed

threatened to evict striking workers. Threats are effective only when they appear real, when they are occasionally actually carried through. In 1936, for instance, the striking workers of Cooper Allen and Company were evicted from the factory settlement. The evicted strikers and their families were seen marching in procession through the city with their household goods loaded on carts.[69]

Managerial discourse drew contrasts between conditions inside the factory and outside, between the city where most workers lived and the factory where they worked. The city symbolised physical degeneration, the factory represented health and vitality. The air in the factory was 'sweet', 'wholesome' and 'pure'. What could be purer than the air in Kanpur factories, one manager suggests: 'A factory in crowded Bombay, surrounded by chawls and tenement houses, cannot possibly have as pure air in its workrooms as one on the banks of the Ganges in Cawnpore . . .'[70] The Ganges thus acquires purificatory powers even in the eyes of an English manager of a leather factory. The 'sanitary surroundings' of the factory were considered far superior to the conditions in the workers' homes.[71]

If the factory environment was pure, time spent in the factory could obviously not be injurious. The health of the worker, managers asserted, was 'much more dependent on his surroundings outside the factory, and the way he spends his time when not working'.[72] Diseases were believed to be invariably contracted in their homes, not in the sanitary surroundings of the factory. Charles Fuller, the medical officer to the Kanpur factories, admitted that eye diseases were prevalent among children employed in the mills, but he asserted that 'they did not catch it in the mills, and if mill life were prohibited for them they would be just as likely to catch and spread it in the bazaars'.[73] Although there were a large number of cases of phthisis in the city, clarifies Fuller, 'this disease

that even family members cannot visit the residents without the owner's permission. KMS Memo. AITUC Papers, File 221/1945–6.

[69] *New Age*, Dec. 1937.

[70] Ev. Allen, *IFLC*, p. 188.

[71] Ev. Woollen Mills, *IFLC*, p. 192.

[72] Ev. North West Tannery, *IFLC*, p. 201.

[73] Ibid., p. 211.

was not prevalent among mill hands'.[74] The mill settlements similarly were considered free from disease. All cases of disease in mill settlements were seen as coming from outside. The Woollen Mills management reported five deaths from plague in its settlement, but it clarified that these were 'imported cases'.[75] There was a similar opinion about the five cases of phthisis in the settlement: 'The settlement had only been recently started and in his [the medical officer's] opinion these cases came in to begin with.' Those living outside the factory and factory settlements are seen as unhealthy, and this 'outside' takes on what are seen as the generic characteristics of its inhabitants. Workers living in bastis in the city are not only physically degenerate but also morally depraved.

The links between dirt, disease and morality that marked official discourse were structured by the urban strategies over the years. In certain areas squalor was taken for granted. Conservancy services were given low priority and dirty nalas were allowed to empty out near land inhabited by lower classes. Working class habitations were seen as blots that had to be eradicated.[76]

Workers' Earnings

Conditions of everyday life and strategies of survival in the city depended a lot on levels of earnings, just as much as the meaning and significance of a specified cash amount was defined by family strategies. If experiences of work and the city were linked to workers' hopes and desires, their dreams were reworked through rude confrontations with an unfamiliar world of hunger, pain and uncertainties. The city could mean dashed hopes, homelessness and joblessness.

How much could the workers hope to earn in the city? Standard descriptions of wage trends based on averages conceal as much as they reveal. Not only do they blur differences, they tell little about what urban wages meant to workers and how they confronted their situation. Yet averages still remain important.

[74] Fuller, *IFLC*, p. 211.

[75] '. . . in some cases the patients were brought into the settlement suffering from plague; in others they were persons who neglected ordinary precautions by living partly in the city and partly in the settlement.' *IFLC*, p. 195. There was a similar opinion about phthisis in the settlement. Fuller asserted that the settlement had started only recently and the cases of disease came in to begin with. *IFLC*, p. 211.

[76] See ch. 1.

They give us a broad picture of trends and fluctuations that affected the everyday life of workers.

The nominal wages of workers seem to correspond to the oscillations in the cost of the living index (see Fig. 18). The rise in the cost of living during the war period, for instance, was followed by an increase in money wages in 1919–20. Similarly, there was an increase in money wages after the rise in prices during the Second World War period. At the time of the Depression, in contrast, the decline in the cost of the living index was accompanied by wage cuts. However, the increase in nominal wages did not automatically follow from a rise in prices. While prices had been rising since the outbreak of the war, wage increases were marginal till 1919; only after the general strike of 1919, was there a rise in the wage level. The decline in wages during the Depression years coincided with a downswing in working class activity. The increases in the post-1937–8 period again were a result of the settlement negotiated after the general strikes of that period.

Since nominal wages increased in periodic spurts following strikes, there was always a lag between the rise in wages and prices. Periods of rising prices saw real wages drop (see Fig. 19). The fall in real earnings that set in after 1912 continued until 1922. When cost of living indices steadied in the 1920s, real wages remained more or less stable. After a relative decline over 1927–9, they moved upwards during the Depression, when agricultural prices slumped, declining again with the revival in agricultural prices after 1934. The rapid inflation during the period of the Second World War neutralised the increase in nominal wages in the post 1937–8 period. Despite additional dearness allowances, real wages fell continuously over 1939–46.

Trends in average wages blur differences between different categories of workers. Wages in different mills, even for the same category of workers, were never the same. Variations in the wages of warpers, and drawers working in the weaving preparatory were wider than those for doffers.[77] Warping, or the preparation of the warp beam for the loomshed, and drawing in—which involved the drawing in of the warp threads through healds and reeds before the beam was fixed on the loom—were occupations

[77] The range of variation in the case of warpers is –42 to +77 per cent from the mean, while for doffers the range is –10 to +13 from the mean. Calculated from *UPLEC Report*, vol. I, part 1, 1946, App. D-2.

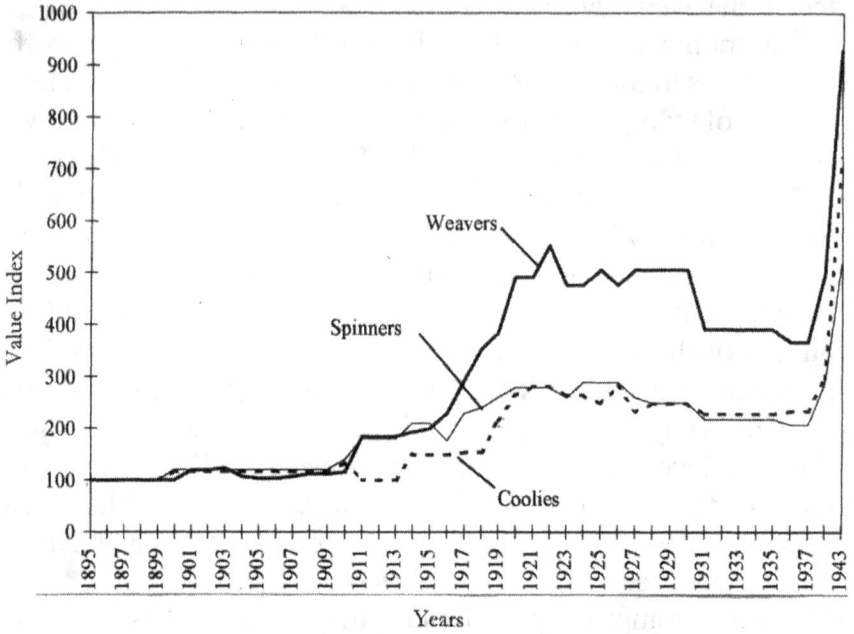

Fig. 18: Nominal Wages (Kanpur: 1895–1943)

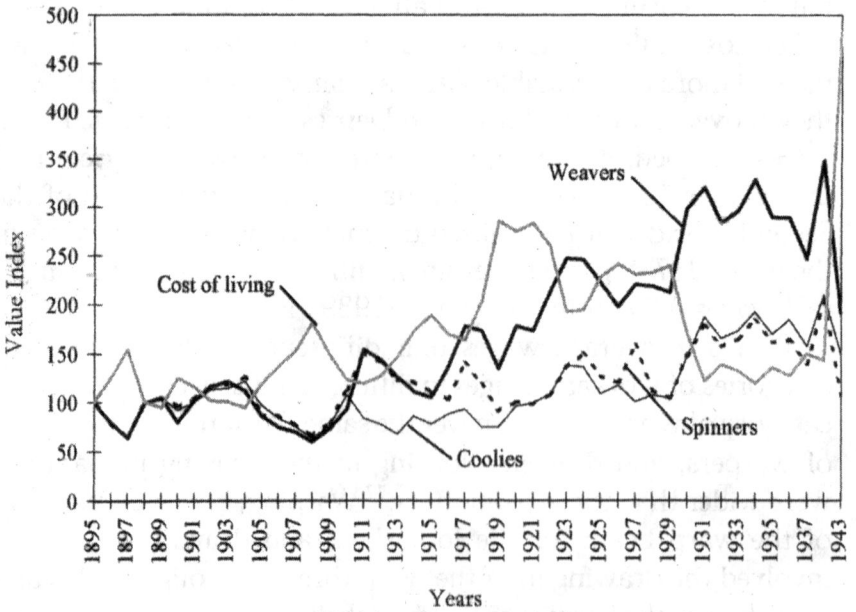

Fig. 19: Real Wages (Kanpur: 1895–1943)

requiring greater skill. Doffing, or the task of removing full bobbins and fixing empty bobbins on spinning frames, was a job on
which little boys were often employed. Wage differentials in the
case of occupations requiring lower skills were lower than for
other jobs. Around 88 per cent of coolies and 58 per cent of reelers
and 45 per cent of doffers employed in fifteen concerns in Kanpur
were concentrated in the wage category of 6–10 as. a day. The
wages of weavers in contrast, had a wider spread. While 50 per
cent earned between 10 and 20 as., 15 per cent earned less than
10 as. and 34 per cent earned over 20 as. per day. The difference
between weavers' wages was partly related to the number of
looms each weaver tended and the kind of material they produced.
Workers in the weaving and weaving preparatory (for example,
warping and drawing) departments in general had skills that were
in greater demand and new mills always tried to lure them away
with higher wages.[78] Technological changes and higher productivity in some mills also had a bearing on wage levels. The average
earnings of winders and warpers, for instance, were higher in
mills with high-speed winding and warping machines.[79]

Table 4: Wage Variations Within Different Categories
of Workers (%)

Wage category (av. daily earnings)	Weavers	Ring doffers	Reelers	Coolies
Less than 6 as.	7	—	14	—
6–10 as.	9	45	58	88
10–14 as.	32	50	15	13
14–20 as.	18	6	13	—
20–24 as.	14	—	—	—
24–32 as.	20	—	—	—

Source: Calculated from LIC: Labour in Cotton Mills, Table XLIV (a), p. 77.

There were also hierarchies in wage levels between different occupations. In the 1930s basic wages ranged between an average of

[78] See ch. 2.

[79] Wage differentials for certain occupations in mills belonging to the JK
enterprises, for instance, were accounted for by the differences in machinery
used and the quality of cotton spun and woven. Ev. Padampat Singhania,
KLIC Progs., UP Ind. Progs., File 1145, 1937, Bundle 110 (UPSA).

around Rs 15 for doffers and Rs 20–25 for piecers in the spinning department to Rs 35–40 for mule minders and weavers and Rs 40–60 for line mistris and electricians. In 1944, around 99 per cent of the double-loom weavers, 34 per cent single-loom weavers, and 27 per cent of the tenters in cotton mills earned a basic wage of over Rs 32 per month, while 50 per cent of the doffers earned a basic of less than Rs 15 per month.

Women workers were concentrated in low-paid occupations like reeling and waste picking and sometimes in the carding, mixing and stitching departments. In the Woollen Mills, women were mostly wool pickers, an occupation which was clearly the lowest paid in the mills.[80] Two women workers, Jamania and Janki, who were interviewed by the Royal Commission in 1929, stated that their earnings amounted to only Rs 2–3 per fortnight.[81] A sample survey taken in 1939 showed that 44 per cent of the women had a monthly income of Rs 9 to Rs 11 and 22 per cent earned between Rs 13 to Rs 15 per month.[82] The disparity between wages for men and women was more apparent when men doing the same job were paid higher wages. In 1944 the basic rate for women reelers varied between Rs 7 and Rs 9, while the rates for men were around Rs 12–13, some being paid as much as Rs 17.8 per month.[83] Women, more than men, were likely to

[80] Women received an average wage of Rs 10–15 as. per month in 1937. Ev. Watt and Bancroft, Woollen Mills, 25.1.1938, KLIC Progs., UP Ind. Progs., 1145, 1937, Bundle 110 (UPSA).

[81] RCL, vol. III (ii), p. 249.

[82] The survey conducted in November 1939 was based on inquiries into the wages of 120 women workers in Kanpur, of whom 32 were employed in cotton mills. 'Report on the Earnings of Women Mill-Workers In Cawnpore', Labour Bulletin, UP, 1:4, p. 247.

[83] Wages for men and women: Percentage difference.

	Year	% diff.*
a)	1896	−47 to−36
b)	1913	−41
c)	1920	−33
d)	1929	−27
e)	1943	−40

*Calculated from LIC: Labour in Cotton Mills, App. xv, p.169.

Note: (a), (b) and (c) refer to figures for the Blowing and Carding Room from the Prices and Wages Series. Since the figures in the series are for

suffer many arbitrary wage deductions. Even in factories that had a regular practice of giving individual wage cards specifying rates and other details, women never received such cards.[84] Patriarchal justification of a higher wage for the male breadwinner as the primary earner of the family was strangely anachronistic in a context when many women workers were actually the sole bread-earners. Women like Marid, winder in Elgin Mills, or Bhoodia, winder in Cawnpore Jute Mills were in the 1890s the only earners for their families. Marid had to support a sick, unemployed husband, and help out her family in the village; and Bhoodia, a single mother, had to look after a twelve-year-old son.[85]

Modes of payment for various categories of workers were different. Lower-paid workers like doffers, reelers, coolies, bale breakers, mixing men, blow-room attendants, openers and scutchers were generally paid time rates. In the spinning preparatory and the spinning main departments, time rates were common though they were not the rule, while in the weaving preparatory and weaving main departments, workers were usually paid by piece. Payment by piece was associated with higher-paid jobs and more respectable.[86] Managements also claimed that the shift enabled them to maintain production levels despite a decline in the numbers employed.[87] There were, however, certain categories of workers in the higher wage groups, workers in engineering departments for instance, who received monthly salaries or were paid by time.[88] For new recruits, substitute workers and coolies,

women workers within the department as a whole, the differential calculated does not necessarily refer to the same category of workers.

d) Refers to wages for women reelers in *RCL III (i)*, App. 1, p. 257.

e) Refers to wages for women reelers in *LIC: Labour in Cotton Mills*, 1946, App. xv, p. 169.

[84] Ev. Bancroft, Woollen Mills, KLIC Progs., UP Ind. Progs., File 1145,1937, Bundle 110 (UPSA)

[85] *IFC*, pp. 68,74.

[86] Ev. Watt, Elgin Mills, KLIC Progs., UP Ind. Progs., File 1145,1937, Bundle 110 (UPSA).

[87] In Elgin Mills, all time workers were put on piece rates after 1928, and the number of workers were reduced from 260 to 188. This, managers claimed, enabled them to maintain the production level despite the reduction in numbers. Ev. Wilkinson, *RCL III (i)*, p 180. However this was a period when managements were not so concerned about improving productivity.

[88] Boiler mistris in the engineering department of the Woollen Mills, for

wages were calculated on a daily basis, excluding Sundays and holidays.[89]

Hierarchies in wages between different categories of workers were associated with sedimented practices, differences in status, and the self-perceptions of workers. In the initial years of the textile industry, workers in the weaving departments of factories in Kanpur were drawn primarily from traditional weaving castes—Julahas and Koris—and they tried to preserve their difference with those from non-weaving castes by demanding higher wages. Certain customary wage levels came to be associated with particular occupations. A weaver would expect more than double a coolie's wage. A woman's wage was often around 40 per cent lower than a man's wage for the same job. Similarly, doffing came to be associated with low wages. Children of around ten to twelve years were commonly employed as doffers. 'Most doffers', the Muir Mills management claimed, 'were adolescents and the low pay they got was really an apprenticeship allowance.'[90] Doffing was seen as an occupation which provided young male migrants an entry to factory work—many were prepared to work for low wages. Such associations between specific jobs and particular communities, gender and age groups defined the social attitudes towards those jobs. Once jobs are thus socially stamped and hierarchies of wages established, these differences acquire a customary sanction; they appear normative and natural.

Average figures, however, tell us little about the experiences of those not employed continuously. Badlis and those employed temporarily as coolies and casual workers had no work for many days in the month. During the Depression years, when production was slack, 'short work', or employment for only a few days a

---

instance, received a fixed salary of Rs 40 a month, while enginemen, oilmen and boilermen were paid fixed-time rate. *BSER: Wages and Labour Conditions*, p. 51.

[89] During the Depression years, when managements were pursuing cost-cutting strategies, workers on time rates were put on daily rates, depriving them of any payment for Sundays and holidays. KMS Memo, KLIC Progs., UP Ind. Progs., 1145,1937, Bundle 110 (UPSA). Watt and Bancroft of the Cawnpore Woollen Mills point out that they paid daily wages to all beginners and later put them on a contract basis.

[90] Ev. Price, KLIC Progs., UP Ind. Progs., File 1145,1937, Bundle 110 (UPSA).

week, was common. The Woollen Mills were running only three–four days a week; the Kanpur Cotton Mills four days; and Muir Mills was closing an hour earlier than usual every day.[91] Even those who had regular jobs could never anticipate with any certainty the amount they would receive at the end of the month. Figures based on the monthly wages paid to Lalloo, a weaver in Elgin Mills, show the wide variations in monthly earnings for weavers. In January 1932, for instance, Lalloo received Rs 39-11-6, while in February he earned only Rs 25-11-6 on the same loom. In his oral representation to the KLIC, Lalloo claimed that he often had no work for some days in the week, being forced to sit idle for three–four days and sometimes for a week every month.[92] To some extent the fluctuations were also because of deductions from wages for breakages and faulty cloth, for 'indiscipline' or other reasons.[93] Workers complained that it was not till pay day that they became aware of various deductions.[94] Changes in the variety of material and in the types of machines used also caused variations in individual income. In the allocation of machines the mistri had an important say—he could transfer a worker from a 'good' machine to a 'bad' machine as a punishment. Thus the amount a worker actually received was being constantly negotiated. It depended on a variety of factors and eventually also on the power equation between the workers and the supervisory staff.[95]

Workers perceived wage differentials, cuts and deductions

[91] KMS Memo and Ev. of Watt and Bancroft of the Woollen Mills, KLIC Progs., UP Ind. Progs., File 1145, 1937, Bundle 110 (UPSA); Ev. of Achcha Singh and other representatives of the Harness and Saddlery Factory Labour Union, *RCL III (ii)*, pp. 242–3.

[92] Ev. Laloo, 7.12.1937, KLIC Progs., UP Ind. Progs., File 1145, 1937, Bundle 110 (UPSA).

[93] See ch. 4.

[94] Zawar Husain, a weaver in the Cawnpore Cotton Mills, complained that workers were not shown the faults with the material they produced. It was only on pay day that they learnt about a deduction for bad cloth. Ev. Zawar Husain, 9.12.1937, KLIC Progs., UP Ind. Progs., File 1145, 1937, Bundle 110 (UPSA).

[95] The introduction of new automatic machines in the Woollen Mills in the 1930s led to significant changes in the earnings of weavers The wages of those making sleeves of sweaters increased by around 20 per cent and for those making bodies of sweaters wages fell by 33 per cent. *BSER: Wages and Living Conditions*, p. 51.

within a framework of what constituted fair wages. Notions of fairness were not defined by assumptions about 'subsistence' requirements and minimum need. Wages were fair if they corresponded to certain expectations of a customary wage for skilled or unskilled workers. Underlying such expectations was a notion of relative wages: a rough comparison of the prevailing bazaar rate. In 1919 when a demand for higher wages was general the plea made by workers was: 'Outside the mills the wages of workmen have almost doubled . . . the wages earned in the mills, both by skilled and unskilled workmen do not compare very favourably with the wages in the bazaar.'[96]

Workers' estimates of wages were based on rough calculations. The prevailing method of calculating wages, the numerous rates for different qualities of material, and the unpredictability of deductions made accurate calculations difficult.[97] Bhola, a weaver in the Woollen Mills, left the calculation to the mistri: 'The mistri knows how much work on which he will be paid. He does not keep an account. But roughly speaking, he gets a certain amount for each piece turned out.'[98] Such attitudes were common. Exact calculations were difficult when workers had no access to information about rates.[99] Besides rates could be changed without notice. The rates of the new varieties of cloth introduced in the 1930s were fixed according to the production of a worker with maximum efficiency and not average efficiency as was done earlier.[100]

But workers had a sense, however fuzzy, about how much they ought to get, a point emphasised by Musahib Ali in his statement

[96] 'Statement on Behalf of Labourers', *Leader*, 14.12.1919.

[97] S.P. Saxena, a KMS appointee to the KLIC and economics lecturer from Lucknow University, pointed out: 'Very few workers could say anything about their wage rates. All they could indicate was their actual earnings.' KLIC Progs., UP Ind. Progs., File 1145, 1937, Bundle 110 (UPSA).

[98] Ev. Bhola, *IFC*, p. 72.

[99] Wage cards specifying the rates were rarely distributed: some managements gave out the cards a few hours before the payment and took them back subsequently, others did not give them at all. KMS Memo, KLIC Progs., UP Ind. Progs., File 1145,1937, Bundle 110 (UPSA).

[100] When productivity increased the rate was often changed by making the calculation on the basis of a higher basic figure of production so as to push down wages. KMS Memo, KLIC Progs., File 1145,1937, Bundle 110 (UPSA).

to the KLIC: 'The average worker was not educated but he could calculate his earnings approximately and detect shortages in his wages.'[101] There was widespread resentment in 1937 against the 'envelope system' of wage payment, according to which their fortnightly earnings were distributed in sealed envelopes.[102] Workers wanted to be given time to feel the coins, examine the amount received, rattle the coins in front of the cashier and see that they were not being cheated. The general feeling that workers were denied a straight deal led to a demand in 1937 for a right to information about wages—for the supply of wage cards showing the rates to each worker.

Many workers moved from mill to mill to mill or from city to city in search of better wages and conditions. Shriram's travels to distant places were motivated both by his wanderlust and the promise of higher wages offered by labour recruiters. Shifts between different mills in the city were common.[103] The shifts were often related to the harsh discipline or low wages in particular mills. However, not all movements were voluntary: workers were arbitrarily dismissed and forced to look for work elsewhere, and for those working as substitutes the temporary nature of the job forced a shift.

For most workers in the Kanpur mills wages earned in the factory alone do not reflect conditions of well-being: for a large number the factory wage did not represent the total family income. The earnings of family members in the village, and the supplements in kind—ghee, grain, etc.—provided by them for urban members need to be taken into account. Those employed in the

[101] Ev. Musahib Ali, KLIC Progs., UP Ind. Progs., File 1145,1937, Bundle 110 (UPSA).

[102] Watt of the Woollen Mills pointed out that they had stopped the 'envelope system' after the strike settlement of 9 August because it was not approved by workers. Ev. 25.1.1938, KLIC Progs., UP Ind. Progs., File1145, 1937 (UPSA).

[103] Bhairon Prasad's father worked in Atherton West, JK, Victoria, Hira Lal in Muir, Laxmi Ratan, Swadeshi, Elgin and Binda Savita in Swadeshi and Atherton West. Interviews Bhairon, Hiralal and Binda Sabita. Ram Charan, a weaver, began work in the Cawnpore Cotton Mills, went back to his village during the communal riots of March 1931, came back and joined Elgin Mills and was finally in Cawnpore Textiles. KLIC Progs., UP Ind. Progs., File 1145,1937, Bundle 110 (UPSA).

factories also worked for short periods in their own or other villages during harvest time. The actual proportion of rural to total income is difficult to estimate. It would depend on the size of holdings, the kind of crops cultivated, the number of family members doing wage work, and various other factors. During the Depression the cost of living fell, real incomes increased, but the decline in rural incomes had an adverse impact on many working class families. Similarly, the wartime price increase brought benefits for some worker families with rural connections. But the gains varied from family to family, depending on the proportion of produce the peasants marketed. The actual impact of rising prices on real wages depended on the extent to which the rise in the cost of living was compensated by the increased agricultural income. Many workers supplemented their wages with other kinds of earnings in the city. Raghubir supplemented his wages in a printing press by buying and selling waste paper.[104] Bhairon Prasad, like others from traditional herding communities, kept buffaloes and carried on business in milk. Like his father, he eventually gave up factory work and did full-time dairy business.

A significant proportion of family earnings for nuclear and joint working class households came from women's work in the factory and outside. This income is not always included in budget surveys. It was common for women from lower-caste backgrounds to work. Most women from lower castes, like Koris and Chamars, worked. Those who were not employed in factories worked in various kinds of cottage industries at home. However, work at home is often misrecognised. Apart from official investigators, women themselves tend to undervalue such work. Jagrani, who came to Kanpur sometime in the 1920s, started her story with: 'Hamne kuch kam nahin kiya. Jo ghar mein apna kam hai chowka bartan kapra' (I did not work. I just did my household work). It was only after a long pause that, she added, she spun yarn on the charkha at home. For her, waged work had an association with the outside; work at home was not significant. The yarn spun at home was sold to weavers.[105] Others rolled bidis at home, or some

---

[104] Interview, Raghubir.

[105] In the 1950s the earning from such work came to around Rs 3–4 a month. Niehoff, *Factory Workers*, p. 42.

went to a contractor's house and did preparatory work for manufacturing bristles out of pig's hair.[106]

Bleak averages also tell us little about how workers experienced
cash wages. Earnings and life in the city were not always what
migrants from the village imagined them to be. Young single
migrants coming to the city did not immediately find regular
work. Some had to take a chance at the coolie market in the city
where labourers from the city and others from the surrounding
countryside sought work.[107]

Yet for peasant migrants who found work after a hard wait,
cash wages had a novelty and significance that they valued.
Shriram had to wait for a year and a half, before finding work as
a doffer boy on Rs 10 a month. This was sometime in the early
1920s. But there was a sense of pride and independence he felt
about his earnings: '*Das rupya mahna niji aay ho gayi*' (Rs 10 a
month was my own earning). Besides, the factory he worked in
was famous: '*Aisee mill mein kam karta tha jo Hindustan mein
Lalimli ke nam se kaphi prasidh mill thi*' (I worked in a factory
which was famous all over the country as Lalimli).[108] The job and
wages gave him a new sense of self-esteem. Despite all the uncertainties and the long wait, a factory job, for many workers from
the old days, was an inheritance to be passed on and treasured.[109]
Ramcharan talked nostalgically of the old days, the 'British
zamana', when they were paid a bonus in silver coins. He remembered the sound of silver coins as they were distributed. The
images of royalty inscribed on the coins gave them a deeper value.
It was almost as if the workers of old days had access to the halo
of royalty through tactile contact with coins stamped with the
images of George V and Queen Victoria. Gold and silver coins
had a value that could not be measured in terms of their nominal
cash value. Stories of wage payment in silver are handed down

[106] Interviews, Sukharani, Bishnu Devi, Lachmipurwa, Kanpur.

[107] Freemantle, 'Report on Supply of Labour', UP Rev. Progs. B, May
1906, no. 90 (UPSA).

[107] Ibid.

[108] Shriram, *Ek Sarvahara ka Jivan Vritanta*, pp. 8–9.

[109] Ganga Devi, whose husband worked in Muir Mills in the 1940s and
1950s, recalled how women like her married to men with regular jobs did not
need to work. Interview.

over the generations.[110] Ram Ratan, whose father worked in Bevis and Company in British days, could not help looking back with amazement at stories he had heard of those days. He said the person distributing coins in his father's factory was blind. The glitter of silver is juxtaposed in his memory with the blindness of the coin disburser. In retrospective accounts the cash value of the coins is much smaller, but its real value to them seems incomparably more. Ramcharan measured the value of the coins in terms of their weight in silver—100 gm each. It was by putting aside those silver coins that Ramcharan could buy six and half acres of land in the village for Rs 500. He spent Rs 1200 in all, including the cost of digging a well, all paid for in silver coins.[111] For him the incremental value embedded in the silver coins was realised in the phenomenal increase in the value of land. Ramcharan is looking at past earnings in terms of the present value of his savings. Land bought for Rs 500 was now worth Rs 80,000.

For women who worked, cash earnings did not necessarily give them a sense of independence from the patriarchal household. Working women in joint households, in particular, had little control over their income and expenditure. Kassia, a reeler in the Kanpur Cotton Mills, handed over her entire income of Rs 13–14 a month to her mother-in-law. Kassia admitted that 'she did not know anything about household matters'.[112] A report on the earnings of women workers in Kanpur categorically asserts: 'No married or unmarried woman has any independent right of spending her income.'[113] The report goes on to add that five of the widows included in its survey also had no independent rights over their income. But this obviously was not the situation for all widows. There were many who lived on their own with their children, looking after the needs of the household. In the late nineteenth and early twentieth century, when child labour was

[110] There was a chorus of voices which clamoured to join in as Ramcharan narrated his story about silver coins.

[111] Interview, Ramcharan, who worked in Muir Mills since the 1940s. Ram Ratan, another worker from Kanpur Textiles, joined in: 'Are tab chalte the angrezon ke zamane mein: chandi ke sikke chalte the.'

[112] Ev. Kassia, *IFC*, p. 70.

[113] 'Report on the Earnings of Women Mill-Workers in Cawnpore', *Labour Bulletin*, 1:4, p. 250.

legal, widows sent their sons off to work in the factories. Seven-year-old Babooa, who worked in Elgin Mills, and fourteen-year-old Ramdeen, who worked in the Woollen Mills, gave over their wages to their widowed mothers.[114]

Patterns of Consumption

If average wage figures provide a slippery basis for understanding the condition of workers, do consumption patterns tell us more about the standards and experiences of workers? On the question of diet and living standards of workers there are two kinds of interpretation in official and non-official accounts: one paints a bleak picture of acute misery and deprivation; the other dismisses such bleak descriptions and points to the adequacy of wages in relation to needs. In 1937, a time when the KMS was raising complaints about the poverty and poor consumption standards of workers, the Employers' Association asserted: 'The prevailing rates of wages in Kanpur were sufficient to enable workers of all grades to maintain working efficiency and a reasonable standard of comfort.'[115] Common to many such statements were assumptions about the meagre needs of workers. A similar premise underlines Freemantle's argument: 'The standard of comfort, the social conditions of mill hands in the mofussil is very low: their needs are few, and such as they are of the simplest.'[116]

How do we arrive at any conclusion about the 'standard of comfort' or the 'needs' of workers? Can we define it in terms of a physiological minimum? On the relationship between poverty and nutrition in India there has been a long debate.[117] But there

[114] Babooa's mother gave him anything between 1 as. to 5 as. out of his earnings during festival times. Ramdeen's mother gave him the cash he needed from time to time. Ev. of Babooa and Ramdeen, *IFC*, pp. 68, 71.

[115] Ev. Employers' Association, KLIC Progs., UP Ind. Progs., File 1145,1937, Bundle 110 (UPSA).

[116] Freemantle, 'Report on the Supply of Labour', UP Rev. Progs. B, May 1906, no. 91.

[117] See, for instance, P.V. Sukhatme, 'Assessement of Adequacy of Diets at Different Income Levels', *EPW*, Special Number, Aug. 1978; *idem*, 'Measurement of Undernutrition, *EPW*, 11 Dec. 1982; *idem*, 'Measuring Increase of Undernutrition: A Comment', *EPW*, 6 June 1981; *idem*, 'On Measurement of Poverty', *EPW*, 8 Aug. 1981; N. Krishnaji, 'On Measuring Incidence of

are problems in analysing the quality of consumption. While the debate is important, the limits of its significance need to be recognised.

The discussion on average consumer intake has its problems. Averages do not take into account the variations in consumption requirements between different gender groups, communities, and classes. Since the energy required to reproduce the same level of activity depends on the nature of work, the caloric requirement of a worker is considerably higher than that of the average consumer referred to in studies on nutrition.[118] Calculations of nutritional intake based on investigations of regularly employed workers give us no clue into the caloric consumption of those not in continuous employment. The consumption pattern of badlis and casual workers was characterised by a continuous oscillation between phases of semi-starvation and extremely low caloric intake, with comparatively higher ones. Such fluctuations are not expressed in average figures. And further, the difference in the nutritional component of male and female diets and the deficiencies in female diets is not reflected in these estimates.[119] An excessive concern with caloric intake glosses over the question of the quality of consumption. Need is not just a quantifiable phenomenon: it is culturally determined. A person consuming a physiologically determined adequate nutritional level may still experience a sense of undernourishment.

In general, consumption patterns varied with the level of income. A working class family in the lowest-income category, of Rs 13 per month, spent 77 per cent of its food budget on flour made of a mixture of wheat, gram and barley, and 16 per cent on arhar dal. But the diet of this family shows no consumption of ghee or oil. Another family with a higher-income, of Rs 20 a month, spent only 48 per cent of its budget on wheat–gram–barley, but a larger proportion, 22 per cent, was spent on arhar

---

Undernutrition: What is a Consumer Unit?' 12 Sep. 1981; *idem*, 'On Measuring Increase of Undernutrition: A Note on Sukhatme's Procedure, *EPW*, 30 May 1981; D. Banerji, 'Measurement of Poverty and Undernutrition', *EPW*, 26 Sep. 1981; V.M. Dandekar, 'Economics of Nutrition', *EPW*, 25 July 1981.

[118] Krishnaji raises these problems in his comments on Sukhatme. Krishnaji, 'On Measuring Increase of Undernutrition', *EPW*, 30 May 1981.

[119] It is difficult to provide figures which show this because available surveys take an adult male as the reference unit.

dal, and 26 per cent on rice and ghee. The caloric content of the two diets does not show any marked variation.[120]But the difference in the quality of food is significant. The consumption of ghee and rice mark off the higher-income groups from the diet of those with a lower-income. The quality of flour consumed by the two income groups also varied: as we move up the income categories the family budgets show a shift from a consumption of coarse flour (mixture of wheat, gram and barley) to finer wheat flour. The quality of consumption however, was not always linked to levels of income. There were cultural preferences. 'Fresh arrivals from the eastern districts', we are told, 'give preference to rice' whereas their west UP counterparts had a taste for wheat flour.[121] Meat was more commonly a part of a Muslim worker's diet than that of a Brahman. Many upper-caste workers who observed restrictions on eating pukka or cooked food in the factory, spent a few extra pies a day on buying parched gram at the mill gate for their midday meal.

The quality of consumption also varied according to family size. A single worker with no family responsibilities could afford a better diet. A worker earning Rs 25, with no dependants, spent 14 per cent of his food budget on meat, 24 per cent on milk and 21 per cent on ghee. But many workers earning a higher salary lived with a larger number of family members. While such families spent more on food, their consumption pattern was not qualitatively superior.

Income levels were important in determining expenses on clothing and other articles of consumption: those from lower-income groups spending more frugally wearing a dhoti, or a lungi and a bandi while others from higher-income categories wore shoes, a shirt and often a coat or a waistcoat when it was cold. However there were important variations. Single migrants from a lower-income category for instance, often spent a larger amount on clothes. Expenditure on smoking was higher for workers in the lower-income group, over 7 per cent, while it was around 3.5 per cent in the case of higher-income groups.[122]Pan supari in contrast was not so commonly consumed by those in lower-income

---

[120] See *BSER, UP: Wages and Labour Conditions*, pp. 66–7.

[121] *RCL XI (i)*, p. 73.

[122] The lower-income group here refers to those earning Rs15 and below and the higher-income group those earning Rs 40–50.

groups. Workers from upper castes, even when they were from a lower-income category, preferred using utensils made of brass or bronze, while those from lower castes used vessels made of cheaper metal.

Different categories of working class consumers were dramatically affected by periodic fluctuations in living standards. A fall in living standards was not necessarily reflected in shifts in the caloric minimum but a change from one kind of consumption to another. A fall in earnings during periods like the Depression, for instance, affected lifestyles. The expenditure on clothes went down and Royal Commission investigators noted how workers in the lower-income categories wore dirty clothes, rarely with a spare set to allow washing. The index figures for the consumption of betel-nut and tobacco plummet after 1931 and do not show signs of recovery till the war period.[123] The sense of deprivation workers experienced in times of crisis and fall in earnings was not just in terms of a decline in caloric intake of food, but other, seemingly minor, shifts in consumption patterns.

Thus, living in the city meant important changes in family and household strategies for migrants to the city. However, contrary to official investigators, there was no necessary shift from joint to nuclear households. Not only did joint households survive, new kinds of extended households emerged. Worker migrants to the city moved precariously between their dream cities and the lived worlds. Survival for male migrants often meant an assertion of a masculinist identity. Standardised accounts of consumption patterns and earnings do not give an idea of the varieties of everyday experience, the different perceptions of factory work and money incomes.

---

[123] Betel-nut consumption declined by 50 per cent and tobacco leaf by 35 per cent between 1931 and 1935. S.P. Saxena, 'Cost of Living Indices at Cawnpore', *Sankhya*, 7: 2, Nov. 1945, p. 183.

CHAPTER 4

Work Culture

——◦⟨═══⟩◦——

A recurring theme in studies on labour in India has been the persistence of pre-industrial work values—in contrast to the West, where rapid cultural transformation produced an industrial work culture. Recent writings on labour make it difficult to sustain this theme of difference.[1] Ambivalences, conflicts, and heterogeneity within the emerging work cultures falsify attempts at a simple contrast. Even in the European context, there existed multiple time-reckoning systems, multiple notions of work and leisure, and multiple strategies of management and discipline.[2]

Moving beyond essentialised contrasts between the rhythms of Western and Indian workers, we need to examine the various processes that went into the making of a work culture among industrial workers in India. I proceed here with the assumption that work culture and discipline are not created by state regulations and managerial strategies alone; these are constituted through sedimented practices, through acts of resistance, through conformity with rules. We need to examine the disciplinary norms which managers sought to impose and the agencies of control which gave meaning to norms in everyday practice. We need to look at the ways in which norms were redefined by workers. And finally the role of trade unions in defining and legitimising specific norms of work are of importance to a full understanding of work culture.

Power at the Workplace

The rhetoric of discipline was important to the public discourse of managers. Rules and regulations expressed managerial attitudes

[1] See Patrick Joyce, ed., *The Historical Meanings of Work* (Cambridge 1987); S.L. Kaplan and C.J. Koepp, eds, *Work in France: Representations, Meaning, Organization and Practice* (Cornell 1986); William Reddy, *The Rise of Market Culture* (Cambridge 1984).

[2] R. Whipp, ' "A Time to Every Purpose": An Essay on Time and Work', in Patrick Joyce, ed., *Meanings of Work*, pp. 210–36.

to work/non-work, they defined how workers were to behave. Discipline ensured more than production efficiency; it was crucial to the constitution of managerial authority.

In the late nineteenth century, managers in Kanpur routinely complained that workers lacked a notion of factory time. Measures to ensure punctuality and restrict absences formed part of the strategy of creating 'committed' workers. Fines could not ensure punctuality. It was only by physically barring late entry, by closing the gates at a fixed time, that the stream of latecomers could be prevented.[3] Those locked out lost a whole day's wages. Rajab, a twelve-year-old employed in the Kanpur Jute Mills, preferred setting off to work soon after the first gong at 4 a.m., reaching an hour before the engines started.[4] Fines were commonly imposed to punish absenteeism. Two days' pay was deducted for a day's absence. In the early years of the industry, specially, when mill jobs were not in demand, managers considered fines—and not dismissals or warning notices—as being effective. Later, with an increase in the influx of labour to the city, dismissals, warning notices and 'forced leave' became more common.[5] Another way in which managements tried to exercise control over absenteeism and desertions was by holding back workers' wages.[6]

Fines were also a way of regulating the quality of work. Faulty produce and an output lower than the minimum specified was categorised as 'bad work' and punished with fines. Fines varied in different mills, from 5 per cent of a worker's wages in some mills to 10 per cent in others.[7] But 'bad work' was a category broad enough to allow a variety of interpretations. It was the unpredictability and erratic nature of these punishments which was resented by workers more than the fine itself. Zawar Husain, a worker in

---

[3] Ev. Babooa, *IFC*, p. 68. The practice of closing the gates on latecomers continued in the 1930s. Ev. Lalloo, weaver, Elgin Mills, KLIC Progs., UP Ind. Progs., File 1145, 1937, Bundle 110 (UPSA).

[4] Ev. *IFC*, p. 73

[5] The practice of giving 'forced leave' became more common after the enforcement of the Payment of Wages Act (1937), which prescribed a ceiling on fines.

[6] Ev. Ghasita and Munir, *RCL III(ii)*, p. 249; Ev. UP Govt, *RCL III(ii)*, pp. 184–5.

[7] Ev. UP Govt, *RCL III(i)*, p. 181.

Kanpur Cotton Mills, complained: 'Sometimes the bad cloth was not even shown to the worker and he realised only on pay day that he had to suffer a deduction. This happened often.'[8] In the 1930s strike leaders were frequently charged for bad work. And this could lead to dismissals.[9]

For child workers, commonly employed till the early 1920s, flogging rather than fines was the usual punishment. When Babooa, a seven-year-old doffing boy, returned after an absence, he was flogged. This upset him more than the wages he lost: he sobbed for an hour in terror and pain. [10] Sheo Audhar, a twelve-year-old working at the throstles, was never fined in his sixteen months at the Kanpur Cotton Mills, but he was beaten up by the mistri each time he broke 'too many' threads.[11] But flogging was by no means confined to child workers; adults too were victims.

There were various other rules regulating the general conduct of workers. Spitting on the walls, eating during working hours, and smoking at unauthorised places were prohibited acts.[12] While chewing tobacco or working with the fluff in the blow-room, it was quite common for workers to spit. For those in positions of authority the act had a different meaning; spitting by subordinates showed a lack of appropriate deference. Sometimes managers confiscated the entrance tickets of workers for offences like smoking.[13] Mobility at the workplace was regulated by rules restricting movement between departments. Such regulations became actually operative in periods when interdepartmental camaraderie was seen as a threat. In certain periods, during the strikes of 1937–8

[8] Ev. 9.12.1937, KLIC Progs., UP Ind. Progs., File 1145, 1937, Bundle 110 (UPSA). In the Harness and Saddlery Factory, ten out of every hundred pieces manufactured were rejected and workers were not paid for these. *RCL III(ii)*, p. 244.

[9] See Kanpur Mazdur Sabha (hence the KMS) Memo, KLIC Progs., UP Ind. Progs, File 1145, 1937, Bundle 10 (UPSA).

[10] Ev. Babooa, Elgin Mills, *IFC*, p. 68.

[11] Ev. Sheo Audhar, *IFC*, p. 71.

[12] *RCL III(i)*, p. 180, KMS Memo, KLIC Progs., UP Ind. Progs., File 1145, 1937, Bundle 110 (UPSA).

[13] Even in the 1960s there were instances of such punishments. Binda Savita, who joined as weaver in Atherton West Mills, recounted how, soon after he became permanent, the manager took his ticket away on the charge of smoking and refused to give it back. Interview.

for instance, there were stringent regulations against workers of one department being seen in another department. Nanhu, a weaver in Swadeshi Mills, and Ram Singh, a piecer in the same mill, were both dismissed on this ground. Nanhu was seen talking to sizers, and Ram Singh was wandering amongst workers in the carding department.[14] Trade union activists often became targets of such charges. Babu Khan, a weaver in Cawnpore Textiles and a KMS activist, for instance, was discharged for neglecting his duties and being away too frequently from his looms.[15]

Managerial attempts at control, in fact, extended to workers' bodies. The time spent in the lavatory during working hours was regulated by mill officials. Such forms of control were obviously more severe in periods when the mills were busy, for example during the period of the First World War. Complaints about the severity of mill regulations were repeated by workers of several mills during the strikes of 1919.[16] Workers of the Woollen Mills complained that a clerk was posted near the factory lavatory to keep track of time. Even a minute's delay was fined.[17] The workers of New Victoria Mills demanded the freedom to use the lavatory any time of the day.[18] There were similar protests by workers in 1937, again a period of labour militancy in Kanpur. Ramcharan, a worker in the Kanpur Textile Mills, complained that workers were not allowed to go to the lavatory after 4.30 p.m. and in his factory twenty-two workers were discharged for this offence.[19]

The object of managerial strategy was thus to define work norms in a particular way. Of course the severity of rules varied from factory to factory, department to department, according to the pressures of production and on the inclinations of the super-vising authority. Discipline within mill departments was enforced through mistris. Mistris were themselves workers, subject to the

[14] *Leader*, 25.10.1937.

[15] Director, Cawnpore Textiles, to Employers' Association, dated 11.1.1938 in KLIC Progs., UP Ind. Progs., File 1145,1937, Bundle 110 (UPSA).

[16] See ch. 5.

[17] *Pratap*, 24.11.1919.

[18] *Pratap*, 1.9.1919.

[19] A chaprasi was posted outside the lavatory and no worker was allowed to spend more than ten to fifteen minutes. Ev. Ramcharan, KLIC Progs., UP Ind. Progs., File 1145, 1937, Bundle 110 (UPSA).

authority of managers, often having to invoke the sahib's orders (sahib ka hukm) to exercise their authority.[20] But the wide discretionary powers in matters relating to leave, fines, absence, etc. allowed them a space within which they could exercise sway. If mistri authority was in a way contingent on the sanction of managers, managerial control was crucially dependent on the power exercised by mistris at the workplace. However, the relationship between the two was one of both interdependence and conflict. The influence of mistris over workers was strengthened through community and regional affinities between them. Their power operated through codes that were different from those regulating relationships between managers and workers. Managerial authority could not legitimise itself through similar extra-workplace sanctions.

An argument commonly put forward is that the mistri system provided an inexpensive mechanism for supervision.[21] Managements themselves admit how investment in supervision was not worthwhile. S.M. Johnson of Muir Mills asserted: 'If they had an amount of supervision which a cotton mill could not ordinarily afford, the outturn would no doubt be higher than without that supervision, but not sufficiently so as to compensate for the extra expenditure.'[22] Managements therefore delegated disciplinary authority to mistris. There is a problem with an argument which sees mistri power as 'derived' and delegated. Managerial will was not the prime source of mistri power. The influence they commanded among workers in a way forced managements to recognise their authority. Workers shared community bonds with mistris, were indebted to them for their jobs, and often for loans and lodging. A sense of obligation sustains submission and respect. Mistris also had technical skills—they served as mechanics or fitters in mill departments—a qualification that gave them considerable bargaining strength. In the first decades of the twentieth century,

[20] Sadasukh, a head mistri in Elgin Mills, took a cut from workers every month saying he had orders from the sahib. *Pratap*, 27.10.1919.

[21] Morris, *Emergence*, ch. 8. On jobbers and workers, see also D. Kooiman, 'Jobbers and the Emergence of Trade Unions in Bombay City', *IRSH*, 22:3, 1977, pp. 313–28, R.K. Newman, 'Social Factors in the Recruitment of Bombay Millhands', in Dewey and Chaudhuri, eds, *Economy and Society*.

[22] Oral ev., Johnson, Muir Mills, *IFLC*, p. 206.

when new mills in other centres were looking for skill and experience, managers frequently complained of desertion by mistris and their gangs—who tried to bargain for better terms elsewhere.[23] Mistris therefore had a powerful voice. Even in matters where the sanction of the manager was essential, it was the counsel of the mistri that prevailed. On the question of dismissal, for instance, Mangali Prasad, a worker in the drawing department in the Kanpur Cotton Mills, noted: 'A mistri could not always pass any dismissal order but the manager always acted on the advice of the mistri. Whatever the *karigar* [worker] said was disregarded.'[24] When workers were punished for 'bad cloth' by the mistri, they did not dare complain. Zawar Husain, a weaver in the Kanpur Cotton Mills in the late 1930s, mentioned the case of two workers in his factory, Bharosa and Iqbal, who did complain. They were not heard. In any case, noted a cynical Zawar Husain, whatever a worker said was 'useless', and it carried no weight.[25]

The limits of mistri authority were never clearly spelt out; they were continuously negotiated. In 1937, workers in Laxmi Ratan Mills said that there was virtual mistri raj in their factory for mistris did not bother about regulations ('*Mistri master kanoon ki koi parvah nahin karte*').[26] 'There are no definite rules,' insisted the Kanpur Mazdur Sabha in 1937, 'it is merely the whim and caprice of a jobber that constitutes an offence or innocence of any workman.'[27] Norms that existed were subject to the interpretations of mistris. This made rules fluid. 'Bad work' was categorised as an 'offence', but what constituted 'bad work' was defined largely by

[23] 'Report on the Supply of Labour', UP Rev. Progs. B, May 1906, no. 91.

[24] Ev. KMS witness, 9.12.1937, KLIC Progs., UP Ind. Progs., File 1145,1937, Bundle 110 (UPSA). These were problems raised in many mills in the 1940s too. Workers complained that the mistri's word was always accepted as the truth. *Samajvaad*, 29.9.1947.

[25] Ev. KMS witness, 9.12.1937, KLIC Progs., UP Ind. Progs., File 1145,1937, Bundle 110 (UPSA). Managements, it was generally accepted, 'were naturally chary of listening to complaints against men who exercised great influence among the hands and with whose services they cannot afford to dispense'. Freemantle, 'Report on the Supply of Labour', UP Rev. Progs. B, May 1906, no. 91.

[26] *Lal Jhanda*, 16.1.1937.

[27] KMS Memo, KLIC Progs., UP Ind. Progs., File 1145, 1937, Bundle 110 (UPSA).

mistris. They could always 'pick fault' when they wanted to, or bend the rules for favourites. On the question of leave, again, mistris exercised discretion. Sheo Audhar, a winder in Elgin Mills, explained the predicament of a worker asking for leave:

> To ask for leave was to face death. [A worker] had to approach the mistri in the first instance and the mistri repeatedly sent him back with scolding and abuse. There was great delay before any leave could be obtained. There were no rules and regulations. To get leave for a period of, say, ten days was in his department a difficult affair. The Manager could be approached only when the work was very urgent. The mistri never gave any facilities and all mistris as a class were hard-hearted in matters of leave.[28]

Leave was sanctioned only after repeated requests, unpleasant encounters and prolonged delays. Mistri power in some ways impinged not just on the time of work but on family time as well. For social occasions, for family festivities, the timing of leave was crucial. When leave was sanctioned ultimately, it appeared more as a special favour granted by a mistri than a right of the worker. And the rituals of delay built into the process were part of the exercise of mistri power.

Abusive language acquires a specific meaning within the structure of power in which it is uttered. Beating up and abuse were visible assertions of hierarchical power over workers. To humiliate, to inflict pain and suffering was the prerogative of those in authority, and authority was constituted through the regular practice of such acts. Beating and abuse were public acts, spectacles meant to intimidate workers and create a sense of fear. Intimidation was expected to produce docile, submissive workers, respectful of hierarchies at the workplace. For new entrants, the gate and the gate-jamadar provided their first encounter with mill authority. Even when the workers were on time the jamadar would display his power by pushing them around, slapping and abusing them if there was a slight delay in showing their tickets.[29] To workers, beating up and abuse meant more than pain and suffering. It caused a sense of injured pride. Zawar Husain, a worker in the Kanpur

---

[28] Ev. Shivadhar, 7.12.1937, KLIC Progs., UP Ind. Progs., File 1145, 1937, Bundle 110 (UPSA).

[29] *Lal Jhanda*, 16.1.1937.

Cotton Mills, was categorical: to slap a worker or box his ears, he felt, amounted to beizzati.[30] A loss of *izzat* (self-respect) or dignity was what hurt most. Workers complained about the tone and manner in which mistris often spoke to them. Sudarshan Chakr recalled how they were rudely driven to work by mistris even before their scheduled rest interval during the night shift was over. Workers were treated like animals, he felt: '*Jaise bhere janvaron ko hankte hain vaise mistri mazduron ko hankte the.*'[31]

Central to the disciplinary code of the mistri was the notion of deference. Even styles had to conform to norms of deference. Hairstyles expressed the difference and the distance of a worker from superior managerial authority. Workers were not allowed to keep 'English-style' haircuts—it was perceived as a sign of disrespect. And mistris whipped workers for this 'offence'.[32]

Mistris demanded various other gestures of respect. Certain payments by workers were considered customary. A refusal to pay was seen as an act of 'insubordination'. Compliance with their demands could secure various favours: obliging workers, for instance, were assigned to better machines or granted leave when they wanted. Factory managers implicitly sanctioned such practices. Consider the case of Raghunath Prasad, a worker in the Empire Engineering Company. Sometime in 1920 he was asked by Ramzan, a mistri, for a monthly payment of Rs 2, in addition to the initial sum of Rs 2 he had taken for providing the job. When Raghunath refused to pay, Ramzan asked the 'sahib' (manager) to dismiss him.[33] Collections from workers were often taken in the form of contributions for religious gatherings, a part of which was appropriated by the mistri.[34] Formally, workers could refuse to contribute, but fear of incurring the mistri's displeasure added an element of compulsion to such demands.

[30] Ev. Zawar Husain, 9.12.1937, KLIC Progs., UP Ind. Progs., File 1145, 1937, Bundle 110 (UPSA).

[31] Interview.

[32] Vishvakavi Sudarshan Chakr, *Kanpur Mazdur Andolan ka Itihaas* (Kanpur 1986), p. 6.

[33] *Pratap*, 3.7.20.

[34] A mistri in Elgin Mills, for instance, appropriated more than half the total sum he collected for organising a katha (religious gathering). Ev. Shivadhar, 7.12.1937, KLIC Progs., UP Ind. Progs., File 1145, 1937, Bundle 110 (UPSA).

Mistris were always men. To assert their power and masculinity they demanded special gestures of submission from women workers. To have access to women's bodies was considered by mistris their prerogative. If a woman worker refused to reciprocate a mistri's overtures, she could lose her job. This was a source of great resentment even in the late 1930s, when the number of women workers in factories had declined. The recommendation by the KMS that women workers be supervised by women officials was considered unnecessary by employers. The Employers' Association witnesses before the KLIC asserted that male jobbers did not misuse their powers against women: 'There was no fear of corruption because it was more or less a family concern in which the women worked side by side with their husbands or relatives.'[35] A story called *Mazdurin*, in a Kanpur paper, *Kranti*, expresses the daily humiliation experienced by women workers.[36] It is the story of a mazdurin (female worker) in a cotton mill. One day when the mazdurin is at work, a mistri called Ram Murat comes and stands beside her. Ram Murat, the story mentions, 'is a mistri, who is aware of his prerogatives as a mistri'. He is furious that the mazdurin does not acknowledge his presence. She does not smile at him or talk. He kicks her and orders her to look at him. When he receives no response, he grabs her by her hand. She pushes him off and abuses him. Ram Murat threatens to fire her if she does not meet him at night. The mazdurin flees. The story ends on a note of despair: a mazdurin cannot always save her izzat; she can be compelled into submission.

The mazdurin here is anonymous. It could be any female worker, many shared similar experiences. The mistri is clearly identifiable, he has a name. His crime is not committed in anonymity. It was a public spectacle through which the mistri asserted his

[35] Ev. J. Tinker and B. Shaw, 8.12.1937, KLIC Progs., UP Ind. Progs., File 1145,1937, Bundle 110 (UPSA). Apart from women supervisors, the KMS suggested that recruitment should be done through a labour exchange, a system that would bring other advantages and protect women: 'Women workers would escape molestation and shame, if jobbers' authority is abolished in this direction.' KMS Memo, KLIC Progs., UP Ind. Progs., File 1145,1937, Bundle 110 (UPSA).

[36] Vijay Kumar Misra, '*Mazdurin*', *Kranti*, Sept. 1939, Pros. Pub., no. 526, NAI. The introduction in parenthesis mentions that the story provides a living description of the predicament of a female worker.

position and his prerogatives. His name, ironically, is Ram Murat: one with the divine appearance of Ram, who personified goodness and virtue.

Arbitrariness in a sense was the basis of mistri power. The lack of definite rules allowed them to exercise their authority in arbitrary ways. But coercion and arbitrariness was only one of the many faces of the mistri–worker relationship. The authority of mistris was tempered by ties of kin and community with the workers they recruited. Codes of mutual help operating between community groups could affect the bending of rules and softening of authority. Mistris played an important part in the mohalla life of workers. They organised kathas (religious discourse) and Ramlilas, and occasions like these helped to bind the participants in a common social world. Their arbitrariness then was not random; it functioned within such cultural codes. But these community bonds could not be taken for granted; they had to be endlessly renewed through reciprocal gestures. The mistri saw himself as a patron who expected repeated signs of gratitude from those who received his patronage. The respect for mistris was ritualised in many ways. Bhairon, a worker in Elgin Mills, recounted the ritual through which he was recognised as a mistri's chela:

Jab maine Ali Husain ko apna guru banaya tha aur mein uska chela bana tha tab bakayada rasm adayagi ki gayi thi. Mujhse kasam li gayi thi; mahmanon ko mithayian tatha dusri chizen batin gayi thi. Maine Ali Husain ke gale mein mala pahnayi thi, unke pair chuye the aur vayda kiya ki aj se guru ki aagya ka aksharaha palan karunga. Is prakar Ali Husain ka chela bana.[37]

On Basant Panchami day many workers ceremoniously paid homage to mistris, presenting them with garlands and turbans after a pooja (worship) held within factory premises.[38] In return mistris gave the workers topis (caps) and vests.[39] Such symbolic

[37] When Ali Husain became my guru and I his disciple, an elaborate ritual was performed and I took an oath and distributed sweets to guests. I garlanded Ali, touched his feet and promised him that I would always obey him. *Samajvaad*, 21.9.1947.

[38] Basant Panchami = a festival to honour Saraswati, the goddess of learning.

[39] Interviews with Shiv Ratan and Sudarshan Chakr.

exchanges were important to the constitution of authority. The offering of turbans and garlands to mistris marked their superior stature and the reciprocal gift of vests and topis was similar to the practice of khilat in Mughal courts, when the emperor presented his robes to subjects who paid homage to him.[40]

There were, however, limits to the exercise of power and patronage. Mistri power was contested in various ways. There were conflicts within the mistri hierarchy. Lowest down were badli mistris who could revert to becoming ordinary workers if the mistri in charge was displeased. Line mistris and assistant mistris exercised supervision over workers in their charge but they were subject to the authority of head mistris. In some mills, subordinate mistris had to give a regular cut from their wages to head mistris.[41] Overall charge within the department rested in the hands of departmental managers, and the mistris' equation with departmental managers was important. Managers had favourite mistris whose recommendations carried greater weight.[42] Mistris would try to win favour with departmental managers by giving dalis (gifts).[43] Sometimes a disciplinary measure against a worker could be overruled by the manager. In the Kanpur Cotton Mills a worker, who had been dismissed by a mistri successfully appealed to the manager for reinstatement.[44]

[40] Citing from the work of Buckler, Cohn emphasises that, 'Robes of Honour are symbols of some idea of continuity or succession . . . which rests on a physical basis, depending on the contact of the body of the recipient with the body of the donor through the medium of clothing.' See Bernard Cohn, 'Cloth, Clothes and Colonialism', in *Colonialism and its Forms of Knowledge: The British in India* (Princeton 1996), pp. 105–62. F.W. Buckler, 'The Oriental Despot', *Anglican Theological Review* 10:3 (1927–8), p. 24 in Cohn, *Colonialism*, pp. 114–15. On the practice of *khilat* and *nazr*, see also Michael Fisher, *A Clash of Cultures: Awadh, the British and the Mughals* (Delhi 1987), pp. 139–40.

[41] In Elgin Mills, for instance, Sadasukh, the head mistri, demanded a regular payment of Rs 5 from mistris and Re 1 from workers. *Pratap*, 27.10.1919.

[42] Ev. Laloo, 7.12.1937, KLIC Progs., UP Ind. Progs., File 1145, 1937, Bundle110 (UPSA).

[43] In some mills, mistris collected funds from workers to give dalis to managers on Christmas. *Pratap*, 15.12.1919.

[44] Ev. Mangali Prasad, 9.12.1937, KLIC Progs., UP Ind. Progs., File 1145,1937, Bundle 110 (UPSA).

In the 1930s, the basis of mistri authority was increasingly questioned. Complaints against 'corrupt' or *rishvat khor* mistris were frequently made. New legal structures created after 1938 provided a possibility of filing cases against 'unfair' mistris. Mistris who received bribes had to abide by their promises. Many workers turned into 'approvers', giving testimony against mistris. Most famous was the case against Ansari and Ali Husain of Elgin Mills. Bhairon, a mistri in the same mill, who himself collected bribes from workers and passed them on to Ali Husain and Ansari, made a daring exposure, giving details of money taken from workers. After collecting amounts ranging from Rs 150 to Rs 400, Bhairon would hand it over to Ansari sahib at cinema halls, outside on the road, at his house or at other fixed rendez-vous.[45] Underlying Bhairon's exposure of mistri practice was not so much an indictment of bribery but of betrayal by mistris who failed in their obligations towards workers.[46]

Worker politics in the late 1930s, and state and managerial discourse, all threatened the old basis of mistri power. There was always an implicit difference between the mistri's 'due' and his unfair extortions. Distinctions between just and unjust demands sharpened at this time. Mistris labelled as *rishvat khor* became an object of attack.[47] The legal discourse of conciliation courts tend-ed to project managerial authority as based on fair and legal

[45] Details of Payments by Workers to Ansari and Ali Husain

	Rs	Installments
Rameshwar	215	3
Baiju	400	3
Kanhai Brahman	310	2
Kanhai Kori	250	5
Yasin	220	2
Mata Prasad	150	

Source: Ev. of Bhairon, *Samajvaad*, 21.9.1947.

[46] He felt very cheated when Khairati, a worker in Elgin, who had paid the customary dues, was not promoted to mistriship by Ali Husain. Evidence of Bhairon, *Samajvaad*, 21.9.1947.

[47] Critique of mistri 'corruption', like the attack on Kanhai mistri for *rishvat khori* by workers of the Swadeshi Mills, was common. *Lal Jhanda*, 16.1.1937. *Rishvat khor* = a person who takes bribes.

sanctions. The authority of mistris, in contrast, appeared extra-legal and coercive. Unlike managers, they took bribes to grant leave: managers, particular about formal procedures, preferred getting written leave applications.[48] This assumption about the relative impartiality of managers underlies the KMS proposal of 1938 to strengthen managerial powers in certain matters. 'The right of punishing a workman,' the KMS proposed, 'should be confined only to the manager who should personally satisfy himself that the complaint against an accused is correct and beyond doubt.'[49] In practice, however, managers tended to reaffirm mistri 'corruption' even while condemning it. In the Ansari case, for instance, managers were part of an elaborate plan to nab mistris in the act of bribe-taking, yet they were reluctant to act on the evidence.[50]

But the image of the manager was not fixed. During the First World War period, when mill discipline was tightened, complaints about managerial authority were widespread. If the relative distance between managers and workers made the former appear impartial, at times this distance evoked images of an impersonal, indifferent and cruel authority. In 1919, a year of major strikes in Kanpur, the rancour against managerial indifference was wide-spread. *Pratap*, a local paper closely linked to the workers' move-ment, carried many stories and poems about callous managers who whipped and abused workers.[51] The inaccessibility of the manager added to the general sense of outrage against mill authorities during a strike in the Kanpur Cotton Mills in 1924. The events of 1924 seemed to affirm the cold-blooded, callous picture of managers.

The Experience of Work

Characteristic of the early years of industry in Kanpur, as elsewhere in India, was the long working day, stretching from twelve to

[48] Ev. Mangali Prasad, 9.12.1937, KLIC Progs., UP Ind. Progs., File 1145,1937, Bundle 110 (UPSA).

[49] KMS, Memo, KLIC Progs., UP Ind. Prog, File 1145,1937, Bundle 110 (UPSA).

[50] *Samajvaad*, 14.9.1947.

[51] *Pratap*, 25.8.1919.

fifteen hours in many factories. Legislative enactments restricted the hours of work to ten by 1922 and nine by 1934, but these regulations were relaxed during periods of exceptional demand.[52] Between 1939 and 1945 the Kanpur mills were exempted from the provisions of the Factories Act and allowed to work upto eleven hours per day.[53] In any case, the increasing use of overlapping shifts after 1935 made it difficult to detect instances of violation of regulations. Each shift had different timings and the machinery hours were spread over different shifts.[54] During the night shift, in particular, many mills worked longer than the stipulated time.[55] In seasonal industries like cotton ginning, violation of factory regulations was much more common. Over 1919–20, for instance, 80 per cent of the total number of prosecutions issued against millowners were against ginning factories.[56]

Managements employed contrasts between the outside and inside as part of its justificatory logic. Some seemed to wonder 'whether a boy is not better off who spends his whole day in the sanitary surroundings to be found in most well-managed mills than he would be if half his day were spent playing in a dirty bazaar, which is usually his home'.[57] The bazaar and the home are synonymous, both imaged as repositories of dirt, disease and vice. Within the factory, infants were looked after, they were not in

[52] Some mills worked continuously for two shifts, i.e., almost twenty-four hours. *Pratap*, 25.8.1919. In many mills workers were denied their normal holidays. The workers of Cooper Allen and Co. complained that during the entire period of the war, the factory was not closed even on Sundays. Statement of workers, *Leader*, 14.12.1919.

[53] *LIC: Labour in Cotton Mills*, 1946, p. 73.

[54] *Reports on the Working of the Factories Act*, 1935 and 1936, pp. 16 and 17. Though the actual hours worked were nine, the spreadover often extended to thirteen hours. KMS Memo, KLIC Progs., UP Ind. Progs., File 1145, 1937, Bundle 110 (UPSA).

[55] Ev. Ramcharan, 7.12.1937, KLIC Progs., UP Ind. Progs., File 1145, 1937, Bundle 110 (UPSA).

[56] *Reports on the Working of the Factories Act* (annual volumes). Instances of prosecution against cotton millowners were fewer: in 1929 four cases were filed against Lala Kamlapat of the JK Cotton Spinning Mills for employing persons and in 1920 and 1923 Horsman of the Swadeshi Mills was prosecuted. *Report on the Working of the Factories Act*, 1923 and 1929.

[57] Ev. Elgin Mills, *IFLC*, p. 215.

danger; the outside, in contrast was full of danger. The Inspector of Factories strongly supported the practise of allowing infants: 'I have invariably assented to this custom. Much as I regret these little ones meeting with an occasional accident, I feel there is no more danger inside the mill when watched by their parents than left unattended in their own homes. The idea that small children are perfectly safe out of a mill, when left to their own devices is entirely erroneous . . .'[58]

Official and managerial writings played on contrasts between work in the factory and that outside, between conditions in the mills and outside, to vindicate the need for long hours in the factory for women workers. Besides, they pointed out, jobs like reeling and winding, on which women were employed in textile mills, were 'easy' and 'better suited' to women than other outside work: 'As a rule the sturdier women took to outside work, and this might account for the apparently low physique of factory women.'[59] In this discourse, the factory, a symbol of modern civilisation, was humane; work in the factory was never excessive, it was civilised not brutal. The outside included all spaces external to the factory; spaces outside represented the pre-modern, uncivilised world. Even the home lay outside this civilised sphere of work: 'In many cases they worked harder at household work than they would in a factory.'[60] In ginning factories women were predominant, a large number of them immigrants from Rajasthan. They provided a flexible labour force that could be dispensed with—when the season was off. Thus, ginning, managers asserted, was 'a woman's job'.[61] Night work for women, which was disapproved even by advocates of long hours for women, was considered legitimate in ginning factories. Ginning managers emphasised that night work was economically necessary for factories with a short working season, and that it was not really injurious to the health and family life of women workers. In the eyes of managers, poor immigrants employed in ginning factories had no proper homes: 'It is more comfortable for them to be in the shelter of these mills at night

[58] Ev. Walsh, Inspector Factories, *IFLC*, p. 222.
[59] Ev. Lt. Col. Baker, Civil Surgeon, Kanpur, *IFLC*, p. 208.
[60] Ev. Baker, *IFLC*, p. 210.
[61] Ev. Z. Meti, *IFLC*, p. 212.

than camping out in the cold weather.'[62]Besides, they pointed out, women employed in ginning factories usually devised alternative strategies to take care of the family while they were at work: 'There exists a regular system, devised by the operatives themselves, according to which certain families or individuals belong to certain gangs and shifts, and as these people take very good care of their own selves, and their household duties, neither the women nor their families are exposed to any hardship or suffering under present conditions.'[63]

To most workers long hours inside the factory meant a sense of unfreedom. Some preferred a shorter rest interval in the day: a longer interval involved working late into the night. 'We want to get home as early as possible,' they said.[64] 'Work is a jail. There is no rest in the day,' emphasised Sheo Shankar, a mule minder in Elgin Mills.[65] The concept of long and short work hours is a relative one and was experienced as such. Around the turn of the century, when a fifteen-hour day was common, to many managers a twelve-hour day seemed short. 'By long hours are meant hours of work of above twelve-hours daily,' stated the management of Elgin Mills in its written evidence to the Factory Labour Commission in 1908.[66] Workers did not always conceptualise the length of the workday in terms of the number of hours worked. It was not just the grind of twelve to fifteen hours which made the day long for them, but the sense of a 'time deprived'. The workday appeared long when work time cut into and absorbed the time they could spend with their family and friends in the mohalla. 'We have no time at home in the evening', complained some spinners

---

[62] Walsh, the Factory Inspector, elaborated how women workers employed in the ginning factories came from as far as Bikaner and had no proper place to stay. Ev. Walsh, Sp. Inspector Factories, Bengal and UP, *IFLC*, p. 222.

[63] Ev. Z. Meti, Jumna Ginning and Pressing Company, Kanpur, *IFLC*, p. 212. Ginning managers from Aligarh pointed to a similar system. 'In case of women their absences are even more frequent, and they are often relieved by other members of their family for hours at a time, it being customary for the husband of other members of the family to take their turn in the day's work.' Ev. Jamasji Pallanji, Alliance Ginning and Pressing Factory, Aligarh, *IFLC*, p. 177.

[64] Statement of fifty spinners and weavers of the Muir and Kanpur Cotton Mills, *IFLC*, p. 218.

[65] Ev. Sheo Shankar, *IFC*, p. 69.

[66] *IFLC*, p. 214.

and weavers of Kanpur in the early years of the twentieth century.[67] Recapitulating his early experience of work, Raghubir, an old worker, talked of the difficult work hours that left him no time for his children. '*Abba tum kahan gaye the*' (Father, where have you been), was the question his children asked him every Sunday.[68] His children were asleep when he left for work in the morning, and they were back in bed when he reached home after dark. Most workers resented coming in to clean the machines on Sundays because it took away the only day they could spend at home. Sunday was the day they met friends, roamed in the bazaar, and did the odd household chore. Sheo Shankar was categorical about a holiday on Sundays: 'I do not care if I get a rupee less, but I want my Sunday holiday.'[69]

For working children the day was long when it left no time to play. By the time Babooa, a nine-year-old working in the 1890s, arrived home, it was dark. 'He has no time to play. He eats his dinner and goes to sleep,' we are told.[70] Play time was long over for Mahabeer, a nine-year-old of Cooper Allen; 'the lamp at home is lighted by the time he gets home'.[71] In the 1890s, most boys employed in the mills came and left with the older men. They were virtually full-time workers.[72] Some had no time to play even on Sundays. Sheo Audhar, for instance, an eleven-year-old boy, who worked at the throstles in Elgin Mills, could never play. On Sundays he worked till midday and then had to help his father with the weekly shopping and other chores.[73] Boys like Sheo Audhar and Babooa had to come in for cleaning machinery on Sundays. Hierarchies of age gave older workers a power over boys. What appeared particularly unfair to Babooa was the fact that 'the boys have to do all the cleaning while the tenters are amusing themselves'.[74]

For women workers like Marid, who worked as a winder in

[67] Statement of thirty weavers and twenty-five piecers residing at Chotumia's buildings, *IFLC*, p. 218.

[68] Interview with Raghubir who worked in the Kanpur mills since the 1920s.

[69] Statement of weavers and piecers, *IFLC*, p. 218.

[70] Ev. Babooa, *IFC*, p. 68.

[71] Ev. Mahabeer, *IFC*, p. 75.

[72] Ev. Babooa, *IFC*, p. 68.

[73] Ev. Sheo Audhar, *IFC*, p. 71.

[74] Ev. Babooa, *IFC*, p. 68.

Elgin Mills in the 1890s, the day started earlier.[75] She woke up at 4 a.m. to cook her lunch and reach in time for work. She always arrived at the time the whistle went, just before sunrise. Like other workers, women like Marid preferred being out of the mill gate during the rest interval. Apart from the midday break, she would often come out twice. Marid, who was the only earning member in her family, had a sick, unemployed husband to look after, without the support of an extended family structure in the city. It was late, around 11 p.m., when she finished with her household work. Often, she had no break even on a Sunday because she had to go and clean the machines. Leave involved negotiation with mistris, and among women this often entailed being subjected to the male power of mistris. Besides, women winders were easily substituted. All the women witnesses before the Factory Commission in 1890 agreed that there were lots of women willing to take their place.

Work was particularly hard during the war years (1914–18). Not only were working hours increased, the pressure of war work led to closer supervision over workers and a greater intolerance of any kind of slackness. In addition, the higher quality of material that was now being produced in some mills demanded greater care and attention.[76] The new disciplinary regime appeared to the workers as arbitrary and inequitable. Fines, they complained, 'are imposed on the slightest mistakes'. Physical violence as a way of enforcing discipline became much more common. A KMS representation to Annie Besant in 1920 drew attention to the inhuman ways in which workers were abused and beaten.[77]

Philanthropists, poets, and Congress leaders expressed concern about the plight of workers in this period. A poem, *Garib Mazdur* by Bhagwati Charan Varma, draws attention by speaking through the voice of a worker.[78]

[75] Ev. Marid, *IFC*, p. 68.

[76] *Pioneer,* 5.12.1919.

[77] *Independent,* 4.2.1920. A report on conditions in factories describes how workers were abused and beaten with leather straps. *Pratap,* 25.8.1919.

[78] '*Ham to kuli mazdur hain, malik janab hazur hain / Nyayi tatha ve krur hain, kis garv mein ve chur hain / Ham pis rahen din rat hain, karte na hamse bat hain / Kaisi anokhi ghat hain, har chal mein shaimat hain / Kaisa hame uphaar hai, kaisa hamara pyar hai, ham mangte ahaar hain, detein hame veh maar hain.*' *Pratap,* 26.1.1920.

We are but workers and coolies / And they—the respected maliks / They claim to dispense justice / But cruelty is their forte / Shrewdness their craft / Their insolence knows no bounds / Indifference no limits / We toil and grind all day and night / What rewards do we recieve? What love do we get? We demand something to eat / We get thrashings instead.

During the Depression and post-Depression years, grievances about the increased workload were articulated within a different context. The retrenchment of workers in some departments, without any corresponding decline in production, meant an increased workload for the remaining workers. In Muir Mills, for instance, ring piecers had to look after 25 per cent more spindles because of the reduction in the number of workers; in the mule room there were six men to a pair of mules, as opposed to eight earlier; and in the weaving room many weavers had to work three looms. Representations by the KMS argued that the process of intensification continued in the post-Depression years. Since the increase in employment in this period was accompanied by the adoption of the double-shift system in most mills, workers still had to work an increased number of looms and spindles in each shift.[79] Many mills introduced the overlapping shift system, which allowed machinery to be run for the maximum possible time. This was very unpopular with workers because it meant an additional burden on each worker for an hour, when one group of workers took their rest interval.[80] The adoption of high draft systems in the speed-frame and in the ring-spinning departments, high-speed winding and warping machines, and self-stripping devices on cards, introduced processes requiring greater vigilance and attentiveness from workers. In small factories, for example in the numerous small establishments that came up during the war years in 1940–1, labour laws were blatantly violated. Under the Defence of India War Regulations, workers were made to work twelve–fourteen hours without any weekly rest day.[81]

[79] KMS Memo, KLIC Progs., UP Ind. Progs., File 1145,1937, Bundle 110 (UPSA).

[80] Ev. Ramcharan, weaver in Kanpur Textiles, 7.12.1937, KLIC Progs.,UP Ind. Progs., File 1145,1937, Bundle110 (UPSA).

[81] *Citizen*, 6.9.1941.

Continuous work in the hot summer months was specially difficult. In the weaving and weaving-preparatory departments that used live steam for humidification, conditions were particularly oppressive. Workers in this department complained about excessive heat even in the winter months because the steam taps were kept running continuously.[82] In the summer, the electric lamps under which weavers worked through the day made the heat intolerable.[83] Weaving was also a department with the highest rate of absentee-ism, with the proportion of absentees going up in the hot and humid month of July. Absenteeism in the department was not always connected with harvest-time departures, since a large number of weavers were from urban dwelling, artisanal castes.[84] Weaving—as Ramcharan a weaver who worked in the Kanpur mills since 1940s, recapitulated—required focused energy:

> *Usme dam lagti hai. Ankhen chalti, gardan alag, pav alag, hath alag, sab chalat hai. Binta ka kam hai, har vakt nazar mare—kahi jane nahi pate, dhyan apka machine par. Char machine chalane mein ye hota hai ki charo ko ek sath chalna chahiye. Band bhi nahi hona chahiye.*[85]

> (You need energy. The eyes move, the neck, the legs and the hands, each part moves. Weaving is done under a continuous gaze—one cannot go anywhere, the focus must be on the machine. When four machines run all four must move together, they must not stop.)

The strain, as Ramcharan elaborated, was particularly heavy on the eyes, which had to focus continuously on the moving shuttle. Workers in other departments experienced the exertion in different ways. Sheo Shankar, a mule minder in Elgin Mills in the 1890s, recalled his days as a boy worker at age fifteen as particularly arduous: 'The mule work is particularly severe for the boys, as they never have time to sit down and are continuously on the move. In all other work the boys get periods of comfort, but in the

---

[82] Ev. Zawar Husain, 9.12.1937, and KMS Memo, KLIC Progs., UP Ind. Progs., File 1145,1937, Bundle 110 (UPSA). Also *Report on the Working of the Factories Act*, 1935.

[83] Ev. Ramcharan, 7.12.1937, KLIC Progs., UP Ind. Progs., File 1145,1937, Bundle 110 (UPSA).

[84] On seasonal fluctuations in absenteeism, see ch. 2.

[85] Interview.

mules never.'[86] Even a job like winding, considered easy and fit for women, could be arduous. The machines required constant tending. The yarn from the ring bobbins had to be wound onto the warper's bobbins and all the broken ends had to be pieced together. If left unattended for a moment, there was a danger of threads getting entangled and production being damaged.[87]

In most mill departments, periods of high heat were also times when accidents increased. The largest number of accidents, according to the Factory Inspector's estimates, occurred around midday.[88] Contrary to managerial and official assertions about the lack of mechanical sense of Indian workers,[89] many of the accidents were a result of managerial indifference to the hazards

[86] Ev. *IFC*, p. 69.

[87] Women working on winding machines in the 1970s, for instance, were emphatic: 'It [winding] is heavy work . . . We are not allowed to put off the machine if we want to relax or drink a glass of water. If we leave them, the threads get entangled and we are severely scolded or charge-sheeted. Except for the half-hour lunch-break, we have to stand and work by the machine all the time.' Interview, Sheela, textile worker, Rohini P.R., Sujata S.V., and Neelam C., *My Life is One Long Struggle: Women, Work, Organization and Struggle* (Madras n.d.).

[88] Time of accidents

Time	Number of accidents
6 a.m. to 9 a.m.	235
9 a.m. to 12 noon	388
12 noon to 3 p.m.	346
3 p.m. to 6 p.m.	222

Source: Ev. Mackay, *RCL III (i)*, p. 229.

[89] The UP Government in its evidence to the RCL asserted: 'The average Indian workman has little idea of the dangers attendant on machinery. His training is negligible. His environment is unmechanical. His traditional dress exposes him to risks. He often takes shortcuts or undue risks because he does not realise their danger. Only a small proportion of the workmen are literate and therefore understand, even if they care to, the meaning of safety instructions and posters.' *RCL III (i)*, p. 166. From a different standpoint, altogether, Chakrabarty's understanding of the relationship between the jute worker and machinery essentialises the pre-modern outlook of workers: 'a religious outlook rather than "science" determined this relationship . . .' *Rethinking*, p. 89.

of work. To keep machines running for the maximum time possible, for instance, workers were often required to clean them in motion. This was risky business, sometimes resulting in fatal accidents.[90] In general, factory accidents tend to suggest a seasonal pattern. The total number of accidents in cotton spinning and weaving mills in UP increased after June, rose more sharply in August, and fell steeply after September. The increase in accidents coincides with the harvest months, when a large number of badlis were employed.[91]

Women from working class families, who were not employed in the factories, worked on a variety of jobs at home and outside. Besides, factory employment was never continuous. Factories often employed women in periods of increased production and then sacked them. Many women, specially those from lower castes, were engaged in bidi making, an important cottage industry in Kanpur. Activities like bidi making employed almost all women in a household through the day. Bidi leaves have to be soaked and then cut, after which they are layered with tobacco. The entire process requires great care and skill. The bidi has to be rolled with the tobacco while it is wet; the quantity of tobacco has to be just right to pass selection by the merchant. In work like this, the separation between industrial time and family time is blurred. The industrial invades and colonises the domestic. In households in which women do waged work at home, the time for domestic chores shrinks: routine jobs are performed as quickly as possible. Women with infants tend to see family time as cutting into the day's earnings. In many households in which adult men are unemployed, women's wages are the only source of income. Waged work in such a context is valorised and domestic chores are seen as an intrusion into the time of work.[92]

How did workers deal with their conditions of work? And how did their everyday experience define the culture of the factory?

[90] In one factory a worker was fatally injured by being caught between the unfenced belt and fast pulley of an inter-frame. *WFA Report*, 1939, p. 10. For a discussion on the hazards of work in other industries, see, Dilip Simeon, 'Work and Resistance in the Jharia Coalfield', in J.P. Parry, ed., *The World of Indian Labour*, pp. 62–7; Janaki Nair, *Miners and Millhands*, pp. 53–61.

[91] See ch. 2.

[92] For an elaboration of this argument, see C. Joshi, 'Making Spaces'.

Everyday Practice

Norms within the factory were continuously negotiated. Various forms of opposition, intended or unintended, shaped the culture of work. Desertion was a common response to oppressive conditions. New recruits who found working conditions unbearable sometimes left in the course of the first six months.[93] Many workers preferred construction and coolie labour to fixed hours inside a factory.[94] Experienced workers could also desert. Around the turn of the nineteenth century, many skilled workers left their jobs in Kanpur and moved to newly established mills in other centres in the hope of easier discipline.[95] About two-thirds of spinners in the Delhi mills were from Kanpur.[96] Experienced workers could exercise greater bargaining power and demand better conditions in new centres which needed their services. The Agra millowners, for instance, preferred workers from Kanpur for their efficiency but found them more troublesome.[97]

The long 12–15-hour day till the early years of the twentieth century intruded into domestic time. Ritual ablutions were performed within the space and time of the factory. Workers carried their lotas, clothes, and angochas into the factory.[98] Since many of the Kanpur mills were located on the banks of the Ganga, workers would take a dip in the river during the day. In the winter months

[93] S.H. Freemantle, *IFLC*, p. 220.

[94] Tula Ram, for instance, was helped out with a job in a textile mill by his brother Beni Ram. But Tula Ram quit the job very soon: he could not stand the fixed hours in a factory. Instead he worked sometimes as a painter, sometimes as a construction worker. See S. Molund, *First We are People,* p. 180.

[95] Freemantle writes, for instance, 'Owing to the necessity for importing hands at the opening of new mills conditions were and are somewhat easier, discipline less strict, and pay somewhat higher.' Report on the Supply of Labour', UP Rev. Progs. B, May 1906, no. 91.

[96] Ibid.

[97] G. Thornley, manager, John's Mill, pointed out how they 'always had a lot of trouble with the Kanpur men'. Ev. *IFLC*, p. 172. In managerial perceptions the Kanpur workers were the main leaders behind the strikes for a shorter working day in Agra.

[98] Lota is a metal pot used for bathing and washing; angocha is a cloth used as a towel. In December 1919 when the striking Elgin Mill workers were locked out by the management, they complained that their lotas and clothes were locked inside the factory. *Pratap,* 1.12.1919.

they washed in the cooling tanks which contained hot water discharged from boilers.[99] To European supervisors and managers, such intrusions of domestic time confirmed images of the factory as a home to workers.

Workers tried to define their pace of work by taking time off for a smoke or a chat and a little rest. Breaks for a smoke, insisted Laloo, a worker in Elgin Mills, had to be distinguished from just 'whiling away' time: 'Workers did not while away their time in latrines but, since no smoking was permitted inside the mill, smokers used to go into the latrines for smoking.'[100] Rajub, a twelve-year-old worker in the Kanpur Jute Mills, went out about seven times in the day for a drink of water from a vendor outside the factory gate.[101] For piece-workers breaks from work meant reduced earnings. Yet weavers and spinners on piece-wages took frequent breaks specially in the hot summer months.[102]

Evidence like this from official inquiry commissions has its problems. Worker witnesses rationalise informal work breaks in terms of physical necessity: it is the heat or the long hours or the need for a smoke which makes a break necessary. Clearly, this was not all that the breaks meant to workers. The times they went out to the lavatory or took a rest were also times when they chatted, gossiped, and exchanged information. These were expressive times, when they teased and joked.[103] They were moments of

[99] Letter, 1.1.1938, from Labour Officer to the KLIC, File 1-L/38, Coll.1, Rajendra Prasad Papers (NMML).

[100] Ev. Laloo, 7.12.1937, KLIC Progs.,UP Ind. Progs., File1145,1937, Bundle 110 (UPSA). Similar forms of 'quotidian' resistance have been elaborated by Ranajit Das Gupta, 'Poverty and Protest', pp. 319–26; R.P. Behal, 'Forms of Labour Protest', *EPW*, 20:4, Jan.1985, PE 19–PE 26. On notions of 'shirking' in factories in more recent times, see Jonathan P. Parry, 'Lords of Labour: Working and Shirking in Bhilai', in Parry, ed., *The Worlds of Indian Industrial Labour*, pp. 107–40.

[101] Ev. *IFC*.

[102] *IFLC*, p. 218.

[103] Ludtke uses the category of *eigensinn* to refer to the everyday acts—the jocular horseplay, the physical expressions of camaraderie among workers, and the evasions of work norms through which workers create space for themselves. For rich insights on this, see the writings of Alf Ludtke, 'The Historiography of Everyday Life: The Personal and the Political', in Raphael Samuel, *et al.*, eds, *Culture, Ideology and Politics* (London 1982); and 'What

communion with other workers, moments when collective identities of the workplace were forged. And managerial attempts at control were often directed at restricting such camaraderie between workers, especially during strikes.

Skilled workers, who worked at piece-rates, could exercise a greater control over their workday. It was customary for weavers in most mills to leave before closing time; [104] and tailors in some mills never came before 7 a.m.[105] The offer of extra payments could not always persuade skilled workers to work long hours.[106] In the wider conflict over the control of work time, skilled workers often countered managerial controls with their own norms. In the North West Tannery, saddle-makers refused to take entry and exit passes when they went out during working hours. Instead, the 'men themselves regulated the going out'.[107]

If managers accused workers of 'stealing time', workers in turn made counter-charges. They redefined the formal limits of the workday and asserted their right to informal breaks, but they demanded from managers a respect for time regulations. They thus expressed a complex and apparently conflicting attitude towards time regulations: questioning as well as reconfirming their legitimacy. Whenever work time intruded into their 'leisure time' they seem to express an acutely calculating attitude. Sheo Audhar, who worked in Kanpur in the 1890s, was sure that the afternoon recess was of half an hour and not the stipulated one hour, for 'he could not get time even to eat all his dry food (chabena) at the recess'.[108] Zawar Husain, who worked in Kanpur in the 1930s,

---

Happened to the "Fiery Red Glow"? Workers' Experiences and German Fascism', in Ludtke, ed., *The History of Everyday Life: Reconstructing Historical Experiences and Ways of Life* (New Jersey 1995). James Scott distinguishes between the hidden transcripts and the public transcript of submission to dominant codes in his *Domination and the Arts of Resistance: Hidden Transcripts* (Yale 1990).

[104] Ev. J.B. Sunderland, North West Tannery, *IFLC*, p. 202.

[105] Ev. Butterworth, Woollen Mills, *IFLC*, p. 197.

[106] The management admitted that 'unless they [the workers] wanted to work they could not be tempted to do so by the prospect of extra payment'. Gavin Jones, Empire Engineering Company, *IFLC*, p. 203.

[107] Ev. J.B. Sunderland, North West Tannery, *IFLC*, p. 202.

[108] Ev. *IFC*, p. 71.

was certain that his mill always started ten minutes before and closed five minutes after time.[109]

Did these attempts by workers to define the pace of work constitute resistance? Notions of what constitutes a slow and a fast pace of work are culturally grounded. A work pace that does not conform to managerial definitions is not necessarily intended as an act of resistance. However, when managers repeatedly punish such actions, categorising them as a violation of rules, and workers persist with their own rhythms in defiance of imposed norms, then their practices do not simply preserve tradition. Defined in opposition to a new disciplinary structure, the affirmation of old norms becomes the basis of contestatory practices.

In these forms of resistance, intended and unintended, the focus of opposition was rules, formal codes. Authority objectified in rules is different from authority personified in individuals. When the actions of individuals violate notions of justice held by workers, the target of opposition is the person. This attack can be of various forms. The person in power can be harassed and humiliated, mocked and ridiculed, or physically attacked. In many different ways, authority is questioned, its limits are sought to be redefined. Protest sometimes took the form of physical violence against those in positions of power. Sudarshan Chakr remembered an instance from the 1920s when workers of the night shift in Elgin Mills beat up an unpopular European supervisor called 'bambai saheb'.[110] He recalls that a common strategy was to plunge the room in darkness, blind the supervisor, cover his head with sackcloth, them thrash him. In Elgin Mills, in the 1930s, when a supervisor known for his strictness was appointed to the night shift, the workers devised their own protest. To mock and harass him, a worker was repeatedly sent to him for permission to use the lavatory. When the supervisor refused, the worker threw a shoe at him.[111] To those in authority, repeated demands for leave are never legitimate; and when they were made in an obviously mocking fashion, an acceptance of the demand would be an admission of managerial weakness. In this case the supervisor,

[109] Ev. Zawar Husain, 9.12.1937, KLIC Progs., UP Ind. Progs., File 1145,1937, Bundle 110 (UPSA).

[110] Chakr, *Kanpur Mazdur Andolan*, p. 7.

[111] Chakr, *Jay Janta* (Kanpur 1965), p. 21.

belonging to a ritually 'clean' caste, was doubly humiliated because the worker harassing him was from an 'impure' Chamar caste.[112] The impudence of a worker from a 'lowly' Chamar caste violated the supervisor's notions of hierarchy; and the attack with a shoe, considered 'unclean' because it was made of leather, defiled his sense of ritual purity: it was the worst indignity a haughty, upper-caste supervisor could suffer. The shoe became a metaphor of protest again when, sometime in the 1930s, workers from the same mill tried to lampoon the gate pass system. They entered the mill gate with passes tied to their shoes. When asked for their pass, the workers showed their shoe to the gatekeeper, displaying their irreverence for his authority.[113]

Experiences at the workplace, the relationship with structures of authority, were important to the shaping of worker identities. Notions of self and identity forged outside the workplace acquired new meaning within the everyday context of the factory. Certain groups of workers were commonly associated with militant traditions and were categorised as more rebellious. Weavers, for instance, had a reputation for militancy. Such stereotypes are not necessarily mythical constructs.[114] Perceptions of skill and assertions of self had an important bearing on the creation of such stereotypes. But it was through everyday acts at the workplace—through attempts to preserve dignity and assert notions of independence—that weavers, saddle-makers, tailors and others gave meaning to these identities.

Rules Defined

If workers mocked authority, managements sought to lay down the parameters of acceptable behaviour. Unions occupied an in-between space, a zone of contact, expressing worker grievances

[112] Ibid., p. 21.

[113] Chakr, *Kanpur Mazdur Andolan* p. 49.

[114] Ranciere, for instance, questions the 'myth' of the radical artisan in the European context. He cites the example of shoemakers, arguing that their militancy was related to the availability of forced leisure time (periods of unemployment) and not their professional skill. Jacques Ranciere, 'The Myth of the Artisan: Critical Reflections on a Category of Social History', in Kaplan and Koepp, eds, *Work in France*, pp. 317–54. Dipesh Chakrabarty

as well as ratifying the codes that integrated workers within a new disciplinary regime of the factory.

How did managers perceive the everyday practices of workers? One can broadly distinguish between three kinds of conceptions in managerial discourse. First, there was the common stereotype of the lazy Asiatic and the vigorous European: 'The Asiatic labourer is incapable of continuous work and however light his task may be, he must have intervals of absolute idleness which are unknown to the vigorous European.'[115] Second, there was the conception that Indian workers had no notion of work discipline; they made no distinction between work time and domestic time. Washing, bathing, shaving and other activities associated with the home were performed in the workplace: 'About 10 per cent of our hands may be seen any time of day bathing, washing garments, smoking or otherwise loitering about the mill compound.'[116] Factory time for managers was production time, and all other activities were categorised as 'idling', 'dawdling', 'loitering'. Third, there was a belief that workers operated with their own notion of what constituted legitimate work and overwork. Managers asserted that workers could not be driven to work. 'If he [the worker] thinks he is being overworked he will cease coming to work,' said one Kanpur manager;[117] 'The average Indian worker cannot be hastened . . . [he] greatly prefers to spin his task out to his own time,' asserted another.[118]

Within this managerial discourse lay two contradictory visions. There was, on the one hand, a desire to reform workers and impose a new disciplinary work regime, and on the other a recognition of the limits to reform. These apparently conflicting strands of argument defined the specific nature of managerial strategy and the work culture of the factory. Implicit in the second assumption is the belief that culture in any society is a given,

---

approvingly cites Ranciere in an essay, 'Class Consciousness and the Indian Working Class: Dilemmas of Marxist Historiography', *Journal of Asian and African Studies*, 23:1–2, p. 23.

[115] Ev. Muir Mills, *IFLC*, p. 204.
[116] Ev. Kanpur Cotton Mills, *IFLC*, p. 197.
[117] Ev. J.B. Sunderland, North West Tannery, *IFLC*, p. 202.
[118] Ev. H.D. Allen, Cooper Allen and Co, *IFLC*, p. 187.

natural attribute; and work discipline must adapt to the natural culture of a society. So disciplinary strategies make no sense because discipline cannot be imposed. Arguments about the futility of reform were particularly dominant in periods when there was pressure for reform, for instance, during the early years of the twentieth century, when the demand for a regulation of working hours was widespread. But this resistance to reform coexisted with the attempt by managers to impose work norms in the everyday life of the factory.

Managers expected these norms of work in the factory. Yet, as I suggested earlier, the responsibility of mistris for day-to-day discipline within the factory made rules flexible. Besides, managerial strategy not only tried to transform old habits and impose new norms, it also accommodated the existing practices of workers and modified rules. New rules often formalised practices that had existed in an informal way earlier. Managerial regulations within the factory implicitly recognised the need to accommodate certain customary practices. It was the custom in most factories for workers to leave their work to the joriwala (neighbouring worker) while they took a break.[119] The joriwala became a taken-for-granted phenomenon. To managements, this practice gave the possibility of uninterrupted production; to workers it gave flexibility within working hours. But in the absence of any formal code, the working of the system depended on the power equation among workers and between workers and managers. Factory dadas could bully their neighbours into looking after their work more often than other workers.

When managers saw the practice as an infringement on their authority, they attacked it. Consider the case of Babu Khan, a weaver in Kanpur Textiles and an active trade unionist. Babu Khan, the management claimed, used to be away from his looms five or six times a day for half an hour or more at a time. His work was carried on by his joriwala. When Babu Khan was charged with neglecting his duties, he replied: 'What does it matter to you what time I spend outside so long as the production comes from my looms?' The management in turn claimed, 'If his co-weaver could look after four looms and get the production from them,

[119] Ev. Ramdeen, Woollen Mills, *IFC*.

there was no particular reason why the company should retain Babu Khan's services.'[120] The deorha (overlapping shift) system in a way formalised a practice that informally existed in the institution of the joriwala. In the deorha system, each worker had to work four looms instead of two for one hour, while another group of workers was allowed rest in this period.[121] Many workers complained that the deorha system led to conflicts between them. Since two workers shared responsibility for work on the same set of looms, there were disagreements over who was responsible for any flaws in the material. The decision often depended on the equation between mistris and workers: those closer to a mistri were more likely to get away without any charge.[122]

Absenteeism became a part of the work rhythm in factories. Workers remained away in their villages for long periods, despite the threat of a loss of job when they returned. Absences could not be stopped, so managements had to devise alternative ways of sustaining production. This they did in several ways. There was the system of employing badlis. The manager of Muir Mills explained: 'There are so many spare hands employed in an Indian cotton mill to provide for absentees that the absence of one or two men need not stop a machine.'[123] In the 1930s, a period when factories were cutting down on the number of workers, in many factories no substitutes were employed in place of absentee workers. The joriwala did the work of the absentee worker.[124] In ginning factories, where women were generally employed on the

[120] Ev. Babu Khan, Elgin Mills, 24.1.1938, KLIC Progs., UP Ind. Progs., File 1145,1937, Bundle 110 (UPSA).

[121] Ev. Ramcharan, 7.12.1937, KLIC Progs., UP Ind. Progs., File1145,1937, Bundle 110 (UPSA). William Reddy points to a similar system of doublage in cotton mills in the Andelle valley in France. There was an outrage against this system in 1860 because workers claimed too many fines were resulting from flaws in the cloth that occurred during doublage. *Rise of Market Culture*, p. 244.

[122] Ev. Ramcharan, 7.12.1937, KLIC Progs., UP Ind. Progs., File 1145, 1937, Bundle 110 (UPSA). Some managers claimed to have introduced a system by which a mark was put to differentiate the work of two men at the same loom. Entwistle, Manager, Kanpur Textiles, ibid.

[123] Ev. Muir Mills, *IFLC*, p. 204. S.M. Johnson of Muir Mills stated, 'they did not however want a full complement [of workers] every day, because the full complement included expected absentees'. *IFLC*, p. 207.

[124] *Lal Jhanda*, 16.1.1937.

night shift, it was customary for husbands or other family members of women workers to act as substitutes when they were absent.[125]

Though managers disapproved of unscheduled breaks during working hours, they could at best regulate such breaks, not disallow them. The ticket system reflects an attempt by mill managers to sanction as well as control such breaks. Workers had to take a ticket each time they left work. The limited number of tickets in circulation restricted the number of workers going out at any given time. By the 1930s, when the hours of work were officially reduced to nine, the legitimacy of such breaks was no longer recognised and the ticket system was discontinued in most mills.[126]

Managers caricatured workers' inability to distinguish between work time and domestic time, yet managerial practice allowed a blurring of distinct times. By providing bathing ghats for workers in the factory compound, many managers accepted a phenomenon which was otherwise a subject of their scorn and ridicule. In the 1930s, however, certain managements tried to restrict the use of bathing facilities and allowed workers to wash at the ghats only during scheduled intervals.[127] Smoking in the mill compound was disapproved by managers: it was not only dangerous because of the fire hazard, but to managements it was synonymous with 'loitering'. Yet smoking during work hours could not be totally stopped. Managements therefore attempted to regulate the space and time for smoking. The cotton godown, for instance, was a prohibited area, and Ishaq Ali, a worker in the Kanpur Cotton Mills, was beaten up for smoking there.[128] In the Woollen Mills there was a special space for smoking within the compound, but no one was allowed there for an hour after the mill started and half an hour before it closed.[129]

[125] Ev. Jamasji Pallanji, Alliance Ginning and Pressing Factory, Aligarh, *IFLC*, p. 177.

[126] Ev. Padampat Singhania, Director, Juggilal Kamlapat Spinning and Weaving Mills, 16.12.1937, KLIC Progs., UP Ind. Progs., File 1145,1937, Bundle 110 (UPSA).

[127] A ghat is a paved area by a river for bathing purposes, Ev. Shivadhar, 7.12.1937, KLIC Progs., UP Ind. Progs., File 1145,1937, Bundle110 (UPSA).

[128] Ev. Zawar Husain, 9.12.1937, KLIC Progs., UP Ind. Progs., File1145, 1937, Bundle 110 (UPSA).

[129] Ev. Woollen Mills, *IFLC*, p. 190.

Unions played an important role in legitimising the discourse of discipline among workers. For managements, unions had two contradictory faces. Unions were synonymous with indiscipline and disruption of work; at the same time, unions were potentially the voice of discipline among workers. Their credibility with the management and ability to bargain for concessions were contingent on their disciplinary power over workers. Successful bargaining gave unions a legitimacy in the eyes of workers, and this made their disciplinary authority more effective.

The language of the KMS in the 1930s reflects the shared assumptions in the discourses of managers and the union. This is particularly interesting since the KMS, the only worker's union in Kanpur of this time, was dominated by communists, and was known for its radical rhetoric. The union played an important role in negotiating with the management, persuading them to concede some of the demands of the workers during the strikes of 1937–8. But the concessions were given on the assurance that the KMS would help in enforcing a disciplinary regime. The KMS of the 1930s was stronger than it was in the earlier decade. And its strength and popularity made its disciplinary voice potentially more powerful.

A memorandum submitted by the KMS to the Kanpur Labour Inquiry Committee during the strikes expressed, in rather unequivocal fashion, the union's attitude towards work discipline in the factory.[130] The KMS operated with assumptions about 'commitment' and 'efficiency' common to the managerial discourse on labour. A 'committed' workforce for the KMS was an urbanised workforce, based permanently in the city. Like the management, the KMS considered 'absenteeism' an 'evil' which hindered the formation of a committed workforce.[131] It suggested measures to reduce absenteeism so that a 'permanent', 'efficient' and 'healthy' labour force could be created.

The KMS notions of what constitutes useful time and wasteful

[130] KMS Memo, KLIC Progs., UP Ind. Progs., File 1145,1937, Bundle110 (UPSA).

[131] 'Frequent returns [to the village] make the formation of a permanent labour force difficult in the city. A permanent labour force is of immense benefit to any industry.' KMS Memo, KLIC Progs., UP Ind. Progs., File 1145,1937, Bundle 110 (UPSA).

time are in terms of the function of time in the productive efficiency of a factory. Time spent away from the machines, even if it was to go to the lavatory, is considered in a sense, wasteful. Lavatories, the KMS suggests, should be located in close proximity to each department so that time was not 'unnecessarily wasted' going to and fro. Shorter hours and weekly holidays were seen in terms of their function within the productive life of the factory. Shorter hours would lead to greater efficiency; holidays were necessary to recoup and work efficiently during the week.

It would be an oversimplification to reduce the attitudes of the KMS entirely to managerial assumptions. Although certain categories used by the KMS were similar to those of the management, it was also trying to renegotiate the terms of discipline. Its legitimacy among the workers it represented was dependent on the respect it gave to their notions of justice and fairness.

The KMS was critical of the punitive strategies of the management. It questioned the categorisation of certain practices as 'breaches of discipline'. 'Bad work', the KMS proposed, should not be punished, unless it was proved that it was a deliberate act; movement from one department to another should be punished only if was not for a 'bona fide purpose'; workers on piece-wages, it argued, should not be punished for 'short work', that is, for producing less than a specified output. Proposals like this reflect a difference between the management's conceptions and those of the KMS. It respected the sanctity of rules but it preferred 'definite' rules of discipline to ambiguities that allowed the possibilities of managerial manipulation. Besides, the KMS was insistent that managements observe certain norms. Corporal punishment and abusive language, the KMS emphasised, should be treated as 'severe breaches of discipline' on the part of managers.

The KMS was thus defining both the limits of managerial authority and worker freedom. The language of discipline embodied in the KMS memorandum was, however, the public voice of the KMS, different from its private, everyday idiom. In the day-to-day life of the factory, individual members of the KMS did not operate with the same notions of efficiency and commitment. Yet the public idiom was not empty rhetoric: it formed a part of the institutional ideology of the KMS and this gave legitimacy to the discourse of discipline in the factory.

Workers' attitudes reveal apparent contradictions: they resist and defy existing work norms, just as much as they reaffirm ideologies of work and discipline. Work, in fact, gave a sense of dignity and identity that was central to their self-conceptions. The relationship between work and notions of dignity are articulated much more sharply in the 1990s, in the context of mill closures, when there are few factory jobs. The despair of worklessness today makes even the act of remembering the grind and toil of the past a moment of pride for old workers.

CHAPTER 5

Confronting Authority

—⊰⊱—

In November 1919 industrial Kanpur witnessed its first general strike. The strike did not begin simultaneously in all factories. Weavers of the Woollen Mills struck work on Saturday, 22 November. Workers from other departments in the factory joined them on Monday morning and before midday the workers of Elgin Mills were on strike. By Tuesday morning the workers of Muir Mills, and by late afternoon the Victoria Mills workers, joined the strikers, with the total number on strike going up to 17,000. Later, workers of the Ganges Flour Mills, Dwarka Dass Jute Mills, Cooper Allen and Company, the Empire Engineering Company, the Government Harness and Saddlery Factory, and the North West Tannery joined the strike and the total numbers on strike swelled to over 20,000.[1] The strike continued for eight days. The strikers won substantial concessions: an increase in wages, bonus, and an improvement in working conditions.[2]

How do we read these events? How were solidarities constituted in November 1919? How do we recover the workers' experience of collective protest and organisation? Evidence on the strikes is framed in such conflicting narratives that it becomes difficult to disentangle the event from the stories. Colonial officials and mill managers denied the significance of any collectivity and pointed to the hidden hand of 'instigators' behind strikes. Accounts by trade union activists, in contrast, are framed within a narrative of

---

[1] *Pratap*, 1.2.1919; *Leader* 3.12.1919, 4.12.1919.

[2] The nature of concessions varied from mill to mill. The wage increases sanctioned to different categories of workers in the Woollen Mills varied between 15 per cent and 100 per cent. The workers of the Elgin, Muir, New Victoria and Cawnpore Cotton Mills were given a 25 per cent increase in wages. *Pratap*, 8.12.1919, 15.12.1919.

trade union organisation. The lineages of organisation are traced to the pre-strike period and the story of the workers' movement becomes a genealogy of organisation. So in reconstructing the past of the workers' movement we have to grapple with opposing myths: the myth of the 'instigator' and the myth of organisation.

Representing 1919

Official and non-official reports see the year 1919 as a temporal marker separating a past of quiescence from a present of worker militancy. In Kanpur and elsewhere, official reports point to the relative absence of strikes prior to this year. The Royal Commission of Labour in 1929 noted, for instance: 'prior to the winter of 1918–19, a strike was a rare occurrence in Indian industry.'[3] Such statements repress the evidence of earlier strikes. There is no evidence of generalised strikes in Kanpur before November 1919 but there were strikes in individual mills. In 1892, for instance, there was a strike in the Woollen Mills over the question of wages.[4] Managers admitted in 1908 that whenever workers found their wages were lower than what they customarily received, they would 'revolt'.[5] Besides there were also other modes of resistance, hidden and public, through which workers expressed their discontent with employers.

If evidence of large strikes in the pre-1919 period is lacking for Kanpur, this was not true of Bombay or Calcutta. There was a series of strikes in the Calcutta jute mills over 1895–6 and 1905–8.[6] Police reports refer to an 'epidemic' of strikes among printers

---

[3] *RCL Report*, p. 333.

[4] *UICC Report*, 1892, p. 91. There were also reports of petty strikes in 1889: *UICC Report* 1889, p. 15.

[5] Ev. Muir Mills, *IFLC*, p. 204. An official giving evidence to the IFLC asserted: 'It might sometimes happen that one or two men had the power to call out the whole staff, and they occasionally demanded an increase in the rates of pay. This, however, was only in individual mills, and there was no organisation to consider questions affecting their general interests, such as the restriction of hours.' Ev. Freemantle, *IFLC*, p. 220. Similar statements were repeated about other regions too. The All India Report of the Commission noted: 'While the operatives fully understand the machinery of local strikes . . . they are as yet unable to combine over any large area with the object of securing a common end by concerted action.' *IFLC*, p. 20.

[6] Sen, *Working Class of India*.

in Calcutta and to widespread railway strikes in 1906.[7] Even in these regions, when officials in 1928 looked back to the history of strikes, the post-war years appeared unquestionably as the beginning of troubled times.

To some extent it was the sweep of strikes in 1918–19, which obliterated the significance of earlier strikes. But the notion of a 'sweep' was itself a product of official imagination. 'Industrial unrest', officials said, was 'sweeping' India 'from end to end'.[8] The 'epidemic strike fever', reports note, was related partly to the 'world political unrest' and the frequent news of strikes in England and Europe.[9] What made the situation more alarming in official eyes was the evidence of coordination and organisation among workers. Officials were concerned at the 'unhealthy lines' on which labour was being organised in the country and the growing presence of 'extremists' among the organisers of labour. Secret reports felt 'the latest phases of labour organisation are entirely undisguised: they are the formation of big unions and of cooperative bodies. These are apparently direct imitations of trade union experiences in England, Canada and possibly elsewhere.'[10] Another report pointed to a tendency towards 'the amalgamation of local unions under Central Committees, which appears to be the present stage of labour politics in Madras and Cawnpore'.[11]

Strikes in Europe transformed attitudes in India. Officials and industrialists were gripped by the prospect of collective action, secret coordination, and spreading conflagration. It is this great fear that led officials to imbue 1919 with a special signification, seeing it as a watershed in the history of industrial Kanpur.

While strikes and labour organisation were not a new phenomenon, they acquired a new meaning in the context of the Bolshevik revolution. The events of 1917 now structure official narratives on labour and the theme of workers' insurrection recurs in these accounts. Strikes were seen as inevitably leading up towards an

[7] Sumit Sarkar, *The Swadeshi Movement in Bengal: 1903–1908* (New Delhi 1977), p. 211. Sarkar refers to reports about Calcutta 'agitators' wishing 'to get control of all the railway employees, and, following Russian examples, to add 'general strikes' to their armoury': p. 220.

[8] HPD Deposit, no. 52, Feb. 1920.

[9] HPD, B., nos 262–6, Dec. 1920.

[10] HPD Deposit, July 1920, File no. 104.

[11] HPD Deposit, Feb. 1920, File no. 75.

insurrectionary situation. 'Outsiders' in touch with workers' strikes are categorised as 'pro-Bolshevik extremists'.[12] Such fears are not peculiar to the Indian context, they underline official writings on labour in this period elsewhere too. But official reports drew consolation from the fact that the situation in India was 'by no means comparable with the present situation in England'. In contrast to England, therefore, the 'unrest' was said to be largely 'localised' and 'sporadic'.[13] The absence of trade union funds and all-India organisations of labour made possibilities of a prolonged movement difficult.

Contemporary accounts of trade unionists in Kanpur share with official narratives this conception of 1919 as a watershed. If officials saw 1919 as presaging a troubled time, trade unionists celebrated 1919 as the marker of a new era. The story of the workers' movement in Sudarshan Chakr's *Kanpur ka Mazdur Andolan* begins in 1919. The entire period before 1919 forms the prushtbhumi (background) of the movement to which one page is devoted in a 390-page-long account. From the prehistory of the movement the narrative moves to the beginnings of the movement after 1917. It is only after the revolution in Russia that the Kanpur workers wake up from their 'slumber'. '*Rus ki lal kirne, Kanpur jaaga*', is how the story begins for Chakr. The strikes of November 1919 are described as the 'first' in the history of the workers' movement in Kanpur. The narrative of the labour movement in many trade union accounts is in a sense a narrative of labour organisation. It opens with 1919–20, the year in which organised trade unionism started in India.

Colonial officials and managers saw no real collectivity behind the strikes of 1919. They pointed to the role of 'agitators' and 'provocateurs' in the spread of the strikes. In contrast to mill

[12] HPD Deposit, no. 75, Feb. 1920. The editors of *Pratap*, G.S. Vidyarthi and others belonged, according to the report, to a group of pro-Bolshevik extremists who 'tried to practice what they preach in the Mazdur Sabha and the Kisan Sabha of Cawnpur'. Official reports on the Kanpur Cotton riots of 1924 raised similar fears: 'It may be worth enquiring . . . whether this is not being financed in part at least, with Russian money.' Report on Cawnpore Cotton Mills Riots, HPD File 153,1924.

[13] Telegram, 25 Oct. 1920, from Viceroy to Secy of State for India, London HPD Progs., part B, Dec. 1920, nos 262–6.

managers, who denied any connection between the strikes and the economic demands of workers, provincial officials acknowledged the genuineness of economic grievances but pointed to 'something more than economic difficulty having moved them'.[14] Had they been related solely to universal economic grievances, they argued, a 'general simultaneous strike' was more likely. Instead they spread from mill to mill in a relay. The 'epidemic' character of the strikes, officials argued, was related to the news of 'world political unrest' and the activities of 'political agitators'.[15]

By identifying an 'instigator', officials and managers make a separation between the 'innocent' and the 'guilty', between the 'good' and the 'bad'. Strike leaders, in their accounts, do not share the problems of ordinary workers. They fabricate grievances and magnify problems; they misrepresent and delude. Such conceptions about strikes are important for the legitimation of authority. Within such a framework there is a belief in the essential stability of, and order within, the industrial system. Workers are contented, obedient and respectful of authority. Discontent and disorder are episodic, ephemeral and external to the working class situation. They are a creation of 'outsiders'.

Who were these instigators that troubled officials? The provocateurs were products of the official imagination. Accounts of the strikes of 1919, for instance, point at different 'instigators', from the pro-Bolshevik extremist and the non-cooperator to the intrepid weaver. Worried by the growing tide of nationalism in India and socialism elsewhere, the imperial mind discovered the hidden role of Bolsheviks and nationalists behind all social

[14] HPD Deposit, no. 52, Feb. 1920. Statements by managers similarly deny the connection between the strikes and economic demands; the strikes were sudden; workers who had been 'constant', 'abundant' and 'willing' earlier were suddenly struck by a 'strike fever'. *UICC Report*, 1919, p. ii. The *Pioneer*, a newspaper with close ties with Kanpur industrialists, similarly suggests that workers struck without genuine grievance: 'The vast majority of men apparently do not know why they have gone on strike or what it is exactly that they want.' The newspaper listed the various facilities being provided by employers, from housing schemes to cheap grain. *Pioneer*, 29.11.1919. Another report in the same paper asserted how reluctant workers were being intimidated into joining the strike. *Pioneer*, 30.11.1919.

[15] HPD Deposit, no. 52, Feb. 1920.

movements. The outsider, in many reports of 1919, is categorised
as the 'pro-Bolshevik extremist'. But the label 'Bolshevik' is used
for virtually anyone associated with peasants and workers'
movements. Thus in Kanpur the editors of *Pratap*, a liberal
nationalist newspaper, are called 'pro- Bolshevik extremists 'who
tried to practice what they preach in the Mazdur Sabha and the
Kisan Sabha of Cawnpur'.[16]

By focusing on the instigator, managers deny that workers had
any grievances, they refuse to recognise the discontents of the war
years. To understand these discontents, we need to look not only
at the economics of the war years but at the workers' experience
of suffering, an experience mediated by their own expectations
and beliefs.

Economic indices show a worsening of conditions by 1919.
Between 1918 and 1919 the cost of living index increased by 43
per cent and real wages declined by 31 per cent in the weaving
department and 30 per cent in the spinning (mules) department.
But the increase in cost of living had started earlier during the war.
Between 1911–12 and 1914, the cost of living index increased by
42 per cent and in 1915 by 52 per cent. Compared to the level in
1911–12, real wages in the spinning department dropped by
twenty-seven per cent in 1930 and thirty per cent by 1919.[17] The
experience of suffering was different in 1919. Continued hardship
when the war had ended created a widespread sense of moral outrage. Quiet endurance gave way to articulate anger. The drop in
real wages in 1919 was clearly not more dramatic than in the war
years.

The prosperity of the industry during the war years was quite
apparent to workers. The factories were receiving large orders.
The production of tent cloth increased by almost 3000 per cent.
Profits showed a more substantial increase after 1918, when war
controls relaxed. Cloth prices shot up in 1919 and the profits of
textile concerns in Kanpur rose despite the high supply price of
raw cotton in this period.[18] The state of the industry and the

---

[16] HPD Deposit, no. 75, Feb. 1920.

[17] Figures are calculated from *BSER: Wages and Labour Conditions in Cawnpore*. See also ch. 3.

[18] See ch. 1.

prevailing rates of wages outside the mills were important in defining workers' notion of fair wages. In public statements of grievances, workers argued that their wages should be doubled because the prices of textile products had more than doubled.[19] They pointed to the sharp difference between the wages of factory workers and of skilled and unskilled labour elsewhere in the city: 'Outside the mills the wages of workmen have almost doubled, the unskilled who used to get 4 as. or 5 as. a day now get 8 as. a day, while the skilled workmen, such as a mason, a carpenter now gets on an average from 9 and 10 as. a day to Re.1 and Re. 1–4 a day.'[20]

Unfair wages and unfair discipline became a focus of the workers' strikes in 1919. The expansion of textile production during the war had meant an intensification of labour: factories worked for longer hours and greater control was exercised over work breaks.[21] Almost all statements of grievance and descriptions of working conditions complained of the clocking of lavatory time by factory officials and the severity of the punishment in case of any violation.[22] The columns of *Pratap* carried reports of many such instances. In the Woollen Mills, a clerk kept a note of time and a minute over the specified ten minutes meant a fine of one anna.[23] Controls over work time were seen as a denial of freedom. Workers demanded the freedom to go to the lavatory when they needed to. They complained their leisure time was constantly snatched away from them, with the mill whistle going even before they could finish eating.[24]

Disease and epidemics made life wretched in the city in the post-war period. Contemporary reports describe the condition of the city in 1918–19. Kanpur was among the municipalities worst afflicted by the influenza epidemic of 1918.[25] The first wave of the

[19] 'Statement on Behalf of Labourers', *Leader,* 14.12.1919.

[20] Ibid.

[21] In some mills the same set of workers had to work two shifts, i.e., work almost twenty-four hours. *Pratap,* 25.8.1919. Cooper Allen and Co. worked all days of the week through the war period. *Leader,* 14.12.1919.

[22] *Leader,* 14.12.1919.

[23] *Pratap,* 24.11.1919.

[24] *Pratap,* 25.8.1919, 1.9.1919.

[25] UP Sanitation Progs., Feb. 1919, no.3 (UPSA).

epidemic lasted from August till mid-September, the second, beginning in October, caused many more deaths. Figures from the Elgin, Muir and Woollen Mills show that over 59 per cent of the workers in these mills were attacked by the fever. Between August and November 1918, 33 workers of Elgin Mills died of influenza, and over a single month there were 134 influenza deaths among workers of the Muir and Kanpur Woollen Mills and Kanpur Sugar Works.[26] The mortality figures for Kanpur, according to unofficial estimates, were around 300 per day as against the 200 recorded in the municipal registers.[27] Contemporary descriptions of death in the city paint a grim picture of long queues in the cremation grounds, the stench of unburnt corpses and the near-choking river with masses and masses of bodies.[28]

The issues raised by the strikers had been the focus of various memorandums and smaller strikes in the months preceding November 1919. Among the demands made were: a doubling of wages, bonus payment, more festival holidays, a nine-hour work-day, weekly payment of wages, fewer fines and an end to corporal punishment.[29]

While colonial officials and mill managers denied the connection between economic grievances and strikes, reports in local papers and accounts by worker activists saw the strikes as a logical outcome of the suffering of the war years. Local papers like *Pratap* emphasised the rise in the cost of living during the war years and the fall in the real wages of workers. Other longstanding non-economic grievances, it argued, made the strikes unavoid-able.[30] There are obvious problems with such a mechanistic connection between economic distress and strikes. What was important

[26] Ibid.

[27] *Pratap*, 28.10.1918.

[28] *Pratap*, 28.10.1918, 2.9.1919.

[29] Workers of New Victoria Mills had been on strike for over a month for some of these demands in September the same year and were promised a wage increase. But the increases were selectively granted only to weavers, and not to other workers.

[30] *Pratap*, 1.12.1919; *Abhyudaya* was critical of the attitude of the millowners: *Malum hota hai milvalon ne soch liya ki hamne mazduron ko mol liya aur ve hamare gulam hai* (The millowners seem to think that they have bought the workers and they are their slaves). *Abhyudaya*, 29.11.1919.

was the way in which suffering was perceived. Many of the problems raised by the strikers existed during the war years but there was no collective outrage against them till 1919. The end of the war brought a change in collective expectations. Falling real wages, long hours and harsh discipline were now experienced as unfair and unjust. Worker grievances now received wider public support. Besides, events in Russia and protests elsewhere in India gave a legitimacy to strikes in the eyes of workers.

The Question of Organisation

The Kanpur Mazdur Sabha was set up around 1919.[31] The exact date of its inception is difficult to establish. It appears that the sabha as a formal organisation had not emerged prior to the strike of November 1919.[32] In trade union narratives, the question of dating remains ambiguous, torn by conflicting pulls. There is on the one hand a desire to celebrate the generative power of 1919, seeing the organisation as a product of the strike itself; on the other is the urge to see the strike as the result of a prior organisation. An account which in one place recounts the initial efforts of the workers to set up a sabha during the strike, in another

---

[31] The initial sabha seems really an extension of a strike committee set up in Elgin Mills around 1919. Later, Congress leaders like Murari Lal and Ganesh Shankar Vidyarthi were invited to address a meeting at which ten representatives were elected to meet the Lt Governor. The committee included workers like Yakub, Lachman Prasad, Mohd. Shafi, Ramji Lal, Sheodarshan, Mathura Prasad and Chedi Lal. Along with them, Murari Lal, Narain Prasad Nigam, Abdul Karim, Wahid Yar Khan and Vidyarthi were chosen as non-worker representatives. J.C. Dixit, 'Kanpur Mazdur Sabha ka Shaishav Kal', in Ramesh Mishra and K.K. Sharma, eds, *Sri Surya Prasad Awasthi Hirak Jayanti Abhinandan Granth* (Kanpur 1973), p. 12. For more on nationalists and the KMS in this period, see ch. 8.

[32] Reports in *Pratap* point to the absence of an organised labour union in Kanpur. *Pratap*, 25.8.1919, 1.9.1919. The KMS was formally registered in July 1920 with Murari Lal as president, Kamdatt and N.P. Nigam as vice-presidents, Wahid Yar Kahn as secretary and G.S. Vidyarthi and Abdul Karim as joint secretaries. *Pratap*, 26.7.1920. The executive committee of the KMS consisted of two representatives from each mill. These were elected at meetings held at mill gates. Mehta to Clow, 2.4.1921, Dept of Ind. and Labour, L-877 (ii), 1922.

pushes the founding moment of the organisation back to a period before 1919. But is it really important to fix a date of inception? For a historian, what seems meaningful is not the untangling of dates from conflicting narratives but an understanding of the processes through which the organisation was constituted.

Workers identify organisations through flags, symbols and slogans. They often recount the story of the organisation through a history of these symbols. By the 1930s the KMS is associated with the red flag bearing a hammer and sickle. In 1919 there was no common symbol: strikers carried a variety of banners they could identify with. Raghubir described how some workers marched with a soop, others carried a chalni.[33] Chakr writes of the heterogeneity of colours and symbols used by the strikers:

> *Rang birange dhwaja uthaye*
> *Laal laal tab jaan na paaye,*
> *Oollen meel oon ko jhanda*
> *Joota tana tannery danda.*[34]

> (The workers carried flags of different hues
> The red flag was unknown
> The woollen mill workers carried a flag of wool
> The tannery workers hung a shoe atop a pole.)

There are two levels of emphasis in Chakr's account. One is the lack of awareness of the red flag: an awareness which, in his scheme, is a necessary part of the working class learning process. Implicitly, tab (then) in Chakr's account is counterposed to ab (now), when they *do* know the red flag. The symbols are thus hierarchised and temporally sequenced: there is a movement from the more transparent, self-evident symbols of the workers' past to the abstract symbolism of the present. Being more aware, workers can now associate with images not directly drawn from their work experience in the factory. The contrast between the heterogeneity of symbols in the past and the homogenising red of the present reflects also a movement from a time of segmentation of the working class with all its particularities, to a time of unity.

---

[33] Soop = a winnowing basket, chalni = a sieve. Interview Raghubir, 8.12.1978.

[34] Chakr, *Communist Katha*, p. 226.

Thus while 1919 marks a shift from individualised to organised protest, it is represented in retrospective worker accounts only as a preliminary stage in a long process towards unity.

Oral testimonies appropriate from a range of symbolism of the past what appears meaningful within their story of the working class movement. The oral testimony on the imagery used seems to be of two kinds. In Chakr's account, the symbols are drawn directly from the urban industrial context in the city, while Raghubir talks of peasant symbols. In Chakr's scheme there is no room for symbols that do not have an association with industrial life. The workers of each factory adopt a distinct sign associated with their work, representing themselves through particular objects which were discreet embodiments of their concrete labours. The peasant symbolism of Raghubir's narrative is of course familiar to most workers. The soop and chalni seem as natural as the symbols associated with work in the city. As a second generation worker in the city, what appears meaningful to Chakr is the transition from fragmentation to unity, a process which takes place within a working class rooted in industrial work. For Raghubir, an older worker, the transition from a peasant consciousness to working class consciousness is of greater significance.

In both Raghubir's and Chakr's account, there is an unresolved tension between the spontaneity of the strikes, the anarchy of symbols used, and the organising role of the KMS in the strikes. Raghubir's story shifts from a description of different flags to the founding of the KMS without giving any fixed chronology. Chakr's written narrative is structured along conventional trade union lines, in which organisation is privileged and given precedence. In his account, the story of the 'first strike' is preceded by an account of the birth of the KMS.[35] Although Chakr admits that there is no consensus about the chronology of the KMS, he infers from oral accounts of workers of that period that the sabha came into being in 1918. He asserts pedagogically: 'It is only when the oppressed workers formed an organisation that they could clench their fists and fight.'[36] The sequence of events here is not drawn

---

[35] See Chakr, *Kanpur Mazdur Andolan*, p. 8.
[36] '*Sataye hue mazduron ka jab sangathan bana tab unki panchon ungliyon ka milkar ghunsa bhi tana.*' Chakr, *Kanpur Mazdur Andolan,* p. 10.

through precise calendar time but according to an assumed teleology of workers' movement. To Chakr, a sequence in which organisation precedes strikes seems natural. Workers' unity is seen on the one hand as a product of prior organisation; on the other, as expressive of the very process of organisation. The relay process through which the strikes spread from the Woollen Mills to Elgin, to Muir and Victoria over three days, described in contemporary newspaper accounts, is erased in Chakr's account.[37] In his narration the strike begins almost with a bang, with all workers collectively putting down their tools. At the stroke of 11 a.m. on 24 November, as planned, all the mills rapidly went on strike[38] ('*Sabhi milo mein mashino ki dharkan band ho gayi*').

There are other ways in which metanarratives of organisation seek to frame the evidence of workers' movements, even as the evidence resists such interpretation. Retrospective accounts of the workers' movement tend to imbue a series of discrete events in the past with a coherence and unity, secularising events and erasing the blurred lines between the sacred and the profane.

The initiation of the KMS is traced in trade unionist accounts to the initiative of Kamdatt, an ex-worker from Elgin Mills and an Arya Samaj updeshak at the local Arya Pratinidhi Sabha. Closely associated with Kamdatt in this effort was Lala Devidayal, also an Arya Samajist and worker in Elgin Mills. Kamdatt, according to these accounts, inaugurated the sabha with the ritual of a havan at Munnu mochi's, a leather worker's house, in Khalasi Lines. Munnu's house became a regular venue for worker meetings. Neighbourhood workers gathered regularly at Munnu mochi's, wrote handbills on worker grievances and pasted them on mill gates.[39] At times meetings were held at the residences of Budhu and Jodha, both of whom were paan (betel-leaf) vendors. From

[37] See for instance, *Pratap*, 1.12.1919. A 'Statement on Behalf of Labourers' published in *Leader* is quite explicit: 'The strike in these mills did not take place simultaneously. It began in the Woollen Mills . . . spreading to other mills on subsequent dates during the course of the last week.' *Leader*, 14.12.1919.

[38] Machines in all mills stopped.

[39] Sadhna Sharma, 'The Organisation, Development and Working of Kanpur Mazdur Sabha', unpublished master's dissertation in Economics, Agra University, 1952.

Khalasi Lines the sabha activities extended towards Gwaltoli bazaar, moving from an old widow's shack to Maiku Lal Sahu's and then to Barku halwai's.[40] The location of the sabha centre in and around Gwaltoli was significant. This was the area where some of the oldest mills were located; it was the geographical centre from where many strikes began.

Havans and kathas were popular modes through which bonds were created between those with shared regional and caste ties in the urban milieu. The organisation of kathas was within the conventions of mohalla social life but it was a mode through which different kinds of messages could be conveyed. In the 1930s, for instance, the local Kureel Sabha appealed to Kureels to organise Raidas kathas where the story of Raidas, a lower-caste saint, would be told instead of the usual story of Satyanarayan. [41] For Arya Samajists, like Kamdatt, the havan accompanied with the chanting of Vedas was a sacred ritual. It purified those who participated in them and created bonds of a political community in which all castes were to be incorporated.

In accounts of worker activists these rituals are represented as part of a secular bonding and integrated to the genealogy of trade union organisation. To Raghubir, who identified closely with the communist KMS of the 1930s, the association of religious symbols with worker organisation in the past appeared as a garb: religious rituals being necessary for secrecy at a time when there were official restrictions on trade union activities. Besides, his KMS does

[40] Chakr, *Kanpur Mazdur Andolan*, p. 10. In 1924 the sabha acquired land and a permanent structure was erected. To trade unionists of the 1930s and 1940s, used to the idea of a fixed union office, its absence in the initial few years, seems anomalous and a reflection of the adversities the sabha had to fight to survive. Raghubir recounted, for instance, how funds for erecting a permanent building for the sabha were raised by getting some workers to sell wood in the sabha compound. Interview, Raghubir. The union was dependent on small contributions of 8 as. to Re. 1 from members. Its small membership limited its fund-raising capacity. In 1929 only 16 per cent of the total workforce were KMS members, a contrast to the Girni Kamgar Union of Bombay, whose membership constituted 45 per cent of the total workforce. But in the early 1920s, the KMS membership was obviously larger, its total funds, amounting to Rs 6000, were four times that of 1929.

[41] Ramcharan Kureel, *Kureel Bhaiyon ki Seva Mein Khuli Chitthi* (Kanpur 1934).

not have a Hindu stamp: it alternates easily between Hindu and Muslim religious rituals.[42] Similarly, Chakr in his description of the havan ritual does not attach any significance to its religious connotation. He adds quickly that workers of all communities, Hindu, Muslim, Christian participated in the havan.[43]

The sites at which the early meetings were held are important: space was provided by Munnu, Budhu and Jodha, all belonging to lower castes. This was a period when Arya Samajists were engaged in a campaign for the moral uplift of lower castes through proselytisation and shuddhi (reconversion) activities.[44] Kamdatt's activities formed part of this Arya Samajist attempt to reach out to lower castes. He and other Arya Samajists emphasised the importance of education and physical culture among workers. Purification of the mind and body was seen as essential to the making of a good Arya.

Religious gatherings were only one of the many ways in which ties were created and reaffirmed. There were various other informal networks in the mohalla and the workplace through which workers shared experiences and forged solidarities. Workers had regular addas where they stopped before or after a shift, exchanged news and chatted over puffs of the hookah. At the workplace, the sly smoke at the lavatory, away from the watchful eyes of the supervisor, and the sharing of jokes about those in authority, forged bonds.

The KMS, like most unions in India, had to constantly grapple with the problems of a fluctuating membership and inadequate financial resources. Its membership in the late 1920s was 3000, it went up to 12,000 by 1938, but by 1930–1 it had dropped to 682.[45] Periods of decline in membership were also times when

[42] Interview, Raghubir.

[43] In his account of the workers' movement in Kanpur, Chakr attaches little significance to Kamdatt's Arya Samaj background. Playing on Kamdatt's identity as a worker, Chakr emphasises the role of an ordinary worker in initiating the sabha and questions traditional assumptions which overlook the workers' own capacity for organising themselves. *Kanpur Mazdur Andolan,* p. 27.

[44] On this, see ch. 7.

[45] Ev. UP Govt, *RCL III (i)*, p. 187, Ev. Harihar Nath Shastri, KLIC Progs., UP Ind. Progs., File 1145, 1937, Bundle 110 (UPSA). Around 2776 workers

its income fell. The total funds with the sabha in 1921 were Rs 6000;[46] by 1929 its income declined and it was left with virtually nothing at the close of the year in 1929.[47] Unions in India never had the resources to provision for strikers. Meetings calling on workers to mobilise funds for strikes often met with a poor response.[48] In Kanpur, as in other industrial cities in India, strikers had to organise alternative sources for themselves. Many returned to their villages, others did odd jobs in the city.[49]

The Depression years (1929–31) were troubled times for workers in the city, times of wage cuts and retrenchment, yet there was a distancing from the KMS in these years. A sense of belonging and identity with the union could only grow in periods when it seemed capable of representing workers' demands. In 1930–1, the sabha seemed powerless: its influence was limited to a few mills in the vicinity of Gwaltoli. The declining membership and the alienation of large numbers of Muslim workers made it more ineffectual. After 1936–7 the KMS became more powerful and identification with the sabha was a source of pride for workers.

Exercising Power

Moments of collective action give important insights into the modes of exercise of power. In many recent studies on labour,

---

were reported to have left the sabha between 1929 and 1930. Annual Report on the Working of the Trade union Act, Dept of Ind. and Labour, L-1524 (17), 1930.

[46] Mehta to Clow, 2.4.1921, Dept of Ind. and Labour, L-877 (ii), 1922.

[47] Its opening balance in 1929 was Rs 4 and after an income of Rs 1033-6-0 during the year, it was left with Rs 15 only after meeting its annual expenses. Annual Report on the Working of the Trade Union Act, Dept of Ind. and Labour, L-1524 (17), 1930, App. 1.

[48] In 1922, for instance, efforts by Ramzan Ali to call on workers to raise strike funds evoked no enthusiasm. The Intelligence Dept noted: 'This call for large funds is not likely to add to their [meetings] popularity.' SAID, 23.12.1922. In 1924, again, Ramzan's efforts to raise strike funds were unsuccessful. SAID, 29.11.1924.

[49] Its members were required to pay a subscription of one pice per rupee earned. The subscription for those earning up to Rs 30–40 a month—the highest-income category in textile mills in the 1920s—came to 8 as to Re. 1 per month. Ev. UP Govt, RCL III (i), 1931, p. 187, Mehta to Clow, 2.4.1921, Dept of Ind. and Labour, L-877 (ii), 1922 (NAI).

structures of power appear all-pervasive. This argument occurs in two forms. In one, managerial decisions play a determining role: they not only influence the formation of the workforce and relations at the workplace; they stifle all possibilities of sustained resistance.[50] In the second, pre-modern structures have a determining influence on the way power is exercised; managerial authority is represented as personalised, arbitrary and excessive.[51] While the two arguments are at one level distinct and opposed, they share certain common assumptions. Both frameworks deny the significance of worker practices and the processes of everyday negotiation in the structuration of power.[52]

A closer look at the ways in which power was exercised reveals its fractured and internally troubled nature. Structures of authority were not monolithic and compact. Different segments worked with different calculations and strategies, creating spaces for conflict and negotiation. At any moment, some in positions of authority could be open to dialogue while others were recalcitrant and repressive. The interests of the state and managers did not always coincide. The moral pressures on the state to be conciliatory at times ran counter to the imperatives of capital. The fissured nature of power often made it possible for the state to distance itself from managers, presenting itself as impartial and just, willing to hear the voices of workers at a time when managers were intractable. All members of the bureaucracy did not share the same attitude towards labour; some were seen as more non-partisan than others.

In 1919 the attitude of the state towards the strikers was important in determining the politics of negotiation. The police was not rushed in to repress the strikers.[53] The provincial governor, Harcourt Butler, met the strikers and expressed his sympathy with

[50] See, for instance, Chandavarkar, *Imperial Power and Popular Politics,* p. 119

[51] Chakrabarty, *Rethinking.*

[52] See ch. 3.

[53] A report in *Pratap* approvingly noted that in contrast to its attitude during the recent Victoria Mills strike, the colonial authorities had remained impartial ('*Victoria Mill ki pahli hartal mein police milvalon ke ishare par dauri dauri phirti thi, parantu is bar vah nahi hili. Acha hai, adhikari jan nishpaksh rahe*'). *Pratap,*1.12.1919.

their demands. His intervention was crucial in forcing managers to come to a settlement. After 1919, the context changed. Factory managers responded to strikes with threats of lockouts, mass dismissals and fresh recruitment. Grievances against harsh and unjust mistris and supervisors, and victimisation, were common to most mills, yet there was no mass collective protest over these issues. The number of strikers and workers involved in each strike dwindled after 1919, reaching the lowest point in 1930–1.[54] The situation in the labour market was reverse. The temporary shortage created by the influenza epidemic and army recruitment eased, the military demand for textiles fell, stocks accumulated and cloth prices declined. The managers of the Woollen Mills threatened to dismiss workers protesting against non-payment of bonus in March 1920.[55] During a strike in protest against an unpopular European overseer in Victoria Mills, the management declared a lockout and threatened strikers with dismissal. The workers returned to work after forty-five days of strike with none of their demands met.[56] In contrast to 1919, managerial recalcitrance now had implicit official sanction.

Although wide collective solidarities were not forged in this period, protests and representations against unfair managerial practices were made and these shaped the way in which power was exercised. Even in times when managements seemed inflexible and unresponsive, the public statements of workers often affirm their refusal to submit to unfair dictates. Petitions addressed to

[54] From Dec. 1919 to March 1920 there were 14 strikes involving a total of 14,000 workers. Over 1921–4 there were 16 strikes involving only 8000 workers. The figures are based on: HPD, part B, File 189,1920; Report on strikes in UP, Dept of Ind. and Labour, L-877 (ii), May 1922, L-877 (5), 1924, L-877 (6), 1924, L 877 (14), 1930; 'Weekly reports on the Labour Situation in India', Dept of Ind. and Labour, L-918 (2),1929, L-918 (24), 1930. Gaps checked from *Pioneer, Leader,* and Ev. UP Govt, *RCL III (i),* pp. 190–1. Many of the strikes immediately after 1919 were over the question of enforcement of bonus and wage revisions given by the strike settlement of 1919. After the mid-1920s the questions of victimisation, the injustices of mistris, and the cruelties of European supervisors became the focus of strikes.

[55] *Pratap,* 1.3.1920. The Elgin management gave a similar threat to strikers protesting against a delay in wage payment. *Pratap,* 31.5.1920.

[56] Dept of Ind. and Labour, L-877 (6), 1924.

managers by workers in the 1920s articulate a sense of resolution, and an attempt to hold out and preserve their dignity and justice in the face of managerial recalcitrance. A petition to the management from the workers of Victoria Mills in 1924 powerfully asserts a notion of workers' rights and their determined resistance to unjust terms.

> Saheb, we have seen your notice of the 29th. Not one among us is prepared to resume work on your terms. As for your talk of dismissing all of us and making fresh recruitment, we totally refuse to accept this.
>   We want to be taken back as old employees so that our existing rights continue . . . If you do not accept the terms and do not give us a reply today, we will announce this to all workers tomorrow. After this the workers will all leave for their villages or look for other jobs.[57]

The tone of the petition also marks an important shift from the abject and humble language in which workers made representations in an earlier period. A representation by fifty spinners and weavers of the Cawnpore Cotton Mills in 1908 has a tone of utter helplessness, a public acknowledgement of their own powerlessness: 'We cannot ask for shorter hours as we cannot combine, and anyone putting himself forward would be dismissed.'[58] The point is not to trace a teleology of change, with workers becoming more assertive in their public statements. Petitions had to follow certain conventions and were often phrased in the legal language of trade unionists, and there is no necessary evolutionary pattern. Yet the way in which they capture the prevalent mood of the workers is significant.

State intervention in issues concerning labour had to take these attitudes into account in framing official policy. Even in repressive situations like 1924 efforts had to be made to heal the wounds of the workers. Official discourse on the Kanpur Cotton Mills strike of 1924 gives important insights into the interrelationship between the state, workers and managers and the complex ways in which

---

[57] Reproduced in *Aaj*, 5.1.1924. A statement by workers of the Baijnath Balmukund Sugar Works conveys a similar attitude: 'If you hope to keep the mill working then we should all be given a holiday on Sundays. We are giving you a notice on the 1st that you must give us a reply or else we will all leave work . . .' Report by Factory Manager, Robinson, encl. by Director, Ind., UP to Secy, Ind., GOI, 26.3.1924, Dept of Ind. and Labour, L-877 (6), 1924.

[58] *IFLC*, p. 218.

power was negotiated and exercised. The strike was described as a 'riot' in official terminology. The workers of the Kanpur Cotton Mills who went on a sit-in strike in April 1924 to press for their bonus demands were described as 'truculent', 'obdurate', 'defiant'. Managerial warnings of dismissal met with an aggressive response: workers smashed windows and threatened to set fire to the stocks of cotton in the factory. A large number stayed inside, despite the pleas of Murari Lal, the KMS president, asking them to leave the compound.[59] When the city magistrate summoned a mounted police force and ordered the strikers to leave, the workers retorted: 'Who can turn us out?'[60] The mounted police charged on the workers, forcing them out of the mill compound. The strikers continued to resist, gathering along the road outside and at the gate, and attacking the police with brickbats. The police fired at the workers. Many were injured. 'Yelling and shrieking the crowd then began to disperse in different directions.' After the firing stopped, the mounted police launched a final clearing operation: 'The sowars galloped their horses and mercilessly charged men in hiding . . . The charge continued for about ten minutes.'[61]

State discourse on the strike was made of contradictory strands. Public statements on the Kanpur Cotton Mills events were overwhelmingly justificatory. There was an emphatic defence of the actions of the local bureaucracy and police. The report of the official inquiry into the riots commended the 'admirable behaviour' of the police and the 'utmost forbearance' shown towards the strikers by the management, the magistrate and the police. It denied the use of any 'unnecessary violence' by the sowars. The police, according to the report, was left with no option but to fire, given the 'rain of missiles' thrown at them by the strikers.[62] The district magistrate proposed that cases be instituted against all those who had shot wounds asserting: '. . . these persons must clearly have taken part in the riot.'[63]

In secret correspondence, official concerns appear to be different.

[59] Cawnpore Cotton Mills Riots: Report of the Magisterial Enquiry, HPD, File 153, 1924.

[60] Cawnpore Cotton Mills Riots Report, HPD, File 153,1924.

[61] 'Non-official statement on the Cawnpore Cotton Mills Riot' Pioneer, 9.4.1924.

[62] HPD, File 153,1924.

[63] DM's interim report 5.4.1924, HPD, File 153,1924.

The defence of police action is overruled by an emphasis on the need for confidence-restoring gestures. Soon after the events, the district magistrate, Clay, declared: 'I have let it be known that no more arrests will be made. We have got 22 men on bail or in hospital awaiting trial which seems enough to satisfy justice. I hope this will restore confidence.' He was convinced that the strikers had been punished effectively and there was no need for further prosecution against rioters. In any case, the district magistrate acknowledged that the case against the rioters was weak: 'The men we prosecute will obviously say they were onlookers and never joined in the brick throwing. We cannot possibly prove they did. It was pitch dark and there was an Ephesian uproar going on.'[64]

The withdrawal of cases against the rioters posed problems. The state feared a loss of authority. Its critics could get a chance to allege: 'The case is obviously false . . . the government has not dared to run it.' The district magistrate rehearsed the scenario carefully, visualising the entire performance. A script was prepared carefully, the actors were given allocated parts. The district magistrate was confident: 'If we can approximate the programme I think it can be staged.' The programme ran as follows:

> The workers should come to me with a deputation praying for mercy on their misguided brethren, now being prosecuted for rioting. I will receive them with sympathy and try to pour some oil on troubled waters and promise to supplicate the long suffering and beneficent Sarkar. Government can then bring out a resolution recapitulating the facts, upholding if it sees fit the action of the Deputy Magistrate and police and finally, in view of the strikers having been misled by agitators, announcing its intention as the result of the DM's intercession and its own long suffering and forbearance, to withdraw as an act of pure grace and pending prosecutions.

A distinction was made, however, between the main 'agitators' and others: the former had no claim to clemency.

These rituals through which power was exercised were important in shaping popular perceptions of the state. Official and non-official discourse on the strike shows the ways in which workers

[64] Clay to Lambert, Chief Secy, UP, 13.4.1924, UP GAD, File 218, 1924, Box 432 (UPSA).

negotiated between contradictory images of the state, between its benevolent and repressive face. In 1919, when the state was sympathetic to workers' demands, the workers saw the state as impartial and just. State violence and the repression of 1924 destroyed this faith in the state.[65] Facing a crisis of legitimacy, provincial officials made gestures of mercy in an attempt to restore confidence in the state. But the brutality of police action against strikers was etched in workers' memories. A favourite tale about 1924 recounted even today describes strikers being thrown into boilers in the factory.[66] In 1923 there were rumours that the mill authorities at Elgin Mills sprayed boiling water on striking workers.[67] The use of water cannon against workers by the police is described in this narrative as a spray of boiling water ('*Kaha jata hai ki milvalon ne mazduron par kholte hue pani ki mar ki*').[68] In worker accounts 'khooni' [bloody] cotton mill episode became a metaphor for state violence—the trauma of 1924 was recalled during other moments of repression. In 1947, when the police fired on a workers' demonstration, the events of 1924 were retold, linking present repression with the past. A worker recounted how in 1924, the mounted police suddenly entered the Cawnpore Cotton Mills compound from a little-used gate at the back, an act of cowardice which magnified the maleficence of the state ('*Mill ke piche vale gate se jo kabhi kabhi hi khula karta tha ghursawar ghus aye*'). When the workers tried to resist the attack by

---

[65] Statements like the following recurred in local reports: 'the massacre of the poor labourers of the Cawnpore Cotton Mill reminds us of the Jallianwala Bagh tragedy. This massacre was apparently organised to crush the new awakening among the labourers of Cawnpore.' *Vartman*, 9.4.1924, press clippings UP GAD, 218,1924, Box 432 (UPSA). The *Kartavya* pointed out that the police authorities 'did not care for the lives of mill-hands otherwise they would not have fired above the waist . . .' *RNP*, 26.4.1924.

[66] Interview, Moolchand, 30.10.1983. Chakr, *Kanpur Mazdur Andolan*, p. 24.

[67] *Pratap*, 30.7.1923

[68] It is rumoured that millowners attacked workers with boiling water. The district magistrate writes in his report: '. . . the strikers refused to leave the mill building they had eventually to be turned out by the police by force . . . the water hose was brought into play with a view to stopping the brick throwing . . .' Clay to Lambert, Commsr, 21 Aug. 1924, UP GAD, 218,1924, Box 432 (UPSA).

throwing coal from a heap in the compound, the sowars let loose their fury ('*Ghursawar mazduron par paglon ki bhanti jhapat pare. Dur dur tak khader kar ghoron se mazduron ko rond dala*').[69]

In recollections of traumatic pasts, no distinctions are made between state and managerial violence or between individual officials—all seem complicit in the acts of repression. Day-to-day negotiations of workers with those in authority were more complex. Even in moments of crisis, there is evidence of workers drawing distinctions between the attitude of different officials. In 1924, a letter by workers to the district magistrate asking for withdrawal of cases against those wounded in the police firing, expresses their faith in him: 'We cannot help mentioning, Sir, that each and every labourer and inhabitant of the city believe that had the news reached you in time you would have no doubt come to the spot and no disturbance of any kind or firing would have taken place.'[70] How are we to understand such statements? The petition is structured along conventions usual to such appeals for mercy. The petitioners claimed innocence and tried to evoke pity in order to ask for clemency. Absolving themselves from blame, the appellants glorified the impartiality of the district magistrate and implicitly legitimised repressive action against those who instigated or committed acts of violence against the state. Written under the direction of colonial officials, the statement cannot reveal the private transcript of workers. What it does show, however, is the significance the state attached to the language of faith, clemency and benevolence. The state sought to represent itself as benevolent, implicating workers in reaffirming this image. But this language had a power in reproducing certain conventions, which structured relations between workers and the state. A repeated use of such language could create ambivalent images—of a benevolent and repressive state power. A look at other evidence shows that these contradictory images were not entirely

[69] Shivdutt Shukla, 'Kanpur Cotton Mill Golikand', *Samajvaad*, 6.1.1948.

[70] Petition of the employees of the Cotton Mills to the DM, File 218,1924 UP GAD, Box 432 (UPSA). Pleading for withdrawal of riot cases against those wounded in the firing, the petition argues: 'You might have come to know that none of these wounded labourers was a ring leader or a lecturer. By chance they became the victims of the shots. . . and are therefore reckoned as accused.'

false. Notions of a beneficent and just state were often sustained through individual officials who came to be identified as humane and just. Officials like Clay in Kanpur, for instance, acquired a reputation for being more judicious and forbearing than others.[71]

Workers' notions of a benevolent sarkar were articulated in opposition to images of managerial malevolence. What accounts for such representations? Kanpur managers came mostly from two kinds of backgrounds: there were those who had acquired wealth and status as indigo planters or Company officials. Others like John Harwood, Atherton West, Francis Horsman, Alexander Macrobert were from ordinary working class families. In Kanpur they became part of the city's social élite and displayed their racial and class status in various ways. This industrial élite, which had been introduced to Kanpur through tales of the 'Cawnpore massacre' and 'native treachery' in 1857, were active in associations like the Cawnpore volunteers, with an exclusively European and Anglo-Indian membership. The Volunteers trained in military combat and participated in mock battles and parades and organised a social life around balls, sports and drinking.[72] Entrepreneurs like Gavin Jones were like virtual heroes who had narrowly escaped killing and come back to rebuild a new Kanpur. Mill managers in Kanpur were known for their conservative views: some like Hugh Maxwell were vociferous in their opposition to Ripon's liberal reforms.[73] In the 1920s, European capitalists in Kanpur pressed for more vigorous action against the non-cooperators. Reports for this period contrast the patience and caution of district officials against the hostile attitude of Kanpur managers towards the Congress satyagrahis.[74]

[71] The *Pratap* counterposed the hostile and intolerant attitude of industrialists towards the Congress boycott campaign with Clay's exceedingly patient and tolerant attitude: *Kanpur ke vartman collector Mr Clay. . . atyant dhairyavan aur sahishnu hai. Pratap*, 29.5.1922. In Elgin Mills, in June 1928, the intervention of the District Magistrate, Munro, was considered crucial in persuading the mill management to accept terms that would be acceptable to the workers. *Leader*, 20.6.1928.

[72] Yalland, *Boxwallahs*, p. 264.

[73] 'The native feeling shown through the native press ought to convince the Government how unfit the native mind is to appreciate and sympathise with European ideas of administering the government of a country and people.' Hugh Maxwell to Tom Tracy, cited in Yalland, ibid., p. 227.

[74] *Pratap*, 29.2.1922. A Kanpur entrepreneur, Thomas Smith, later director,

Managerial authority, Chakrabarty has argued, was based not just on its repressive powers but on their paternal mai-bap image. The managerial sources from which Chakrabarty derives his description of jute managers in Bengal naturally magnifies the benevolence of managers. From Kanpur we hear of stories of McRoberts sitting on a charpoy with workers in their settlement, of Butterworth giving the healing touch to injured workers, and of John Stewart (Harness and Saddlery Factory) holding a durbar with workers at the back of his bungalow.[75] Although much of this evidence is drawn from managerial sources, the fact that this self-image was important to them and that they took pride in their ability to establish proximity with workers, is significant. Appreciation for the services of McRoberts of the Woollen Mills or Watson of Cooper Allen and Company in local papers like *Pratap* tends to reaffirm this paternal self-image of managers.[76] The typical mai-bap was someone like Butterworth—no different from the jute manager in Calcutta—who was both a father figure and one who carried a swagger-cane under his arm which he used whenever he spotted workers breaking rules.[77]

Colonial officials had a different perception of managers. They pointed to the lack of personal contact between mill managements and workers: 'Every mill at Kanpur keeps a petition box into which written representations intended for the manager can be dropped.'[78] Written representations are here being counterposed

Muir Mills, was one of four Europeans to sit on the Hunter Commission of 1919, to inquire into the Jallianwala Bagh massacre. Smith was ostracised by members of the Cawnpore Club for being too harsh on Dyer. Yalland, *Box-wallahs*, p. 418.

[75] Yalland, *Boxwallahs*, pp. 239, 245, 425. Stewart made a great personal effort to organise famine relief for workers in 1877, affected gravely by the famine that year. Stewart, Yalland writes, 'had earned for himself the title *Ma-Bap*' (p. 239).

[76] In a powerful piece on the strike of 1919, entitled '*Hartal kyon hui*', indicting mill managers for their failings, Vidyarthi pays tribute to McRoberts and Watson: '*Ye dono sajjan anya mill valon se kahin udar aur durdarshi hain. Aur unhonne apne dhang se mazduron ke kalyan ka kam itna avashya kiya hai . . .*' (these two gentlemen are far more liberal and farsighted than other millowners and they have in their own way done a great deal for workers' welfare. *Pratap*,1.12.1919.

[77] Yalland, *Boxwallahs*, p. 249.

[78] Oral ev. UP Govt, *RCL III (ii)*, p. 194.

to verbal communication between managements and workers. While verbal contact was direct, written petitions were impersonal and indirect. The government witness to the Royal Commission was dismissive of industrialists' claims of regular and easy contact between managers and workers: 'As for the view of the Chamber, the witness quipped 'it should hardly expect it to be any different . . . after all they are employers and naturally would take up that line.'[79]

Worker witnesses to the Labour Inquiry Commission in 1938 shared a similar view and emphasised the inaccessibility of managers.[80] Such images become more powerful in moments of crisis when the distance between workers and mill authorities widens. In strikes after 1919, managers appeared intractable and unrelenting. In many instances a demand by workers to directly negotiate with managers was sternly repressed. Even those typified as paternal could be vilified at such moments. At the Woollen Mills in March 1920, when the manager physically took one worker aside from a group gathered outside his office, there was general alarm that the worker was being beaten up. To the workers, the body language of the manager suggested impending violence. The workers became belligerent, abused the sahibs, and refused to leave when the mill authorities tried to lock them out. Ultimately the sahibs pushed out the workers from the compound with the support of the police ('*Police bulai gai aur sahebo ne dhakka dena arambh kiya. Ant mein mazdur zabardasti nikale gaye*').[81] In the Cawnpore Cotton Mills, the manager refused to negotiate with the workers. When they insisted on a meeting, and organised a demonstration, the mill superintendent pulled out his gun and fired shots in the air, terrifying the demonstrators. He then locked the factory and called in the police.[82]

[79] Ibid.

[80] Ramcharan, a weaver in the Kanpur Textiles, for instance, complained: 'The manager could not be approached . . . because there was a notice to the effect that he could be approached only through the mistri and the departmental in charge.' Similarly Zawar Husain, a weaver in the Kanpur Cotton Mills, was not aware of any system by which workers could approach the manager with a grievance. KLIC Progs., File 1145,1937, Bundle 160 (UPSA).

[81] *Pratap*,1.3.1920

[82] Mehta, to Clow, Dept of Ind. and Labour, L-877 (ii) May 1922.

Ties of race that linked managers and European supervisors together in the exercise of authority in the mills were reaffirmed during situations of crisis. Managerial interventions in defence of the unfair practices of supervisors deepened the chasm that divided them from workers. Managers gave wide discretionary powers to European supervisors in the day-to-day relationships in the factory. In the 1920s, the question of assault by European officials was frequently raised. In Victoria Mills in 1923, workers demanded the dismissal of C.W. Taylor, a European overseer, on these grounds. In Elgin Mills in May 1928 workers went on strike against the beating up of a worker by Rider, a European supervisor. The mill management came to the supervisor's defence and denied the charge altogether.[83] At such moments, class solidarity was reaffirmed through racial ties between managers and supervisors. There were instances of counter-violence, with workers physically assaulting harsh supervisors. Surajpal, a worker in Elgin Mills, assaulted a mill official taking his rounds, hitting him on the head.[84] A supervisor nicknamed Bambai Sahib in the same mill was violently attacked by workers during the night shift.[85]

Disciplining Labour

Questions of control and the maintenance of order troubled not just managers and the state but also trade union leaders. Nationalist leaders associated with the KMS in the 1920s were concerned with keeping workers under control. Underlying this concern was a dread of workers' violence. 'If a strike is prolonged there was always a fear that starving workers could become violent'—this was a belief shared by many KMS leaders.[86] To prevent such situations from arising, they argued, timely intervention by the

[83] The Managing Director, Taylor, asserted: 'It is obvious that a strike having been decided on, the alleged assault was an invention to justify the action of the workers.' *Leader*, 13.6.1928. No action was taken against Rider. Police records were tampered and reports noted that the victim Badlu's complaint with the police accused one Kattai Sahib and not Rider. *Leader*, 16.6.1928.

[84] *Pioneer*, 4.2.1927

[85] Chakr, *Kanpur Mazdur Andolan*, p. 7.

[86] *Pratap*, 26.1.1920.

state was necessary. [87] Violence questioned the legitimacy of the leadership and the limits of their disciplining powers. The events of the 1920s threatened repeatedly to disturb the leadership that had emerged in 1919. In each of these situations there was an effort by worker militants and trade union leaders to define the boundaries of workers' actions and leaders' functions, their mutual rights and obligations.

The KMS constitution of the 1920s was explicit that the main aim of the sabha was the promotion of goodwill between labourers and employers, the maintenance of industrial peace through a relationship of harmony. The sabha constitution tried to ensure that workers acted only with its sanction.[88] The KMS leadership also proposed the setting up of an arbitration board, with representatives of employers and workers to settle disputes.[89] Such a board, they argued, would eliminate the need for strikes and prevent harm to industry. Though slogans like '*Punjivad ka nash ho*', *Karkhanay kiske? Mazduron ke, Zamin kiski? Kisanon ki,* figured on the walls of the KMS office in the mid-1920s, they had little meaning in the sabha politics of the period. Sabha leaders were categorical that the language of class was inappropriate, even 'dangerous', for the nation.[90] District officials appreciated the role of Murari Lal as president of a sabha which did not encourage strikes as a part of its programme: the KMS representatives were duly acknowledged as not being 'agitators in the usual sense

[87] The state they suggested should provide conciliation boards consisting of employer and worker representatives, which could resolve problems before they were aggravated. *Pratap*, 26.1.1920.

[88] The sabha byelaws stipulated that there would be no strike in any mill without its sanction and without the support of 75 per cent of the workers. Mehta to Clow, 2.4.1924, Dept of Ind. and Labour, L- 877 (ii), 1921. In January 1929, the KMS negotiated a settlement in which it promised that it would not allow 'lightning strikes' in future. *Pioneer*, 19.1.1929. In a settlement following a strike in Elgin Mills (May 1928), the KMS secured recognition for itself on the guarantee that it would not 'permit' or 'countenance' any strike without fifteen days' notice. The KMS also agreed to reaffirm the right of employers to engage such hands as they thought 'fit'. *Pioneer,* 20.6.1928; *Leader,* 20.6.1928.

[89] *Pratap*, 2.2,1920; Murari Lal's speech at the Kanpur District Conference. *Leader,* 22.4.1920.

[90] *Pratap*, 1.12.1926

of the term'.[91] These principles also became a basis of the disenchantment of workers with the KMS leadership by the late
1920s. In the 1930s these principles were overruled as the sabha
was pushed into a more militant role.

Fears of worker violence were linked to the fragile basis on
which the legitimacy of the leadership rested. The role of Murari
Lal and other KMS leaders as mediators in 1919 had given them
some legitimacy within the union, but this had no firm basis.
There was continuous conflict between the more militant worker
leaders like Ramzan Ali and Shiv Balak and moderate leaders like
Murari Lal.[92] Others like Vidyarthi had a reputation for being
more sympathetic towards labour. Tributes to him portray Vidyarthi as a person who was always ready to oppose tyranny and
injustice from the capitalist, the government or the 'mob'.[93]While
he was ready to support struggles against injustice, he was wary
of any form of coercion, and strikes, in his view, could become
coercive.[94] Although Vidyarthi strongly defended the legitimacy
of a strike in November 1919, he was critical of strikes later. In
June 1928, when the workers of Elgin Mills protested against

[91] Cawnpore Cotton Mill Riot Report, HPD, File 153,1924.

[92] During a strike in Victoria Mills in Dec. 1923, it was reported: 'The more
moderate elements of the Mazdur Sabha headed by Dr Murari Lal have been
making some endeavours during the past week to persuade the workmen to
return, but their efforts have been frustrated by the action of the more
extremist agitators headed by one Shivbalak and Ramzan Ali . . . ' Secy,
Victoria Mills to DM, Kanpur, encl. in DM to Clow, Dept of Ind. and Labour,
L-877 (ii), 1924. During the Kanpur Cotton Mills strike of 1924, again, a
witness before the Inquiry Committee reported: 'I saw Shiv Balak Vaid—it
was about 12.15—outside the mill gate with a crowd of 250 or 300 men,
strikers. He was shouting to them, "Brothers do not go away, keep on here.
If you leave the mill gate you will get neither bonus nor pay. What does it
matter if you stay 4–5 days. I am there to feed you, bring gram and gur".' Ev.
Mohd.Abdul Jalil, Depy Supdt, 7.4.1924, 94,1924, Dep. XVIII, Jud. Crim.,
ERR, Kanpur.

[93] Leader, 21.2.1924.

[94] Soon after the November strikes, for instance, an editorial in the Pratap
was categorical: 'We do not approve of repeated strikes. A strike should be
the last weapon of the workers. The workers have decided in their meeting
that they will not strike against the permission of sabha. Then why have they
done this?' Pratap,15.12.1919.

being frequently thrashed by European supervisors, Vidyarthi criticised workers' actions as 'too hasty' and taken on 'trifling grounds'.[95]

The relationship between trade union leaders and workers was fraught with conflict. To freeze this relationship in terms of fixed categories of 'babu' and 'coolie', with the coolie tied through absolute loyalty and subordination to the babu, is to miss out the inner dynamics of tension within it. The power of leaders to dictate terms and conditions was questioned especially in periods of worker militancy. The point is not to necessarily celebrate and valorise the spontaneity of workers against the language of legalism of trade union leaders. The ways in which leaders sought to represent themselves was never given. What we need to examine is the process of dialogue through which power was reconstituted and leadership reinvested with authority. The experience of Murari Lal in 1924, the mocking and ridiculing of his authority, can be seen as part of such a process. His attempts to placate workers in 1924 had the opposite effect. The strikers were reported to have 'howled down' Murari Lal, who had to finally leave in despair. 'Brothers, I am going away,' he said. As he left the strikers could be heard shouting, 'let him go . . . clear a path for him'.[96] In situations like this workers and leaders confronted each other to define the limits of their authority. The experience of Murari Lal in the Cawnpore Cotton Mills can be read almost as a theatrical performative practice, which played a role in the way power was defined. Murari Lal threatened to withdraw his leadership in a dramatic gesture to coerce workers into submission. The threat to withdraw was premised on a self-conception of his own power. By shouting 'let him go . . .' the workers denied the premises of his authority. As he was leaving Murari Lal could be heard telling a local merchant that the strike was the work of

[95] *Leader*, 3.6.1928.

[96] Ev. Mohd. Abdul Jalil, Depy Supdt Police 7.4.1924. File 94,1924, Dep. XVIII, Jud. Crim., ERR, Kanpur. Other witnesses gave similar evidence: 'I heard a Muhammadan workman get up and say that he did not wish to hear Dr Murari speak as it was the Doctor who had spoilt the strike at the Victoria Mills.' Ev. Mannilal Awasthi, 9.4.1924, Cawnpore Cotton Riots Commission, File 94,1924, Dep. XVIII, Jud. Crim., ERR, Kanpur.

'agitators'. He thus tried to retrieve lost prestige by asserting his distance from workers' actions and strike leaders, whom he label-led as 'agitators', making a clear distinction between respectable leaders like himself and 'agitators'.[97]

Working class histories often narrate a story of the great mo-ments they forget or erase times of fragmentation and repression. The collectivity of workers, however, does not unfold in a linear teleological history. It is true that after 1919 there were no industry-wide strikes till 1937-8. The upsurge of 1919 was fol-lowed by a series of strikes in individual mills, violence and repression, and then the quiet of the Depression years. But the experience of repression, defeat, silence is part of a process of identity formation—part of a learning process through which workers construe the limits of their power, the constraints on their activity.[98]

Traumatic experiences of repression and police attack, as in 1924, were passed down generations to enrich other stories of martyrdom and sacrifice. Remembering the event more than two decades later, a worker in the same mill dwelt on images of mount-ed police trampling on defenceless workers. The motif of cavalry police is charged with power—the repressive force of the state. The account, based on the memory of survivors, blurs chronology. The happenings in the Cawnpore Cotton Mills are fixed in 1922. In oral accounts from recent times, when memories of 1924 are virtually extinct, fragments of motifs from 1924 still recur. Images of workers being thrown into boilers are interwoven into narratives about the general strike of 1955.[99] Moments of collective struggle and an eighty-day strike are overshadowed with memories of repression of 1924. In accounts of trade unionists like Arjun Arora, the first memory of the workers' struggle in Kanpur is associated with 1924 ('*Mere liye Kanpur ke mazduron ki kahani san 1924 me hui jab Kanpur katan mil ke mazduron par goli*

[97] Ev. Mohd. Abdul Jalil, Depy Supdt Police, 7.4.1924, Cawnpore Riots Commission, File 94,1924, Dep. XVIII, Jud. Crim., ERR, Kanpur.

[98] I discuss elsewhere how periods of slump in working class activity did not necessarily mean an absence of protest. Other forms of resisting and confronting authority were a part of everyday relations at the workplace See ch. 4.

[99] See epilogue.

chalne ke sansanikhej samachar se sare shahar mein stabhtha cha gayi).[100]

The Depression years in Kanpur were very troubled. Large inflows of job seekers from rural areas made negotiations at the workplace fraught and difficult. There was a visible increase in the numbers of the unemployed and homeless in the city. They were out there sleeping every night on canal banks and other such places. Police reports saw a direct connection between rising crime figures in the city and the numbers of homeless, workless poor. Workers moved between spells of work and non-work, between factory work and vending and petty trade and criminal activity. The palpable hostility between different communities made life in the city more precarious, and workers and the labouring poor tended to retreat into a ghettoised existence. The apparent tranquillity of the Depression years conceals a great deal of pent-up anger against wage-cuts, retrenchment, and other cost-cutting managerial strategies.

Memories of collectivities like that of November 1919 were, however, not erased by the experience of defeat or with the intervention of traumatic times. These were periods of concentrated activity which became a sedimented part of workers' experiences. Workers recall great strikes in different ways at various points: sometimes with a sense of nostalgia for lost collectivities, at other times to legitimate the present by linking it to the past, tracing an uninterrupted heroic history. In periods of fragmentation, memories of such moments are often suppressed and the past is constructed along a temporality in which the experience of repression, of crushed aspirations, dominates. In other periods a continuous rebellious time of worker heroism and opposition is constructed and memories of defeat seem forgotten.[101]

---

[100] A. Arora, 'Kanpur ka Mazdur Andolan Jo Yad Raha', in A. Arora, *Shri Suraj Prasad Awasthi Hirak Jayanti Abhinandan Granth*, p. 19.

[101] Stories of strikes for men and women are often different. Periods of strikes for women often were moments of trauma, remembered as a time when they were done out of factory jobs.

CHAPTER 6

Lal Kanpur

The general strike of 1938, lasting 52 days, involving more than 46,000 workers, was the longest strike in pre-independence Kanpur. Decades later workers returned repeatedly to 1937–8 with a sense of nostalgia. These dramatic years became the most amplified moments in their representations of the past. Old workers I met in the 1980s invariably celebrated the years as unique, and felt proud of their association with the movement.[1] It was as if they were the bearers of a special history, surviving witnesses of a lost time. In trade unionist accounts too, 1938 represents a climactic moment of working class organisation in Kanpur: never again, not even during the anti-rationalisation general strikes of 1955, was the intensity of the 1938 experience replicated, never again were such solidarities forged.

Solidarities

The strike upsurge of 1937–8 took place after a period of relative quiet during the years of the Depression. Although industries in Kanpur were not as severely affected by the slump in business as in other centres, there was a decline in profits.[2] Production did not drop sharply but managerial strategies to check declining profits affected workers' jobs and incomes. Many badlis and casual workers lost their jobs. According to KMS estimates, direct and indirect cuts in this period amounted to a total of 40 per cent.

---

[1] By the late 1990s, however, memories of Lal Kanpur were restricted to a few old workers. Living in the pessimism of the lockout years, the younger generation had no interest in returning to moments of past struggles. See ch. 9.

[2] Statistical evidence shows a continuous increase in mill production during the Depression years. See ch. 1.

Around 20 per cent of the decline was through direct cuts by a reduction in rates and stopping of bonus payments. Indirect cuts
took various forms: short work or the closure of mills for two or
three days in the week; the nine-hour regulation; the conversion
of certain categories of time workers to the daily-wage system; the
introduction of new machinery and new varieties of cloth in some
mills. Real wage figures, which show a steady increase up to 1931
due to a fall in the cost of living index, mask the actual decline in
income that results from reduction in employment. These figures
also do not reflect the decline in rural earnings that constituted an
important component of the gross income of working class families.[3] Moreover, incomes were declining in a period when the intensity of work increased. In many mills fewer weavers had to
tend more looms; ring piecers had more spindles to look after; in
some there were fewer minders to a pair of mules and more cards
per worker in the carding room. An increase in workload on old
machines obviously meant greater physical exertion for workers.

Wage cuts, retrenchment and intensification were some of the
pressing issues that were raised during the strikes of 1937–8.
There were no major strikes over these issues during the Depression
years. Collective opposition to the cost-cutting strategies of managers is much more difficult in periods of slump. Added to this, the
trauma of the communal riots of 1931 in Kanpur had a lingering
effect, creating barriers between communities and affecting the
formation of wider solidarities between workers.

By 1937 the situation changed. There was an upsurge of strikes
against a background of the renewed expansion of industry, and
recovery of industrial profits with the increase in market demand.
Most factories ran double shift after 1934 and made some im-
provements and additions to their machinery. A demand for
higher wages and an end to the Depression cuts and economies
now appeared just to workers. The political context made hopes
of a better world seem more real. The campaigning by Congress
candidates in labour areas, the election of a Congress government

[3] In many of the districts from which the workers were drawn, the
percentage decline in rural wages varied between 31 and 44 per cent. *Report
of the Fifth Quinquennial Wage Census of the United Provinces* (Allahabad
1936), Statement VI, p. 16; Note on Agrarian Situation in UP, File no. 14,
1931, AICC Papers.

in UP, and the radical rhetoric of communists inspired faith in the imminence of change.

A nineteen-day strike in New Victoria Mills in June 1937 was followed by a series of strikes through July in the JK Jute Mills, Maheshwari Devi Jute Mills, Muir, Swadeshi and Kanpur Textiles Ltd. Each factory had its specific problems over which the workers struck, but issue of declining wages and increased workload was raised by all the strikers. When efforts at negotiation between managers and strikers failed, the strikes resumed with greater intensity by 6 August. Strikers carrying red flags and shouting slogans gathered at mill gates, openly defying prohibitory orders under section 144.[4] Attempts by the police to disperse the crowd outside the Elgin Mills in the Gwaltoli–Khalasi Line area, with a lathi charge, were resisted aggressively, with strikers throwing brickbats at policemen. Large crowds in the Gwaltoli area were seen as a threat to the neighbouring Civil Lines inhabitants. The crowd finally dispersed and moved southwards towards working-class concentrations in the Darshanpurwa and Cooperganj area. Spaces and boundaries seemed more fluid as workers trudged from one end of the city to the other, mobilising others. Strikers forced their way inside the Kanpur Cotton Mills and the JK Mills, smashing windowpanes and damaging mill machinery. The police opened fire wounding several workers.[5] As stories of police repression spread, the ranks of demonstrators on the streets swelled. Bands of strikers went from mill to mill demonstrating and persuading others to join them. The slogan shouting built up a strike fever. A crowd of over 12,000 gathered outside the LR Mills. Additional police were brought in from outside the district to keep the crowds in control. Over a thousand policemen could be seen patrolling the factory areas.[6] But there was no stopping the strike, which spread like a contagion. Beginning with the Victoria Mills, it moved rapidly to the Elgin and the Kanpur Cotton Mills and then to others. By 9 August, workers of the local oil

[4] SAID, 14.8.1937; *Leader*, 11.8.1937.

[5] SAID, 7.8.1937, *Leader*, 8.8.1937. On Pant's defence of the police action, see ch. 8.

[6] *Pioneer*, 8.8.1937; Yusuf, 'Cawnpore General Strike', *New Age*, Dec. 1937.

mills, soap factories, flour mills, match factory, iron foundry joined in, sending the numbers on strike up to 40,000.[7]

The announcement of a settlement on 9 August added to the militancy of the strikers. The Employers' Association agreed to recognise the KMS, withdraw cases against workers, and appoint an inquiry committee to investigate workers' grievances. The acceptance of these terms was conditional on the workers resuming work by 10 August. The strikers were indignant. Not only was the acceptance of their demands contingent on their rejoining work, but they were denied the right to strike till the official inquiry committee reported its findings.[8] Crowds of over 30,000 gathered on the streets and went on a rampage, attacking leaders associated with the settlement. At a meeting at Parade Grounds on 9 August, where over 35,000 workers were present, the strikers launched a tirade against communist and Congress socialist leaders of the KMS for not making the strike committee a party to the negotiations.[9] Communist leaders like Aiwaz Ali, who tried to defend the settlement, were assaulted by the crowd. Newspaper hawkers selling copies of papers, announcing the settlement at the meeting, had their cycles snatched away and papers destroyed.

Although sporadic strikes continued during the tenure of the inquiry committee, they did not draw wide public sympathy. Solidarities were at times fractured along communal lines. Support for the KMS from Muslim workers was hesitant and halting. To many of them, the KMS, like the Congress, appeared to be an organisation dominated by Hindus. Communist trade unionists tried to mobilise Muslims by giving them important positions in factory-level organisations. Yet there were tensions. In Elgin Mills, Sami, a Muslim head jobber in the weaving department, known for his opposition to the strike, was grievously assaulted.[10]

The situation changed dramatically when the Kanpur Employers' Association rejected the recommendations of the Inquiry Committee in May 1938.[11] In a sense the rejection was predictable.

[7] Yusuf, *New Age*, Dec. 1937.

[8] *Leader*, 12.8.1937.

[9] *Pioneer*, 10.8.1937, 11.8.1937; *Leader*, 12.8.1937; HPD, 12/1/1937.

[10] *Pioneer*, 30.11.1937; SAID, 11.12.1937.

[11] Among some important recommendations of the Inquiry Committee

While workers had some faith in the committee, industrialists felt it was partisan, with no one representing their voice. The idea of including a representative each from the KMS and the Employers' Association was abandoned after the initial sessions. Of the three-member committee that prepared the final report, the industrialists trusted only Rajendra Prasad, the president.[12] But Prasad was unwell and unable to participate in the proceedings.[13] The manner in which the proceedings were conducted deepened the anxieties of industrialists. Worker witnesses representing the KMS spoke out against managers and jobbers. Some even came to the sessions wearing red shirts, asserting a spirit of defiance. Editorials in newspapers like the *Pioneer* articulated the industrialists' fears and expressed doubts over whether Rudra and his colleagues were being allowed a free hand in preparing the report. The *Pioneer* was categorical: 'We do not want a report that has been drafted with one eye to the Congress left-wing and to which sops have been added to keep the extremists quiet.'[14] To them the contents of the report only confirmed these apprehensions.[15]

---

were: a graded wage increase for different categories of wage earners, standardisation of wages, the setting up of a labour exchange, improvement in working and living conditions, and the recognition of the Mazdur Sabha as the only representative labour organisation of textile workers in Kanpur.

[12] The other two members were S.K. Rudra, Professor, Allahabad University, and B. Shiva Rao, a trade unionist. Originally, Tracy Gavin Jones and Harihar Nath Shastri were appointed as representatives of employers and workers, respectively, but were subsequently replaced by a technical adviser with no rights as a member. *Leader*, 4.5.1938.

[13] In May 1938, Rudra wrote to Rajendra Prasad: 'I think had you come up to Cawnpore, and seen the Employers, much if not all, would have gone well. They all especially the English, hold you in esteem and reverence. But your health has been our misfortune.' Rudra to Prasad, 7.5.1938, Rajendra Prasad Papers, File I-L, 38, Coll I. Earlier Kanpur industrialist Gavin Jones, expressing his misgivings about the committee, wrote to Rudra: 'I must reiterate my contention that the Enquiry Committee as at present constituted cannot function properly and will do nothing but harm.' 13.12.1937, RP Papers, File IX,1937, Coll 1 (NMML).

[14] *Pioneer,* 16.3.1938

[15] The 'downright condemnation' of the employers and 'reluctant criticism' of the KMS, according to the *Pioneer*, showed the biased nature of the Report. *Pioneer*, 26.4.1938.

In May 1938 the Employers' Association rejected the report. A wave of protest swept through the city. Workers of all textile factories went on strike. In contrast to 1937, when the strike spread gradually through a relay effect, in May 1938 the strike began almost simultaneously in all the factories. Once the workers struck, the KMS extended its support. Picketing was done in an organised and co-ordinated way, with picketers wearing red bands and carrying red flags guarding roads leading to the factories. Strikers went around mill settlements and mohallas, appealing to workers to stay away from work. The houses of clerks and jobbers, known for strike-breaking, were kept under constant watch. Outside the gates of Cooper Allen and Company, the Kanpur Cotton Mills and Laxmi Ratan Mills, workers lay on the road, blocking possible entry into the factory. Boats patrolled the riverside to prevent strike-breakers entering factories through the rear gate.[16] The numbers on the street swelled continuously, fresh batches of picketers quickly replacing those arrested by the police.[17]

What marked the events of Lal Kanpur from other times of collective struggle was the significant presence of women and children. More than 200 women—a large majority factory workers—joined the demonstrations and picketing.[18] Bal tolis (squads of children) picketed mill gates and the houses of managers. A procession of over 500 children went around mazdur bastis.[19] Although women had participated in strikes earlier, it was not usual for them to picket at mill gates.[20] In official and non-official descriptions women usually appear as unwilling participants, passive and submissive, their actions controlled by male leaders.[21] It is as

[16] *Pioneer*, 28.5.1938.

[17] *Aaj*, 20.5.1938; *Leader*, 21.5.1938; *Pioneer*, 19.5.1938.

[18] Only about 5 per cent were not factory workers. See P.C. Joshi, 'Cawnpore—A Report', *New Age*, Sept. 1938. *Pioneer*, 27.5.1938, 28.5.1938. *Leader*, 30.5.1938.

[19] This was an event that stood out in Raghubir's recollection of the strike, more than forty years later.

[20] In 1922, for instance, eighty women workers struck work for more pay. Dept of Ind. and Labour, File L-877 (II),1922.

[21] Reports describe how women picketers were 'posted' outside the JK Cotton, JK Jute, JK Manufactures and Laxmi Ratan Mills gates to prevent strike-breakers from entering. *Pioneer*, 27.5.1938. Similarly, *Leader* reported how women picketers were 'enrol(led)' in the picketing. *Leader*, 28.5.1938.

if strikes and picketing by women are assertions of masculinised power—a role that cannot be reconciled with the image of a gentle, compliant, female figure. Notions that equate femininity with cowardice, however, were dramatically reversed during the strike. Clerks entering the mills from the back gate were stated to be 'like women'[22] while women refused to give way to pressures from strike-breakers. Women, in fact, were posted at the gates of newer mills of the JK group where strike-breaking was more persistent. Outside the JK Jute Mills, women picketers lay on the ground to stop motor vehicles from entering. Ultimately the men on strike had to persuade the women to relent and allow the lorries in.[23]

Officials were wary of dealing with women picketers.[24] Strike-breakers and mill officials were hesitant to violate a cordon drawn by women picketers. At the Cooper Allen gate the District Magistrate, Superintendent of Police, and other officials arrived with a large police force and mounted constables to deal with the impossible situation created by women picketers. A company official, who struggled for a long time trying to find a way in between the outstretched bodies of women picketers, had to finally give up and go home.[25] The participation of women structured crowd action in important ways. A large crowd of spectators gathered

---

In June 1955, similarly, reports noted: 'Latest stunt is the employment of women to lead the band of picketers in *ahatas* and mill gates to prevent peaceful non-striking workers from going to work . . . Why should there be any necessity at all for picketing and much less for picketing by women if the strike is spontaneous?' *Pioneer*, 14.6.1955. At the same time, women strikers were seen as more 'tenacious' and 'intractable' as picketers than the men. For a discussion of the contradictory notions of women's militancy in the context of jute mill workers of Bengal, see Samita Sen, *Women and Labour*, ch. VI.

[22] Millowners are reported to have 'denied allegations that they had asked clerks not to come from the back door like women but through the main entrance . . .' *Leader*, 8.6.1938.

[23] *Pioneer*, 28.5.1938.

[24] The Superintendent of Police enlisted the services of sixteen women police to handle the situation created by the participation of women picketers. *Pioneer*, 3.6.1938. Another report mentioned: 'This is perhaps the first occasion in India when women have been enrolled to do police work.' *Pioneer*, 8.6.1938.

[25] *Pioneer*, 1.6.1938.

wherever women picketed.[26] Reports noted that there was always a danger of ruffling crowd sentiments if women were violated in any way. The defence of female honour became an important issue in such situations.[27]

The Lal Kanpur days built up a tradition of the active involvement of women in demonstrations and picketing. During strikes in January 1947 and again in 1955, women were militant and active. In 1947, Saraswati, a woman worker in the JK Jute Mills who marched on despite threats of police attack, succumbed to bullet wounds.[28] In the general strike against rationalisation in June 1955, militant picketing by women workers became a way of shaming strike-breakers.[29]

Mohalla solidarity was expressed in different forms. Strike-breakers were socially boycotted, ridiculed and humiliated. Norms of purity and pollution that were so important for the maintenance of social status were used to mobilise solidarity and sharpen the distance between strikers and non-strikers.

Sweepers boycotted the houses of 'loyal' clerks and jobbers, an action particularly significant in a context where excreta had to be daily removed by the sweepers. Accounts describe how strikers emptied buckets full of excreta into the houses of strike-breaking jobbers, defiling their living spaces.[30] Polluted with excreta,

[26] 'Due to the novelty of picketing by women the crowd on the roads though mobile was dense . . .' *Pioneer* 27.5.1938. A large crowd gathered outside Cooper Allen and Co., where women picketers prevented mill officials from entering. *Pioneer*, 1.6.1938.

[27] . . . 'any real or supposed discourtesy to a woman picket might flare up the standing multitude and lead to trouble.' *Leader*, 30.5.1938.

[28] '*Saraswati jaloos ki neta thi. Uske seene mein goli lagi—phir bhi us virangana ne kadam na hataya. Uske dusri goli lagi aur vah larkhara kar shahid ho gayi*' (Saraswati was the leader of the demonstration. A bullet hit her chest yet the brave woman did not surrender. When the second bullet hit her she succumbed to her injuries). Raja Ram Shastri, 'Kanpur ka Golikand aur Am Hartal', *Samajvaad* (*Shahid Mazdur Ank*), special issue commemorating the martyrs of 1947, 6.1.1948.

[29] *Aaj*, 10.6.1938. In June 1955 a group of women picketing near Elgin Mills reportedly beat up a strike-breaker with chappals, others got aggressive with a worker on a cycle, pushing him off. *Pioneer*, 8.6.1938.

[30] Chakr, *Kanpur Mazdur Andolan*, pp. 60–1.

strike-breakers became 'untouchable'; hostility and opposition to them thus acquired a ritual meaning.

Wider solidarities were also constituted. The barbers of Parmat held a meeting where they decided to give free shaves to strikers.[31] Local sweepers' organisations promised to provide 300 volunteers for picketing.[32] The local motor drivers' union showed their solidarity by refusing to bring in strike-breakers to the factories.[33] Traders and shopkeepers observed Kanpur Strike Day on 29 June by remaining closed.[34]

Local Congress leaders, who had been lukewarm in their support to the strikers in 1937, now participated actively in picketing, in raising funds and food for the striking workers. Pressure from local Congressmen like Balkrishna Sharma was important in compelling the state leadership to pass a resolution in support of the strikers.[35] Solidarity meetings for the strikers were organised in towns in UP and elsewhere.[36] Appeals for strike funds were made and resolutions in support of the strikers passed. The GKU appealed for a boycott of textiles from the Kanpur mills till a settlement was arrived.[37] Labour leaders from other cities visited Kanpur during the strike.[38] Muslim organisations like the Ahrars, Ittihad Millat and the Muslim League supported the strikers.[39]

An important way in which different organisations tried to mobilise solidarity was through the collection of grain for the strikers. The *chutki andolan*, the collection of a pinch of ata a day from each household, was symbolically significant for the strikers. Entire neighbourhoods were drawn around such expressions of solidarity. In the Juhi area, around forty households contributed matkas of flour towards the strike. For many Congress volunteers this seemed an extension of activity that was part of their

[31] *Aaj*, 12.6.1938.
[32] *Aaj*, 4.6.1938.
[33] *Leader*, 24.6.1938.
[34] *Aaj*, 1.6.1938.
[35] *Pioneer*, 22.5.1938. Balkrishna Sharma was the president of the City Congress Committee.
[36] SAID, 4.6.1938.
[37] HPD, 18/6/1938.
[38] SAID, 25.6.1938.
[39] SAID, 28.5.1938.

campaigns during the Civil Disobedience Movement in Kanpur.[40] The Muslim League actively mobilised around the food distribution campaign. Ward leagues collected grain and set up relief
centres to distribute food.[41]

Order and Disorder

Contemporary accounts draw a distinction between the form of
activity in 1937 and 1938: between the organised and peaceful
strikes of 1938 and the unorganised, spontaneous and violent actions of 1937. Official accounts of 1937 refer to 'mobs of workers' being 'defiant', 'violent', 'unruly' and 'threatening'.[42] Reports
on 1937 in nationalist papers like *Aaj* echo the language of officialdom, stigmatising worker violence and rationalising police
repression. The strikers are described as upadravi (rowdy), engaging in senseless violence, while the police is stated to have
'fired in self-defence'.[43] Papers like the *Pioneer* always expressed
the managerial voice. Violent, aggressive, unruly are recurrent
terms in the *Pioneer* descriptions.

In 1938, in contrast, orderly, peaceful, quiet, non-violent are
the key words in most descriptions of the strikes. Official accounts
approvingly note the absence of violence in 1938.[44] *Leader*, which

[40] For many workers the chutki andolan (chutki=literally, movement for
a pinch of grain) during the civil disobedience campaign in Kanpur was their
first initiation into political activity. Raghubir recounted how he was asked
to collect ata for the chutki andolan when he was a boy of fifteen, working
in a printing press: '*Mere mohalle mein ek neta ne mujhe satyagrahon ke liye
kuch ata ekatha karne ko kaha. Ganesh Shankar Vidyarthi ka chutki bhar
andolan chal raha tha. Ye kam mujhe bahut achha lagta tha*' (A local leader
from my mohalla asked me to collect flour for the satyagrahis. That was the
time of Ganesh Shankar Vidyarthi's chutki andolan in Kanpur. I loved doing
this work). Interview.

[41] *Aaj*, 12.6.1938. Food distribution became crucial to the communal
politics of the League in the wartime scarcity period, helping to mobilise
support around separatist demands.

[42] SAID, 14.8.1937; Ramsay Scott to J.G. Laithwaite,1.11.1937, HPD,
12/1/1938.

[43] *Aaj*, 8.8.1937. Another report carried a headlines: 'Kanpur mein phir
Upadrav'. *Aaj*, 7.9.1937.

[44] Home officials noted that the strikers 'have shown no violence'. HPD,
18/5/1938.

censured workers' violence in 1937, describes the 'perfect quiet' and 'peaceful' picketing by the strikers.[45] *Aaj* criticised the haste with which workers struck work yet dwelt on the fact that picketing was peaceful, with picketers moving about in an orderly way in twos and threes to avoid a violation of prohibitory orders under Section 144.[46]

Accounts structured around such contrasts between the unruliness of 1937 and orderliness of 1938 share certain common assumptions about order and violence. To Congress supporters of the strike, notions of order are linked with issues of non-violence and organisation. In 1937 the strikers' actions are criticised for their unruliness and because they are not sanctioned by their union. In 1938, in contrast, the strikers were well organised and leading Congress and communist members of the KMS—Hariharnath Shastri, Balkrishna Sharma, Sant Singh Yusuf, Aiwaz Ali, Arjun Arora and others participated actively in the strike. The orderliness of the strikers is attributed by local Congress leaders to the influence of the Congress principles of non-violence. Balkrishna Sharma, the city congress president, in a self-congratulatory tone, noted: '*Congress mazdur andolan ko puri sahayata de rahe hain aur mazdur congress ke ahimsa-siddhant ka palan kar rahe hain.*'[47] It was as if the order of 1938 itself signified the power of non-violence and hegemony of the Congress.

The order of 1938 was deceptive. Seen through the violent events in 1937, the peace of 1938 appears reassuring. So the politics of the period created a rhetoric of orderliness. The local Congress leadership was committed to support the workers if the Employers' Association refused the recommendations of the Inquiry Committee. Forced to go along with the strikers' decisions, the local Congress leadership justified its support by working with the KMS to ensure greater discipline among strikers, and by valorising the orderliness of the strike. Periods like Lal Kanpur, however, were turbulent times when workers' actions inverted given assumptions, when notions of order were questioned and

[45] *Leader,* 26.5.1938.

[46] *Aaj,* 20.5.1938, 22.5.1938.

[47] 'The congress is giving full support to the workers' movement and the workers are abiding by the congress principles of non-violence.'*Aaj,*1.6.1938.

reconstituted. If order meant a respect for hierarchy and organisation, then behind this appearance of order lurked the threat of
disorder.

In 1938, as in 1937, workers were seeking to build a new order,
often overruling established structures of authority. Periods of
upsurge like this are times when workers feel empowered, when
authority within organisations is questioned, when organisational
decisions have to be legitimated through popular sanction.

This sense of power was palpable in public meetings during the
strikes of 1937–8. Meetings were unusually large and charged
with excitement. At Parade Grounds on 16 May 1938, more than
30,000 workers assembled at 5 p.m. The meeting continued till
10 at night. Much before the meeting, workers 'gathered in
knots', talking animatedly. Noises, gestures, created a feeling of
bonding between those who gathered. Each time a vote was
taken, hands went up in unison and there were shouts in support
of an immediate general strike. Mounting the rostrum did not
imbue speakers with the halo of power. The legitimacy of leaders
had to be continuously reaffirmed. Speakers had to feel the pulse
of the crowd. When the audience felt the KMS president was
advocating a delay in the strike, they 'began shouting and drown-
ed his voice'. Soon the rostrum was 'captured' by workers in
favour of a strike and 'it was impossible for any Mazdur Sabha
leader to obtain a hearing'.[48] 'Orator' after 'orator' came up from
the crowd amidst loud cheers and clapping. Eventually the KMS
leaders had to go along with the decision of the crowd and support the strike.[49] Earlier, in August 1937, similar scenes were witnessed at meetings, with strikers openly attacking trade union
leaders for the terms of the settlement.[50]

[48] *Pioneer,* 17.5.1938.

[49] In August 1937, the KMS had publicly announced its decision to call off
the strike and managerial acceptance of the strike settlement was conditional
on this. To retain its legitimacy the union tried to deny the existence of opposition and persuaded workers to go back to work.

[50] *Pioneer,* 10.8. 1937. The strikers were indignant that the strike committee
had not participated in the negotiations. An official inquiry committee was
appointed to investigate workers' grievances, but managerial acceptance of
the settlement was conditional on the strikers rejoining work by 10 August.
The day after the meeting (10 August), most workers did not go back to

Newspaper reports described speakers at meetings becoming more aggressive and defiant as the strike proceeded. There was a spirit of carnival about the meetings: loud sloganeering, recitation of poems, cheering, clapping. Worker orators followed certain expected codes of address at such meetings: 'When a worker mounts the rostrum he invariably begins "*Bhaiyon, ek martaba khub zor se nara lagaiye*", and from the assembled throats peal out the memorable slogans, "*Inquilab Zindabad; Sarmayadaron ka nash ho; British hukoomat ka nash ho, Lal Jhanda uncha ho*", thrice repeated.'[51] The chorus of slogans created a sense of oneness in the crowd. Speakers had to keep up the mood of the moment to hold together the excited audience.

Public meetings provided a space where new leaders tried to win the crowd, each trying to outbid the other in oratory and passion. Often, ordinary worker leaders could hold sway only after the departure of Congress bigwigs. Meetings became more spirited and speeches more belligerent after the departure of party officials. At one meeting, as soon as luminaries like Mohan Lal Saxena and Hassan Zaheer left, there was a sudden change in the mood of the crowd *Leader* reported: 'The young lions of the Mazdur Sabha roared as they had never roared before and the louder they roared the louder grew the applause till between this violence to lungs and hands it seems as if the very heavens would fall.'[52] At other times workers openly mocked at leaders, asserting their right to speak. When the president of the meeting asked a worker to finish his speech quickly, he retorted before leaving: '*Yeh leader log jo barsati medhak ki tarah yahan jaman huai, kya bhala ham mazduron ko kyon bolne denge.*'[53]

These were tumultuous times when authority had to be constantly relegitimated. However, inversions of authority at public meetings did not question the gendered basis of power. Mass meetings appear as male gatherings, demonstrations of male

---

work; only two factories could resume work and one of them with only 15 per cent of its usual workforce. HPD, 12/1/1938.

[51] *Leader,* 10.6.1938.

[52] Ibid., Mohan Lal Saxena was President of the UPCC in 1938.

[53] 'These leaders who have gathered here like frogs in the rain, why on earth will they let us workers speak.' *Leader,* 10.6.1938.

collective strength; women remain curiously absent in all reports on public meetings. Worker leaders who captured the rostrum were 'young lions'. No women orators are seen mounting the rostrum. The erasure of female faces from the crowd seems anomalous in times when women appear unusually active in picketing on the streets. Women as picketers are valorised, their strength and tenacity is counterposed with the cowardice and effeminacy of strike-breakers. It is unlikely that women who were so active in the streets did not form part of the audience at such gatherings. But their presence goes unrecorded.

Notions of order, continuously questioned at an everyday level in the factory, were dramatically altered during the strike.[54] Authority and order within the factory was premised on the observation of certain norms of work and codes of deference in speech and action. Resistance to these norms was not peculiar to periods of strikes, negotiation of power was part of the everyday life within the factory. But the form it took in periods of strike upsurge was different.

Acts of resistance in factories in 1937 were public enactments. The actors were not anonymous; they proclaimed their identity. Practices that were considered unfair by workers, like the oiling and cleaning of machines after working hours, were openly resisted. In the Kanpur Cotton Mills and Swadeshi Mills, workers refused to clean and oil machines.[55] Staying on in the factory after work to clean machines was always resented, yet it had become a norm.[56] When workers protested against the practice, managers saw it as a violation of factory rules. Workers of the Kanpur Textiles Limited protested against the ten-hour overlapping shift in the carding department. The Intelligence Department reports of 'the complete disregard of mill rules' overstate the magnitude of resistance.[57] What they feared, however, was the undermining of mill authority. The attempt by managers to isolate a few 'instigators' was both an effort to check militant protest and reinstate authority

[54] See ch. 3.

[55] HPD, 12/1/1938; *Leader,* 25.10.1937.

[56] KMS Memo, KLIC Progs., UP Ind. Progs., File 1145, 1937, Bundle 110 (UPSA).

[57] HPD, 12/1/1938.

within the factory. Thus, Ram Singh of Kanpur Cotton Mills was punished for 'instigating' workers to refuse cleaning machines.

Respect and fear, the two premises of authority within the factory, were embodied in codes of verbal etiquette observed by workers towards their superiors. The violation of these codes in 1937–8 was an assertion of both irreverence and the lack of fear of authority. Unpopular mistris were publicly mocked and ridiculed. Disrespect towards supervisory authority was more visible in the actions of worker militants, Babu Khan. When a weaver in the Kanpur Textiles, Babu Khan, was reprimanded for loitering and being away from his looms, he responded to disciplinary threats with complete nonchalance.[58] Another, Amrit Lal, who protested against the overlapping shift system, spoke out against the manager, declaring publicly that the European should cross the seas and return home: 'We do not want him here in India. We are not going to work the overlapping shift under any circumstances'.[59]

The Lal Kanpur days were times when institutions of order at the factory level were refigured and re-established. Popular institutions in the factory and neighbourhood—mill committees and hata committees—became active bodies which reflect the popular mood.[60] Although existing relationships built around akharas, tea-shops, Ramlila mandalis, and caste panchayats were important in mobilising workers, solidarities forged through mohalla and hata committees during the strikes went outside the bounds of existing neighbourhood networks. New relationships were forged, outlasting the moment of the strike. Neighbourhood organisations during the strike were not inward looking. Hata boundaries seemed to dissolve as workers moved across the city, linking up with other neighbourhoods. Distances between Juhi and Gwaltoli, lying at opposite ends of the city, seemed to shrink in the camaraderie of the strike. Mill committees were shopfloor organisations, similar to strike committees formed in November 1919. The formation of such collectivities allowed a questioning of existing

[58] Director, Kanpur Textiles, to Employers' Association, 11.1.1938, KLIC Progs., UP Ind. Progs., File 1145, 1937, Bundle 110 (UPSA).

[59] *Pioneer*, 25.10.1937. See also ch. 4.

[60] P.C. Joshi recounts how mohalla committees were set up in 1937 because of prohibitory orders under Sec.144 that made gate meetings difficult. P.C. Joshi, 'Cawnpore: A Report', *New Age*, Sept. 1937.

structures of authority. The power and authority of mistris within the factories, for instance, were considerably weakened, with workers claiming that incidents of beating up by mistris were fewer since mill committees were set up.[61]

Communist trade unionist accounts celebrated these institutions as *their* creations. Shriram, who worked in Muir Mills, recounts: 'Maulana (Yusuf) called a gate-meeting and asked workers to form a committee . . . and soon after a committee was formed.'[62] The president was usually chosen by a unanimous vote—in the way Juggan Baba was in Muir Mills. Juggan Baba, we are told by Shriram, 'was a person, who could get mill officials and workers to do what he wanted, who never quarrelled with anyone, and whom everyone loved'.[63] The events of 1937–8, however, invested these institutions with a new meaning. Factory committees became bodies that reflected the popular mood. Mill managers complained that mill committee members brazenly violated norms and disregarded authority within the factory. Mill committees also provided a space for the emergence of new militant leaders who questioned the decisions of trade unions. Although in retrospective accounts communist trade unionists applaud the role of mill committees, their potential for subversion created anxieties within the established leadership.[64]

These anxieties are articulated in the ambivalence about workers' action in communist discourse. At times, the communist leadership tactically supported independent action by workers, outside the framework of their union.[65] Yet they were worried and

[61] Ev. Zawar Husain, Cawnpore Cotton Mills and Ramcharan, Kanpur Textiles, KLIC Progs., UP Ind. Progs., File 1145, 1937, Bundle 110 (UPSA). Another worker narrated how mistris formed their own 'Mistri Kamgar Union' in November 1938 in retaliation. Interview, Raghubir.

[62] Shriram, *Ek Sarvahara ka Jivan Vritanta*, p. 14.

[63] Ibid.

[64] In these accounts the history of communist organisation is authenticated by the workers' initiative in creating new institutions. P.C. Joshi, for instance, describes how after the first strike 'workers spontaneously formed mill committees without any direction from above, even by the communists'. P.C. Joshi, *New Age*, Sept. 1938. This celebration of spontaneous initiative in Joshi's account is in a period when the communists see themselves as heroes who had led the successful strike of 1938.

[65] In 1936–7, when the communists were trying to carve out their influence in Kanpur, they supported independent initiative by workers, outside the

critical of independent action when it seemed to threaten their legitimacy and leadership. Communists like Arjun Arora, and S.C. Kapoor joined in with Congress and socialist leaders of the KMS in their critique of spontaneity. 'Sporadic' action by workers, they argued, would fritter away their energy without resolving their main problems. They urged 'planned' action against 'individual' strikes and emphasised the need to represent grievances through the KMS. Communist narratives shared with the nationalist certain assumptions. For both, order was a measure of the strength of the movement, and organisation expressed as well as ensured order. Partly, these contradictory attitudes towards the question of spontaneity and organisation reflect real tensions the communists were faced with. Lack of support to independent initiative meant a loss of legitimacy, while affirmation of workers' action threatened organisational discipline.

These anxieties are reflected in attempts by the KMS leadership to reorganise the sabha and bring mill committees under closer control of the union in the post-strike period. Mill committees were given a constitutional status within the 'reformed' sabha in 1938. The new constitution of the KMS stated clearly: 'The mill committees will function under the discipline of the General Council [of the sabha] and will obey the rules regarding their income expenses, policy and programme framed by the General Council.' [66] The mill committees were accepted as constituent bodies of the union, but at the same time their independence was curbed.[67]

Partly, the changes in the KMS constitution were also a response to pressures from the Employers' Association to reform

---

union. During a strike in the Cooper Allen works in November 1936, the communists pressed for continuing the strike, despite an agreement calling off the strike. Statement of Yusuf, *Pioneer,* 28.7.1937. In July 1937, they rejected a settlement negotiated by the KMS, for the JK Jute Mills. *Pioneer,* 23.7.1937.

[66] The constitution also stated that the mill 'should increase the membership and try to bring the workers more and more under the Mazdur Sabha flag'. See KMS Constitution, AITUC Papers, File 135 (NMML).

[67] On the right to strike the constitution stipulated: 'The General Council, the representative of all mills, shall only have the right of declaring a strike, but it will be essential to take the opinion of all mill committees and the workers of the mill before hand.' AITUC Papers, File 135 (NMML).

the KMS and check worker militancy. The employers made re-form a precondition for recognition of the union. The new constitution of the KMS thus emerged out of the conflicting needs of a trade union for organisational discipline and managerial demands for industrial order. While arguing for greater discipline, the sabha leadership resisted changes in the language of the constitution recommended by the employers. Communist office-bearers of the KMS were firm about not including a clause stating that the sabha should 'aim at promotion and maintenance of harmonious relations between workmen and employers'.[68] They also refused to incorporate any clause in its constitution on co-operation between the sabha and the Labour Office or on the right of the Labour Commissioner to conduct a ballot before a declaration of a strike.[69] Even while making recognition of the KMS conditional on reform, the employers seemed sceptical about a restrained and transformed sabha. Caricatures of a feminised KMS, under the guardianship of a newly established office of the Labour Commissioner, expressed their cynicism. A cartoon in the *Pioneer* shows the new Labour Commissioner, Kharegat, striding along confidently while the KMS, caricatured as a petite, sari-clad woman with a KMS parasol, walks gingerly behind. (Fig. 24). Two employers look on, expressing a sense of disbelief in the feminised KMS. They acknowledged the need to recognise the reformed and softened sabha, yet shared an underlying scepticism. The images of KMS radicalism played on their minds.

Images of Radicalism

Workers' efforts to refigure structures of power and authority in 1937–8 were reflected in a wider rhetoric and imagery of radicalism. The metaphor 'Lal Kanpur' in popular accounts evokes the mood of the period. Anti-capitalist slogans and references to

[68] They argued that the primary object of any trade union is to safeguard the interests of the worker and to bring about harmony between labour and employers. *Pioneer*, 28.9.1938. Among its stated aims the sabha constitution no longer talked of a 'peaceful' settlement of all trade disputes. The prefix 'peaceful' was now deleted and the object of the Mazdur Sabha was now 'to secure the settlement of all disputes between employers and their employees' KMS Constitution, AITUC Papers, File 135 (NMML).

[69] *Pioneer*, 28.9.1938.

the coming workers' raj all seemed more meaningful in a milieu where change was taking place.[70] The coming to power of the Congress in 1937 coincided with a shift from socialist to communist influence within the KMS, an upsurge in strikes, and the constitution of factory-level organisations. The radical rhetoric corresponded in many ways with workers' lived experience. It defined the nature of experience, just as their experience gave meaning to the rhetoric.

In speeches at gate meetings and in their writings communist leaders continuously drew analogies between the Bolshevik revolution and the events in Kanpur.[71] Names of Soviet leaders became a part of popular discourse. A Lenin week was celebrated in Kanpur in January 1938, during which speeches on Lenin and the Russian revolution were given and the imminence of a revolution in India was talked of.[72] During the general strike in 1938, communist leaders emphasised that the main object of the strike was the abolition of capitalism and imperialism. The strike, they stated, would continue till the workers took over factories and peasants controlled land.[73] The red army, communist leaders declared, would be used to take possession of all mills.[74] Film advertisements in Kanpur captured the prevailing mood. In July 1938 the film running in Imperial Talkies was *Rangeela Mazdur*, advertised in the local papers as '*Garibon ki bastiyon mein andolan uthane vala tufhani neta dekhna nahin bhuliye.*'[75]

[70] Anti-capitalist slogans and the association with the red flag were not new to the workers' movement in Kanpur. Papers like the *Mazdur* had numerous writings on communism and class struggle and workers' raj in the early 1930s and socialist slogans. See ch. 5.

[71] SAID, 19.9.1936, 26.9.1936. At other meetings mill committees were described as the beginnings of a soviet form of government. SAID 5.2.1938.

[72] SAID, 29.1.1938.

[73] SAID, 18.6.1938.

[74] SAID, 17.9.1938. A new weekly from Kanpur, in Urdu and Hindi, was started with the object of propagating communist ideas. Its cover carried the communist emblem and the motto: 'Workers of the world unite . . .' The opening page carried a poem which urged workers to fight the battle of freedom and equality '. . . Workers are born in poverty and starvation is their lot. Hunger and fetters are for them. But how long are they to remain poor. They should wave the red flag for the day of liberty is nigh.' *Lal Jhanda*, cited in SAID, 18.10.1938.

[75] 'Do not miss seeing the fiery leader stirring up revolt in the *mazdur*

The symbolism of the colour red, so important in official and non-official representations of the strikes shaped workers' self-perceptions as well as official and managerial attitudes towards them. The red flag was associated with the KMS even in the 1920s but it did not carry the significance it acquired in the late 1930s. In narratives of workers this signification is derived from their own local experiences. Fact and fiction are woven together in stories of the heroism of worker militants overpowering all opponents. One such story is about a time when managers' goondas stormed into a meeting at the Swadeshi Mills gate addressed by the communist leader Daud Khan, beat up workers, tore up the red flag and set it on fire. The injured Daud Khan called on workers to fight, at which large numbers rushed in to retrieve the burning flag. Remnants of the burnt flag, workers believed, were preserved in the KMS office as a tribute to the workers' bravery.[76] In solidarity with the Swadeshi workers, other textile workers in Kanpur hoisted red flags, pieces of cloth dyed in their own factories. In the account of Sudarshan Chakr, it is through such acts that the metaphor Lal Kanpur acquired a reality. Another story narrated is about Ilahi Baksh, a worker from Elgin Mills, dismissed by the management for wearing a red shirt to work. The KMS organised a meeting in protest at the Parade Grounds. Theatrical rituals of solidarity were performed. More than 20,000 workers, we are told, ceremoniously dipped their shirts into large drums of red dye. Collectively, they resolved to go to work clad in red the next morning. Alarmed at this protest, the Elgin managers reinstated the dismissed Ilahi.[77] In other stories the victory of red-shirted militants is celebrated with a symbolic burning of black shirts, signifying their triumph over blacklegs.[78]

Stories of Lal Kanpur have resonances from folklore: tales of encounters between the forces of good and evil and the moral

---

bastis'. *Pratap*, 27.7.1938. The reference is probably to *Mazdur*, a film directed by Mohan Bhavnani, scripted by Premchand and produced by Ajanta Studio in 1934. The film got into problems with the Censor Board for being too inflammatory—there was a near riot situation in Lahore—but was re-released in 1938. For details, see Ashish Rajadhyaksha and Paul Willemen, *Encyclopaedia of Indian Cinema* (New Delhi 1999), p. 259.

[76] Chakr, *Kanpur Mazdur Andolan*, p. 62.

[77] Ibid., p. 60; interview, Raghubir.

[78] Ibid., p. 62.

victory of the good are retold. In some, the strikers' red brigade is endowed with extra-human powers, punishing its opponents and rewarding supporters. The manager of a hosiery factory has to make a public apology at a meeting for insulting a KMS activist. In another incident, the brigade calls for a boycott of a leading trader of Gwaltoli bazaar because he was reported to have ridiculed the workers' movement. The boycott is lifted only when he apologises to Shivratan Tripathi, a worker and an active KMS member. In yet another incident, the red brigade sabotages efforts of managers to organise an anti-communist league. Red brigade members dressed in plain clothes stormed the league meeting and cried 'Inquilab Zindabad'. Soon after, we are told, the league disappeared, almost by magic. Tales from Lal Kanpur, celebrating the invincibility of workers and the vulnerability of opponents, turn the world upside down, empowering workers and disciplining those in authority.

The languages of radicalism in 1938 created real fears. Kanpur industrialists were gripped with panic. The communist sweep in the KMS elections in August 1938 seemed to confirm their fears.[79] Frightened of the colour red, the Associated Chamber of Commerce saw the red flag as symbolic of violence and disorder.[80] Change in the colour of the flag was seen as emblematic of larger changes. The industrialists now talked of the KMS as a 'red body', keen on building 'red workers' armies', involved in organising 'savage demonstrations', and raising slogans which were full of 'ferocity' and 'hatred'.[81]

[79] The communists won 8 out of 10 office-bearers' posts, 20 out of 30 seats on the sabha executive committee, and 80 out of the 120 seats on the General Council of the Sabha. *Pioneer*, 23.8.1938.

[80] 'Resolution regarding the growth of communistic propaganda', Assoc. Chamber of Commerce, Calcutta, Dec. 1938. Encl. by Secy, Chamber to Secy, GOI, HPD, 7/1/1939.

[81] Horsman, the president of the UICC, similarly expressed concern at 'the increasing influx to the United Provinces and particularly to Cawnpore, of the apostles of the Communist creed from other provinces'. 'Report on the Growth of Communistic Propoganda'. Discussion at the Annual General Meeting of the Associated Chambers HPD, File 7/1/1939. The UICC, in its annual report, notes that the KMS since its elections (1938) had openly become 'a Communist organisation exploited by outsiders for personal, political and revolutionary motives'. *UICC Report*, 1938, p. 4.

Memories of workers' upsurges in other places and other times fed into the general panic among industrialists and colonial officials. In Kanpur, district officials feared a reenactment of events in Bombay: 'Developments are similar to those in Bombay in 1929 and 1930, and the Collector apprehends that the situation may develop into a war of attrition between capital and labour.'[82] Analogies are drawn with the Soviet experience: the workers' red army, like the Soviet army, symbolises victory for the workers. In sounding general alarm, official reports create images of workers' power that tends to converge with the workers' self-perception of themselves in this period.

Beneath the order of 1938, industrialists saw violence brewing. Newspapers like the *Pioneer* articulated the fears and apprehensions of industrialists that the labouring classes were intrinsically dangerous and unruly, that striking workers were always on the brink of violence. Under the headline 'VIOLENCE THREATENED' the *Pioneer* reported that volunteers and picketers were behaving in the most 'objectionable manner'; cases of 'intimidation' and 'coercion' were frequent; workers were taken to secluded places 'roughly handled' and beaten.[83] The picture that emerges from reports of the Intelligence Department is somewhat similar. Speeches at labour meetings were reported to be 'objectionable' and 'intemperate'. Violence always appeared imminent. Labour leaders, we are informed, threatened a long-drawn-out struggle: the object of the strike was the abolition of capitalism and imperialism.[84] A letter to the editor of *Leader* expressed anxiety about the 'misuse of red pieces of cloth' by workers: 'just wear them and compel a law abiding citizen to cry halt at any place'.[85] The letter ridicules the red brigade yet it acknowledges their power in the city.

The anxiety of mill managers is expressed in a series of caricatures published in the *Pioneer*. Many of these cartoons lampoon the KMS, but in the process they reveal a deep fear of the growing KMS power and reaffirm that power. The *Pioneer* of 2 June 1938

[82] HPD, 18/10/1937 (ii).
[83] *Pioneer*, 24.5.1938.
[84] SAID, 11.6.1938, 18.6.1938.
[85] *Leader*, 26.6.1938.

carried a facsimile of three passes issued by the KMS permitting the bearer to enter the mills. An accompanying cartoon shows a weary traveller from Kanpur standing outside the gates of heaven, his entry blocked by St Peter who asks for the KMS pass. The expressed fear is obvious (see Figs 20a and b) .[86] Another cartoon shows a new KMS recruit, a Scot, marching towards the sabha headquarters with a communist flag, tempted by the offer of free shaves. English parochial sarcasm of 'celtic economic conscience' is used here to mock the expansion of KMS power. Another cartoon jibes at the Congress for its protest against police action against picketers, and its disregard of the breakdown of order and the machinery of disciplinary control (Fig. 22).[87] Yet another shows how Congressmen were being coerced by goondas into supporting the strike (Fig. 23). It was as if the expanding social support of the strikers was illusory: no individual voice of dissent could be heard in a context where lumpens held sway. The cartoon ridicules the powerlessness of the Congress leadership, its complete failure to ensure normal life in the city. The effort to misrecognise KMS power articulated the insecurity of mill managers, the voice that laughed through the cartoons, was a tense and nervous one. The industrialists' fear of Lal Kanpur, the repressed nervousness of their mock laughter, attested the power of workers. A look at themselves through the eyes of managers could only deepen their sense of self and confidence in their capacity to fight.

The outcome of the strike seemed to confirm this sense of self-confidence among the workers. The acceptance of their demands by mill managers was empowering. Not only did they agree to the demands for increased wages, and an improvement in working and living conditions, they were forced to recognise the KMS— an organisation that had become symbolic of worker militancy during the Lal Kanpur days. But if recognition of the KMS was an

[86] The *Pioneer* reported that a journalist was prevented from visiting an industrialist by picketers, mostly women and children. They demanded a sabha 'pass' from him. *Pioneer,* 11.6.1938.

[87] Papers like the *Pioneer* were critical of the local police for being too mild with the strikers. A report in the paper noted how instructions had been given to policemen not to regard picketing as an offence unless picketers gathered in a crowd. *Pioneer,* 24.5.1938.

Fig. 20a: [Maz]door Pass, Please!

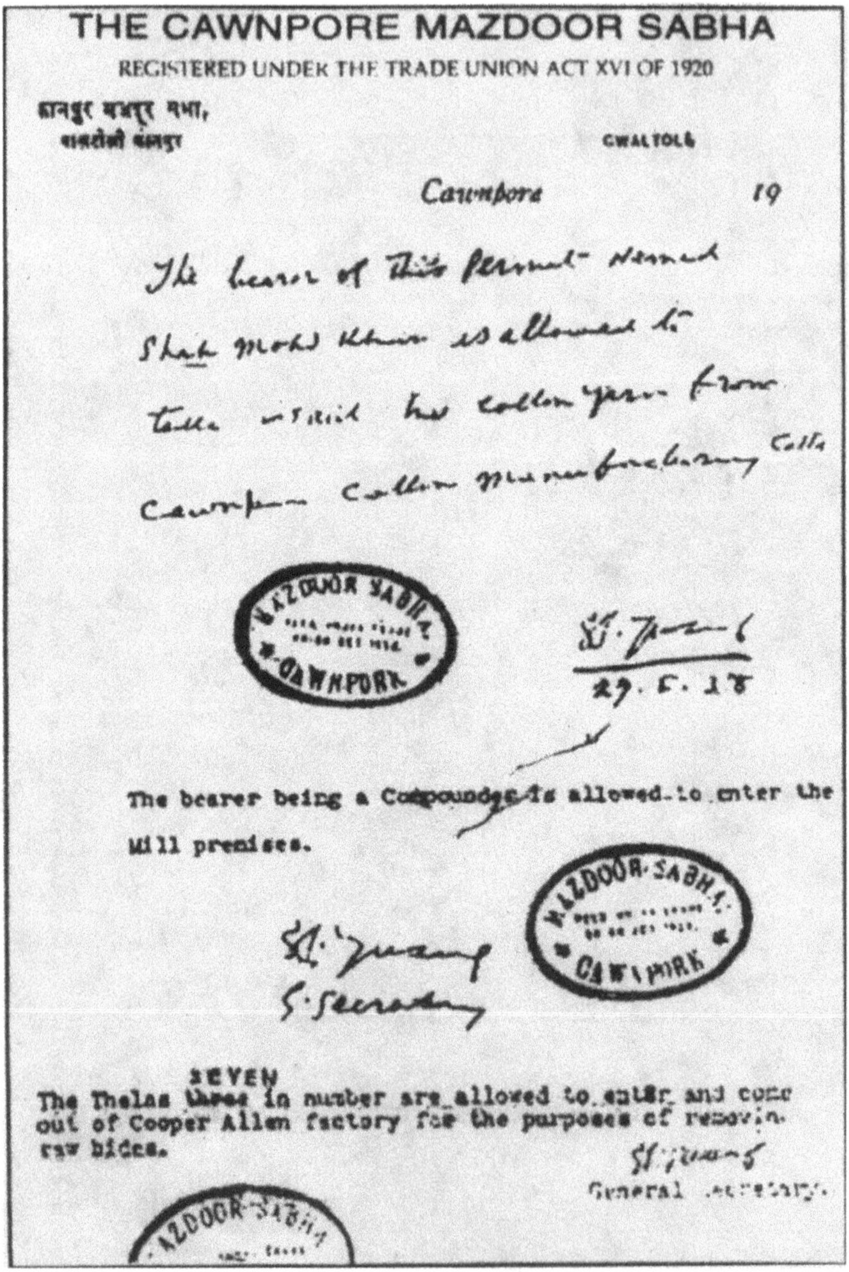
THE CAWNPORE MAZDOOR SABHA

REGISTERED UNDER THE TRADE UNION ACT XVI OF 1920

कानपुर मजदूर सभा,
ग्वालटोली कानपुर

GWALTOLI

Cawnpore 19

The bearer of this permit named Shah Mohd Khan is allowed to take with him cotton yarn from Cawnpore Cotton Manufacturing Co.

MAZDOOR SABHA CAWNPORE

27. 5. 38

The bearer being a Compounder is allowed to enter the Mill premises.

MAZDOOR SABHA CAWNPORE

G. Secretary

SEVEN
The Thelas three in number are allowed to enter and come out of Cooper Allen factory for the purposes of removing raw hides.

General Secretary.

MAZDOOR SABHA

Fig. 20b: A composite facsimile of three permits issued by the Kanpur Mazdur Sabha

Fig. 21: The New Recruit

Fig. 22: The Right to Obstruct

Fig. 23: The Congressman who Objected to the Strike

Fig. 24: Nice to know, Now

Fig. 25: Out of control

affirmation of workers' power, its reorganisation and reconstitution also defined the limits of this power.

In the post-1938 period the strength of the KMS and the workers' movement in Kanpur declined. Partly, the People's War politics of the communists and their support to the British War efforts led to a thinning of its ranks. The Defence of India Rules and the restrictions on political activity during the war years made organisation difficult. A resurgence of strikes occurred only in the post-war period, in 1946–7, when the Congress ministry was again in power. But it was only during the anti-rationalisation strikes of 1955 that something of the spirit of Lal Kanpur was recreated.[88]

Lal Kanpur remained a unique moment to which workers returned in other times of struggle. But moments like this are never indelibly inscribed creating a continuous time of memory. The learning process of workers is infinitely fractured, continuously disturbed. If in moments of struggle memories of past solidarities are dramatised, recalled and deployed, forging a collective unity, at other moments—when the impossibility of struggle paralyses the working class, dramatic moments from the past fade from memory—the links with them are ruptured, the temporal distance with the past appears unbridgeably extended. If at some moments the past appears almost contemporaneous, at others times it is infinitely stretched, almost forgotten.[89]

[88] In 1955, more than 46,000 workers went on strike for 80 days in protest against rationalisation. Six rival unions came together to form the Suti Mill Mazdur Sabha, which organised the strike.

[89] See ch. 9.

CHAPTER 7

Ties of Community

—+⥿⥿⥿+—

The politics of class and nation discussed in the earlier chapters was mediated by ties of community and religion. Discussions on community consciousness have oscillated between reductionist arguments which see culture as a reflection of, and structured by, the economy, and culturalist frames which reify culture, seeing it as a static given. While the culturalist turn has broadened historical perspectives, underlining the power of culture in ordering society, it has often denied to culture a history of change.[1] Culture appears as primordial, a past that defines the lives of workers without being redefined by them. I proceed with the assumption that culture is continuously constituted and reconstituted in a variety of ways. Ties of religion and community among workers were reworked in everyday practice, at the mohalla and the workplace, through redefinitions of community identities, through conflicts and confrontations, and through the larger politics of communal movements.

Religion, Ritual and Everyday Life

The organisation of space in the neighbourhood, the clustering and segregation of castes and communities at the workplace and outside, the celebration of festivals, the observance of rituals and

---

[1] Chartier, for instance, looks at the processes of appropriation of culture and emphasises the centrality of cultural practice to the study of history. In a different way, Bourdieu makes the question of practice central to the argument of culture. Roger Chartier, *Cultural History: Between Practice and Representation* (Oxford 1988); Pierre Bourdieu, *Outline of a Theory of Practice* (Cambridge 1977).

norms of purity and pollution, all helped to preserve a familiar milieu for workers even while they worked in the city.

Urban space came to be spatially segregated, with different communities inhabiting different areas. The pattern of distribution reflects two kinds of separation: between Hindus and Muslims, and between lower- and upper-caste Hindus. Areas like Butcher Khana, Anwarganj and Patkapore had a predominantly Muslim population—they constituted 85 per cent, 76 per cent and 81 per cent of the total population in the areas. Hindus were more spread out and scattered in almost all parts of the city. But certain areas were virtually 'Hindu areas' with few Muslims.[2] The communal riots of 1931 widened the distance, with Hindus fleeing Muslim areas and vice versa. Outside this broad pattern there was intermixing of Hindu and Muslim workers, but they rarely lived within the same hata. Muslim workers usually lived in all-Muslim or in Muslim-dominated hatas.[3] The second kind of separation was between upper- and lower-caste Hindu workers. Workers from lower-caste groups were generally excluded from hatas where Brahmans and Thakurs were predominant.[4] In rare instances, when workers from 'low' castes happened to be living with other 'high'-caste workers, special arrangements for segregation were made. Such hatas usually had some rooms with entrances facing outwards, instead of the usual opening into the walled-in courtyard, and it was in these rooms that low-caste workers lived.[5]

The system of recruitment through mistris, their role in providing lodging and loans, shaped the organisation of space in the neighbourhood. Mistris arranged cultural events like kathas and

[2] *UP Census*, 1931, part II, pp. 172–83.

[3] Neihoff, *Factory Workers,* p. 50.

[4] Even in the 1950s, Niehoff's survey shows that, despite housing problems, there was 'a definite tendency for different caste groups to keep together as much as possible and to keep out, or segregate, the less desirable castes'. Niehoff, *Factory Workers,* p. 49. A similar pattern was prevalent in Madras, where the 'untouchable' Adi-Dravidas lived in cheris segregated from workers of other castes and Muslims had their own cheris. E.D. Murphy, *Unions in Conflict: A Comparative Study of Four South Indian Textile Centres, 1918–1939* (New Delhi 1981), pp. 44–5.

[5] Niehoff, *Factory Workers,* p. 52.

Ramlilas, occasions that helped to bind participants in a common social world.

The imperatives of urban life, however, qualified the rigidities of segregation between communities. High rents and chronic housing shortage, for example, forced many to share lodgings. Among single male migrants this became a common feature and sometimes involved sharing rooms with workers of different castes. Yet even in these cases, the partners usually belonged to the same village, and upper castes shared their quarters only with those whose ritual status was not low enough to be totally impure.[6] Regional clusterings became a part of the industrial landscape. Many Banarsis, for instance, lived in close proximity in Changa Mal ka Hata and groups of them shared rooms and meals together.[7] Confronted with a situation where community boundaries seemed to blur, workers sought to redraw the limits of their socialisation: defining a new sense of community, incorporating some castes and excluding others.

In the mill settlements, similar processes were at work. At one level, workers of different castes and communities had to live together. But workers struggled to retain some form of community identity. As an official report on labour supply noted in 1906: 'Men like to live among their own caste-fellows and this is a point to which attention is always drawn when houses are allotted.'[8] At a much later period, too, similar preferences were expressed. Higher-caste workers were reluctant to go to the Allenganj settlement where the inhabitants were mostly Chamars.[9]

At the workplace too, norms of purity and pollution informed

[6] Ibid., pp. 78–9. See also ch. 3.

[7] Banarsis were those from Benares. In the present context, however, the term encompasses all those from the eastern districts of UP. Interviews with Prem Narayan, employee in Swadeshi Cotton Mills, Kanpur, and Praga Dutta, worker in Kanpur Cotton Mills.

[8] Freemantle, 'Report on the Supply of Labour', UP Rev. Progs. B, 1906, no. 90.

[9] Ev. Carnegie, BIC, KLIC Progs., UP Ind. Dep. 1145,1937, Bundle 110. By the time of Niehoff's survey in the 1950s there was a mixture of castes at both Macrobertsganj and Allenganj, but sweepers were generally kept out. In Allenganj, they were eventually given quarters facing away from the rest. Niehoff, *Factory Workers*, p. 52.

relationships in important ways. In leather factories, Chamars and Muslims were dominant.[10] Managers preferred Chamars because of their 'traditional' skills in the occupation, and middle- and higher-caste workers shared a prejudice against leather as 'unclean'. The small proportion of upper castes employed in leather did the relatively clean jobs, such as storing and packing finished shoes. In the vegetable tannery department, where hides were soaked, workers from a non-Chamar background handled chemicals but refused to touch wet hide.[11]

The caste composition of the workforce in the textile industry was more diversified, but even here there were caste and community clusterings.[12] In the late nineteenth century, Julahas and Koris were predominant in reeling and weaving, Ahirs in carding, and Brahmans in the weaving preparation section. Only during the late 1930s was there a greater diversification of castes employed within the textile industry. But pollution taboos were far from absent. The preponderance of Koris and Muslims in weaving was related, amongst other reasons, to the dangers of ritual pollution in a job which required the sucking of yarn into the shuttle each time a weft bobbin had to be replaced.[13] The taboo against jutha was deeply rooted in the psyche of most Hindu workers, and contact with untouchables was considered unthinkable. Workers devised strategies to grapple with the perceived threat of pollution.

[10] Castes Employed in the Leather Industry (1944)

Religion and caste	Percentage of total
Chamar	63.54
Brahman	0.46
Kayastha	0.18
Muslims	32.27

Total no. of workers in the sample=1094

Source: *LIC: Report on Labour Conditions in Tanneries and Leather Goods Factories* (Simla 1946), p. 29.

[11] Niehoff, *Factory Workers*, p. 55.

[12] See also ch. 2

[13] In Bombay and Madras in contrast, 'untouchable' castes were excluded from the weaving sheds. Morris, *Emergence*, p. 79; Murphy, *Unions in Conflict*, p. 44.

The story ran that an upper-caste worker nicknamed 'Vichari Maharaj' carried his own little pipe which he fixed onto the shuttle each time he had to suck in the yarn, refusing to touch the polluted yarn with his lips.[14] Upper-caste women rarely transgressed the prohibitions against factory work. Only women from a Kori and Chamar background worked in textile mills.

Within the factory, some flexibility in norms was accepted, but rules of commensality had a rigidity of their own. The early decades of the twentieth century, in the memory of many workers, were times when norms of chhut-pat were more rigid.[15] Workers recounted how any violation of norms in the city was concealed from the community in the village.[16] Sudarshan Chakr, for instance, looked back with amusement at an incident in the 1930s, when a shopkeeper refused to sell him gaya marka colour for laddoos, thinking it was an ingredient made from cow's flesh. Others recalled these as times when most upper-caste workers avoided contact with lower castes during mealtimes. Even within lower castes there were taboos against touch pollution. A Kori worker avoided any contact with Nats or Pasis.[17] Higher-caste workers considered it almost their caste prerogative to be reimbursed in cash if a Chamar or a Muslim worker defiled their rotis.[18] Many Brahman workers refrained from carrying cooked food into the factory. Lunch for them consisted of uncooked food like dry chabena, not subject to the same pollution taboos.[19] Because of these attitudes, dining sheds provided in the mills were not popular with most workers. Only a few used the Elgin Mills dining shed, and Brahman workers stayed away from it altogether. Mangali Prasad of the Kanpur Cotton Mills felt a common dining space was of no

[14] Interview, Chakr. Vichari in this context refers to one who is fastidious about pollution taboos.

[15] Chhut-pat = pollution taboos. Interviews, Raghubir, Moolchand, 30.12.1983.

[16] Interview, Chakr.

[17] Moolchand, a worker, recollected how Koris would throw away food that had been touched by a Nat (those from a community of jugglers and acrobats and ranked low in the caste hierarchy).

[18] Interview, Shriram.

[19] Chabena = parched grain. Ev. Sheo Shankar and Sheo Audhar (workers), *IFC*, pp. 69, 71.

use all; he himself would not eat there if a Bhangi cleaned it. He preferred a Kahar for the job. Mangali Prasad, incidentally, was a mill committee member and appeared before the Labour Inquiry committee (1938) in a red shirt. Sheo Audhar, another witness before the Committee, had no objection to a common dining shed, provided he did not come in physical contact with any other worker. Lalloo of Elgin Mills preferred a separate dining shed for Hindus. The Kanpur Cotton Mills' shed proved more functional because of a provision for separate spaces for Hindus and Muslims. Two separate shops for food articles were also provided—one run by a Hindu and the other by a Muslim.[20]

Within the factory, religion became a site for a new kind of contestation—the struggle to define work time and festive time. Collective action around the issue of festival holidays reaffirmed religious identities at the workplace. The workers of Elgin Mills refused to work on Shab-i Barat in October 1937 because it was customarily a holiday.[21] Most mills remained closed on Kartiki Purnima, but when the Maheshwari Devi Jute Mills continued to work on that day, a large number of workers stayed away and the management subsequently declared a lockout. The KMS was critical of this action: 'If a mill works on such an important festival as Kartiki Purnima they [the management] must reckon with a more than usual percentage of absenteeism and this cannot be made a pretext of declaring a lock-out.'[22] The participation of mill workers in festivals was so important that managements could fix festival dates by closing the mills on a particular day. The UICC suggested, for instance, that the conflict over the timing of the Ganga Mela could be resolved by fixing the Ganga Mela holiday

[20] Ev. Wilkinson, Caterall and Tinker (employers); Mangali Prasad, Sheo Audhar, Lalloo (workers), KLIC Progs., UP Ind. Dep., 1145,1937, Bundle 110 (UPSA). Fear of pollution surfaced even in moments of collective struggle. During the stay-in strike in the Kanpur Cotton Mills in 1924, Mohd Shafi, a worker in the mills, recounted how their leaders implored them to continue the struggle with the threat: 'If we ran away we Muslims would eat pig and the Hindus cow.' Cawnpore Cotton Mills Riots Inquiry, HPD, 153,1924.

[21] Gen. Secy, KMS to Secy, KLIC, 16.11.1937, KLIC Progs., 1145, 1937, Bundle 110 (UPSA).

[22] KMS Memo on MD Jute Mills lockout, KLIC Progs., 1145,1937, Bundle 110 (UPSA).

for factory workers: 'The mere fact of closing the mills could result in 50000–60000 people going to the ghats that day. Even if certain sections of the community wished to hold the mela on another day, they would not manage to bring sufficient people.'[23]

The organisational activities of workers were sanctified through sacred rituals and practices.[24] The KMS in its early days arranged gatherings of workers by organising kathas and maulud sharifs. This provided a cover against police surveillance but the choice of the ritual was significant—the katha and havan accompanied with the chanting of Vedas and distribution of prasad to the participants.[25] Prominent among the early organisers of the KMS was Pandit Kamdatt, an ex-worker in Elgin Mills, and an Arya Samajist. Kamdatt performed Vedic rituals at sabha meetings. These rituals were played out in a sacred site. Workers recalled how Bhaironghat, on the banks of the Ganga, was where meetings were held and an oath in the name of the Ganga was taken. The rites of initiation, the havan, the chanting of Vedas and the sacred oath marked the KMS with a religious stamp. A library set up for workers by Kamdatt focused primarily on religious books and Arya Samaj literature.[26] A religious idiom forms a part of akhara culture so integral to the mohalla and workers' lives. Devotion to Hanuman (and the gada, a round stone attached to a stick or club) is common in akharas. In the Mazdur Sabha akhara too, slogans of Bajrang Bali were a regular feature. The religious idiom did not give akharas an exclusivist orientation. Muslim workers were also actively associated with the KMS akhara.

Religious symbols and images structured the discourse of workers in significant ways. The writings of workers like Sudarshan Chakr, who like his father worked in the Kanpur mills, are framed in a religious mode. Chakr was born in Choti Manoh village in Kanpur district and, like many other workers, spent his childhood in the village.[27] The choice of his pen-name, Sudarshan Chakr, the invincible weapon of Vishnu, is symbolic. In one of his major

[23] Letter, 17, 1934, *UPCC Report*, 1934.

[24] See also ch. 5.

[25] Chakr, *Communist Katha*, p. 227.

[26] *Pratap*, 9.6.1919.

[27] Surya Prakash Tripathi, *Vishvakavi Shri Sudarshan Chakr* (Kanpur 1973).

works, entitled *Communist Katha*, Chakr tries to replicate the structure of the Ramayana. The chapters, seven in number, with titles such as 'Marx Kand', 'Rus Kand', 'Chin Kand', 'Bharat Kand', are reminiscent of the seven 'Kands' in the Ramayana. The metrical form, using the doha and chaupayi, are again similar to those in the epic.[28] In one of his epic poems, entitled *Vishwamaha-bharata*, Chakr focuses on the struggle between the rich and the poor, the exploiters and the exploited, and the eventual victory of justice over injustice. For a worker like Chakr, legendary heroes like Rama and Krishna were so intimate a part of the social world that allusions to them figure in all his poems. Often, the names of workers are used metaphorically, symbolising characters from the Ramayana: '*Siriram Ravana ranranga/Dekhatinheh shatru matibhang*' (Seeing Shri Ram, a miltant worker, on the battlefield against Ravana, the enemy disappeared). From various allusions in his poems, it appears that the spectrum of figures—Rama, Vyas Muni, Lenin, Stalin, Gandhi—on the cover illustration of his book *Vishwamahabharata* is not coincidental. To him, all of them in their own way, were avatars who had struggled against evil and injustice: '*Krishna hee Karl Marx ban gaye, vahi Lenin ban kar tan gaye. Vahi the Stalin avatar, gaya jisse Hitler tak har*'.[29]

In such a context, religious slogans —'Bajrang Bali ki Jai' and 'Allah-o-Akbar'—had a powerful familiar appeal. Decades after 1931, trade union leaders remembered how cries of 'Allah-o-Akbar' from bastis dominated by Muslims and 'Bajrang Bali' from bastis with mainly Hindu workers, were frequently heard, during and after the riots.[30] To left trade unionists this appeared as a time when radical slogans like 'Inquilab Zindabad' (Long Live Revolution) were unfamiliar to workers. When this slogan

---

[28] Doha = a couplet; chaupayi = four-lined rhymes.

[29] The poet describes Karl Marx, Lenin and Stalin as incarnations of Krishna with his invincible strength. S.Chakr, *Vishvamahabharata* (Kanpur 1977), p. 96. Chakr considers himself a nastik and he looked back with amusement at an incident in the 1930s, when a shopkeeper refused to sell him gaya marka colour for ladoos thinking it was an ingredient made from cow flesh. Ironically, Chakr himself was quite disturbed by reports about the use of beef tallow in cooking oil in the 1980s. Interview, Chakr. Marka (brand name) is confused here with marke (to kill).

[30] Interview, Arjun Arora.

was raised in 1936, the response two hundred yards away, was 'Lanklat Vrindavan'. The reference to 'lanklat' (long cloth) and Vrindavan is meaningful: while the general emotional zeal and rhythm of the slogan 'Inquilab Zindabad' is captured, it is expressed in an idiom familiar to the workers.

In describing the past as a time of chhut-pat, a time when pollution taboos were all-powerful, working class memory tends to erase traces of difference and change. A closer study shows the complex processes at work. Workers struggled to retain certain norms of purity and pollution in their daily lives, trying to set the limits of change, yet everyday practice transformed and redefined the very categories with which they apprehended their social world. In histories of the everyday life of workers, the notion of an 'inner' protected space of tradition is hard to retain.[31] There was no pure space of tradition untainted by negotiations with the new industrial milieu. Instead of an opposition between the inner and outer—one closed and the other open to change—there was a continuous process of dialogue and conflict in both spaces, within the home and outside, in the neighbourhood and workspace. What was retained in workers' lives was an allegiance to certain notions, categories which may represent a continuity with the past and which allowed workers to see themselves as belonging to tradition even as they were reworking each of these categories. So the category of pollution came to be emptied of content. A language of purity and pollution was continuously used, creating a sense of an unchanging tradition and of a simple continuity with the past.

Mobilising the Community: Assertion of Caste

While the ordering categories of everyday life were being reworked at one level, at another the identities of communities were being

---

[31] The idea that colonial subjects confront modernity by protecting an inner space of tradition and spirituality has been strongly argued by Partha Chatterjee, *The Nation and its Fragments* (Princeton 1993), pp. 3–13. In a different way, the relationship between the outer and inner space has been discussed by Tanika Sarkar, *Hindu Wife, Hindu Nation: Community, Religion and Cultural Nationalism* (Delhi 2001), pp. 23–52; and in Dipesh Chakrabarty, *Provincializing Europe: Postcolonial Thought and Historical Difference* (Princeton 2000), pp. 214–36.

redesigned. The internal contours of identity were not pre-given;
they were redrawn through processes of mobilisation and
redefinition within the urban context. There was a variety of ways
in which the attributes of communities were reshaped.

The preponderance of lower castes in the working class population in Kanpur meant that the question of caste remained important to the process of identity formation.[32] Reform activities
whether initiated by upper or lower castes, had to direct their
energies towards the working population in the city and incorporate them. Arya Samajists, Congress and dalit organisations
mobilised lower castes in different ways, articulating in the
process the limits and possibilities of reform.

Nationalist leaders in the 1920s tried to draw workers from the
Chamar, Kureel, Kori and other ritually impure castes towards
Congress activities through programmes of social reform. In
1924, the Kanpur Hindu Sabha organised an Arya Swaraj Sabha
chaired by Jawaharlal Rohatgi, a local Congressman, to work
among 'untouchable' castes.[33] The sabha set up schools in achut
mohallas. The educational programme in the schools laid special
emphasis on the teaching of religion and nationalism. Provisions
were also made for setting up akharas in various localities. Organised sport could draw children to the KMS and weld a sense of
belonging and community among the participants.

The Hindu Sabha tried to reach out to dalit children through
the Hindu Bal Sabha. At Bal Sabha meetings participants recited
verses from the Ramayana and Hanuman Chalisa and gave discourses on Hindu religion and its contemporary distortions.
Young enthusiasts were given books and sweets as inducements
to memorise verses from the Ramayana.[34] Among the important
office-bearers of the Bal Sabha was Arjun Arora, who later joined
the Communist Party and became an important trade unionist.[35]
Congress and KMS leaders like Ganesh Shankar Vidyarthi attended
some of the sabha meetings.[36] The sabha set up libraries for dalit
children in Patkapur and Sadar Bazaar.[37] On Sundays, bal sabhas

[32] See ch. 2.
[33] *Pratap*, 7.9.1924.
[34] *Vartman*, 28.4.1927.
[35] Ibid., 17.12.1927.
[36] Ibid., 26.8.1927.
[37] Ibid., 1.8.1927, 1.12.1927.

in various localities organised debates so that children could acquire oratorial skills.[38]

The anxiety about dalit welfare among Arya Samajists and Congress members was motivated by considerations that were similar. They were concerned about the conversion of lower castes to Christianity and Islam. Congressmen like Vidyarthi expressed fears about the conversion activities of tabligh organisations.[39] Arya Samajists passed resolutions to intensify shuddhi and welfare activities among the depressed castes. Contemporary papers reported several cases of shuddhi in Kanpur.[40] The constant refrain in dailies close to the Congress, like *Pratap* and *Vartman*, was that dalits should resist conversion to Christianity and Islam and improve their material conditions within Hinduism. Organisations engaged in welfare activities among the Harijans, implicitly, however, assumed the 'uncleanliness' of these castes. The 'unclean' had to be cleaned, the impure purified. A significant aspect of the activities of the Arya Swaraj Sabha in Kanpur consisted in the free distribution of soap and datuns in achut mohallas.[41] Hygiene and personal cleanliness was considered crucial for the uplift of depressed castes. The focus of Hindu Sabha activities was not so much on a critique of caste Hindu discrimination against dalits but on education and purification as a means to uplift. Dalits could be incorporated within the Hindu hierarchy only if they cleansed and purified themselves. Even those like

[38] Ibid., 22.11.1928.

[39] '*Is samay . . . 2000 Hindu prati saptah isai hote hain. Musalman bhi ve dharadhar ho rahe hain . . . Yadi hinduon mein shithilta ghati nahin, aur unme nyaya ka bhav jaga nahin, to choti jatiyon ke sab log, jo aj Hindu jati ke ang hain, usse kat-kat kar alag ja paregein, isai ya musalman ho jayengein.* (At present around 2000 Hindus convert to Christianity every week. Islam is also claiming many converts. If Hindus remain weak then almost all members from lower castes will become Christians or Muslims). Vidyarthi, *Kranti ka Udgosh*, p. 797.

[40] See, for instance, *Vartman*, 8.11.1928, 10.11.1928. On Arya Samaj activities in Kanpur see also, S.Vidyalankar, *Arya Samaj ka Itihas*, vol. 2, p. 242.

[41] Pratap, 7.9.1924. Datuns = twigs (commonly neem twigs) used for cleaning teeth; achut = untouchable. For a discussion on a similar programme of reforms advocated by Hindu Mahasabha leaders in Punjab, see Vijay Prashad, *Untouchable Freedom: A Social History of the Dalit Community* (Delhi 2000), pp. 82–3.

Vidyarthi who defended the Arya Samaj against its critics in other contexts, were sceptical of its reforming activities among lower castes.[42] The prescriptions for uplift of lower castes offered by the Arya Samaj, Vidyarthi emphasised, only reaffirmed unjust caste practices. It mobilised lower castes by holding out the promise of a higher status signified through the wearing of the sacred thread: practices which legitimised discriminatory practices in Hindu society.[43]

The 1920s was also a period when attempts at self-assertion and organisation were made by lower-caste groups in Kanpur and outside.[44] Swami Achutanand, Ramcharan Kureel and other ideologues of the movement spoke in a language radically different from that of other upper-caste reformers. Achutanand traced the decline in status of Chamars and other lower castes to conquest and enslavement by Aryan invaders.[45] The injustices perpetrated by Aryans, according to him, led ultimately to the subjugation of Aryans by Muslim rulers.[46] Adi-Hindu reformers were deeply influenced by the devotional ideas of the Bhakti movement. They propagated the worship of Bhakti saints and the celebration of

[42] Vidyarthi reacted sharply to the critique of Arya Samaj sectarianism by Gandhi and argued how the Samaj emerged in a context when Hindus were being attacked from all quarter. G.S.Vidyarthi, *Kranti ka Udgosh: Ganesh Shankar Vidyarthi ki Kalam Se*, ed. Radhakrishna Awasthi, p. 714. See also Vidyarthi, 'Hindu Sabha aur Uske Musalman Alochak', in *Kranti ka Udgosh*, p. 802. See also ch. 8.

[43] Vidyarthi, 'Hinduon ki Kup Mandookta', *Kranti ka Udgosh*, pp. 797–8.

[44] On the ideology of lower-caste movements in UP in this period, see Nandini Gooptu, 'Caste and Labour: Untouchable Social Movements in Urban Uttar Pradesh in the Early Twentieth Century', in Peter Robb, ed., *Dalit Movements and the Meanings of Labour in India* (Delhi 1993).

[45] On Achutanand's ideology, see also R.S.Khare, *The Untouchable as Himself: Ideology, Identity and Pragmatism Among the Lucknow Chamars* (Cambridge 1986), pp. 81–7. On the Adi-Hindu movement in Punjab, see Mark Juergensmeyer, *Religion as Social Vision: The Movement against Untouchability in 20th Century Punjab* (California1982). On lower-caste politics in North India see also Vijay Prashad, *Untouchable Freedom*; Owen Lynch, *The Politics of Untouchability: Social Movements and Social Change in a City of India* (Columbia 1969).

[46] Ganesh Shankar Vidyarthi, 'Adi Hindu Andolan', *Kranti ka Udgosh*, pp. 799–800.

festivals commemorating important figures associated with the Bhakti movement, like Ravidas.

Regional and local organisations among lower castes appropriated and interpreted the ideology of the Adi-Hindu movement in different ways. The writings of lower-caste leaders like Ramcharan Kureel, who were trying to reach out to the working class population in Kanpur, incorporate the politics of caste discrimination into the language of class. Prominent among such lower-caste organisations were the Kureel Sabhas which came up in Kanpur, Unnao and neighbouring villages. In pamphlets and literature circulated by the Kureel Sabha, the decline in the status of Chamars in society was attributed to a loss of skill. Ramcharan Kureel elaborates how a class of self-interested (*svarthi log*) people had deprived Chamars of their skills.[47] Dispossessed of their traditional expertise, they were reduced to the position of ordinary labourers. Describing the activities of lower castes in the villages, Ramcharan narrates how they did months of hard labour through the year, in the hot sun and through bitter cold, sowing, harvesting, threshing grain, and then cleaning and painting landowners' houses. Later, the grain was ground and made into flour by wives and womenfolk from untouchable households. He drew contrasts between the toil and sweat of the lower castes with the easy, languorous life the upper castes enjoyed all through the year: '*Jara, garmi, barsat mein pair pasarkar sukh se soven* . . .'[48]

Lower-caste leaders like Ramcharan ridiculed and attacked the taboos against untouchables in contemporary society. He pointed to the irony of the fact that artisanal products made by lower-caste artisans were widely used yet there were all kinds of prohibitions against touching the people who produced them. The grain ground into flour by lower-caste women was saturated with their toil and sweat, both literally and metaphorically; it was consumed by upper-caste masters without any fear of pollution. Yet pollution taboos were used to prevent physical proximity with lower castes. When there were situations requiring the

[47] In a powerful piece, *Anyaya se Achut,* Babu Ramcharan Alekhakar describes how 'untouchables' became *kala kaushal viheen* (without any skill) (Danakhori, Kanpur n.d.).

[48] Winter, summer, rains, they stretch out and sleep. Babu Ramcharan Alekhakar, *Anyaya se Achut.*

zamindar's intervention, lower-caste labourers were told to stay at a suitable distance: '*Alag se bat kar kahin chu ne lena alag rah kahin ham chuhtere ne ho jayen . . .*' (Stay away: do not touch us or we will be polluted). Any transgression of these codes was met with relentless physical and verbal violence. Acts of repression, Ramcharan argues, were justified through an ideology which condemned certain castes as 'untouchables' and attributed their social position to their birth. Repeated violence against lower castes denuded them of all self-esteem: they began to believe in upper-caste myths of domination and saw themselves as lowly by birth.[49]

The speeches and writings of lower castes seek to create a new identity for Chamars both by questioning Brahmanical notions of pure and impure and by valorising their work and their skills. Ramcharan Kureel, for instance, narrated new myths about the social origins of Chamars, negating and inverting upper-caste myths.[50] Contrary to dominant caste notions which stigmatised leather work, and attributed the fallen status of Chamars to their unclean occupations, Ramcharan glorified their work. He emphasised that Raidasis alone possessed the special gift of creating beautiful and useful objects out of the hide of dead animals. It was for this reason that Chamars had enjoyed a special status in ancient times: some among them were venerated as saints. Unlike lower-caste myths which claim dignity by tracing a ritually pure and high-caste lineage for themselves, Kureels like Ramcharan assert the dignity of leather work. He invents a past where leather work had a different status. In his account the fallen status of

[49] Lower castes began to understand their social status in terms of divine dispensation: '*Hamko ishwar ne neech hi paida kiya . . .*' (God created us as lowly). Ramcharan Alekhakar, *Anyaya se Achut*.

[50] For a wider discussion on lower-caste myths of origin, see Rosalind O' Hanlon, *Caste, Conflict and Ideology: Mahatma Jotirao Phule and Low Caste Protest in Nineteenth-Century Western India* (Cambridge 1985); Robert Deliege, 'The Myths of Origin of the Indian Untouchables'), *Man* (new series), 18, 1993; Ranajit Guha, 'The Career of an Anti-God in Heaven and on Earth', in Sugata Bose, ed., *Credit, Markets, and the Agrarian Economy of Colonial India* (Delhi 1994); Saurabh Dube, *Untouchable Pasts: Religion, Identity, and Power among a Central Indian Community, 1780–1950* (New York 1998).

leather work in contemporary society was a sign of social degradation. In other countries, Ramcharan Kureel argues, Chamars were respected: the Soviet leader Stalin and the British Prime Minister Lloyd George were Chamars.[51] In his representation all those working with their hands are Chamars. The term chamar (leather workers) is transformed into a generic category incorporating all workers. Chamars come to be seen as workers and workers as Chamars. What binds the two and erases their difference is the act of labour. Ramcharan Kureel was also making an effort to reach out to the working class audience in Kanpur by categorising labour leaders from a working class background as Chamars.

In contemporary society, he argues, their skills were devalued: leather work was considered unclean and Raidasis were treated with contempt. Ramcharan traces the decline in their status to the de-skilling of Chamars and their transformation into ordinary labourers. Chamars were forced into begar labour and had no access to education or the means to improve their social status. He suggests that it was by elevating their work and skills, by educating their children, that Chamars could improve their social position. Chamars, he argues, should set up leather factories which could employ the unemployed in their community.

Like other lower-caste organisations, Kureel sabhas tried to create a sense of solidarity among caste members by unifying them around new forms of worship. Kureels were asked to boycott corrupt Brahman pandits with their rigid notions of purity and pollution. Instead of the usual Satyanarayan katha where the story of Satyanarayan was narrated by a Brahman pandit, Kureels were encouraged to organise Ravidas kathas where the story of the Bhakti saint Ravidas was told and prayers offered to him. The idea of Kureel brotherhood and solidarity was propagated and all Kureels from different localities and regions were represented as part of the same family.[52]

Lower-caste organisations tried to define a new identity for themselves by doing away with the signs of low status. Opposition

[51] Extract of speech of Ramcharan Kureel, reproduced in *Unnao Zila Conference Report*, 7.12.1929.

[52] Ramcharan Kureel, *Kureel Bhaiyon ki Seva Mein Khuli Chitthi* (Danakhori, Kanpur, 10.9.1934).

to caste norms was expressed through a violation of codes of dress which served to differentiate lower castes from others. Lower-caste men, for instance, were not allowed to wear trousers and jackets; and women were not to wear *lehengas* and *dupattas* bordered with gold or silver and anklets.[53] In the case of lower-class men and women, dull and dirty clothes made their lowliness visible from a distance: '*Hamari jati ko jabardasti se bhadesil jevar ve maile kapre pahanne ke rivaj dalne ki koshish karte the jisme dur se hi dhikhne me bure malum pare.*'[54] Dullness was not only their natural state of being, a corollary of their poverty, it was an imposed marker of their identity, signifying their difference with upper castes. Kureel panchayats in the 1920s tried to create a new self-identity and critiqued existing caste codes. They pointed out how lower-caste men and women could not dress attractively even if they could afford it. Fear of censure and punishment by upper castes often forced them to submit to existing codes of dress. Transgression of these was traditionally penalised by upper castes.[55] The way in which low-caste women presented themselves was particularly important as a marker of status. In the 1920s and 1930s. Kureel sabhas asserted the right of lower castes to dress in ways they considered pleasing. Kureel panchayats

[53] Pamphlet entitled *Achut Bhaiyon ke Liye Shubh Sandesh* issued by Bhavani Prasad, Tamsenganj, Sitapur. The leaflet cites instances when women from low castes were forced to shed their anklets by upper castes. The author points out how achuts could not wear clean and respectable clothes even out of their own savings ('*Apni hi kamai se saph suthra kapra pahanna aur apni striyon ke pahanava adi sudhar karna bara hi kathin hai . . .*') On clothes as a marker of identity, see Robert Hardgrave, 'The Breast Cloth Controversy: Caste Consciousness and Social Change in Southern Travancore',*IESHR*, 5:2, June 1968; Bernard Cohn, 'Cloth, Clothes and Colonialism: India in the Nineteenth Century', in *Colonialism and Its Forms of Knowledge: The British in India* (Princeton 1996); Uday Kumar, 'Self, Body and Inner Sense: Some Reflections on Sree Narayana Guru and Kumaran Asan', *Studies in History*, 13:2, July 1997.

[54] Our jati was forcibly made to wear hideous jewelry and dirty clothes so that we appeared repulsive from a distance.

[55] Kureels invented their own rituals of purification. If a Kureel married a woman who was ritually inferior, she had to be purified with gangajala (water from the Ganges, considered pure, in Brahminical Hinduism). Interview, Moolchand.

criticised prohibitions on dress and passed resolutions encouraging members of their community to dress as they pleased, and smoke and eat anywhere. Conflicts over such issues were not only between higher and lower castes but within low castes as well. Kureel men often imposed repressive codes on women, disallowing anklets and bright clothes. An open letter signed by Raidasi Kureels scathingly attacked the restrictions imposed by Kureel men on women. While the men wore churas (bracelets) and dressed as they pleased, women were humiliated and abused if they did so. To disallow women from adorning themselves, Raidas Kureels argued, was to accept dress codes imposed on them by upper castes.

Even in rebelling against upper-caste norms, lower-caste organisations appropriated upper-caste rituals and practices. Kureel sabhas appealed to caste members to stay clean, dress well and avoid eating the meat of dead animals. A sabha in the vicinity of Kanpur proposed a fine of Rs 25 on those who consumed objectionable meat.[56] Similarly, in a leaflet issued before Holi, Ramcharan Kureel appealed to lower castes to celebrate the festival in a clean and dignified way without throwing mud and dirt on each other.[57] In celebrating festivals commemorating bhakti saints like Ravidas, Kureel sabhas appropriated elements of popular rituals like the Ganga snan, the ceremonial dip in the Ganges. Kureels were urged to light up their houses on Ravidas Jayanti just as was done on Diwali.[58]

Working class politics of this time sought to incorporate the politics of caste into the language of labour and class. Working class leaders like Kamdatt tried to reach out to dalits in 1919–20. Lower-caste workers like Moolchand were associated with the committee constituted to negotiate a settlement in 1919. In order to involve lower-caste workers more actively with the KMS in the 1920s, efforts were made to organise Sunday meals at the sabha office. Hindus of all castes and Muslims were to eat together. But the food served on these occasions consisted of dry chana (gram),

[56] *Kusambhi ke Charmkar Bhaiyon ki Panchayat,* issued by Master Bhushan Ram, Unnao (Kanpur n.d.).

[57] Ramcharan Kureel, *Holi ka Premuphar,* 26.3.1938.

[58] *Bhagwan Raidas ka Janm,* issued by Ravidas Janmotsav Samiti, Coolie Bazaar, Kanpur.

that is, food in a natural state, not subject to the usual prohibitions.[59] Even in opposing norms of purity and pollution, the KMS
was reaffirming them by observing Brahmanical prohibitions
about cooked food. The Harijan Sewak Sangh which carried on
welfare activities among sweepers, emphasised norms of cleanliness
and urged Chamars to give up un-Hindu customs like eating beef,
carrion and leftovers, as well as other 'unclean' habits.[60]

In the 1930s, the discourse of class became more powerful in
the public language of the communists. Muslims workers, who
were increasingly alienated from the KMS in the late 1920s and
lower-caste workers, were drawn to the radical rhetoric of the
communists. Koriana, for instance, where Koris were dominant,
remained a communist stronghold till the 1960s. The symbolism
of the red flag and the wearing of red shirts in the days of Lal Kanpur had a powerful appeal among lower castes who were rebelling
against signs of low status by wearing bright colours.[61] For many
workers the defiance with which they entered the mills in red was
both an expression of class solidarity and caste rebellion.

But there were also conflicts and tensions in the relationship
between lower-caste workers and others. During the strike of
1938, many lower-caste workers were critical of the KMS for its

[59] *Chana bhoj itvar karaven, Hindu Muslim sang chabaven,*

Yadapi vishesh aj nahi koyi vahi din bari bat yah hoyi
Hamhun sang pita ke javen, jeevbrahm ko bhed mitave.

(On Sundays a meal of chana is arranged where Hindus and Muslims eat
together. Though not as significant today, it was big occasion in those
days. I went along with my father and participated in this attempt to do
away with distinctions between people). Chakr, *Communist Katha*
(Kanpur 1961), p. 227.

[60] *Harijan Survey Committee Report, 1933–34* (Kanpur 1934), p. 57.

[61] The Report of the Ad Dharma Mandal for Punjab, for instance, says
'Red colour is the symbol of the Ad Dharma. It is the color of the original
inhabitants; the Aryans took it and prohibited Untouchables from wearing
it. We request the government to allow us to wear red colors. In fact, we insist
on it: red is our rightful color.' Cited in Mark Juergensmeyer, *Religion as a
Social Vision*, p. 53. Juergensmeyer elaborates that the wearing of red in
areas of Punjab that bordered on Rajasthan as a 'direct affrontery, since
upper caste Rajputs there considered it to be the color of their own military
royalty . . . ', p. 54.

lack of sensitivity towards their problems. Some of them became a part of the Dalit Mazdur Sangh. The union appealed for separate representation of depressed castes before the Labour Inquiry Committee.[62] In protest against the discrimination they suffered from caste Hindu practices. Many lower-caste workers refused to accept relief from the strikers. They argued that the strike affected them more severely than other workers. While caste Hindus could find alternative modes of livelihood by vending sweetmeats and other edibles, lower castes, who were considered impure, were denied this option. The Dalit Mazdur Sangh workers passed a resolution demanding that they be allowed to set up *khomchas* without interference from caste Hindus.[63]

An issue that created conflict between dalits and other workers was also the attitude towards the colonial state and imperialism. Dalit organisations continued to affirm a faith in British rule and distanced themselves from nationalist propaganda. Writings by depressed caste leaders which appealed to caste members to support British rule were circulated and dalits were cautioned against Congress propaganda.[64]

In a poem called 'Pheku', written as a tribute to a dalit worker, Chakr articulates some of the ambiguities in the relationship between communists and lower castes. Pheku is known as a communist and active in the workers' movement in Kanpur. His name 'Pheku' (literally one that can be thrown) personifies his low-caste status. Besides, Pheku was physically disabled, orphaned as a child, and poor. Lower-caste workers like Pheku experienced a

[62] The Dalit Mazdur Sangh passed a resolution that the KMS was not truly representative of the workers employed in the Kanpur mills because there were no representatives of the depressed workers in the executive. *Pioneer,* 5.5.1938. The union also demanded representation in the welfare centres for workers. *Pioneer,* 10.10.1938.

[63] *Pioneer*, 12.6.1938.

[64] '*Congress ki chikni chupri batein our kameti mein kabhi nahin bhag lena chahiye*' (Do not be carried away by the sweet talk of the Congress and do not participate in their activities) sd. Bhawani Prasad, Sitapur. '*Achut Bhaiyon ke Liye Shubh Sandesh*'. In another leaflet, all untouchables, Koris, Chamars, etc., are told that they can only progress and improve their conditions under British rule. *Sat Karor ki Pukar*, sd. Jiya Lal Chowdhary (Kanpur 1923). At the Dalit Mazdur Sangh meeting in May 1937 the Collector, Owen, was a special invitee. *Pioneer,* 5.5.1938.

new sense of dignity and freedom, being part of a communist 'commune', living with other comrades and cooking for them in their collective kitchen in the days of Lal Kanpur.[65] The poem ends on a tragic note: '*Marne ke bad bhi na koi ahsan kare / ardhi mein kandhe ka sahara nahin chahiye.*'[66] The meaning of the lines somewhat obscure but Chakr explains elsewhere that communist leaders refused to identify Pheku's corpse and give him a funeral.[67] Chakr recounted sadly how these were comrades for whom Pheku had cooked in a commune in the Lal Kanpur days. The ambivalent nature of this relationship between communists and lower castes was expressed in communist attitudes at his death. There are possibly other versions of what happened to Pheku. What is important, however, is the way communist activists like Chakr construed the tragedy of Pheku's life, his experience of injustice and caste discrimination.

The assertion of caste identities in the city meant important realignments and changes in the constitution of these identities. Efforts were made to forge larger solidarities among all castes categorised as untouchables, for example, between Koris, Chamars, Gangaparis, Jaiswaras, Dusadhs, Raidasis.[68] Links were also made between lower castes in the city and the villages in and around Kanpur. These assertions of solidarity were important in articulating a critique of 'begar' labour and zamindari exploitation in the villages.

Conflicts and Confrontations

Ritual and community practices shaped community identities, but the boundaries and lines of difference between religious communities were drawn through conflicts and confrontations. Conflicts between communities often swept aside the divisions between

[65] '*Gardan utha garv se chalne laga*' (He walked with his head high). Chakr, 'Pheku', *Shahidon ki katar*, p. 26.

[66] 'Pheku', *Shahidon ki Katar*, pp. 26–7. The story is that comrades who had been part of the same commune as Pheku refused to identify or claim his body when the police brought it to them.

[67] Interview, Chakr.

[68] See, for example, leaflet titled *Sat Karor ki Pukar*, Tract no.1 (Kanpur 1923).

upper and lower castes, redefining notions of 'us' and 'them' in terms of Hindus and Muslims. But these divisions were again never fixed: they were remade in different contexts. A community forged through a shared experience of opposition to the state could subsequently fragment and regroup. In the plague riots of 1900 and the Machli Bazar riots of 1913, the target of attack was the state. In 1931 there was a major confrontation between Hindus and Muslims.

The main issue, which provoked a violent outburst by a large cross-section of the city populace in April 1900 was the implementation of plague regulations. According to these regulations, patients for whom segregation was not possible at home were to be put in plague camps.[69] This, according to official reports, affected particularly those of a 'low social position',[70] a large proportion of whom were mill workers living in congested and insanitary conditions in the local bastis and hatas. The news about segregation and the use of the police to enforce it led to a violent reaction. Rumours circulated about men, women and children being taken away from their homes under the pretext of plague and used as slaves, that the water supply was being poisoned, that patients were being burnt, and other such stories.[71] All this added to the growing resentment among both Hindus and Muslims, and there appeared a growing solidarity between the two communities. Reports noted signs of 'unusual friendliness' between Hindus and Muslims on Bakr Id on 11 April. The Hindus joined in the festivities and provided sherbet at the Idgah, and the Muslims did not sacrifice cows. At a meeting at the Idgah a general alarm was raised that a boy had been kidnapped to be burnt alive at the plague hospital. Immediately a crowd of over fifteen hundred

[69] Extract from Plague Regulations, Home Public Progs. A, June 1900, no. 298. On plague policy and reactions to it, see also Chandavarkar, 'Plague Panic and Epidemic Politics in India, 1896–1914', in *Imperial Power and Popular Politics,* pp. 234–65; I.J Catanach, 'Plague and the Tensions of Empire, 1896–1918', in David Arnold, ed., *Imperial Medicine and Indigenous Societies* (Manchester 1988), pp. 149–71; David Arnold, *Colonizing the Body: State Medicine and Epidemic Disease in Nineteenth-Century India* (California 1993), pp. 200–39.

[70] Telegram, 17.4.1900, Home Public Progs. A, June 1900, no. 298.

[71] *Pioneer,* 11.4.1900, Home Public Progs. A, June 1900, no. 298.

attacked the plague camp. The police, who had helped in the forcible removal of plague patients from their homes and from the railway station, became special targets of attack: five of them at the camp were killed. The huts of the plague hospital and the segregation camp were set on fire. Volleys of police bullets eventually dispersed the crowd, which moved to the city.[72]

Many of the plague victims were mill workers and the areas affected by the riots—Sisamau, Lachmipurwa, Gwaltoli Bazaar—were areas inhabited by a large number of workers.[73] Their 'inflammable temper', it was argued, made the enforcement of the plague regulations more difficult and reactions more violent. Among the workers who were reportedly very active and who are mentioned in various reports of the incident by their caste names were the butchers in the leather factories and Chamars in leather and textiles.[74] The day of the riot was a holiday, and thousands of workers were out in the streets.[75] The local authorities were particularly apprehensive of an attack on the mills. Troops were dispatched to guard the North West Tannery and the Victoria Mills area, and arms were provided to the volunteers at various factories.[76] These incidents disrupted the life of the city. Bazaars were closed for a week and business came to a standstill.[77] Some mills tried to keep their workers within the factory premises so as to prevent any loss of production. The Woollen Mills, and one or two other establishments, could remain open by giving double wages, but there was strong picketing outside the mills and they were reported to be in a state of virtual siege.[78] For several months after the episode, millowners complained that the labour supply

[72] Home Public Progs. A, June 1900, no. 298; *Pioneer*, 15.4.1900.

[73] Freemantle, 'Report on the Supply of Labour', UP Rev. Progs. B, May 1906, no. 90.

[74] Home Public Progs. A, June 1900, no. 298.

[75] C. Hope, DM, Kanpur, 28.4.1900, UPGAD, 86C, 1900, Box 105 (UPSA).

[76] Correspondence relating to the positioning of troops in App. IX, UPGAD, 86C, 1900, Box 105 (UPSA).

[77] Commsr, Allahabad Div. to Chief Secy, NWP and Awadh, UPGAD, 86C, 1900, Box 105 (UPSA).

[78] *Pioneer*, 15.4.1900.

to mills remained irregular and unsatisfactory.[79] Many of the workers left for their villages for fear of police enquiries that followed the riot.

The hostility to the plague regulations, dismissed by colonial officials in terms of the 'preposterous superstitions' of the lower classes, was linked up with notions of death and domestic space. Death in unfamiliar surroundings was always dreaded. Besides, segregation in the plague camps meant a violation of some of the important coordinates of social existence. For most women, who lived in the seclusion of their hata and domestic space, the idea of forcible removal to a plague camp was horrifying. For men and women alike, the idea of cohabitation in a hospital with those from castes and religious communities other than their own was abhorrent.

The upsurge against the plague rules was also linked to a deep-rooted suspicion of Western medicine. The system of diagnosis practised by indigenous hakims and vaids interfered little with women's notions of modesty. Officials could not ignore such attitudes in the formulation of plague regulations. In order to placate the sentiments of various communities the revised plague regulations issued after the riots stipulated that the health officer would be assisted by a panchayat of Hindu and Muslim residents which would include a vaid or a hakim among its members. Plague hospitals were to be used only as a last resort if segregation in caste hospitals was not possible.[80]

In the Machli Bazaar Mosque riot of August 1913, local Muslims came up against an encroachment by the state into their place of worship. The mosque, located between Halsey Road and the Mall, one of the most congested parts of the city, became the centre of controversy because of the implementation of a new

[79] *UICC Report*, 1900, p. iv.

[80] *Pioneer*, 18.4.1900. Official statements reflect the concern about making plague regulations acceptable: 'No system of plague administration can be successful which does not carry the people with it. From this point of view any rigid system of plague measures is to be deprecated, and he is the most successful plague administrator who is able to gauge the temper of the particular class of people he is dealing with.' Chief Secy, NWP and Awadh to Secy, GOI, 25.4.1900, Home Public Progs. A, June 1900, no. 298.

road scheme which required the demolition of the dalan of the mosque.[81] This sacred place of worship was also a focal point of community interaction and centre of educational activity—a place intimately connected with the daily life of a Muslim. Road-building activities amounted to desecration and cemented the solidarity within the community both in the city and outside.

On 1 July 1913, as soon as news of the demolition of the dalan reached the mills, 'large crowds of julahas left their work and went to the spot . . . '[82] All sections of the Muslim community, the government noted with concern, were being united 'into a common belief that their *Deen* is in danger'.[83] Soon prominent Muslims from various parts of the country poured in to inspect the mosque. Pamphlets on the desecration of the mosque were widely circulated.[84] A meeting to discuss the problem held on Sunday, 3 August 1913 was attended by almost the entire Muslim community of the city. The day was specially chosen so that mill workers could add to the crowds. At the end of the meeting 'the crowd surged out of the Idgah and proceeded towards the city. They were wearing black flags, reciting the kalima, and walking barefoot and bareheaded; there were, it was estimated, 10,000 to 12,000 men and boys.'[85] When the crowd reached the Machli Bazaar Mosque, cries of 'Banao banao' (build it up) rent the air. A number of men began to pick up the material of the demolished dalan and piled it up at the edge of the mosque courtyard. Violence ensued when an attempt was made to prevent them from doing so. The police was ordered to fire and the sowars were signalled to charge at the crowd. The police surrounded the mosque and captured the inmates. The Lt. Governor explained later that

[81] The dalan was the bathing space, consisting of a raised platform with a drain running through it. *Pioneer*, 30.7.1913; Minute of Lt. Governor on Cawnpore Mosque Riot, HPD Progs. A, Oct. 1913, no. 112.

[82] Minute of Lt. Gov., HPD Progs. A, Oct. 1913, no. 112.

[83] Letter, 2.9.1913, HPD Progs. A, Oct. 1913, no. 113.

[84] *Pioneer*, 7.8.1913.

[85] Azad Subhani in his speech to the crowd proclaimed: 'Every Muhammadan house in Kanpur has sent all his men and boys. There are 47,000 Muslims in the city and only women are left in our houses . . .' *Pioneer*, 7.8.1913. Hazan Nizami, *Kanpur ki Khuni Dastan* (Meerath 1913).

police arrangements had been made since the 3rd morning because they were uncertain about the conduct of a 'mob' recruited 'largely' from mill workers.[86] Official reports quite characteristically related the violence of the crowd in the mosque episode and the earlier riots of 1900 to the uncivilised character of the mill workers and 'lower orders' in general.

The violence of the rioters in 1913, as in 1900, was directed against the state and not against any particular community. However, the Machli Bazaar episode became symbolically important to the construction of a Muslim identity. A sense of threat to sacred space provided an opportunity to Muslims leaders from outside the city to rally around and forge community linkages across regions. Most of the leaders who made a representation to Meston, the Lt. Governor of the province, were from outside Kanpur and were actively involved in provincial and all-India Muslim politics. The mosque riots thus came to be remembered in later narratives as an important landmark in the crystallization of a communal rhetoric in North India.[87]

The riots of March 1931 occurred at a time when relations between the two communities were increasingly fraught with tension, especially since August 1927 after a conflict over a tanzim procession. This estrangement dovetailed the developments in nationalist politics in Kanpur. There was growing disenchantment among many Muslims with the Congress, which came to be identified increasingly as a Hindu organisation, since many of its members were actively participating in 'revivalist' movements. Meanwhile, Muslim communal organisations were also becoming more active. Tanzim processions grew in number and frequency. Revivalist activities among both communities widened the social distance between them and created an atmosphere of mutual distrust, even hatred. Religious festivals now tended to become obtrusively demonstrative. News of riots in other places—in Benaras and Mirzapur, for example—began to disturb the communities deeply. In this atmosphere an attempt to forcibly close

[86] Ibid.

[87] On the links between the Machli Bazaar incident and the emergence of 'a new rhetoric of communalism for North Indian Muslims', see also Sandria Freitag, *Collective Action and Community: Public Arenas and the Emergence of Communalism in North India* (California 1989).

Muslim shops as a part of a general hartal against Bhagat Singh's execution was severely resented by Muslim traders.

On 24 March 1931, signs of trouble were evident from the morning, when Congress volunteers and sympathisers tried to bring life in the city to a standstill. Traffic was being forcibly stopped at Badshahi Naka and Gillisbazaar.[88] At Halsey Road, Muslim women were forced to get off their tongas and walk. The real trouble began around midday, with 'a sudden and wild rush' down the Mall, of volunteers from the Congress youth organisation—the 'Vanar Sena' (monkey brigade)—smashing the windows of big shops. An attempt was made to forcibly close the shops behind the Kotwali and at Moolganj, Thateri Bazaar and Sarrafa.[89]

Reaction and counter-reaction followed such attempts to extend the hartal. Wild rumours about Muslims beating up any cow coming from Hindu galis, and Hindus attacking men in pyjamas indiscriminately, spread panic. Muslim shops at Joota Bazaar were looted, the Ban Bazaar Mosque was partially destroyed, and the Bazaza Mosque set on fire. News of an atttack on the Machli Bazaar Mosque created an uproar. In the fighting that followed, the Meston Road temple was put aflame.[90] Soon the riot engulfed the whole of Kanpur.

By the 25th the intensity of rioting increased and the communal frenzy spread from the central parts of the city to areas like Gwaltoli, Sisamau, Parmat and Sadar Bazaar. At Sisamau armed bands of Muslims were reported to have killed defenceless passers-by. There was looting and arson at Gwaltoli, Sadar Bazaar, and Subzi Mandi. By the morning of the 26th, Gwaltoli Bazaar was a mass of flames, and houses were burning in Sisamau.[91]

Reverberations of the riot were heard in the outlying villages. Early on the 27th some ten to twelve Hindus were seen crossing over to the fields on the Unnao side of the Ganges. Together with about forty others from Unnao, they set fire to the fields, huts and

[88] See Report of the Congress Inquiry Committee into the Kanpur Riots, 1931, AICC Papers no. 68, 1931 (NMML). This has been subsequently published. See N.G. Barrier, ed., *Roots of Communal Politics* (Delhi 1976).

[89] Barrier, *Roots of Communal Politics*, p. 266; UP Home Police, File 1263, 1931, Box 211(UPSA).

[90] Barrier, *Roots* of *Communal Politics*, pp. 270, 283–4, 286, 288.

[91] Cmd. 3891, East India: Cawnpore Riots, pp. 24–7.

grain stacks of Muslims, murdered about seven of them, including women and children, and scattered their bodies in the fields and huts.[92] Attacks were reported from several other villages—from Kalyanpur, Fatehpur Kachar and Gabraha.[93]

Nearly 400 people were reported to have died and another 1200 were injured.[94] Each community highlighted the atrocities committed on its members. Hindus reported that in mohallas like Chamanganj, Baconganj and Talak Mahal, entire Hindu families were massacred.[95] Muslims stressed that 'the butchery committed on Cawnpore Muslims is unthinkable . . . not one Muslim has been left in mohallas which are predominantly Hindu'.[96] The madness of the violence touched all—workers, non-workers, women, children, rich and poor were victims.[97]

On the 25th morning very few workers reported to work at the factories. By 10 a.m. that morning rioting spread to the area around Gwaltoli where the New Victoria, the Elgin, the Woollen Mills and the North West Tannery were located.[98] Army officials noted that there was 'general uneasiness' among the mill workers since the morning and soon after the mills closed there was 'rioting' on Mall Road near the Woollen Mills.[99] By the evening of the 25th, reports noted that 'the whole of Gwaltoli has been burnt to ashes'.[100] At Gwaltoli there was brickbatting, looting and arson all day. Basheeruddin Ahmad, the Municipal Commissioner, in his evidence to the Riot Inquiry Committee talked of threatening groups of 'rioters' emerging from the mill settlements around the Sisamau–Colonelganj area.[101] At Parmat, Muslim houses were reportedly surrounded by Hindu millhands, who threatened to

[92] Ibid., p. 30.

[93] Note by Hafiz Hidayat Husain, MLC Kanpur, 16.4.1931, HPD, 10/19/1931.

[94] Barrier, *Roots of Communal Politics*, p. 11.

[95] Copy of Telegram encl. in R.P. Bagla to Crerar, 6.4.1931, HPD, 10/19/1931.

[96] Note by Hafiz Hidayat Khan, 16.4.1931, HPD, 10/19/1931.

[97] Some like Hoon, MLA, suggested that the quarters attacked were mostly those occupied by mill workers and labourers. HPD, 10/19/1931.

[98] Cmd. 2891, East India: Cawnpore Riots.

[99] *Leader*, 25.4.1931.

[100] 'An account of a student from Govt Textile Institute', *Leader*, 14.4.1931.

[101] HPD, 10/19/KW1931.

kill them.[102] The mills remained closed for a few days after the riots. They opened gradually after the 29th, though it was only on 1 April that 'good attendance' was reported.[103]

The riot affected the politics of labour in the city. Muslim workers were clearly alienated from the KMS.[104] They were disenchanted with the predominantly Congress leadership of the KMS. [105] In an effort to placate Muslim feelings, Fazal Husain Hazrat Mohani was made a member of the executive committee of the sabha.[106] In the late 1930s communists in Kanpur tried to mobilise Muslim workers into trade union activity through a rhetoric of class. Many Muslim workers became mill committee leaders, a fact which gave communists and the KMS a new legitimacy in the eyes of Muslim workers.[107] Yet even the communists had to rely on the appeal of their Muslim comrades to reach out to Muslim neighbourhoods: Sher Khan, Zakir, Akbar and Aiwaz Ali were among those who campaigned in Muslim bastis.[108] Communists had to make their distinction from the Congress palpable through codes of dress: they were not allowed to enter Muslim galis in khaddar, which had come to acquire a Congress/Hindu connotation in Kanpur.

At the workplace too there were conflicts and confrontations between communities. Ties between workers of a particular community both helped in forging solidarities against millowners and in fragmenting and creating sectional unities. Muslim weavers, for instance, had a reputation for militancy, for initiating strike action and holding out longer than other workers.[109] Community ties were a basis on which strike-breakers could mobilise support and fragment wider solidarities. In the Elgin Mills strike in June 1928, for instance, a group of around seventy Muslim workers broke the strike and rejoined work.[110] Jobbers often provided the

[102] *Leader*, 4.5.1931.

[103] Telegram from DM Kanpur, 1.4.1931, HPD, 10/19/1931.

[104] In October 1931 Muslim workers made plans to start a sabha of their own at the office of the *Gharib*, an Urdu newspaper. SAID, 30.10.1931.

[105] Interviews, S.P. Awasthi, S.C. Kapoor, S.S. Yusuf.

[106] SAID, 21.11.1931. Interviews, Raghubir, Aiwaz Ali.

[107] See ch. 6.

[108] Interviews, Raghubir, Aiwaz Ali.

[109] See p. 267.

[110] *Leader,* 31.5.1928, 2.6.1928, 13.6.1928, 15.6.1928; *Pioneer*, 21.6.1928.

leadership in such actions. In November 1937 an attempt by a Muslim head jobber, Sami, to break a strike in Elgin Mills led to a major confrontation, culminating in his murder. Sami's murder created acute communal tension between workers and in the city as a whole.[111]

On a day-to-day basis there were numerous instances of conflict. The ways in which power was exercised within the factories, the bending of rules or the hardening of authority, were influenced by kinship and community considerations—a fact which often created hostility and conflict. In Muir Mills, for instance, a confrontation occurred when a Muslim gate jamadar reported a Hindu worker for not carrying a mill ticket. The jamadar became a focus of attack and larger violence between Hindu and Muslim workers and stone throwing followed.[112]

The notion of the self and perception of the other was constantly redefined. In the context of the plague riots a broader notion of community was constituted. Different communities came together to assert perceived collective values and norms against intrusion by the state. In 1931 the lines of opposition were drawn between communities articulating a different notion of 'us' and 'them'. In the collective memory of workers, both forms of community action occupied an important place. These different pasts were recalled at different times to give meaning to the present.[113] No one memory was permanently valorised.

Crime, Violence and Communal Riots

A familiar argument which recurs in official and non-official writings on religious riots explains the madness of rioters in terms of the peculiarities of Kanpur—a city with a reputation for 'turbulence'. Kanpur always had a large flow of migrants in search of

[111] *Leader,* 3.12.1937; *Pioneer,* 30.11.1937; SAID, 11.12.1937.
[112] SAID, 15.4.1939.
[113] The politics of recall becomes important in understanding nationalist propaganda. The Congress inquiry into the riots celebrated the past of communal harmony. Before the riots the report noted, the participation of Muslims in the festival of Holi was very significant. 'During the Holi nights, the Kunjras [fruit sellers], the Kasais [butchers], and all those other Muslims who now take part in Hindu Muslim fights, organised swangs [farcical tableaux] in honour of the Hindu festival.' Barrier, *Roots of Communal Politics,* p. 236.

jobs. This flow was particularly marked during the years of the Depression, a time of shrinking employment. The unemployed poor in cities like Kanpur were seen as specially prone to violence and crime. In official eyes this floating population, which had no 'fixed abode', drifted easily between a life of crime and casual employment.[114] Many among these homeless 'vagrants' were identified as 'bad characters', engaged in activities such as cocaine smuggling and gambling, often in the service of local goondas. Regularly employed by rival candidates during elections, they were seen as a class of people who were 'ready to commit even murder for a few annas'.[115] In Kanpur, officials asserted it was this 'smuggler of contraband' who 'played the communal bully, looter and slayer' during the riots.[116] The district authorities in Kanpur demanded greater powers against such 'law breakers', and it was in this context that the Goonda Act was framed for Kanpur.[117]

The term 'goonda' used for the rioters, was an all-inclusive category which included those classified as professional goondas, whose names figured in the history sheets maintained by the Kanpur police, workers in the mills and outside, rural immigrants in search of jobs.[118] Various stereotypes seemed to feed this image of a goonda, with all the groups sharing one common feature— a propensity for violence. Statements before the Riots Inquiry

[114] Supdt Police, Kanpur, 3.4.1930, UP Home Police 412,1931, Box 206 (UPSA). In similar vein, the District Magistrate noted: 'The mill population was turbulent and had no mohalla or other ties, being shifting.' *Leader*, 19.4.1931.

[115] Supdt Police, Kanpur, 3.4.1930, UP Home Police 412,1931, Box 206 (UPSA).

[116] Note on Goonda Act for UP by Commsr, Allahabad, 21.10.1931. UP Home Police 412,1931, Box 206 (UPSA).

[117] The act, which was modelled on the lines of a similar law in Bengal (Bengal Act no. 1 of 1923), empowered the DM to recommend action against any person who appeared to be a goonda, and had committed or was likely to commit or assist in committing any non-bailable offence against a person or group of persons implicated in an offence against a person or property, or an offence of 'criminal intimidation'. In addition, any person or group of persons implicated in an offence involving a 'breach of peace' could be charged under the Act. UP Home Police 412, 1931, Box 206 (UPSA).

[118] The goonda was described as the 'communal bully', a 'looter' and a 'slayer'. Commsr, Allahabad, 21.10.1931, UP Home Police 412,1931, Box 206 (UPSA).

Commission described the 'poor uneducated' mill population as 'good material for communal explosion.'[119] Besides, the very nature of work in the mills, some argued, made mill workers as a class 'more in love of excitement' than ordinary people.[120] Sale, the District Magistrate, for instance, believed 'millhands develop *badmashi* because they are an industrial population'.[121]

There were other stereotypes that shaped narratives on communal violence. In some, lower-class Muslims as a whole were represented as an 'excitable class of people'. They were seen as frequenting toddy shops, in the neighbourhood of which incidents of violence during riots took place. The notion of the excitable Muslim drew on familiar stereotypes of the 'troublesome' Julaha, which recurs in official and non-official writings on artisans and workers. The 'aggressiveness' of the Julahas, traditionally associated with weaving, was linked in official characterisations with their 'zealous', 'fanatic' and 'clannish feelings'.[122] Similarly, workers from Kasai (butcher) and Chamar backgrounds were described as 'notoriously of a turbulent disposition'.[123]

Official discourse on goondas in the 1930s bore close similarities to the discussions on criminal tribes in the nineteenth century, when entire communities were stigmatised as naturally prone to criminal activities. The links between the floating population, mill workers and criminality were never demonstrated. The mere existence of a working class population and crime in the city is

[119] Statement of D.N. Nigam, Hony. Mag., HPD, 10/19/1931 KW.

[120] Ev. A. Hoon, MLA, 10/19/1931.

[121] *Leader*, 19.4.1931.

[122] See, for instance, C.A. Silberrad, *A Monograph on Cotton Fabrics Produced in N.W.P. and Awadh* (Allahabad 1898), p. 1; Freemantle 'Report on the Supply of Labour ', UP Rev. Progs. B, 1906, no. 90. Local proverbs express popular representations of Julahas: 'How should a weaver be patient'; 'A weaver by trade and his name is Fatah Khan' (victorious chief). H.A. Rose, *A Glossary of the Tribes and Castes of Punjab and North-West Frontier Provinces* (Delhi 1970), p. 414. See also W. Crooke, *Tribes and Castes of North Western India*, vol. III (Delhi 1975), pp. 70–1. In an important essay, Gyanendra Pandey links images of the 'bigoted' Julaha with the long-drawn-out struggles by weavers in different places to preserve and improve their social position in the context of a decline in traditional occupations. 'The Bigoted Julaha', in *The Construction of Communalism in Colonial North India* (Delhi 1990).

[123] Home Public A Progs., 1900, no. 735,

asserted as proof of a connection between the two. Note, for instance, a statement of the Deputy Collector, Kanpur: 'The industrial population of Cawnpore throws into the life of the city a large number of persons of very desperate character—a factor not to be found in any other city of UP. Gambling and cocaine smuggling are very rampant and extremely profitable. These institutions of the city offer protection to a large number of undesirable characterless persons.'[124] In some statements the presence of job seekers was seen as a 'screen' for criminal activities: criminality was the real occupation and jobs were a cover.[125]

Official descriptions also tend to project the goonda as an outsider—as someone who came in from Unnao, across the river from Kanpur, or from further-off places like Farukhabad and Fatehpur.[126] The danger to the city came from outside. The identity of the outsider was unknown—they came and went, committing acts of violence. In order to protect the city from such 'criminals' officials proposed the extension of the Goonda Act to the neighbouring areas. History sheets of goondas from Kanpur, based in Unnao, were drawn up. Police records affirm the essentially criminal character of the men on their list through a use of stock terms and phrases: 'hazardous', 'dangerous' 'uses dangerous weapons unhesitatingly'—descriptions which tend to create a terrifying image of the criminal.[127] Those charged with crime did

[124] Statement of Rameshwar Dayal, UP Home Police 412,1931, Box 206 (UPSA).

[125] Statement of D.S. Barron, ICS, UP Home Police 412,1931, Box 206 (UPSA).

[126] S.M. Raza, Mun. Commsr, recounted how he heard Gangaputras and Mahaputras coming by boats from the Unnao side, creating havoc in Parmat, and that badmashes also came from Farukhabad and Fatehpur. Written Statement, HPD 10/19/1931. In the discussions around the Goonda Act of 1933, the provincial officials noted: 'The goondas residing in Unnao, being just opposite to Cawnpore city across the Ganga and at a distance of only one or two miles from it, manipulates through their agents or through surreptitious visits, the communal disputes and labour troubles in the city of Cawnpore, and are thus a danger to the peace of that city even after their externment from it.' Note by Depy Secy, 6.9.9.1938, File 4 (3), 1938, Box 282 (UPSA).

[127] Note, for instance, a description of Babu, alias Ismail: 'Is a typical goonda . . . Hazardous and unhesitatingly uses force and dangerous weapons. Took active part in the riot case of 1939. Was suspected in burglary case and

try to escape police surveillance by fleeing the city. However in official eyes there was a generalised fear of those outside municipal limits as perpetrators of urban crime.[128]

This is not to construct a romanticised picture of working class innocence, untainted by criminality. Workers like individuals from any social background, could for a variety of reasons be associated with crime. Workers often straddled different worlds. The story of Kallan Khan, as one who moved from a life of crime to communist trade union activity, is remembered and recounted by many workers.[129] In the self-perception of communist activists, trade union activity sanitised and purified them of their criminal past. However, a categorisation of the mobile, industrial population as potentially more criminal, in official narratives, shows a different bias. Such classifications reveal more about the mentality of those who classify—their fear of the 'floating population' as a dangerous class.[130]

Communal Politics

The intensity of communal violence in 1931 needs to be understood in terms of the growing communalisation of local politics by the late 1920s. The boundaries between communities were more sharply drawn. Each community tried to protect itself by defining

---

was arrested in the gambling cases.' Similar details are cited about other goondas on the police history sheets. Appendix showing details of goondas, UP Police 4 (3), 1938, Box 282 (UPSA).

[128] The Supdt Police, Kanpur testified that 'the figures for cases run under Section 109 Criminal Procedure Code, which deals mainly with bad characters from outside, were the highest for any city in the Province for 1929 and 1930.' SP, Kanpur to DM, 14.10.1931, File 412,1931, Box 206 (UPSA).

[129] See ch . 3.

[130] The fear of 'dangerous classes' formed an important part of nineteenth-century official and non-official narratives on industrial cities in Europe. Fears about the dangerous classes, the 'evil' character of 'the mob', 'the populace' were articulated in the writings of Victor Hugo, Balzac and others in France; the threat from 'the nomad poor' in nineteenth-century London was a focus of official and non-official concerns. See Louis Chevalier, *Laboring Classes and Dangerous Classes in Paris During the First Half of the Nineteenth Century* (Princeton 1973); Gareth Stedman Jones, *Outcast London: A Study in the Relationship between Classes in Victorian Society* (Harmondsworth 1971).

its own space and defending its religious symbols against assault by others. Rituals which were part of everyday life became, in moments of crisis like 1931, a basis of conflict.

From the mid-1920s the 'revivalist' activities of communal organisations gained strength in Kanpur. Various Hindu organisations mushroomed: the Sanatan Dharma Mahamadal Sabha, Hindu Rakshini Sabha, Seva Dal, Mahabir Dal, the Hindu Sabha, figure in the list.[131] The Arya Samajists carried on an aggressive programme of shuddhi, while Muslims organised a Tabligh-ul-Islam to propagate Islam.

The involvement of several leading Kanpur Congressmen with the Arya Samaj and Hindu Sabha left its imprint on the politics of the city. Murari Lal Rohatgi and Narain Prasad Nigam, two Congressmen connected with the Mazdur Sabha, were closely involved with the local Hindu Sabha. In fact Congressmen themselves admitted that only a small minority were above communal feelings. Many were members of the Hindu Sabha and took an active part in shuddhi activities.[132] A note of dissent appended to the Congress Committee Report by Zafarul Mulk reveals some significant details.[133] It shows how Congressmen who were 'truly secular' constituted a 'microscopic minority' within the organisation in Kanpur. Among those interviewed by the committee, some seemed to believe that four out of the thirty prominent Congressmen were above communal feeling; one witness was convinced the number was even smaller.

The politics of the Kanpur Municipal Board added to the growing hostility between communities. Muslim traders criticised the board for openly espousing Hindu business interests. The increase in the powers of the municipality since the passing of the Municipality Act of 1916, many believed, worked to the detriment of Muslim traders. The eviction of Muslim timber merchants

[131] Statement of Mohd Fazal Husain, editor, *Al Barid*, in HPD 10/19 KW.

[132] The secretary of the local congress committee pointed out: 'Formerly Shuddhi was limited to the Arya Samaj,. . . now the entire Hindu community, that is, even the orthodox Sanatanists, joined it.' Barrier, *Roots of Communal Politics*, p. 245.

[133] The note, the signatory, Zafarul Mulk, clarifies, consists of passages which formed a part of the Congress Inquiry Report but were subsequently deleted. Barrier, *Roots of Communal Politics*, p. 462.

from Cooperganj, attempts to evict Muslim kunjras from the Subzi Mandi, the attempts to evict hide merchants form Pech Bagh with the support of the Improvement Trust, the licensing of hide godowns and the increase in octroi rates were also seen as testimony to the communal bias of the board.[134] Witnesses before the official Riots Inquiry also criticised the board for helping Hindu communal organisations to set up akharas where the participants were trained in the art of using lathis, chhurries and swords.[135]

A large section of Muslims in Kanpur and in other parts of the province, already quite estranged from the Congress since the retreat of the Non-Cooperation Movement, were more embittered by the early 1930s. The Civil Disobedience Movement 'had come to be regarded in Kanpur [more definitely] than in any other city of the province as a Hindu movement, with Muslims actively or passively in opposition.'[136] Many found it difficult to distinguish between the Arya Samajists and Congressites. In fact, on one occasion a Congress procession was mistaken for an Arya Samaj procession and stoned. Most Muslims were conspicuously absent from the Congress activities during the Civil Disobedience Movement. Muslim traders, cloth merchants and liquor shop owners resented the attempts at forcible closure of their shops by Congress picketers and not for business reasons alone. The attempts by some Muslims at organising themselves took the form of a revival of the tanzim organisation.[137] This religious mission assumed the form of a political counter to Congress demonstrations. Meetings addressed by Muslim nationalist leaders under the auspices of the

[134] Ev. Mohd. Hanif, hide merchant at Pech Bagh, 1 May 1931, 10/19/1931 KW. Muslim kunjras (fruit and vegetable sellers) felt: 'their old business of fruit and vegetable selling was being snatched by Hindus with the help of the Municipal Board', Statement of Khan Basheruddin Ahmad, Mun. Commsr, Kanpur, 20.4.1931, HPD, 10/19/1931.KW.

[135] According to one of the witnesses before the official inquiry, the teachers at the akharas were paid out of municipality funds. Ev. Khaliluddin (Hony. Mag.), 22 April 1931, HPD, 10/191931 KW.

[136] Resolution of the Government of UP on the Report of the Commission of Inquiry into the Cawnpore Riots, 1931, HPD, 10/19/1931.

[137] Ev. Lal Dewan Chand,Principal DAV College, Kanpur Riots Inquiry Commission, HPD, 19/19, KW 1931.

local Congress committee met with a hostile reaction from local Muslims.[138]

Theatrical displays of communal fervour in religious processions fanned communal feelings. As the processions wound their way through the streets, people from various mohallas joined in. Tanzim processions paraded every day, accompanied by large bodies of men carrying flags, lathis, ballams and kantas, raising cries of 'Allah-o-Akbar'. They sang songs charged with religious hatred: *'Jhagarna marna aur lootna kafir ka jayiz hai/ Zarasi bat mein amada-i-takrar ho jao.'*[139] Arya Samajists took out processions and sang songs which attacked Muslims as aliens. Muslims were told to flee back to their homeland in Mecca:

Yeh Arab hai na Ajam, Faris na Turkistan hai,
Hinduon ke rehne ki jaghai hai, yeh Hindustan hai,
. . . Gar Musalman hai to fauron chor Hindustan ko,
Bhag Makke ki taraf rakh deen ko, Iman ko.[140]

The aggressive communal fervour of these processions provoked hostile reactions. The songs and speeches propagated the language of hatred. Each community tried to assert aggressive, masculinised notions of the self. Threats, counter-vengeance, and retribution were the terms in which songs and slogans were phrased. Stereotypes of the other were created, shaping perceptions of 'us' and 'them'. Attacks on Hindu iconic figures like Sita and Draupadi in maulud sharifs, taunts against the namaz ritual and the customary beard worn by Muslims, offended religious sentiments.[141]

Each community tried to appropriate space and time in its own

[138] Written statement of Babu Brijendra Swarup, Advocate and Mun. Commsr, HPD, 10/19/KW/1931.

[139] It is lawful to quarrel with an infidel (as also) to kill him and plunder. On trivial provocation be ready to fight. Cited by Hirday Narayan, Riots Inquiry, HPD, 10/19KW/1931.

[140] Barrier, *Roots of Communal Politics*, p. 240.

[141] Note, for instance, songs like:

Ham hastiya Muslim ko duniya se mita denge,
Is Om ke jhande ko kabe pe chaddha denge
Dadhi muda ke chutiya rakhaiye
Bas ho chuka namaz musalla uthaiye.

(We will wipe out the existing Muslims and plant the Hindu banner [banner of Om] atop the Kaba in Mecca. Shave off your beards and let

way. Boundaries were drawn between areas considered exclusively Hindu or Muslim. Moolganj, for instance, which lay in the heart of the city, on the border line dividing the 'Hindu' and 'Muslim' areas, was considered a particularly dangerous zone—an area where most communal riots began.[142] Transgression of borders and violation of sacred spaces and sacred times became an important part of the communal politics of the period. Arya Samaj processions were deliberately provocative, making long halts in front of mosques.[143] In the late 1920s festival times became critical times when a defence of community rights became charged with a new political meaning. The overlap between the Hindu marriage season and Moharram in 1927—the conflict over procession routes—made the situation very tense.[144]

Stories of violence between communities travelled fast. There was news of rioting in Sandila, Maurawan (Unnao district), and Ballia in 1927, and from Basti, Benares, Mirzapur and Agra in 1931. Official reports from Lucknow in September 1927 noted: 'Communal tension overshadows everything and seems to dominate every public act and private opinion.'[145] And from Aligarh: 'It seems absolutely appalling to what length communal bias has been allowed to enter into the life of the district.' In Lohta village, in Benares district, the local Julahas and Thakurs came to blows after the Julahas threw shoes at the Thakurs. In Kheri, the arrival by train of twenty-six cattle dealers from Bijnor district led to the rumour that hundreds of Muslims were pouring in to kill Hindus. Ripples of the Calcutta riot of 1926 travelled to Kanpur. 'Wild rumours' created a 'nervous fear' and there was panic about an Arya Samaj procession on 21 April 1926. Anticipating trouble, workers from several mills asked for leave to go and protect their homes.[146]

---

your chutiya [pigtail] grow, your prayers are over, fold your prayer cloth.) Statement of Munshi Mazhar Uddin, HPD, 10/19/KW/1931.

[142] Mooganj was also considered a haunt of goondas, who came here to solicit prostitutes residing in the area. Links were often drawn between the presence of goondas, prostitution and the locus of communal riots in the area. S.P. Mehra, 'Shall We Exile Prostitutes', *Citizen*, 19.12.1940.

[143] HPD, FR 32/3/1927.

[144] HPD, 32/7/1927.

[145] HPD, FR 32/9/1927, Sept. (i), UP.

[146] Official reports noted how this was an annual affair and rarely called

How were workers affected by such propaganda? Witnesses before the Inquiry Commission mentioned how many tanzim processions were taken out on Sundays to enable mill workers to join them. During the riots and after, cries of 'Allah-o-Akbar' from bastis dominated by Muslims, and 'Bajrang Bali' from bastis with a Hindu majority were heard long after the riots. In the early 1940s, a large section of Muslim workers in Kanpur, especially those in the leather industry, were drawn towards the Muslim League. The communists had to work closely with the League in this period in order to mobilise the support of Muslim workers.[147]

The politics of communal organisations was not all. The lack of effective intervention by the state during riots and the divisive tactics of mill managers were a common grievance. Most accounts of 1931 dwell on the lack of timely action by the local administration to quell the rioting crowd.[148]Labour representatives point repeatedly to evidence of mill managers trying to provoke communal tensions during moments of collective struggle. In 1938, the trade unionist and labour representative on the Labour Inquiry Commission was categorical that the employers were playing 'a dirty game', inciting Muslim workers against the KMS leadership.[149] Recruitment policies were often manipulated by managers in order to weaken worker solidarities. After the strike of 1938, many managements were wary of employing castes which held a dominant position in the factory: Brahman workers

---

for much notice but a fear that a similar procession had been the cause of riots in Calcutta caused anxiety. Reporting on the situation the DM commented: 'The state of panic is extraordinary. I have had telephone messages this morning from several mills in which the mill hands have asked leave to go and protect their homes' HPD, FR 112/IV/1926.

[147] During a strike in the Kanpur Tannery in 1945, the communists supported the mediation of the League because the majority of the workers and the owner of the establishment, Abdul Jabbar, were all League members. *Citizen*, 15.12.1945. On the relationship between the League and communists, see also *Citizen*, 12.9.1942, 3.10.1942, 15.1.1944, 26.6.1944, 15.7.1944.

[148] Cmd. 3891, East India: Cawnpore Riots. On the 1931 riots and the inefficacy of state action, see also Gyanendra Pandey, *The Ascendancy of the Congress in Uttar Pradesh, 1926–34: A Study in Imperfect Mobilization* (Delhi, 1978), pp. 131–42; Sandria Freitag, *Collective Action*, pp. 239–48.

[149] Shiva Rao to Srinivasan, editor, *Hindu*, Shiva Rao Papers, 1938 (NMML).

in Elgin Mills, Koris in JK Mills and Julahas in the Cawnpore Cotton Mills.[150] In the Cawnpore Ordnance Depot, retrenchment strategies were applied in a discriminatory way, affecting Hindu workers and not others.[151] Many Indian businessmen in Kanpur had close links with communal organisations: tannery owners were members of the Muslim League and the Singhanias were closely connected with the activities of the Hindu Sabha.[152] In 1940, the Singhanias demanded compulsory contributions to the Hindu Mahasabha, though after widespread criticism the contributions were made voluntary.[153]

In conclusion I wish to emphasise two general points. One: workers did not live 'singular' or 'unitary' lives. To see them as embedded in community culture alone is as reductive as to suggest that their identities were forged in the economics of the production process. Workers bear the marks of multiple identities, a multiplicity not captured in the neatness of homogenising categories. Two: cultural identities were continuously refigured. Patterns of residence and work in the mills had an impact on caste identities. The rigidities of separation between castes broke down, but new lines of separation were created. Caste movements among lower castes widened the limits of interaction between them and made their relationship with upper castes more hostile and antagonistic. At another level, these differences seemed to dissolve during communal riots, when non-Muslims of all castes—Chamars, and upper castes—were pitted against Muslims. Communal riots in the city altered relationships between communities, sharpening existing differences and creating a wider gulf through changes in residential patterns. The militant anti-imperialist politics of communists in the 1930s tried to subsume all differences, emphasising the need for class unity. However, solidarities of class in 1919 or in 1937–8 did not rupture ties of religion, they did not secularise inner selves. Contradictions and inner conflicts remained. Yet this

[150] Interview, Arjun Arora.

[151] This created a situation when the Muslim Workers' Association opposed the COD labour union's demand for a strike. *Citizen*, 23.11.1946.

[152] Padampat Singhania was the President of the Hindu Sangh in Kanpur and was very active in the anti-Pakistan movement in the city in 1941. *Citizen*, 5.5.1941, 7.3.1942.

[153] SAID, 22.10.1940.

did not mean paralysing a plurality of identities: an inner ambivalence that was impossible to reconcile. All identities—workers are no exception—are always hybrid, torn by ambiguities. Workers had to negotiate these oppositions in different situations, repressing parts of their selves while giving expression to other parts.

CHAPTER 8

The Politics of Labour and the Languages of Nationalism

—⊹⊱⊰⊹—

The events of Lal Kanpur provide points of entry into the world of labour and nationalism. The politics of the period—the interplay between the rhetoric of leaders, working class activity, and the paradoxes of power—brings out the complex processes through which a space for labour was negotiated within nationalist politics. Once Congress came to power in 1936–7, its populist rhetoric lost its edge and the provincial government's need for order complicated the relationship between nationalists and labour. But by 1938 events in Kanpur radicalised the language of the local Congress. The communist strategy of united front in this period minimises the difference between the Congress and the communists. The logic and genealogy of these shifts and their implication for labour politics need to be understood.

Nationalists in UP and elsewhere seriously engage with labour in the post-war context of 1919–20 The terms in which nationalists conceive of the nation and its constituents in the early 1920s is different from the 1930s. The discourse of nationalism in Kanpur was made of divergent strands, and the relationship between community, nation and class was defined in a variety of ways by nationalists at different points of time. There were tensions within individual thought, between the broad universalist paradigms within which the nation was defined and in the sense of commitment and identity with the specific interests of a community. In the 1930s the tension between community and class in nationalist rhetoric is less apparent as the language of class becomes dominant in the public discourse of nationalists.

Ambivalences of the Nationalist Self

In November 1919 local Congress leaders acted as mediators in the negotiations between workers and managers. By the late 1920s, all important office-bearers in the KMS were closely associated with the Congress. Leaders like Murari Lal, Ganesh Shankar Vidyarthi, Narain Prasad Nigam and Wahid Yar Khan, for instance, were involved in the Home Rule League, Khilafat and Non-Cooperation activities in Kanpur district.

Murari Lal Rohatgi and other nationalists within the KMS were not professional trade unionists: labour was one among their diverse concerns. Murari Lal was a doctor by profession, who, like many others supported the boycott call of 1921–2 by giving up his government medical practice. Apart from being a member of the local municipal board, the provincial legislative council and assembly, Murari Lal was active in various other bodies in the city. Unlike the trade unionists of the 1930s, who lived in mazdur bastis and had a plebeian image, Murari Lal stood out as a khaddar-clad nationalist who travelled in a motor car.[1] To many contemporaries, his identity as KMS president was quite marginal; it was as a protector of Hindu interests that Murari Lal is remembered. A volume felicitating him pays him tribute for his role as an organiser of the shuddhi movement in the city, and for giving Hindus courage and direction at a time when Kanpur was besieged by Muslim terror.[2] Murari Lal was an active Arya Samajist who was among the founders of the DAV College in Kanpur, and was closely associated with the organisation of an ashram for widows, a Hindu orphanage, and with Arya Swarajya Sabha activities among dalits.[3]

Ganesh Shankar Vidyarthi's style presents a contrast to city élites like Murari Lal. Biographical reconstructions portray Vidyarthi as a leader whose figure was inscribed in working class memory: 'The Kanpur workers can never forget Vidyarthi's lean figure

---

[1] '*Un dino khaddar ki poshak ke log motoron par nahi dikhai parte the is liye maine kuch gaur se unhe dekha*' (Those days, people dressed in khadi were not seen travelling in motor cars, therefore I looked at him closely). Reminiscences of Shambhu Nath Srivastava in *Jawaharlal Rohatgi Abhinandan-Granth* (Allahabad 1969), p. 163.

[2] *Rohatgi Abhinandan-Granth*, p.163.

[3] Ibid., *Pratap*, 7.9.1924.

running about in the sun. Whenever there is a strike or any other crisis Vidyarthiji comes to workers' rescue . . .'[4] He is universally portrayed as a crusader for justice who worked selflessly for the poor and oppressed.[5] Deeply influenced by Gandhi, ascetic ideals were crucial to his conception of self and its presentation in everyday life. He was among the only non-worker Congress leaders of the 1920s who had a sustained involvement with the problems of workers. An interesting feature of the paper *Pratap*, which he edited, was the space it gave to workers' grievances in its columns.

Another type of nationalist of the 1920s straddled a middle ground: between city notables of the Murari Lal variety and Gandhian nationalists like Vidyarthi. Nationalists like Narayan Prasad Arora formed part of the literary and educated class but mingled with plebeians in akharas. Arora, who came from a family of cloth merchants, taught in various schools and colleges in Kanpur and outside and was associated with various local bodies. He wrote extensively on the problem of child marriage, untouchability, widow remarriage, the position of women in contemporary India, and on social inequalities.[6] Arora's popularity, however, rested primarily on his image as a wrestler. He was an akhara veteran, who not only participated in all important local tournaments but actively propagated wrestling by organising a kushti prachar mandal to revive the sport in the 1940s.[7] Arora was inspired by local figures like Pratap Narayan Misra, who wrote pieces glorifying wrestling in his journal *Brahman:*

[4] Surendra Sharma, 'Nirbhik Lekhni ki Kahani', in B. Chaturvedi, et al. eds, *Ganesh Smarak Granth: Amar Shahid Ganesh Shankar Vidyarthi* (Kalpi 1960).

[5] Devrata Shastri, *Ganesh Shankar Vidyarthi* (Delhi n.d.), pp.19–20; Surendra Sharma, 'Nirbhik Lekhni ki Kahani', pp. 135–42.

[6] In an essay 'Duniya ke Mazduron ka Bolbala' Arora focuses on the injustices in contemporary Indian society and draws hope from successful workers' movements in Europe particularly Russia. *Narayan Nibandhavali*, p. 73. In another essay, 'Samajik Vishamta ka Yudha', he writes that inequalities would soon be removed because the poor and oppressed of the world were now struggling to change their condition. *Narayan Nibandhavali*, p. 114.

[7] Kushti prachar mandal = organization for the propogation of wrestling. Uma Shankar Dubey, 'Kushti Premi Aroraji', in *Narayan Prasad Arora Jeevanvret* (Kanpur 1951).

Yah sab koi manta hai ki dhanvan aur vidvan ki bhanti balvan bhi desh ki shobha hai. Kisi riti se pahalvano ko sahai karke unka utsah bharana desh ki sharirik unnati me ek paramyogi kam hai.[8]

For nationalists like Arora, politics and physical culture were linked: physical well-being signified the health of the nation. Patriotism and nationalism in his writings were closely connected with a culture of masculinity. To be true sons of the soil and protectors of the nation, physical strength was necessary. Physical strength was considered essential to defend Hindus from others. Akharas became important to Congress politics in the intensely communalised context of the late 1920s, when the culture of violence increasingly determined local politics. The emphasis on physical culture now became a part of the official ideology of the Congress and a gymnasium was set up to train Congress volunteers.[9]

In contrast to leaders like Murari Lal, Vidyarthi and Narayan Prasad Arora, nationalists associated with the KMS in the 1930s were professional trade unionists whose relationship with the working class movement was conceived in different terms. The political context and the basis on which trade union leaders functioned and presented themselves changed. Harihar Nath Shastri, who was president of the KMS over 1931–7, was actively associated with various provincial and all-India trade union associations. Although his rhetoric and politics was different, socialists like Shastri shared similarities in political style with communist trade unionists of the 1930s. Shastri lived in the mazdur basti of Gwaltoli.[10] Living in a working class neighbourhood gave a different legitimacy to middle-class leaders like Shastri: it meant a symbolic transcendence of class difference.

If socialists like Shastri set the tone for this period, communist leaders like Yusuf, with their bohemian style, came to symbolise the militant unionism of the Lal Kanpur period. Yusuf had worked with trade unions in Punjab, Ahmedabad, Bombay and Delhi. He

[8] 'Everyone recognises, like the rich and learned, the strong and powerful are also important to the nation. To help and encourage wrestlers is vital for the physical progress of the nation.' Reproduced in N.P. Arora and Lakshmi Kant Tripathi, *Pratap Narayan Misra* (Kanpur 1947), p. 39.

[9] Ganga Sahai Chaube, 'Ganeshji ki Sharan Mein' in B. Chaturvedi, et al., eds, *Ganesh Smarak Granth*.

[10] Harihar Nath Shastri, *Amar Shahidon ke Sansmaran* (Kanpur 1981).

arrived in Kanpur in the mid-1930s, during a period of upsurge in the labour movement, when his populist style had a special appeal. Known originally as Sant Singh, the title Maulana Yusuf was partly to dodge the state intelligence, but also to reach out to Muslim workers in Kanpur. Trade unionists like Yusuf gave a different meaning to Gandhian ascetic ideals. Renunciation for them was a way of bridging the social distance between middle-class leaders and workers. However, communists in Kanpur demarcated their difference from Gandhian nationalists by not wearing khadi. In the communalised context of the early 1930s khadi in Kanpur had acquired a peculiarly Hindu connotation. Contemporary trade unionists recounted how they would be lynched in Muslim bastis if they appeared in khadi. Dress codes became important for an assertion of secular credentials and to gain acceptability as leaders.

The period of Lal Kanpur was for many workers one in which communist egalitarian ideals were being realised. For a fleeting moment the distance between leaders and workers seemed to narrow. Ordinary workers dreamt of themselves as leaders. To many the dreams came partly true. Workers who became leaders within factory-level institutions thrown up during the strikes felt a new sense of dignity and empowerment. Note, for instance, the experience of a worker chosen as secretary of a mill committeee:

> *Kanpur mein bare aur mane jane netaon mein pandit Balkrishna Sharma, Maulana Yusuf, Hazrat Mohani, aur Pyarelal Agarwal ka nam ek dam shikhar choti par tha aur inhi sab netaon ke sath meri bhi ganana ho rahi thi . . .*[11]

To be counted along with respected leaders was to realise the impossible.

Representations of the 1930s often tend to erase memories of conflict and differences between workers and leaders, and emphasise the camaraderie and spirit of bonhomie. For many workers the experience of living in shared accommodation in the late 1930s created a sense of community between worker leaders and others. Households consisting of male migrants to the city were not a new phenomenon. But to many radicals these collectivities

[11] My name now figured with all the well-known and respectable leaders in Kanpur, like Balkrishna Sharma, Maulana Yusuf, Hazrat Mohani, and Pyarelal Agarwal. Shriram, *Ek Sarvahara ka Jivan Vritanta*, p. 17.

now carried a new meaning. These male households were referred
to as 'communes'—a term which to them was evocative of communist egalitarianism.[12] These fantasies of egalitarianism were
sometimes transferred to other contexts. In Chakr's account, the
experience of prison with communist comrades is imagined as
different from days in prison with others. Comrades in prison
transcended hierarchies in prison life through a spirit of sharing:
communist leaders in B class jails shared goodies like butter with
comrades in C class, deprived of such luxuries.[13]

A schematic view of shifts between the 1920s and 1930s conceals the conflicts, and ambivalences in each period. Local leaders
continuously negotiated between different identities and different
constituencies. Ganesh Shankar Vidyarthi, editor of the local *Pratap*, labelled as a Bolshevik in official reports of the early 1920s,
was upheld as a staunch defender of Hindu interests (*Hindu hiton
ka kattar pujari*) by Lajpat Rai[14] and was represented as the only
truly secular Congressman in Kanpur in testimonies before the
Riots Inquiry Committee of 1931. How do these different identities
play themselves out in Vidyarthi's politics?

In Vidyarthi's writings of the early 1920s the emphasis is on
broad, universalistic identities: the boundaries of a nation are not
defined by caste, community or religion. In a powerful essay on
rashtriyata, Vidyarthi staunchly opposed the idea of a Hindu
rashtra and was emphatic that the theory of a Hindu rashtra was
based on certain misconceptions.

> *Kuch log Hindu rashtra chillate hain . . . ve ek bari bhari bhul kar
> rahe hain. Aur unhone abhi tak rashtr shabda ke artha hi nahin
> samjhe . . . ab sansar me hindu rashtra nahin ho sakta hai kyonki
> rashtra ka hona tabhi sambhav hai jab desh ka shasan desh valon ke
> hath me ho, aur yadi yeh man bhi liya jai, ki aaj bharat swadhin ho
> jaye, . . . to bhi Hindu hi bharat mein sab kuch na hongen.*[15]

---

[12] Note for instance: 'A special feature about the communists was that
they set up communes in Gwaltoli and Gandhinagar in which communists
stayed together' (my translation). Chakr, *Kanpur Mazdur Andolan*, p. 41.

[13] Chakr, *Kanpur Mazdur Andolan*, p. 41.

[14] *Pratap*, 21.11.1926; *Vartman*, 14.11.1926.

[15] 'Some people have been demanding a Hindu nation . . . they are committing a grave error. They have not yet understood the meaning of the term
rashtra . . . now a Hindu *rashtra* is not possible in the world today. A nation
is possible only when the government is in the hands of the people. Even if

He was equally critical of Muslims whose loyalties he believed were towards Islamic sacred places in Kabul, Mecca and Jeddah.

Vidyarthi seems to suggest an irresistible, natural movement of history towards the growth of nationalism. With the decline of religious values in modern society, he argues, patriotic ideals took precedence over religious ideals. The shift had a liberating and progressive impact on the development of culture and civilisation. There is an explicit dichotomy here between secular national values and religious values: one liberates and takes forward, the other constricts and fetters.

Like many others in his times Vidyarthi was influenced by the tide of socialist ideas. In essays like 'Aagami Mazdur Mahakranti' he focuses on workers' solidarity and the inevitability of a workers' revolution.[16] He traces the beginnings of the workers' movement in Europe to the seventeenth century and the industrial revolution to the sixteenth century. The long history of the movement gives workers' struggle a legitimacy in Vidyarthi's description. The achievements of the workers' movement in the twentieth century were a product of centuries of struggle and suffering. The Soviet revolution gave a new confidence to workers all over Europe. Socialist ideas were now spreading so rapidly that there was a possibility of a worldwide revolution. A revolution seems logical and imminent in his description. Similarly, in *Garib Parvari* Vidyarthi ridicules officialdom which attributes peasants revolts to intervention by outsiders. He sees revolt as almost natural in the condition the peasants were living in. Reform and betterment of peasants' conditions was not a product of official will and initiative but a result of their own struggles.[17] In another context Vidyarthi is categorical that Bolshevism and conspiracy carried different meanings. What was seen as a Bolshevik conspiracy by those in power was to the poor and downtrodden an attempt to improve their social conditions and a step towards the establishment of people's power (*loksatta*).[18]

India becomes independent Hindus alone will not exercise power.' Radha Krishna Awasthi, ed., *Kranti ka Udgosh: Ganesh Shankar Vidyarthi ki Kalam Se*, p. 145.

[16] *Kranti ka Udgosh*, p. 501.

[17] He argues in a similar vein in 'Desh ke Mazduron ki Dasha', *Kranti ka Udgosh*, p. 517.

[18] 'Mazdur: Mahattam Samaparvartak', ibid., p. 525.

Yet it is important to distinguish between the socialism of Vidyarthi and that of later socialists. While inspired by socialist ideals, for Vidyarthi there was always a potential danger in socialism. Such differences notwithstanding, there are uncanny similarities between Vidyarthi's narrative and contemporary official descriptions. The prospect of Europe-wide strikes is almost inevitable yet dangerous and fearful (bhayanak).[19] In essays like 'Bolshevism ki Lahar' and 'Bolshevik Khatra' Vidyarthi writes about measures to prevent the 'poison' and 'contagion' of Bolshevism from touching Indian shores. A socialist identity for workers seems natural and acceptable, yet it is alien and portends danger: '*Ham hraday se chahte hain ki, Bolshevism ki chut hamare pavitra desh ko na chue. Yah bhumi madhya asia ki barbar jatiyon aur asabhya logon ki akhet sthali na ban jaye.*'[20]

In his later writings Vidyarthi's nationalism is articulated differently. The shift is related partly to the growing communal antagonism of the 1920s. The nation, he feels, is endangered and has to be defended.[21] It can be saved only by restoring the voice of sanity and strengthening its constituent basis. Vidyarthi is categorical that goondas and cowards cannot constitute a nation. Acts of violence and aggression by goondas were responsible for the communal madness. Vidyarthi ridicules the emasculated Hindu male and emphasises that the meekness and cowardice of victims breeds goonda violence. Who are the goondas and cowards in Vidyarthi's characterisation? He identifies cowardice as a Hindu and aggression as a Muslim attribute. Muslim goondas symbolise violence, danger, unreason and madness. Not all Muslims are goondas: there are sharif Muslims who embody sanity. But Hindu cowardice silences this voice. Cowards do not attract respect or sympathy. In his characterisation of Hindus Vidyarthi makes no distinction between the good and bad, sharifs and others. If goondas are others, all Hindus are intrinsically good, yet too weak to make the nation. To become true patriots Hindus must be valiant and courageous. Although in popular accounts it is the emasculated, lean figure of Vidyarthi which is

[19] 'Aagami Mazdur Mahakranti', *Kranti ka Udgosh*, p. 501.

[20] We sincerely hope that Bolshevism does not endanger the purity of our nation. This land should not become a playground of the barbarous and uncivilised people of Central Asia, ibid., p. 570.

[21] 'Majhabi Pagalpan', *Kranti ka Udgosh*, pp. 720–2.

iconised, his later writings have resonances of the virile, masculinised nationalism advocated by the proponents of akhara culture.

The boundaries of rashtriyata in Vidyarthi's earlier writings are wide and inclusive. Later, the boundaries of the nation narrow down. The nation no longer stands above particular interests: the interests of the community and nation are synonymous. The apparent basis for exclusion and inclusion within the nation are not dramatically altered. Muslims cannot be easily assimilated— not because they are Muslims but because they lack the necessary moral attributes. It was possible for meek Hindus to transform themselves and become good patriots, but Muslim goondas lack this potential in Vidyarthi's characterisation. Hindus seem to naturally form a part of the nation-building project, despite all weaknesses: Muslims pose a danger from the outside and cannot be assimilated within. Conversion activity by Muslims is seen as a threat to the 'purity' of the nation. Conversion which was not voluntary but through force, abduction, deceit, was sinful. The nation has to be protected from Muslim goondas, abductors of women and children. The purity of the nation is implicitly identified with the preservation of the Hindu order. Vidyarthi defends the Arya Samaj against its critics and boldly asserts his difference with Gandhi on this issue. Vidyarthi considers Gandhi's critique of Arya Samaj parochialism discriminatory and unfair. If in Gandhi's view Muslim fanaticism was a reactive phenomenon, so was the sectarianism of the Arya Samaj. Vidyarthi explains that the context in which the Arya Samaj emerged was one in which the Hindus were falling prey to predators from all quarters. The counterposition between the image of the Hindu and the masculine Muslim predator is common. Vidyarthi goes a little further: Hindus were not only feminine, they were soft—like fresh butter being lapped up by all and sundry: '*Hinduon ka to yah hal tha jo taje makhan ka hota hai. Jo chahta hath marta, aur jahan se jitna chahta, utna nikal leta.*'[22] He opposed separate electorates because of similar apprehensions about growing Muslim power. With separate electorates the number of Muslim representatives would be far greater than was justified by their numerical strength.[23]

[22] *Kranti ka Udgosh*, p. 715.

[23] Vidyarthi found it anomalous that a municipality which was financed

The discourse of Vidyarthi and the Hindu Sabha shared certain similarities. Against Gandhi's attack on the Arya Samaj, Vidyarthi made an aggressive defence of Hindu interests. At other moments, however, Vidyarthi had sharp disagreements with Arya Samajists. Vidyarthi staunchly opposed the involvement of the Hindu Maha-sabha in local elections, arguing that the election of Hindu Sabha candidates to local bodies would legitimise communal represent-ation and intensify religious and caste conflicts. However, in critiquing Sabha politics, Vidyarthi reaffirmed an essential identity of interests between the sabha and himself. The politics of the Sabha, he argued, would fragment the nation and ultimately harm the interests of the Hindu community. In response to the Maha-sabha charge that Congress representatives in local bodies would endanger Hindu interests because they were not '*kattar* (staunch) Hindus', Vidyarthi asserted the pro-Hindu credentials of the Congress: '*Jo Congressvadi Hindu hain, vah na to Hindu hain aur na Hindu hit ke virodhi.*[24] To protect Hindu honour and Hinduness, he felt, it was best that electoral politics was left to the Congress.[25]

But Vidyarthi's peace-making role during the communal riots of 1931 and his final act of martyrdom transform the way in which he is represented. All subsequent assessments of Vidyarthi are refracted through this halo of martyrdom. Vidyarthi now stands apart from other local leaders as the apostle of peace and communal amity. Remembrances eulogise him:

> He was one who could be counted amongst angels. He was an ornament not only of the Hindu but also of the Musalman com-munity. Humanness personified, embodiment of social morality,

---

primarily by contributions from the city's Hindu population should have a larger representation of Muslims. He warned that the value of Hindu voters would fall since four Hindu voters would become equivalent to one Muslim, according to the new system of representation. 'Municipal Bill par Andolan', *Kranti ka Udgosh*, pp. 221–2.

[24] Congressmen who are Hindus, are not opponents of Hindu interests. Vidyarthi, 'Hindu Sabha Ya Congress', *Kranti ka Udgosh*, p. 858.

[25] Yet in order to protect Hindu honour we feel that the day Hindu sabhas take elections in their hands it will be the end of Hindu organisation. *Kintu ham, Hindupan ki raksha aur hindutva ki aan ke nam par yah kahna avashyak samajhte hain ki jis din sabhayen chunavon ke kam ko apne hath mein le lengi us din Hindu sangathan ki atyeshta kriya ho jayegi.*' 'Hindu Sabha Ya Congress', *Kranti ka Udgosh*, p. 857.

standard-bearer of unity, he, whom we savages and enemies of humanity knew as Ganesh Shankar Vidyarthi, was seen restless and full of anguish, now in Hindu quarters, and now in Musalman localities, sometimes protecting the Hindu and sometimes defending the Musalmans.[26]

Communal violence disturbed Vidyarthi deeply and in this moment of crisis he worked selflessly, protecting both Hindus and Muslims from the fury of the rioters. Images of Vidyarthi in his final moments are truly moving:

> On the 25th March when Ganeshji reached Patkapur he was bareheaded and barefooted. There he appealed to both Hindus and Musalmans to live amicably. . . . When they reached near Bengali Mohal they saw brickbats raining from all sides. Ganeshji cried out at the top of his voice, 'What are you doing?'. . . As soon as they entered they saw a head separated from the trunk, and the dead body of a child which had been pierced through with a spear. Seeing this Ganeshji wept loudly . . . Chhotey Khan who heard him crying like this was so much affected by Ganeshji's words that he also began to weep . . . Ganeshji clung to Chhotey Khan, and both of them wept . . .[27]

Through his death Vidyarthi is refigured. Subsequent nationalist chronicling removes all traces of sectarianism and intolerance in Vidyarthi. He becomes a mythic figure, invested with all the idealised moral qualities of a popular hero in times of trouble. He is represented as selfless, working tirelessly to help people, confronting violence fearlessly without any feelings of anger or retribution. He stands out as the only Congress member in Kanpur who was truly secular.[28] In these retrospective accounts Vidyarthi appears as a feminised, angelic figure, an embodiment of humanity and morality. The ambivalences in Vidyarthi's discourse, the tensions between his belief in a secular ideal of nationalism and his sectarian critique of Muslim aggression, his belief in non-violence and his critique of the emasculated Hindu male, are erased from such recollections.

[26] Statement of Maulana Riaz Ahmad, a Kanpur merchant, cited in Barrier, pp. 324–5.

[27] Barrier, pp. 318–19.

[28] One of the witnesses before the Riots Inquiry Committee for instance: 'No other prominent Congressman at Cawnpore is so much above communalism as Ganeshji was . . .'

Radical Rhetoric of the 1930s

By the 1930s the rhetoric of the KMS changed. The nationalism of the KMS was now defined through a discourse of socialism. The language of socialism was not completely new. Vidyarthi, Narayan Prasad Arora and others in the KMS made frequent allusions to socialism and the creation of a just and better world for workers. But this was not central to the discourse of the 1920s.[29] The mutations in the languages coincided with a period when professional trade unionists like Harihar Nath Shastri and Raja Ram Shastri became important within labour politics in Kanpur. Harihar Nath Shastri wrote impassioned pieces on class war and the inevitability of conflict between capital and labour.

> Class war means that, there are only two communities in the world. On one side is the capitalist, who enslaves millions of labourers to achieve his selfish ends, while on the other, there are labourers and farmers, who have been for ages downtrodden and victims of oppression. The war that is to be in the world will not be between the Hindus and Muslims, nor between one country and another, but between the capitalists and the united labourers of the world, be they Hindus and Muslims, Indians or Europeans, to avenge the wrongs propagated against them through centuries . . .[30]

The *Mazdur*, a weekly paper of the KMS edited by Harihar Nath, frequently carried essays on the coming workers' raj. Writings in the *Mazdur* pointed out how swaraj under the leadership of the Congress, a party controlled by the capitalists, could not be true swaraj.[31] The *Pratap* press in Kanpur brought out publications on the Russian revolution. In a pamphlet on *Trotsky and the Russsian Revolution,* Shiv Narain Tandon paid glowing tributes to Trotsky and his theory of revolution. Tandon argued that the revolution was the outcome of a general awakening among the people; their courage and determination provided sustenance and inspiration to leaders.[32] He was dismissive of critics who saw Bolshevik rule

[29] In a piece called 'Duniya ke Mazduron ka Bolbala', for instance, Arora, writes about the inequalities in society and argues that there could be no peace in the world till social inequalities were removed and each worker had enough for himself and his family. *Narayan Nibandhavali*, pp. 73–4.

[30] B.N. Datar, ed., *Harihar Nath Shastri: Life and Work* (Bombay 1968).

[31] RNP, 30.11.1931, 10.11.1931.

[32] Shiv Narain Tandon, *Bolshevik Russia* (Kanpur 1932), Pros. Pub., nos 320–2, NAI.

as a reign of terror: 'what injustice have the Bolsheviks done by establishing a rule which was based on the will of the majority . . .'[33]

KMS publications of the 1930s incorporate the socialist message. The struggle for freedom is represented as a struggle for the emancipation of workers; the red flag is a symbol of struggle for freedom. In a poem, *Mazdur Jhande ka Awahan*, the strong, virile, masculine image of workers contrasts with the nurturing yet helpless and agonising mother/nation image.[34] Workers are the saviours who can rescue the nation from misery and doom. The poem implores workers to be true to their mother's milk, be ready for sacrifices and demonstrate their courage. They must terrify the enemy that sucked their blood and starved them. Almost as a last act to save their honour, men are asked to commit jauhar, the act of self-immolation usually associated with the preservation of female honour. Links are drawn between the nation's suffering and workers' exploitation; the poem ends with a call for revolution.

Another publication in the series, *Mazdur Jhande ki Prarthana*, is addressed to the workers' red flag. The author of the poem is Avdesh Sitapuri, a worker in the cotton godown at Elgin Mills.[35] The poem declares unequivocally that the red flag, inscribed with a hammer and sickle, is the one which destroyed the tyranny of tsardom in Russia. There is no ambivalence about the socialist message; it is emphatic and has a sense of urgency. The poem calls on the red flag to awaken the sleeping nation with the lessons of communism and create a fearful revolution.[36]

---

[33] Ibid.

[34] '*Mat ab aur adhik rone do, mukh ne aasuyon se dhone do
Ma ka man ne malin ne hone do, kyon phatti ne dard se chhati
Ab ne dud uska sharmaon
E mazdur jawano aao.*'

(Do not let her [mother] cry do not any more. Let her not be morose. Her bosom is bursting with pain, do not shy away from her milk. Come forward, brave workers.) *Mazdur Jhande ka Awahan*, Pros. Pub., no. 552, NAI.

[35] The proscribed pamphlets do not cite the name of the author, Chakr provides this information in his *Kanpur Mazdur Andolan*, p. 39.

[36] *Samyavaad ka path patha do, soya bharat bhagya jaga do
Bharkar bhishan kranti macha do anyayi sarkar mita do.*

(Wake up sleeping Bharat, teach the lesson of socialism. Make a fearful revolution and remove this unjust government.) *Mazdur Jhande ki*

As opposed to the conciliatory language of earlier trade union leaders like Murari Lal, trade unionists like Harihar Nath Shastri, in the late 1920s, brought in a new militant language which emphasised the legitimacy of strikes to secure workers' demands. Shastri was critical of the Madras trade unionist Shiva Rao's advice that workers should adopt constitutional methods of struggle: 'When the employers do not hesitate to adopt unconstitutional ways, only Shri B. Siva Rao can understand how far it is proper to advise workers to use constitutional means.'[37] There was a close similarity between the language of communists and those of leaders like Harihar Nath Shastri. In publications like *Duniya ke Mazduron Ek Ho*, brought out by the UP Communist Party, the emancipation of workers is linked with the end of British rule. It argues for the formation of a strong organisation of the poor to lead people towards freedom. The pamphlet warns against following the Congress leadership too blindly—there is a danger that the affluent leadership of the Congress would abandon the working class in the final stages of the struggle.[38] Similarly, a workers' and peasant party publication from Gwaltoli in Kanpur, *Ham Bhukhe Nangen Kyon Hain*, analyses the roots of existing social problems and, like other left writings in this period, ends with a note of hope: '*Zamana samyavaad ki taraf ja raha hai.*'[39] It visualises a future in which there was swaraj with panchayati raj, that is, communal ownership of property and the elimination of zamindars, capitalists and landowners. Yet it was by asserting their difference with other trade union leaders that the communists established their influence over the movement. By the late 1930s, the politics of Harihar Nath Shastri came to be seen by officials as moderate compared to that of the communists, who were labelled as 'agitators'.[40] Papers like *Leader* approvingly testify to

---

Prarthana (Kanpur 1930), Pros. Pub., no. 552, NAI, published by S.P. Awasthi for the Mazdur Sabha.

[37] Cited in S.P. Misra, 'Mazdur Andolan ka Itihas', in Krishna Kant, ed., *Harihar Nath Shastri Smarak Granth* (Lucknow 1969).

[38] *Duniya ke Mazduron Ek Ho Jao* (1937), a bulletin of the UP Communist party.

[39] *Ham Bhukhe Nangen Kyon Hain* (Kanpur 1935)

[40] Ramsay Scott to J.G. Laithwaite, 1.11.1937, HPD, 12/1/1938.

this: 'One of the reasons why Mr Hariharnath Shastri, President of the Mazdur Sabha, is not such an attraction with the mob is that, he keeps his head on his shoulders, and however bitter his criticism may be of the employers, he never really lets himself go.'[41]

In Sudarshan Chakr's account, the entry of communists brings an important change in the nature of the workers' movement. 'Other leaders were merely interested in bringing about some reforms in the conditions of workers, the communists saw workers' struggles as a step towards a workers' and peasants state.'[42] Unlike other leaders, who opposed foreign managers and not Indian millowners, communists he argued, made no distinction between the two and attacked all employers. The dominance of communists in the KMS coincided with a labour upsurge in Kanpur. The radical nationalist rhetoric was now enriched and inscribed with a new meaning. It was a context in which workers felt empowered: mill committees were formed, large rallies and meetings were organised, and codes of authority and power within factories were challenged. Workers' raj and swaraj, red flag and national flag, all seemed synonymous in this moment of militancy. Workers' opposition to managers was expressed in a language of anti-imperialism. Communist leaders emphasised that the main objective of the general strike was the abolition of capitalism and imperialism.[43] Workers like Jan Mohammad drew an idyllic picture of Congress rule: 'Congress stood on the strength of peasants and workers and aimed at the destruction of capitalism and the establishment of a Soviet form of government.'[44]

[41] *Leader*, 10.6.1938. Haig noted a change in Shastri's politics: 'Though he has given a good deal of trouble in the past, showed signs of being helpful and anxious to work with the Government in connection with the present strike situation.' Haig to Linlithgow, 6.8.1937, Haig Papers (NMML).

[42] Chakr, *Kanpur Mazdur Andolan*, p. 52.

[43] See ch. 6.

[44] SAID, 5.2.1938. Communist speakers at workers' meetings emphasised that the main object of the strike was the removal of the British government. SAID, 18.6.1938. Revolutionary songs at meetings raised a call for freedom: 'Let there be a cry for freedom / . . . The capitalists and imperialists depart as their end has come / We shall remember the cruel story of exploitation / Let peasants and workers realise that they are the future rulers.' SAID, 5.2.1938.

The languages of socialism were appropriated by nationalist discourses, just as much as nationalism became the language of socialism. Class politics in the 1930s was articulated through a language of nationalism: the notion of a workers' state could not be conceptualised without seeing it as swaraj. Moments of working class upsurge like 1937–8 allowed loyalties to fuse under the banner of class. The methods of mobilisation used by communists in this period played an important role in harnessing community loyalties and integrating them to wider ties of class.[45] But this was not an easy process: solidarities were always being made and unmade. The tensions between the communist-dominated KMS and sections of dalit workers, who formed their own labour organisation, was expressive of the conflicts which were integral to the process of negotiation between community, class and nation.

The Paradoxes of Power

Once the Congress came into office in July 1937, the logic of power was important in shaping its attitude towards labour. But the processes through which power was legitimated were complex. In its election campaigns the Congress made promises to labour for better working conditions and an improved standard of living, and these were included in its manifesto. This built hopes of determined action. Millowners and officials feared the extravagant promises and the spate of strikes soon after the formation of the new ministry confirmed their fears. The Chamber of Commerce seemed to believe that the 'irresponsible' promises of the Congress created illusions among workers that in future industries would be owned and controlled by them.[46] Much before the Congress came to power, colonial officials like Haig expressed anxieties about popular expectations from the Congress ministry: 'Among the common people there was a feeling sedulously fostered by successful Congress candidates and other Congress workers, that Congress raj was coming which they were apt to interpret as being inconsistent with British raj.'[47]

---

[45] See chs 6 and 7.
[46] Presidential address, *UICC Report,* 1937, p. 12.
[47] Haig to Zetland, 7.4.1937, Haig Papers (NMML).

A series of strikes in Kanpur in July 1937 provided a testing ground when the conflicting pulls and pressures on nationalists became more apparent. The government could not deny the legitimacy of the workers' demands. But Congressmen like Katju were convinced that strikes were unnecessary when the government was sympathetic to workers' demands.[48] The contemporary press reflected a similar attitude—it was sympathetic to worker grievances yet hostile to strikes. Aaj expresses an opinion which was widely held: 'The welfare of workers today lies in their remaining quiet even if they are provoked. They should increase their strength, and thus make the Congress government successful and give it an opportunity to legislate in their favour.'[49]

On 6 August the police made lathi charges and fired on striking workers. The presence of the police in the city was obtrusive— more than a thousand patrolled the industrial areas. There were violent exchanges between the police and strikers: the strikers resisted police action with stone throwing. Repressive action by the government created a crisis of legitimacy. The strength of the strikers increased rapidly, and numbers of demonstrators in the streets swelled.[50] Crowds numbering between 12,000 and 20,000 gathered at mill gates. Among the strikers there was a growing sense of anger against government action. The announcement of a settlement did not restore their faith in the government. A settlement negotiated without consulting the strike committee, they believed, had no legitimacy. A large section of workers felt they were betrayed by the Congress and the KMS leadership.[51] Their militancy intensified.

Pant denied there was a lathi charge. The term lathi charge, he argues, is justifiable only if 'regulation' lathis are used.[52] On the firing, Pant again makes a technical distinction between the police 'opening fire' and the police 'firing' a single shot: 'The police did not open fire. One sub-inspector, being hard pressed by a mob

[48] Statement of Katju, Minister for Industries, Pioneer, 6.8.1937.

[49] Aaj, 4.12.1937. Similar opinions are echoed in Hamdam, RNP, 21.8.1937 and Vartman, RNP, 14.8.1937.

[50] Yusuf. 'Cawnpore General Strike', New Age, Dec.1937.

[51] Leader, 12.8.1937.

[52] On 6 August, Pant explained that light cane lathis of one inch thickness were used. Legislative Assembly Debates, 10 September 1937.

numbering over 5000, fired one shot resulting in an injury to one man.'[53]

Contrary to 1924, when there was widespread condemnation of police firing on the Kanpur Cotton Mill strikers, the criticism of government action was not so widespread in 1937. Communist trade unionists, who had softened towards the Congress, ignore the events of 6 August altogether,[54] others try to absolve the ministry by attributing responsibility to the colonial bureaucracy.[55] Papers like *Aaj* and *Pratap*, which unequivocally condemned police action in 1924, now censured the strikers for their violence and aggressiveness.[56] A contrast is drawn between thousands of riotious strikers, trouble makers (upadravi) and a single police daroga who fires and injures only one worker.

The defence of government actions against strikers is framed within a larger discourse of 'order' and 'stability' and development of the province. As a popular government, the Congress had to consider the demands of the workers. Yet the protection of industries was equally important to nationalist conceptions of development.

Kanpur as the largest industrial centre in the province was symbolic of development.

> Cawnpore is the only industrial centre in our province. It is a place where thousands of labourers find employment. If the relations between employers and labourers are not harmonious and if we do not succeed in restoring peace where there has been lately a rift and a cleavage, the disorder that will result and which will not be confined to Cawnpore is hard to conceive. It will then be beyond the capacity of any of us to control matters. We look at the question from the point of view of those who want their province to get rich, who want unemployment to be wiped out, who want industries to flourish and who want men to be made as happy as inspite of handicaps it may be possible for us to do.[57]

[53] Ibid.

[54] This is characteristic of accounts by communist trade unionists. A blow by-blow account by Yusuf makes no reference to the police action of 6 August 1937. *New Age*, Dec. 1937.

[55] Interview, Arjun Arora.

[56] *Aaj*, 8 Aug.1937.

[57] *UP Legislative Assembly Debates*, vol. II, 6.9.1937. In a statement reported in *Leader*, the UP govt clarifies: 'The maintenance of order and

In this discourse, order was identified as natural for all interested in the prosperity of the province.

Pant recognised the legitimacy of the workers' demands and emphasised the government's commitment to resolving their problems.[58] He was critical of the obduracy of the millowners and was categorical that the solution to the crisis in Kanpur depended more on employers than on labour, 'for they were in a position to give while the latter were in a position to take only'.[59] He emphasised the need for transparency and dialogue: 'They [employers] should take labour into confidence, show them their balance sheet and tell them that both were engaged in the same industry and that their interests were identical.'[60] Pant's intervention was important in persuading the employers to agree to the appointment of an inquiry committee and recognise the KMS as a representative union. The government displayed firmness in dealing with the violence of the strikers but this was not without considerable inner tensions within the minds of Congress leaders. Pant showed a respect for democratic principles and in his exchanges with colonial officials he was insistent that labour activists should be dealt with 'by argument and not by restraint'.[61] Preferring to tread cautiously, he refused to be persuaded by the demand of officials that the activities of 'Communist agitators' be curbed. Soon after the events of 6 August 1937 he admitted to Nehru: 'We have been throughout exercising a restraining influence on the Collector and he himself was anxious not to do anything embarrassing to

---

tranquillity is the primary duty of . . . it is his [the District Magistrate's] duty to see to it that the present dispute does not degenerate into disturbances and riots and that public order and tranquillity is firmly maintained.' *Leader* 9.8.1937.

[58] See, for instance, Pant's appeal to the JK Mill strikers in *Aaj*, 24.7.1937.

[59] *Pioneer*, 13.11.1937. In a letter to Nehru, Pant sharply criticised the obstinacy of millowners: 'Katju went there personally and the matter was all but settled . . . but for the stupidity and pugnacity of Gavin Jones.' Pant to Nehru, 7.8.1937, Nehru Papers, vol. 79 (NMML). Clearly, Pant did not seem to be in agreement with industrialists like Padampat, who 'asserted that there was no grievance so far as the labourers are concerned and the mistris had fomented this trouble'. Pant to Nehru, 20.7.1937, Nehru Papers, vol. 79 (NMML).

[60] *Pioneer*, 13.11.1937.

[61] Haig to Linlithgow, 23.8.1937, Haig Papers (NMML).

us. But there were some unfortunate incidents yesterday and one man was injured.'[62]

The attitude of Congress leaders like Nehru reflects similar ambiguities. In the late 1920s and 1930s, Nehru was seen by colonial officials as a sympathiser of labour under a liberal mask, as one who 'stirred up labour trouble'.[63] In 1937–8 his role had changed. His visit to Kanpur had, in fact, a 'tranquilizing' effect on labour. In his appeal to Kanpur strikers he advised them not to interfere with the smooth working of the mills: 'The workers should not forget that, after all, their wages are paid out of the profits made by the mills and factories. Whatever therefore is injurious to the working of a mill ultimately proves detrimental to the interests of the worker.'[64] He was critical of strikes against victimisation and he defended as a general principle, the employers' right to dismiss workers.[65] His defence of the right to dismiss, at a time when victimisation of worker activities in Kanpur was a common complaint, meant in effect a delegitimisation of strikes. It was as if labour and capital were tied through a mutuality of interest, not through conflict. The need of the time was to maintain the authority and prestige of the Congress government. In private, however, Nehru expressed a deep anxiety about the functioning of Congress ministries and a fear that they were 'tending to become counter-revolutionary'.[66]

[62] Pant to Nehru, 7.7.1937, Nehru Papers, vol. 79 (NMML).

[63] Haig to Linlithgow, 7.10.1937, Haig Papers (NMML). During the Golmuri Tinplate workers' strike in Jamshedpur, for instance, Nehru was more sympathetic with the strikers, emphasising: 'You will no doubt appreciate that no worker looks forward light-heartedly to a strike which must necessarily mean considerable suffering for him . . . But a long strike must necessarily be based on a conviction that there are substantial grievances.' Nehru to Shaw Wallace and Co., 10.9.1929, AICC Papers, File G-71/1929 (NMML).

[64] 'To the Kanpur workers', original text in Hindu published in *Pratap*, reproduced in *Selected Works of Jawaharlal Nehru*, ed. S.Gopal (New Delhi 1975), vol. 8, p. 333. He also went on to say 'the right to dismiss a worker who does not do his work well should be conceded to the mill manager. No one should question this right. No institutions or mill can function properly without discipline.' *Selected Works*, vol. 8, p. 332.

[65] *Selected Works*, vol. 8, p. 332.

[66] He added how the general attitude of the ministries was 'static': 'We dare not be static for that means that we are merely carrying on the traditions

Conflicts over the attitude of the Congress ministry towards labour caused deep divisions within the party. Murmurs of discontent became louder by the end of 1937. A large number of complaints against the government action were received at the AICC office. A letter from Najibabad captured the shock and dismay of many sympathisers and followers of the Congress when they heard Pant's defence of the repressive actions:

> I shall not depart from the truth if I hold the view that had any ministry but that of the Congress been in power a storm of protest and condemnation were sure to be raised as has always been the case and you too would have vehemently condemned it. . . . You should know Panditji, how your statement was responsible for making the opposition benches tongue tied in the Bengal Assembly the other day, and their objecting to the police lathi charge at Calcutta on Andaman Day, when one of the members of the Ministerial Party referred to your statement at Kanpur incident.[67]

By December 1937, criticism of government policy became more widespread. The left within the Congress and outside was extremely critical of the restrictive orders against strikers.[68] The City Congress Committee too was riven with conflict over the strike. By May

---

(with minor variations) of previous governments. Indeed one cannot remain static for long for the world is not static. Inevitably the choice has to be made and I fear the choice too often is of the wrong kind.' Nehru to Pant, 25.11.1937, Nehru Papers, vol. 79 (NMML).

[67] Letter, 20.8.1937, Chhotey Lal Jain, Najibabad to Pant, AICC Papers, File G-76, 1937 (NMML). Such anguish about Congress policies was expressed by others too. S.G. Patkar, a Bombay communist, in a letter to Nehru, expressed the dilemmas confronting working class leaders: 'Hitherto we had the common bond of struggle against foreign rule, we were all suppressed, and this very suppression held us together. How are we to explain to the worker that it is still the same foreign power we have to fight against? What reply are we to give when we are asked as to why the war against the working class alone is continued in the same old way?' AICC Papers, File G-76/1937 (NMML).

[68] *Leader* reported: 'It is an irony of fate that the severest critics of the Congress ministries . . . are a section of Congressmen themselves.' 12.12.1937. See also statement of Harihar Nath Shastri in *Leader,* 10.12.1937. The Home Dept drew attention to the growing criticism in the left wing press, of the 'reactionary policy' of the government, particularly of the adoption of repressive measures. HPD, File 18/12/1937 Dec (i) UP.

1938, radicals within the Congress constituted the dominant voice in the local party. They played up to the popular mood and pushed for strong action against opponents of the strike. Ram Ratan Gupta, director, Laxmi Ratan Cotton Mills who actively opposed the strike, was threatened with suspension of his membership from the City Congress Committee and his office of vice-president of the committee. Younger Congress members were pitted against older Congress leaders who objected to severe sanctions. But the latter were clearly marginalised.[69]

The recommendations of the KLIC, made public in April 1938, had wide support within the KMS and outside. Although the report of the committee was ambivalent on the question of wage cuts, it was sympathetic to many of the issues raised in the KMS memorandum. The rejection of the recommendations by the Employers' Association led to widespread protest by workers.[70] The ministry was now in a moral bind. It was torn between its commitment to the recommendations of the inquiry committee and its perception of strikes as disrupting 'peace' and 'harmony'. To the majority of local Congress members, support to the strikers seemed imperative. It could not retract from its commitment to abide by the terms of the Inquiry Committee, but it was apprehensive of strikes. The legitimacy of local leaders depended on their ability to influence the provincial government. A complex of pressures was at work on the Congress ministry while Pant groped along with what Haig characterised as a 'gradual' and 'tentative' approach.[71] Eventually the local situation—the mass outrage and protest against the rejection—forced a swing in Congress politics. Younger and more radical members of the City Congress Committee made populist speeches in support of the strike.[72] In some ways the events of May 1938 helped to blur the

---

[69] *Leader* reported: 'The old Congressmen who opposed haste in this decision have no power in the Committee and although lip service is paid to them they command really no respect, their opinions have ceased to carry any weight of late . . .' and the mere fact that they remained studiously aloof or were not sufficiently prominent in the labour strike has lost them whatever little respect they commanded with their younger followers.' *Leader*, 27.6.1938.

[70] See ch. 6.

[71] Haig to Linlithgow, 9.12.1937, Haig Papers (NMML).

[72] *Pioneer*, 22.5.1938.

difference between political groups. The strike became a mass festival in which communists, Congress members, Muslim Leaguers, Ahrars, workers, women, children, families, entire working class mohallas participated.

The surge of militancy narrowed down differences between communist trade unionists and the Congress left. Active support to the strikers by local leaders like Balkrishna Sharma endeared them to communist leaders. P.C. Joshi was all praise for the 'inspiring leadership' provided by Sharma to the strike. In Joshi's account, Sharma's role in the strike was integrated to his narrative of the proletarian movement: 'Under Sharmaji's leadership the Cawnpore congress has . . . given the proletarian struggle the strength of the whole people and built the united front in practice.'[73] Local Congress leaders like Balkrishna Sharma defended their attitude to the communists: 'I want to assure capitalist friends that the communist is not such a dangerous animal as he is often represented to be. He has passed through fire. He has gained experience. He has come to grips with realities. And of all people it is he who today realizes that mere fire-eating will not do.'[74]

The support of the provincial Congress to the strikers was a more cautious one. Sharma and other local leaders extended their support to the strikers much before the provincial leaders gave official sanction. Pant and others in Lucknow were like spectators, watching the actions of local leaders.

Critics of the Congress saw the entire provincial Congress swinging leftwards . A cartoon in the *Pioneer* caricatured Pant as an eagle in a spin, expressing his helplessness to Gandhi: 'Its terrible Mahatmaji I've lost control of my left wing and its going twice as fast as I want it to' (see Fig. 25).[75] In a piece titled 'Red Influx into Cawnpore' the paper described the UP ministry being

[73] *National Front*, 2.6.1938. Communist Party publications of this period are replete with statements like: 'The Congress is our organisation and therefore the Congress ministers are people's ministers. Experience has shown that they can be moved by the pressure of mass mobilisation. Therefore while definitely rejecting the tactic of confining political action to the constitutional plane, we must at the same time boldly come out in defence of any progressive measure initiated by the Congress ministers.' *National Front*, 17.4.1938.

[74] *National Front*, 11.9.1938.

[75] *Pioneer*, 15.7.1938.

driven by communists.[76] It warned the government against the dangers of leniency and approvingly cited the actions of Munshi and Sardar Patel in Bombay, who had 'effectively silenced communist propaganda'.[77] The *Pioneer* was here articulating criticisms and concerns increasingly being voiced by the representatives of industry. The Associated Chambers of Commerce scathingly criticised the 'virtual tolerance' of communist propaganda in UP and urged provincial governments to take 'stringent precautions' to discourage Communism.[78]

European millowners were not alone in their criticisms of Congress policies. Indian capitalists like the Singhanias of the Juggilal Kamlapat group and Ram Ratan Gupta of the Laxmi Ratan Cotton Mills were equally severe in their condemnation of Congress politics. In June 1938 Padampat Singhania urged the Congress to give up its role of leading the strikers and to play the role of a mediator instead.[79] The Juggilal Kamlapat group threatened to withdraw capital from new enterprises planned for Kanpur, to safer centres, with no history of labour troubles, outside UP. Kanpur capitalists saw this as a logical outcome of Congress policies.[80] The government could not ignore criticisms from the Singhanias or Ram Ratan Gupta, both of whom had been Congress supporters and had always contributed generously to its funds.

The colonial state was alarmed at the militancy of the working class movement in Kanpur, yet it preferred to allow the ministry

[76] *Pioneer,* 3.9.1938. *Leader* echoed a similar opinion, 8.6.1938.

[77] *Pioneer,* 3.9.1938.

[78] Secy, Assoc Chamber to Secy, GOI, Home Dept 31.12.1938, HPD, File 7/1/1939. At a meeting of the Employers' Association, the Chairman Tracy Jones was unequivocally critical of the UP govt: 'The attitude that the UP Government is taking up in all matters with which we have to deal with is leading to disaster in this province. Indiscipline is rampant throughout both the countryside and the towns; communal tension and riots are on the increase and communism in its worst and most violent form is spreading rapidly.' *National Herald,* 6.4.1939.

[79] *Pioneer,* 26.6.1938.

[80] *National Herald,* 6.4.1939. The decision to relocate three factories, a steel rolling mill, a factory for manufacturing bakelite goods and straw board mill, meant according to some estimates a loss to Kanpur of capital worth Rs 3,000,000 and unemployment to about 2000 workers. *Pioneer,* 13.7.1938.

to handle the situation.[81] Haig, the governor of UP, was critical of the employers' refusal to negotiate with the KMS in 1937 and appreciated Pant's efforts to resolve the problem by supporting the comparatively moderate leaders within the KMS.[82] Although Haig consistently advised the ministry against the dangers of growing communist militancy in Kanpur, he did not interfere with Pant's general principle of dealing with the communists by argument and not restraint.[83] Owen, the District Magistrate, was in basic agreement with Haig, although he made careful plans of dealing with 'disorder' and was categorical that he would arrest extremist leaders in case of any 'serious disorder'.[84]

Visions of the Nation

Did the rhetoric of nationalism touch the lives of workers? How did workers perceive swaraj? In nationalist narratives which subsumed all movements of workers, peasants and tribals within the larger story of the national movement, the question of worker consciousness was not problematised. Their participation in nationalist activities appears self-evident. Similarly, in trade union-centred accounts, trade union involvement in nationalist activity was equated with worker nationalism. The shift away from nationalist metanarratives in recent writings is marked by a denial

[81] Haig to Linlithgow, 23.9.1937 and 6.9.1937, Haig Papers (NMML).

[82] 'The employers showed, I thought, a rather unwise attitude of peevishness after the settlement had been reached, and complained that it had been forced on them and that they had no confidence in the Mazdur Sabha.' Haig to Linlithgow, 23.8.1937, Haig Papers (NMML). Later in 1938, again, Linlithgow wrote to Hallett, 'Whatever faults there may be on the side of the employees, the employers also—European and Indian alike—are adopting an unnecessarily stubborn attitude and that some pressure should be brought to bear upon them.' Linlithgow to Hallett, 3.6.1938, Linlithgow Papers, Corr. with Governor UP, vol. I, Jan.–Aug. 1938 (NMML).

[83] 'The new Ministry could not be persuaded that there was any danger in communism and a number of communist agitators and agents of some importance were released . . . I keep on pressing upon him the dangers of ignoring communist activity.' Haig to Linlithgow, 6.9.1937 Haig Papers (NMML).

[84] Haig to Linlithgow, 22.9.1937, Haig Papers (NMML).

of any real significance of nationalism to working class lives.[85] In these writings the strength of primordial ties and sectional interests limits the possibilities of wider identities.

In Kanpur, as in many industrial centres, there was no apparent convergence between the rhythms of nationalist activity and working class activity. Apart from 1919–21, when intensified nationalist activity coincides with a period of intense working class activity, there is a disjunction between the two.[86] The widespread strikes in Kanpur in 1919 had no links with the Home Rule League or Congress activities in this period. The one-day hartal in support of the Khilafat agitation on 19 March 1920 was perhaps the only occasion when the mills closed down for an overtly nationalist issue.[87] Demonstrations in Kanpur against the Simon Commission failed to attract the mill workers. An attempt on the part of boycotters to call out the workers proved unsuccessful.[88] The efforts of Congress leaders to persuade workers to keep away from work in support of the call for civil disobedience did not meet with any success.[89] Workers were expected to participate in a meeting and procession on 10 June 1932, in connection

[85] Dipesh Chakrabarty, for instance, argues that the language of nation-building, of citizen's rights is the preserve of elite classes, while the lives and aspirations of the subaltern classes have been enmeshed in relationships of power, authority and hierarchy which pre-date the coming of colonialism and importation of the idea of 'citizenship'. 'Invitation to a Dialogue', in *Subaltern Studies IV*, ed. Ranajit Guha (Delhi 1984). Although arguing from different assumptions, Raj Chandavarkar similarly suggests that workers were too mired in their own narrow, sectional interests for larger imaginings like nationalism. Trade unions and political groups involved in a strategy of confrontation with the state were drawn to the anti-colonial rhetoric of the Congress. 'Opposition to the state provided a focus around which a fragmented and sectionalised working class could at times coalesce, though not necessarily behind the banner of the Congress—indeed more often under the hammer and sickle of various communist and socialist groupings.' Chandavarkar, *Imperial Power and Popular Politics*, p. 319.

[86] The Civil Disobedience Movement (1931–2) was a period of lull for the working class movement, and apart from stray strikes in 1942 there were no major strikes in Kanpur. HPD, FR File 18/8/1942, Aug. (i & ii) UP.

[87] *Pratap*, 22.3.1920.

[88] *Pioneer*, 5.12.1928.

[89] *Pioneer*, 10.5. 1930. The Kanpur workers were not exceptional in their lack of response to the Congress agitation in 1930. In Bengal, apart from the

with Gandhi's arrest, but the event never took off.[90] The KMS meetings organised in connection with the Civil Disobedience Movement did not evoke an enthusiastic response.[91]

It is not as if Congress leaders did not make efforts to mobilise workers around nationalist issues. At KMS meetings Congress leaders like Murari Lal, Narayan Prasad Arora and Ganesh Shankar Vidyarthi appealed to workers to support nationalist campaigns: to participate in events like the satyagraha divas, to vote for Congress candidates in municipal elections and wear khadi.[92] A swadeshi cloth store was opened in the workers' neighbourhood of Gwaltoli. The shop sold cheap cloth and tried to enlarge KMS membership by offering a special discount to sabha members.[93] At Congress meetings, speakers talked about local strikes and workers' problems.[94] Workers attended Congress meetings. In the mid-1920s many workers enrolled as Congress volunteers and marched in processions.[95] Virtually all the factories in Kanpur remained closed as an expression of solidarity with the Khilafatists in March 1920. Resolutions in support of Vidyarthi's candidature for the municipal elections were passed at workers' meetings.[96] KMS volunteers participated in swarajya demonstrations. The demonstration on 10 March 1929 was a spectacle. At its head were volunteers on horseback, followed by cyclists and tailed by thousands of marchers on foot. The demonstrators sang patriotic

---

strikes by 8000 workers of Budge Budge on 15 April 1930, following Nehru's arrest and the active participation of the workers of these mills in the picketing of liquor shops in August the same year, labour remained largely unaffected by the Congress agitation. Tanika Sarkar, 'The First Phase of Civil Disobedience in Bengal, 1929–31', *IHR*, 4:1, July 1977, pp. 83–4.With the exception of the GIP Railwaymen's Union, the Bombay workers were not involved in the Civil Disobedience agitation. Ravinder Kumar, 'From Swaraj to Purna Swaraj: Nationalist Politics in the City of Bombay 1920–32', in D.A. Low, ed., *Congress and Raj: Facets of the Indian Struggle, 1917–47* (New Delhi 1977).

[90] HPD, FR File18/1/1932, Jan. (i), UP.

[91] SAID, 2.8.1930.

[92] For instance, *Pratap*, 20.11.1922, 25.9.1922, *Vartman*, 25.2.1925.

[93] *Pratap*, 9.10.1922.

[94] *Leader*, 21.4.1920, 22.4.1920, *Pratap*, 27.11.1922.

[95] *Pratap*, 30.11.1926.

[96] *Vartman*, 14.11.1926.

songs and carried banners with slogans against foreign cloth and imperialism.[97] How do we read the meaning of such actions? Evidence of worker participation in collective spectacles does not quite reveal the structure of consciousness that lies behind their actions. Moving beyond the visible, the public, to the interior of their thought is difficult.

Why were the Kanpur workers unresponsive to nationalist efforts to mobilise them? Why did protests against European mill-owners in Kanpur not take the form of an opposition to the colonial state in general?[98] The relationship between workers and the state was marked by ambivalence. At certain moments there is an implicit faith in the impartiality of the colonial state, as opposed to the venality and injustice of employers. Appeals to the Lt. Governor to mediate in the strikes of November 1919 reflect a faith in the benevolence and impartiality of the state.[99] The effective intervention by the state to persuade Kanpur managers to give concession to workers in 1919 sustained its credibility. At other times, as in the Kanpur Cotton Mills strike of 1924, the repressive character of the state was quite apparent. But official discourse on the strike suggests that once it had crushed the strike and demonstrated its authority, it was keen to refurbish its image and promote better feelings in labour circles in Kanpur.[100] But

[97] *Vartman*, 13.3.1929.

[98] On racial and class conflicts between European railway authorities and Indian railwaymen taking on an anti-colonial character in the early 1920s, see Lajpat Jagga, 'Colonial Railwaymen and British Rule: A Probe into Railway Labour Agitation in India, 1919–1922', in Bipan Chandra, ed., *The Indian Left: Critical Appraisals* (New Delhi 1983), pp.103–45.

[99] A resolution passed at a workers' meeting apppealing to the Lt. Governor to mediate stated: 'We pray intervention, relying on His Honour's sympathy with poor people'. *Independent*, 29.11.1919.

[100] Lambert, Chief Secy, UP, to Commsr Allahabad Div. UPGAD, File 218,1924, Box 432 (UPSA). A petition to the DM, signed by 56 employees of the Kanpur Cotton Mills, asking the government to withdraw the cases against those injured in the riots. The signatories to the petition expressed their confidence in the DM and their conviction that had he been present the situation may not have become as ugly. Petition n.d. UPGAD, File 218,1924, Box 432 (UPSA). See also ch. 5. In other regions too, similar attempts by the state to maintain an 'impartial' image in the eyes of the workers are evident. During the strikes in the Golmuri Tinplate Company in 1929, the provincial

such faith rested on fragile grounds. The large participation by workers in the plague riots of 1900 and the Machli Bazaar Mosque riots of 1913 directed against the state demonstrated the limits of its legitimacy. By the late 1930s, such notions of a just state were clearly losing ground. Socialist propaganda in this period drew links between the struggle against capitalism and freedom from imperial domination.

What was the nature of this rhetoric and what was its relationship with worker imaginings? Is it possible for a historian to recover workers' notions of swaraj? Are the voices we hear authentic? What appears as expressions of worker nationalism can easily be read as rearticulations of middle-class nationalism. Writings by worker nationalists are layered with images and metaphors drawn from official nationalist writings. In a sense a search for an authentic, untainted worker voice can only be elusive.

Although workers were only marginally involved in key events—the non-cooperation or the civil disobedience movement—what is important is the significance of nationalism to their imaginings. Statements at workers' meetings, and poems and writings by workers suggest how nationalist imagery and rhetoric defined their discourse. At meetings during the general strike of 1938, speakers emphasised that the main object of the strike was removal of the British government.[101] Worker leaders like Jan Mohammed drew an idyllic picture of Congress rule: 'Congress stood on the strength of the peasants and workers and aimed at the destruction of capitalism and establishment of a Soviet form of Government.'[102]Revolutionary songs at workers' meetings

---

government was keen that it 'must stand apart and see that there is no violence or breaking of the law and if possible by an attitude of strict impartiality retain the confidence of all parties.' J.T. Whittle, Statement in the Bihar and Orissa Legislative Assembly, 7.8.1929, Dept of Ind. and Labour, L-918 (24) 1930.

[101] SAID, 18.6.1938.

[102] SAID, 5.2.1938. P.C. Joshi, in a statement in the *National Front*, eulogised the role of the Kanpur Congress: 'Under Sharmaji's inspiring leadership the Cawnpore Congress has done more to help the strike than any Congress Committee has ever done before and thus given the proletarian struggle the strength of the whole people . . .' *National Front*, 12.6.1938.

evoked anti-imperialist feelings: 'Let there be a cry for freedom / . . . the capitalists and imperialists depart as their end has come / we shall remember the cruel story of exploitation / Let peasants and workers realise that they are the future rulers.'[103]

In speeches and writings by workers, foreign rulers and capitalists are portrayed as aliens from across the seas. The boundaries of the nation are drawn by the sea. Reports mention how workers opposing the overlapping shift system in 1937 made dramatic speeches telling European managers to cross the seas and go back.[104] In statements like this, all managers European and Indian alike come to be seen through the anti-imperialist prism. Occasionally there are references to workers making an emotional plea for swadeshi. In a letter to *Abhyudaya*, Ram Sewak, a worker from Khalasi Lines, expresses an emotional longing to die in his own homeland: '*Tamanna hai ki markar ho/kafan apna swadeshi ho/hamari maut se pahele/vatan apna swadeshi ho.*'[105] The opposition between home and outside, between foreign and indigenous, is not unusual in references to death. Death at home, in familiar surroundings, is preferred to death outside, in a foreign land or in a hospital and in the absence of familial relations. Indigenous control in Ram Sewak's piece is ambiguously defined. He begins with a verse which makes an association between the territorial space of the nation and indigenous control, and shifts to prose in which the autonomous space is limited to the space of the factory: he demands indigenous control over all industrial enterprises and asserts that workers will be willing to work for lower wages in swadeshi enterprises.[106]

[103] SAID, 5.2.1938.

[104] See ch. 6. A poem by Sudarshan Chakr using similar imagery says that workers had the strength to drive away foreign rulers: '*Tumhare pas mazduron! /hai takat ki dava aisi / samandar par se aye / samandar par ho jayen*' (Workers you have the strength—the strength to drive back those who have come from across the seas). *Sachi Kavitayen*, p. 7.

[105] *Abhyudaya*, 20.3.1920.

[106] Ram Sewak concludes with a statement on behalf of 20,000 workers from Kanpur for an end to exploitation by foreign millowners and makes an appeal to Indians to invest in setting up factories in the sacred territory of Kanpur. Indians could enjoy the double satisfaction of earning wealth and doing a sacred duty, for 20,000 workers in Kanpur were willing to work for them at lower wages. *Abhyudaya*, 20.3.1919.

We need to probe deeper into the structure of discourse, the images and metaphors employed in the languages of labour, in order to understand how workers expressed their nationalist imaginings. I focus on a selection of writings by Sudarshan Chakr to examine the differences and the shared terrain between 'élite' and popular discourses. The introduction to a collection of his poems describes Chakr as a 'worker poet' who had little formal schooling, a claim that seeks to represent him as an 'authentic' voice of the workers and marks his distance from the educated élite. In Chakr's poems there is a complex interplay of many voices. Chakr was a worker, employed in the Elgin and Victoria Mills for many years. He grew up in a Vaishnavite milieu as a worshipper of Rama, but the influence of Arya Samaj ideas in the 1920s made him iconoclastic. He was a nationalist associated with local Congress activities from his boyhood and was drawn to the socialist ideas of trade unionists like Raja Ram Shastri since the 1920s.[107] After his close association with communist comrades in jail, he joined the Communist Party in 1940. Chakr's writings redeploy some of the complex influences to which he was subject; addressing many audiences, he uses conventional religious and nationalist symbols and refigures them.

The structure of Chakr's *Kanpur ka Mazdur Andolan* shares certain similarities with official communist publications. He begins by tracing the genealogy of class struggles to slave uprisings in ancient Egypt and ancient Rome and goes on to make connections between events in Kanpur and the Russian revolution. Workers' struggles in Kanpur are thus located within the wider struggle for communism. At the same time, Chakr is deeply nationalist, and in his narrative the workers' movement in Kanpur is seen as part of the anti-imperialist movement. The general strike of 1938 is represented as a step towards freedom and the strikes of 1941 are seen as an attack on the British raj.[108] Differences,

---

[107] Chakr was part of a Congress youth organisation, the *Vanar Sena*, during the Civil Disobedience Movement and was associated with the Mazdur Bal Mandal, an organisation for working class children. Surya Prakash Tripathi, *Vishvakavi Shri Sudarshan Chakr* (Kanpur 1973), p. 8.

[108] Chakr's poem on 1938, 'Alha Am Hartal', ends with a hope that freedom would be attained soon and imperialism would collapse. Cited in *Kanpur Mazdur Andolan*, p. 59. On 1941 see *Kanpur Mazdur Andolan*, p. 75.

conflicts between communists and the Congress are played down;
all seem united in the wider struggle against imperialism. The
conflicting pulls and pressures created by the communist slogan
of 'Peoples' War' in 1942 are not queried.[109] Despite similarities
in the sequencing of the events with official publications, Chakr's
history is an alternative account which gives a space to anonymous
local activists in the movement, along with well-known leaders.[110]

Chakr's poems of the late 1930s to the early 1950s are laden
with nationalist imagery; but in his usage dominant nationalist
images are turned upside down, questioned and subverted. In a
collection called *Shahidon ki Katar*, Chakr weaves in the local and
the national, invoking familiar national figures like Mangal
Pande, Kunwar Singh and Jhansi ki Rani, Gandhi, Maulana Hazrat Mohani, together with anonymous local figures like Pheku
and Azizan Randi. The collection is significant for the insights it
gives into the interplay between the politics of gender, caste and
class in the imagination of a working class nationalist. In Chakr's
'Jhansi ki Rani', published in 1939 and confiscated as seditious
literature by the state, a familiar nationalist icon acquires a different meaning.[111] In contrast to images of a mardani (masculinised) queen leading the rebel forces,[112] Chakr celebrates female
valour. Rani Laxmibai is iconised as Chandi (an incarnation of
Durga), Durga who kills all demons (foreigners) and as a lioness

---

[109] There is a tangential reference to the lack of enthusiasm for strikes
among communists in this period and the circulation of the paper 'Lokyudh'
(Peoples' War') by the Communist Party in this period. Chakr, *Kanpur
Mazdur Andolan*, pp. 80–1. Devi Babu an ex-worker in a Kanpur mill, talked
about the dilemmas of communist politics in this period.

[110] Note references to Cde. Pheku, p. 275, Cde. Manjoor and his mother,
p. 174, Cde Sher Khan, p. 192. It is significant that Chakr does not rationalise
the party position in 1942 and is sharply critical of party leaders on the Pheku
episode. *Kanpur Mazdur Andolan.*

[111] Pros. pub., nos 612–14, by Sudarshan Misra 'Chakra', 'NAI'. The
short poem, 'Jhansi ki Rani' in the collection *Shahidon ki Katar*, by the same
author, is a different poem.

[112] See, for instance, the famous lines of Subhadra Kumari Chauhan's
'Jhansi ki Rani': *Khub lari mardani voh to / Jhansi vali rani thi* (Bravely she
fought like a man, she was the Rani of Jhansi). Valour here is a masculine
virtue: it could be a female attribute only to the extent that she was 'male'.

(*singhni*) who attacks jackals.[113] The Rani plays a double role in Chakr's story. She is a conventional widow, weeping helplessly when her husband dies, and she is strong, assertive and aggressive, taking the form of Chandi and Durga when Dalhousie's troops take over Jhansi. Chakr ends by paying tribute to her womanhood: '*Nari hokar narsinghon mein apna nam likhaya tha, ablaon mein kitna bal hai duniya ko dikhaya tha*' (Even as a woman she was a like a lion in human form, she showed the world that an abla [one without strength] stood for strength). Female aggression in Chakr's *Jhansi ki Rani* does not negate an intrinsic femininity in a woman.[114]

In contrast to many nationalist writings that see conquest as a story of weak, strife-torn Indian rulers falling prey to foreign invaders, the British in Chakr's representation wage a coward's battle. Unlike the Rani who fights bravely, facing enemy forces, the white foreigners attack and kill the Rani from the rear: '*Usi samay ek gore ne piche se us par bar kiya/rani ne marte marte us kayar ko bhi mar diya.*'[115] The metonyms used for foreign rulers—*siyar* (jackal), *daitya* (demon), *sanp* (snake)—are the opposite of the imageries he uses for the nation. Foreigners are depicted as treacherous, deceitful, cruel, cowardly and venomous; they lack the heroic attributes associated with conquerors; they could conquer only through guile and deceit, not through martial

[113] *Ran karne ko raniyon ban kar ran chandi nikal par
jyon daityon ka badh karne ko durga devi svayam barhi.
pili singhni syaron mein ek dam se dhava bol diya*

(On the battlefield it seemed that the rani was Chandi incarnate / Durga devi strode forward to kill the demons . . . the yellow lioness charged at the jackals), Chakr, 'Jhansi ki Rani', p. 5.

[114] Ibid. Chakr's construction of womanhood shares similarities with nineteenth-century nationalist repersentations which glorify the heroism of Rajput princesses, demonstrating that martial characteristics were not a male privilege. Femininity was refigured as an embodiment of courage and heroism. On nationalist constructions of femininity, see Indira Chowdhury-Sengupta, 'The Effeminate and the Masculine: Nationalism and the Concept of Race in Colonial Bengal', in Peter Robb, ed., *The Concept of Race in South Asia* (Delhi 1995).

[115] A white soldier attacked her from the back, even as she struggled with death, the Rani killed the coward. Chakr, 'Jhansi ki Rani', p. 7.

skill. In the gendering of the nation, Chakr again complicates normal representations. The nation, Bharat, as *duniya ka sartaj* (pride of the world), the interplay between the identity of the nation as Bharat and Hind Ma, in Chakr's verse, all suggest a fluidity. In the world outside, the nation is male, Bharat being grammatically fixed as masculine in gender. The interior of the nation is symbolised by the figure of a nurturing, caring mother who feeds and shelters all. Chakr's imaging of the nation reproduces conventional oppositions between inner and outer, the home and the world, and the gendered nature of these spaces.

Chakr's poem 'Azizan Randi', which pays tribute to a prostitute as a martyr of 1857, inverts nationalist conceptions of gender and sexuality. By using the term *randi* in the title of the poem, as opposed to the usual bai, Chakr valorises Azizan's image as a prostitute, while refiguring it. Contrary to the image of a chaste, virtuous, de-eroticised woman that nationalist narratives celebrate, Chakr represents Azizan's struggle as expressing the purity within sin: '*Pap ka punya rup, jo swatantrata ke liye lara.*' As in his '*Jhansi ki Rani*', Chakr plays on the femininity of the female image he employs. His randi is not projected as a masculinised horse-backed warrior woman, but as one who appeared fearsome and powerful without being on a horse. Sounds of her dancing bells can be heard even when she is imagined in the battlefield, shooting arrows at the enemy ('*Cham cham cham cham ke sadhe tir jab thirak rahe the sangar mein*'). Abla, a term personifying the figure of a fragile and powerless woman, comes to symbolise strength in Chakr's invocation of 1857 ('*Abla ke bal se atankit angrez kilo ke andar mein*'). If the figure of the woman stands for courage and valour, young men appear timid and weak-hearted.[116] Chakr's celebration of Azizan as a symbol of 1857 is specially meaningful in a context when the figure of the prostitute in nationalist discourses was commonly stigmatised, symbolising disease and vice. Concerned about the link between prostitutes and goondas in the city, nationalists sought to control and reform prostitution.[117] Nationalist discourse drew upon colonial official

[116] '*Bujdil darpok javano ko balvan banaya randi ne*', Sudarshan Chakr, *Shahidon ki Katar*, p. 11.

[117] The Congress inquiry into the communal riots of 1931 made a special note of this connection: 'Cawnpore also possesses an unusually large number

conceptions which saw prostitutes as a source of disease and trouble, a threat to the moral fibre of society and the health of the Company soldiers. Linked to 'turbulent elements' in the city, they were held responsible for the notoriety of Moolganj as a trouble spot. Proposals to remove prostitutes from the central localities of Kanpur city had been put forward since 1915 and were revived after the riots of 1931.[118]

In the post-First World War period, as the working class became more vocal, the Congress felt the need to create a space for labour in its visions of the nation. In industrial cities in particular, nationalist leaders had to be in touch with workers' grievances and intervene in situations of conflict. Nationalists like Vidyarthi gave labour an important voice through his writings, and papers like *Pratap*, published by him, regularly featured columns by

of prostitutes—open and private. They are as at other places, fruitful sources of quarrels, which when the Hindu–Muslim feeling runs high, easily take a communal turn.' N.G. Barrier, p. 233. Reports in *Pratap* note the association between prostitutes and respectable families with a sense of dismay. Although relieved that dance shows by prostitutes at the Budwamangal and Barahdevi melas had been put an end to, a *Pratap* report expressed a deep sense of regret that a local notable was not only connected with organising performances by prostitutes at the Kailash temple but had a relationship of intimacy with them. *Pratap*, 12.4.1914. See also report on dance show at the bungalows of local gentry, for instance at Biharilal Bhajan Lal, by Hira Panna, at which various respectable men were present. *Pratap*, 24.5.1914.

[118] The Under Secretary, Municipal Dept, was voicing a commonly held opinion when he argued: 'The recent riots have shown that trouble of every kind invariably starts from this locality, and it is believed that, if the prostitutes were removed much of this turbulent element would disappear from Moolganj.' Under Secy, Mun. Dept to Chairman Imp. Trust, File 43,1931 (Imp. Trust), Mun. Dept, Box 51(UPSA).The Municipal Dept suggested the removal of these prostitutes to a more secluded locality where greater control could be exercised over them. Eventually the proposal to relocate prostitutes was abandoned on the grounds that the Moolganj area was not 'an area of great respectability'. Note by Supdt, Mun. Board, 22.2.1936. 43,1931 (Imp. Trust) Mun., Progs., Box 51.The question of removal of prostitutes from municipal limits came up again in 1939–40, when some members of the Municipal Board passed a resolution to remove them. Criticising the proposal, Mehra, editor of a local daily, *Citizen*, thought it was a foolish plan. 'Prostitutes,' he asserted, 'are necessary to protect the morals of the society.' *Citizen*, 19.12.1940.

workers and editorial pieces sympathetic to labour. In periods of crisis, however, when labour was more militant the legitimacy of nationalist leaders like Vidyarthi and Murari Lal was questioned, worker actions spilled outside their restraining influence.

In times like 1937-8 the relationship between the Congress as a party of nationalism and workers is deeply problematised. The neatness of the conceptualisation gets disturbed and destabilised and is threatened by the politics of power. The need to mobilise workers against imperialism came into conflict with the demands for order and discipline, of making workers responsible members of the provincial community. Nationalist conceptions about labour were disturbed as the Congress anticipated the problems of the future—just as much as the experience for the workers was a presaging of the times to come. Till then repression had been associated with managers and the state. It now came to be associated with the Congress. Yet workers imagine their own nation, sorting out the relationship between gender and community, working it out in different ways, grappling with it.

CHAPTER 9

Despair

—◦═══◦—

Since the late 1980s, the situation in Kanpur is much changed, with the cotton textile being an industry in a crisis. Most Kanpur mills have been closed, workers have been retrenched in large numbers. Some continue to be on the pay-rolls but there is no work. Salaries have been levelled to a flat minimum, pay is cut for all holidays. Workers have been forced to turn to other work: rickshaw-pulling, paan, vegetable and fruit vending, begging. The line of difference between the formal and informal sector, always thin and questionable, seems to have disappeared altogether. The decline of the factory industry has been accompanied by a mushrooming of cottage industries: the myth of a linear transition from the cottage/domestic sector to factory production, from proto-industrialisation to industrialisation, seems to have been reversed. In the pre-independence period a phase of stagnation was followed by a phase of growth and boom. But now there seems no hope of recovery. Economic experts have announced the end of cotton textile factory production in Kanpur, and the death of its working class.

After the growth of the 1950s, cotton textile production in India steadily declined. From 4.34 billion metres in 1972 it dropped to 3.4 billion metres in 1983, declining at an annual rate of around 1.5 per cent. The number of working looms reduced from 144,000 in 1971 to 133,000 in 1987. Since the 1960s the demand for coarse varieties of cloth has dipped. Per capita consumption of coarse varieties, which had gone up in the 1950s, fell after the 1960s due to increased durability of synthetic blends and decline of real income in rural areas.[1] Per capita consumption of cloth

[1] C.P. Chandrashekar, 'Growth and Technical Change in Indian Cotton-Mill Industry', *EPW*, 19:4 (1984), PE 22–PE 39.

showed a continuous decline between 1970 and the 1990s from 13.5 metres in 1969–71 to nine metres in 1989–91. The market that cotton textiles lost, synthetics gained. Per capita purchase of synthetic textiles and blended fabrics increased at the rate of about 100 per cent per year in the period between 1973 and 1989.

Since the 1990s, changes in state policies have led to a rapid restructuring of the textile industry and a growth of the export market in cotton textiles. However, a major part of this demand is supplied by the informal sector, primarily by powerlooms.[2] The relative share of mills in cotton textile production declined rapidly since the mid-1980s, from 18 per cent in 1985–6 to 10 per cent by 1990–1 and 6 per cent by 1995–6, while that of powerlooms increased from 63 to 78 per cent over the same period. The figures for exports show similar trends. The share of mills in cotton textile exports declined from 59 per cent in 1985–6 to 38 per cent by 1990–1, coming down to 23 per cent by 1995–6, while that of powerlooms went up from 34 per cent to 76 per cent in the same period.[3] The revival, limited to the powerloom sector, has meant no lease of life for textile mills.

While markets shrank, costs increased. The fixed costs of the National Textile Corporation (NTC) mills are astoundingly high and rapidly increasing. In 1993–4, fixed costs as a percentage of sales had mounted to 80 per cent in the NTC mills compared to a mere 21 per cent in other mills (in 1888–9 it was 56 per cent). All NTC mills, except the ones in Pondicherry and Tamil Nadu, are making losses. Their sales are insufficient to cover the variable costs and wage bills. In most NTC mills, losses are over four times their net worth. The accumulated losses of the British India

---

[2] Reports from the Textile Commissioner's office pointing to a 'phenomenal growth' in installed spindleage, yarn production and output of cloth, are somewhat misleading because the growth has not offset the decline in the mill sector apart from a small segment catering to new consumer tastes in cotton casuals, denims, etc. See *Compendium of Textile Statistics 1997* (Mumbai n.d.). On the growth of the market for cotton casuals see Tirthankar Roy 'Economic Reforms and Textile Industry in India', *Economic and Political Weekly*, 33: 32, 1998, pp. 2173–82.

[3] Tirthankar Roy, 'Economic Reforms and Textile Industry in India', op. cit.

Corporation (BIC) amount to 3.3 times its net worth, while Kanpur Textiles losses were twenty-five times its net worth.[4]

Composite mills which produced both yarn and cloth were the worst affected. The early phase of Kanpur industrialisation was based on the expansion of the composite mill sector. Not only were they cost efficient, but managerial control over the entire process of production of cloth was easier. Now powerlooms in India appear more cost efficient in terms of fixed costs, raw material use, and energy consumption. Economists consider most of the old composite mill units bankrupt and obsolete.

In this context of declining profits, private industrialists in Kanpur found it more profitable to invest in new expanding industries in centres outside Kanpur, where wage costs were lower and where such a long tradition of trade unionism was absent. The Jugglilal Kamlapat group, for instance, set up a rayon factory in Kanpur and cement and plastic units in Rajasthan; the Jaipurias started five textile units in other regions. Disinvestmest in textile mills in Kanpur was accompanied by cost-cutting strategies directed primarily at workers. Wages were held back for months, provident fund, insurance and other benefits were cut, workers were laid off and retrenched. Workers' anger against these policies led to a series of strikes in the 1970s.[5] Managements were inflexible, preferring their units to be declared 'sick' and taken over by the state. It was against this background that the Laxmi Ratan, Atherton West, Swadeshi, Muir, and New Victoria Mills were taken over by NTC. By 1981, BIC, Kanpur Textiles and Elgin Mills were nationalised by the central government.

How do workers confront this crisis? What are the strategies with which they negotiate their situation?

For working class families living in Kanpur for several decades, the closure of textile mills means more than just a problem of

[4] Omkar Goswami, 'State owned Enterprises in India', mimeo for OECD Paris. See also Goswami, 'Sickness and Growth of India's Textile Industry: Analysis and Policy Options', *EPW*, 25:44 and 25:45.

[5] See 'Report of the Citizen's Committee for Inquiry into the Kanpur Massacre', 23.2.1978. See leaflet issued by workers of JK Manufacturers Ltd. '*Kailash Mil Mein Sangarsh ka Elan: Sabhi Mazdur Bhaiyon ke Nam Ek Apil*' (Kanpur n.d.).

survival. Their lives are so intertwined with work in the mills that a life without the mills seems unthinkable. Mill closure can mean death: a belief which underlines Niamat Rasul's fears: '*Agar mill band ho jai to hamari maut hai.*'[6] Niamat Rasul worked as a weaver in Elgin Mills 2 (earlier known as Cawnpore Cotton Mills), like his father. Niamat's father came to Kanpur from a village in Barabanki district and they still have relatives there, but like many second-generation workers he identifies completely with the city and cannot conceive of an alternative.[7]

Ties with their native villages are important for most rural migrants, but the possibilities of work and life in the village are not always open to those who move to the city with their families. Besides, it is not easy for rural migrants to reintegrate themselves with village life once they have lived in the city for several decades. Most rural migrants come from families with small holdings, income from which has to be supplemented with wage labour. Unemployed workers past their fifties saw themselves as too old for arduous toil in the fields. The loss of jobs was seen as a loss also for descendants. In working class families, skills in factory work were handed down through the generations. A mill job was almost like an inheritance which provided a sense of security. It was a way of ensuring a reproduction of skills, the basis of worker identity and pride. Shriram Sharma, who like his father was a spinning line mistri in Elgin 2, felt this strongly: 'The closure of mills will render us and our future generations unemployed' ('*Millbandi se ham, hamari pidiyan bhi bekar ho jayengi*').[8]

The absence of work in the present imbues the past with a different significance. The drudgery and travails of work in the past have no space in these narratives. Mill work is glorified. The pain of work is represented in retrospect as pain which was fulfilling. Work on the machines wore them out, yet there was a bonding with the machine and a pride in their work. Niamat asserted that the mill authorities claimed that the workers were inefficient and lazy. This was not true. Workers in his mill produced around

[6] If the mills shut down, we will die. Interview, Niamat Rasul.

[7] '*Agar main jaun to kahan jaun, yahin marna jeena hai*' (Where can I go? I have to live and die here). Interview, Niamat Rasul.

[8] The closure of mills will render us and our future generations unemployed. Interview, Shriram Sharma, Elgin 2.

120,000 metres of cloth.[9] Another worker, Pramod Awasthi,
boasted that the amount of cloth he had produced during his
years of service could take a person holding one end of it to Delhi
more than 2000 times.[10] Muhammad Said was proud that the
looms never stopped running in his mill: 'If we struck work for
even a day the entire BIC management would try to negotiate.'[11]

There is in these narratives a distancing from the oppressiveness
of work discipline in the past. The long hours, the absence of work
breaks, especially in the war years, are remembered now with a
sense of male pride and achievement. Strict discipline is presented
as an index of efficiency. Ramcharan, who started work in Muir
Mills in 1946, talked of the times he worked four machines often
on a meal of gur and chana alone: 'We have seen those days, those
days when we were not allowed to go to the lavatory during work.
To go to the lavatory was impossible for us.'[12] He contrasts it with
the present when there are no controls. Workers take frequent
breaks for five–ten minutes, sometimes they stay away for half an
hour at a stretch. This was read not as evidence of greater worker
freedom, but of disinterested management.

Workers entering their fifties feel a sense of weariness about
looking for alternative possibilities of work. Their bodies feel
worn with age, with the daily wear and tear on the machines. In
a context of worklessness, work was seen as physically empowering; non-work created a sense of physical disability.[13] Images of
decay and ageing are used alternately for the machine and the
body of the worker. 'We are worn out like the machines. When I
joined the mill there were no lines, no signs of age on my face,
Today I am grey and old.'[14] Besides, work elsewhere would not

[9] 'Yahan ka mazdur nikamma nahin hai. Yahan ka worker bahut mahanti
hai. Yahan ka worker itna production karta tha ek lakh bees hazaar metre
kapra banaya karta tha.'

[10] Pramod Awasthi, dye house worker, Elgin 2.

[11] Mohd. Said, weaver, Elgin 2.

[12] 'Voh zamana hamne dekha. . . . voh zamana tha jab pishab karne ke liye
nikal nahin sakte the. Pishab karna mushkil ho jata tha ham logan ko.'

[13] 'Kahil pan mahsoos hota hai, shamta sheern hoti hai' (There was a sense
of weariness and loss of a capacity to work.) Interview, S.P. Awasthi, weaver,
Elgin 1.

[14] 'Hamari sari ghisai pitai yahin ho gai hai. Yeh machine bhi ghis pit gayi
hain, ham bhi ghis pit gayi hain. Hamari rekhe nahin aayi thi jis samay ham

have the same meaning.[15] Like the machines and the people who worked on them, the structure of the mills conveys a picture of dilapidation. The sprawling Lancashire-style mills in Kanpur are crumbling structures in a state of disrepair, with fallen roofs and broken walls.

The daily routine for most workers now consists in reporting at the mill gate for their attendance. Although most mills have been closed for eight-to ten years, workers crowd around mill gates at shift times, thrice a day in some mills like Kanpur Textiles, twice in others. Some move off to their gambling addas near the gate, others gather around union leaders for news, rumours, plans. The daily ritual is also a collective affirmation of anxieties, fears, hopes, and uncertainties. Although workers on the rolls in a state-controlled mill are paid wages, there is no certainty when they will be paid or how long this will continue.[16] The threat of total closure hangs like a noose. Dates are changed and extended. Even those hoping that the mills will reopen once again feel tormented by the uncertainty.[17]

There was always a hope that millowners would pay arrears before festival time: 'We had pegged our hopes to Diwali. We got nothing. We waited for Eid there was nothing. We hoped Holi would bring something.'[18] Descriptions of the city as khandhar, as an ujra hua shahar,[19] carry in their narratives images of desolation and devastation. The magnitude of loss in their accounts is obviously greater than can be expressed in official estimates. Naresh Chauhan recounted the times when the mills employed around 70,000 workers. In addition, around 300,000 were employed in industries sustained by textiles. Official estimates show

---

yahan bharti hue the, aaj hamari saphedi aa gai hai.' Interview, Naresh Singh Chauhan, cloth room worker, Elgin Mills.

[15] '*Ab hame service mil bhi jati hai to hame service karne mein maza nahin hai.*' Interview, Niamat Rasul.

[16] On an average, most workers receive around Rs 2000 a month, paid at irregular intervals, usually once in three months.

[17] Naresh Chauhan was insistent: 'Why do they not give a final yes or no?'

[18] '*Diwali ka sahara lagaye the. Usme nahi mila. Id ka sahara lagaye tha. Usme nahi mila—Holi ka sahara lagaye the.*' Interview, Hari Lal, oilman, Kanpur Textiles.

[19] Dilapidated, ruined.

that textile mills in Kanpur never employed more than 50,000 workers, even at the best of times. This overestimation of numbers in worker accounts emphasises the meaning the city had in their lives. If was as if Kanpur was of the workers: workers constituted the city. And now the vanishing workforce signifies the destruction of the city, its death. The changed context of the present is apparent in the street life of areas like Gwaltoli, where a large number of mills are located. Thousands of workers had once walked in and out at shift time. Panna Lal, who worked in the cloth godown in Victoria Mills, recollected the times when it was difficult to walk in Gwaltoli without rubbing shoulders with people. Now there is only silence.[20] Panna Lal runs a small tea stall and finds it hard to get customers. Even the tea stalls and tobacco shops are connected with the running of the mills. Closure of mills means deserted streets.

Worker narratives move between articulations of despair and resignation to an assertion of their power. This sense of power expresses itself at times through threats of retribution, street violence, murder, looting and dacoity: 'If this mill is shut the revolt will spread to the streets, killings will begin, isn't that so? If we die of hunger we will throttle you and kill you. No car will be allowed to move, no bus, there will be looting and violence. There are no two views on this. When I am hungry I will snatch your spectacles from your eyes.'[21] Yet there is an ambivalence in this voice of retribution. It slides easily into a despairing, helpless voice: I am forty years old . . . I am a substitute . . . and I am old today. Where can I go? There is no respite. I cannot live or die. It is better to set myself on fire and die.[22]

For women workers the despair runs deeper. Most women workers were employed on a contract basis and not treated as

[20] Interview, Panna Lal.

[21] 'Yadi yeh band kare [mill] to kranti sarkon par phailegi, mar-kat shuroo hoga, nai shuroo hoga kya? Bhookhe marenge tumhara gala dabakar mar dalenge tumko. Ek gari nahin niklegi, na hi bus niklegi. Loot paat hogi. Isme koi do rai nahin hai. Jab main bhookha hoonga to apka chashma bhi noch loonga.' One worker from a group at a mill gate.

[22] 'Chalees saal ki umar ho gai. Ab main aujidaar hoon . . . aur ham budhe bhi ho gaye hain. ab ham kidhar jayenge. na goli chal sakegi, na maut mar sakenge. Kisi tarah chain nahin. Aag lagakar marna thik hai.'

regular mill employees. Even the older workers, who were regular employees earlier, were turned into contract workers in the 1970s. Munni Devi, who was a regular employee at the Swadeshi Cotton Mills, remembers how the main gate through which all workers entered was suddenly closed to women workers. After a long dharna, women were allowed entry from a separate gate as thekedar's (contractor's) employees, not company employees. Most likely, this was before a major struggle in the Swadeshi Mills in 1978, when several workers were killed in the police firing, when the golikand (firing) happened and women were ordered out: 'We had access to only one gate, we could not use any other gate. We were turned out.'[23]

For many workers today, stories about struggles in the past seem unreal and distant. In their narratives there is a constant return to the present, as though remembering the past might take them away from more pressing, immediate concerns. Younger-generation workers today have only heard stories about the great strikes of the 1930s or 1950s, not personally experienced them. This was equally true of many workers I met in the early 1980s. The most recent experience of collective struggle was the rail blockade of 1989, when workers stopped the movement of trains to and from Kanpur for over four days in protest against the proposed rationalisation and workload scheme. But the proximity in time of this event was not evident from their recollections: they were reluctant to recount details. What makes the remembering and retelling of these stories difficult in the 1990s and now is a sense of futility in relation to industrial struggles. Even those who personally participated in the strikes of the past gave a sketchy outline of them. For Ramcharan, who started work in Muir Mills in the 1940s, queries about the major eighty-day strike against rationalisation of work in 1955 initially evoked no response. His memory cued in only after a reference to tikadde vali hartal (strike for a three-loom system). For workers like him, moored within an oral tradition, such symbols and images—and not chronology—provide markers around which their past is organised.[24] Ramcharan's focus was not so much on details of the strike, the

[23] 'Ham logan ka sirf ek gate the. Aur jagah nikalne ki nahin thi. Ham logan ko bahar nikaal diya gaya.'

[24] The general strike of 1955 is also remembered locally as the alu vali hartal (potato strike). This a former student activist from the 1950s explained

militancy of the strikers, or the scale and spread of a strike which lasted eighty days. He talked only of his experience of the work and rigours of the four-loom system, opposition to which was one of the major demands of the strikers. Others like Niamat Rasul, who had heard about the 1955 strikes from his father, dwell on moments of repression. In his recounting, stories about the Kanpur Cotton Mill strikes of 1924 are woven in those of 1955: 'One day the English ordered a mounted police attack on workers. Many workers were thrown into boilers. My father told me that four workers were thrown into boilers.'[25] Two moments of state repression are here fused into one, and he rereads the events as moments of repression, not as heroic moments of worker solidarity. He fuses fantastical stories of repression in 1924 with memories of surveillance in working class neighbourhoods by mounted police in 1955.

Feelings of anger and retribution are tied up with workers' understanding of the crisis in the mill industry. The crisis appears as unreal in their narratives: a fabrication of corrupt managers. They repeatedly draw contrasts between present decline and past prosperity. Prosperity is attributed to efficient management, present decline to managerial inefficiency. A series of contrasts between then and now are drawn: managerial efficiency versus inefficiency; incompetence versus competence; industrial discipline versus laxity; morality versus immorality. These contrasts are explained by two other contrasts: private management and government control; European managers and indigenous managers. At times the latter two oppositions fuse; private management appears as a distant past, it becomes a past when managers were European, the decline begins with indigenous management.

---

was because of the uproar over the pegging of the cost of living index with potato prices in 1955. Workers complained of major discrepancies in the calculation of the dearness allowance.

[25] '*Andolan chal raha tha. Meeting hoti thi. Ham chote the, itni samajh nahin thi. meeting hoti thi tab angrezon ne ghore dora diye. Tamam boiler ke andar dal diye the. Hamare bap batate the char admiyon ko boiler ke andar dal diya.*' On working-class memory, see Michel Bozon and Anne-Marie Thiesse, 'The Collapse of Memory: The Case of Farm Workers', *History and Anthropology*, 2, 1986, pp. 237–59, Luisa Passerini, *Fascism in Popular Memory: The Cultural Experience of the Turin Working Class* (Cambridge 1987).

Fig. 26: Inside the weaving shed

Fig. 27: Images of disrepair and desolation

Fig. 28: Sprawling mill compounds wear a deserted look

Fig. 29: KMS office at Gwaltoli

Managers in the past were technical people, they knew their job;
today, civil service officials on managerial chairs have no clue
about their work: 'Mill officials today do not know how to handle
a wrench. They have no knowledge about their job. They have to
ask the mistri how a machine should be fixed only then are they
able to write the job on paper. Are these supervisors?'[26]

When the mills were under private control, managers were
upright and honest; mill profits were *their* profits—a product of
their capital, *their* efforts. With state control, managers no longer
identify with the mill. The company's loss is no longer seen as their
own loss.[27] The capital belonging to the state exists to be embezzled
and appropriated. Now mill officials take fat commissions on
orders to raw material suppliers, they trade in coal supplies coming in for use in the mills, they adulterate raw material supplies
with waste products, they fill up supervisory posts with
incompetent relatives.[28] In the past, managers were conscientious
and factory discipline was closely supervised: bobbins were never
empty, looms never stopped.[29]

Within the present scenario, different strategies have been put
forward by economic experts, the state, and workers. The state
has to negotiate between market pressures from the new global
order to close sick mills, and demands from labour representatives
to keep the industry going. In the context of these pressures,
decisions are deferred and dates for final settlement postponed.
The merger of unviable units into healthy units, the modernisation
of some mills, a freeze on retrenchment—these restructuring
plans were to be financed through the sale of surplus land in the
mills. But for pro-liberalisation economic experts, who now
dominate, state-controlled textile mills are sick and beyond
redemption. Plans to revive mills with a long history of 'low productivity', 'disinterested labour' and 'poor managerial supervision'
are 'fairy tale schemes'.[30] The merger of two sick units, they point

---

[26] '*Inhe wrinch pakarna nahi maloom. Technical knowledge nahi hai.
Mistri se pooch rahe hain, machine kaise banegi. Jab mistri batata hai to
yahan ke supervisor job likhte hain. To yeh supervisor hain.* Interview,
Naresh Singh Chauhan.

[27] '*Ab sab sarkari—kisi ko kisi ke maal par dard nahin.* Mohd. Said.

[28] Interview, Phool Singh, Elgin 1.

[29] Interview, Mohd. Said.

[30] Omkar Goswami, 'State-owned Enterprises in India'.

out, cannot produce a healthy unit; and prohibitive costs make restructuring plans unviable.

For trade union activists the closure of mills spells their own demise. Workers and trade union activists support alternative schemes for revival. Those working with the BIC group of mills (Elgin 1, Elgin 2, Kanpur Textiles) felt that workers from the three units could all be employed in one unit.[31] Voluntary retirement schemes (VRS) are not seen as a real solution. Most trade union activists are emphatic in their opposition to the VRS. Among ordinary workers, the opposition to VRS schemes is not always unequivocal. Some seemed to feel that they could escape the uncertainties of the present by opting for the VRS; others felt the compensation amount should be increased. Many workers still on the rolls were wary of such schemes. Used to small earnings, they fear lump-sum payments: such money is bound to disappear, leaving them destitute. They recounted stories about workers who turned homeless after opting for the VRS: the money was grabbed by scheming relatives and wayward, unemployed sons.

So workers prefer the fiction of factory work. They go to the factory every day to report their attendance and collect their pay even when it comes after months of wait. Despite the irregularity of wage payments, being on the factory rolls appears to be important for the male sense of self. To accept the VRS was to be formally unemployed, a status male workers found difficult to accept. To be classed as a berozgar was particularly humiliating for males.[32] In such a situation, regular subsistence for the family comes from women's waged work at home. In Muslim neighbourhoods, women are employed in sewing burqas. Many women, in both Muslim and Hindu neighbourhoods, work as out-workers with leather companies and make uppers for leather sandals.

Many labourers have now shifted from work in the mills to work in home-based industry. At one level, a shift from the factory to the home homogenises labour, erasing gender distinctions based on work at home and work outside: factory work, the source of male pride, is denied to working class men. Yet gender

[31] The total strength of workers in all three units is now only 4000. Earlier each unit employed betwen 4000 and 5000 workers.

[32] Premnath of Elgin Mills, for instance, protested vehemently when his wife described him as unemployed. Prem Nath, who worked in the dye house in Elgin 2 for nineteen years, took VRS and retired in 1997. Interview.

distinctions within the new work milieu continue. For instance, in hosiery units which have mushroomed in Kanpur mohallas, women do not work on the sewing machines. Men cut and sew vests and hosiery goods; women clean out the thread from the finished product, fix labels and do the ironing. Women's earnings are never more than a couple of rupees per day. Men in hosiery production earn up to Rs 100 per day.[33] Other jobs like bidi making and wrapping toffees, are usually done at home by lower-caste women.

By the 1980s the characteristics of the workforce began to change radically. Up to the 1950s and 1960s, peasants moved from fields to factories; now there is a reverse movement—back to the villages for those who have land. If earlier the unemployed in the city—artisans and migrant peasants—fed the factory labour force, or moved between the 'informal' and 'formal' sector in a circular movement, now factories show no promise of reabsorbing labour. The factory, in fact, steadily feeds the labour market, dissolving boundaries between factory workers and others. Many ply rickshaws, adding to the scores of rickshaw-pullers in the city. The teleological notion that industrialisation is marked by a shift from the domestic to the factory sector has now been widely questioned: domestic industries, we know, continued to flourish through the period of industrialisation in the West.[34] What we see in Kanpur today is not a coexistence of different forms of production, but rather a reverse movement from factory to domestic industries.

At the turn of the twentieth century, when factory employment has shrunk and male workers are unemployed, the spaces through which working class men in the city derived their identity are under threat. If the factory was the sphere within which notions of masculinity were constructed, their dislocation in the present has unsettled these identities. Workless men at home appear an

[33] Interview, Phoolmati.

[34] See, for instance, Ronald Aminzade, 'Reinterpreting Capitalist Industrialisation: A Study of Nineteenth-Century France', in Kaplan and Koepp, eds, *Work in France*, pp. 393–470; Maxine Berg, *The Age of Manufactures, 1700–1820* (London 1985); Pat Hudson, *Regions and Industries* (Cambridge 1981).

intrusion into spaces occupied earlier by women and children during a large part of the day. In women's stories, men idling at home all day disturb notions of time and domestic order. Even in domesticity, women had a different regime of time. For men, being berozgar means a double loss—a collapse of their worlds outside, and a diminished patriarchal presence in the household. For women, in contrast, the domesticisation of waged work in a context when men are unemployed is important in creating a sense of relative empowerment.

In a scenario where traditional large-scale industries are in retreat and crisis, the nature of the labour force is being rapidly transformed. If the phase of industrial expansion was accompanied by a masculinisation of the labour force, today a feminisation is possibly taking place at two levels. First, there is a shift from male to female labour with the displacement of men from factory work, and the employment of women in domestic industries. This female labour, however, remains invisible from public view. Not only is it engaged in invisible forms in home-based industries, it is unrecorded in official statistics. Second, there is a change in the social psychology of the workers—as we noted, a sense of loss of masculinity. Loss of work today implies more than economic hardship. It means also an emasculation of their selves and a destabilisation of their authority within the household.

Perhaps there is something to be said for this partial reversal of traditional gender roles. But not *that* much, in the end: at bottom, this is not the death of masculinity, which, as has often been shown, resurrects itself in new forms; it is, ultimately, the death of a world, a whole way of life, of a cultural form which was once seen as the backbone of urban, industrial India. It is a lost world, and this book is only what E.M. Forster might have termed 'one of the slighter gestures of dissent'—an attempt, against the grain, not to forget that world.

List of Sources
for Graphs, Illustrations,
and Cartoons

—‡⟞══ ══⟝‡—

Sources for Graphs

Figs 6 & 7: *Financial and Commercial Statistics of British India* for the relevant years.

Fig. 8: *Statistical Abstract of British India* for the relevant years.

Figs 9 & 10: *BSER: Wages and Labour Conditions*, pp. 15–16.

Fig. 11: *The Investor's India Yearbook* for the relevant years.

Figs 12 & 13: *Statistics of Large Industrial Establishments* for the relevant years.

Fig. 14: S.H. Freemantle, 'Report on the Supply of Labour to UP and Bengal', UP Revenue Progs. B, no. 91.

Fig. 15: *UP Census*, 1931, Part I, App. A, Table II.

Fig. 16: *IFLC*, pp. 198–9.

Fig. 17: *Indian Labour Yearbook* for the relevant years.

Figs 18 & 19: K.L. Datta, *Report on an Enquiry into the Rise in Prices in India*, vol. III; *Reports on the Working of the Factories Act in Uttar Pradesh* for the relevant years; *BSER: Wages and Labour Conditions*; *Report UPLEC*; *LIC: Labour in Cotton Mills*.

Sources for Illustrations

Fig. 1: From Zoe Yalland, *Traders and Nabobs*, p. 43.

Fig. 2: Maria Sherwood, *The History of Little Henry and his Bearer*, frontispiece (London 1815).

Figs 4 & 5: *Upper India Chamber of Commerce: Golden Jubilee, 1888–1938*, pp. 10–11.

Figs 26–9: Courtesy Mukul Mangalik.

Sources for Cartoons

Cartoons are reproduced from the *Pioneer*, 1938, of the following dates: 2 June (Fig. 20a & b), 3 June (Fig. 21), 9 June (Fig. 22), 22 June (Fig. 23), 6 July (Fig. 24), 13 July (Fig. 25).

Bibliography

MANUSCRIPT SOURCES

1. India Office Library, London

Files and proceedings of the Municipal and Sanitary Departments of the Government of North West Provinces and Awadh; Board's Collection: correspondence, between the Board of Control, London and Company administration overseas; vernacular literature and proscribed publications.

2. National Archives of India, New Delhi

Files and proceedings of the following departments of the Government of India: Home Judicial, Home Political, Home Public, Home Sanitary, Commerce and Industries, Industries, Industries and Labour, Military.

3. Uttar Pradesh State Archives, Lucknow

Files and proceedings of the following departments: General Administration, Home Police, Industries, Local Self-Government, Medical Sanitation, Municipal, Political, Revenue.

4. Criminal Investigation Department Office, Lucknow

Secret abstracts of the Intelligence Department for United Provinces and Awadh (weekly).

5. Kanpur Collectorate Records

Files of the Labour, Judicial (Criminal), Municipal, Police and Sanitation departments.

6. Kanpur Municipality Records

Annual Reports of meetings, administration reports and files of the Miscellaneous Department.

7. Factory Records

Muster rolls and miscellaneous data on wages, workers employed and machinery from JK Spinning and Weaving Mills and Elgin Mills.

8. Private and Institutional Records

Ahmedabad Textile Labour Association Papers (NMML).

AICC Papers (NMML).

AITUC Papers (NMML).

Harcourt Butler Papers (IOL).

Narayan Prasad Arora Papers (NMML).

N.M. Joshi Papers (NMML).

Hallet Papers (IOL).

Haig Papers (NMML).

Jawaharlal Nehru Papers (NMML).

Linlithgow Papers (NMML).

Meerut Conspiracy Case Papers (NMML).

Govind Ballabh Pant Papers (NAI).

Rajendra Prasad Papers (NAI).

Satya Bhakta Papers (NAI).

B. Shiva Rao Papers (NMML).

M.N. Roy Papers (NMML).

Purshottam Das Thakurdas Papers (NMML).

9. Newspapers

Aaj (Benares).
Abhyudaya (Allahabad).
Capital (Calcutta).
Citizen (Kanpur).
Congress Socialist (Bombay).
Independent (Allahabad).
Lal Jhanda (Kanpur).
Leader (Allahabad).
National Front (Bombay).
National Herald (Lucknow).
New Age (Madras).
Peoples' War (Bombay)
Pioneer (Lucknow).
Prabha (Kanpur).

Pratap (Kanpur).

Samajvad (Kanpur).

Sankhya (Calcutta).

Sansar (Kanpur).

Satta Sangharsh (Kanpur).

Shramik (Kanpur).

Sukavi (Kanpur).

Vartman (Kanpur).

10. Oral Accounts

Oral accounts from working class families have been collected over the years between the late 1970s to the present. Among the accounts of workers used here are those of Shriram (worked in textile mills in Kanpur and outside), Raghubir (Swadeshi Cotton Mills), Devi Babu (worked in textile mills, and later ran a teashop), Sudarshan Chakr, Shiv Ratan 'Daddu' (New Victoria Mills), Devi Datt Agnihotri (Kanpur Textiles), Moolchand (Cawnpore Cotton Mills), Mahadeo (Swadeshi Mills), Prem Narayan (Swadeshi Mills), Anarsi (New Victoria Mills), Rama Kant Misra (New Victoria Mills), Paras Nath Yadav (JK Cotton Mills), Praga Dutt (Swadeshi, Kanpur Cotton and Atherton), Phool Singh (Elgin Mills 1), Panna Lal (alternated between work in textile mills and driving a push cart—thela), Naresh Singh Chauhan (Elgin Mills 2), Mohammad Sultan Khan (Elgin Mills no. 2), Ramcharan (Muir and then Laxmi Ratan Mills), Hira Lal (Elgin Mills 2), Pancham Lal (Elgin Mills 2), Cde. Zaif (JK Jute), Taufiq (Kanpur Textiles), Ashraf Ali (Elgin Mills 2), Sukhrani, Mannoo, and Vishnu Devi (Rame Babu ka hata, Lachmipurwa), Munni Devi (Swadeshi Cotton Mills), Radha Rani and Lachmi (Kishan Pyari ka hata, Shakkar mill Khalua), Ram Pyari, Ganeshi Devi, Susheela, Sheela and Indira 'bidi vali'(Chuna Bhatiya), Tehrunissa and Shakeela (Nur Mohammad ka hata), Rasheeda Begum (Fazalganj), Shyama, Krishna and Ganga Devi (Mathiya vala hata), Asha (Devi Deen ka hata), Tijiya, Sunita, Gangotri, Phoolmati (Bisati ka hata, Lachmipurwa), Ruksana, Sona Devi, Rajbunisa and Badarjahan (Tannery ka hata).

Trade unionists interviewed were Aiwaz Ali, Arjun Arora, S.P. Awasthi, S.C. Kapoor, R.R. Shastri, Dev Sena, Ravi Sinha, S.S. Yusuf.

11. Official and Semi-official Publications

Annual Reports of the Sanitary Commissioner, North West Provinces and Awadh (Allahabad annual).

Annual Report on the Working of the Indian Trade Unions Act, 1926 (xvi of 1926) in the United Provinces (Allahabad annual).

Annual Statement of the Seaborne Trade of British India with the British Empire and Foreign Countries (Calcutta annual).

Briggs, G.W., The Chamars (Calcutta 1920).

Bureau of Statistics and Economic Research, United Provinces: Agricultural Prices in the United Provinces, by R.B. Gupta (Allahabad 1933).

Bureau of Statistics and Economic Research, United Provinces: Wages and Labour Conditions, by S.P. Saxena (Allahabad 1938).

Census of India, 1881, vol. xvii, Part I, Report, North West Provinces and Awadh (Allahabad 1882).

Census of India, 1891, vol. ix, Part 16-1, Report and Provincial Tables, North West Provinces and Awadh (Allahabad 1894).

Census of India, 1901, vol. xvi, Part I, Report, North West Provinces and Awadh (Allahabad 1902).

Census of India, 1911, vol. xv, Part I, Report, United Provinces of Agra and Awadh (Allahabad 1912).

Census of India, 1921, vol. xvi, Part I, Report and Part II Tables, United Provinces of Agra and Awadh (Allahabad 1923).

Census of India, 1931, vol. xviii, Part I, Report and Part II Tables, United Provinces of Agra and Awadh (Allahabad 1933).

Census of India, 1941, vol. v (Simla 1942).

Census of India, 1951, vol. ii, Part I -A, Report (Allahabad 1953).

Chatterjee, A.C., Notes on the Industries of the United Provinces (Allahabad 1908).

Chaturvedi, S.C., Rural Wages in the United Provinces (Allahabad 1947).

Compendium of Textile Statistics, 1997 (Mumbai 1998).

Crooke, W., Tribes and Castes of North Western India, vol. III (Calcutta 1896; rpt Delhi 1975).

Datta, K.L., Report on the Enquiry into the Rise of Prices in India (Calcutta 1914).

East India (Cawnpore Riots), Report of the Commission of Inquiry into the Communal Outbreak at Cawnpore and the Resolution of the Government of UP, Cmd. 3891 (London 1931).

Employers' Association of Northern India: Silver Jubilee, 1937–1962 (Kanpur 1962).

Financial and Commercial Statistics of British India (Calcutta annual).

Freemantle, S.H., Report on the Supply of Labour to the United Provinces and Bengal (1906).

Gracey, H.K., *Final Report on the Seventh Settlement of the Cawnpore District of the United Provinces 1903–6* (Allahabad 1907)

Indian Industrial Commisssion, vol. i, Report 1916–18, vols ii–iv, Evidence (Calcutta 1918).

Indian Labour Yearbooks (Simla annual).

Indian Law Reports (Allahabad annual).

Indian Tariff Board: 1936–37, vol. I, Report; and vols ii–iii, Evidence (Delhi 1936–7).

Indian Tariff Board: Cotton Textile Industry Enquiry: 1927, vol. i, Report and *vols ii–iv Evidence* (Calcutta 1927).

Indian Tariff Board: Cotton Textile Industry Enquiry: 1934, vol. i–iv, Evidence (Delhi 1934).

Indian Worker: A Changing Profile, 1947–67, National Commission on Labour (Delhi 1969).

Investor's India Yearbook (Calcutta annual).

Joint-Stock Companies in British India and in the Indian States (Calcutta annual).

Labour Bulletin, UP (Allahabad annual).

Labour Investigation Committee: Report on an Enquiry into Conditions of Labour in the Woollen Textile Industry in India, by S.R. Deshpande (Simla 1946).

Labour Investigation Committee: Report on an Enquiry into Conditions of Labour in the Principal Municipalities of India, by S.R. Deshpande (Simla 1946).

Labour Investigation Committee: Report on Labour Conditions in Tanneries and Leather Goods Factories, by Ahmad Mukhtar (Simla 1946).

Labour Investigation Committee: Report on an Enquiry into Conditions of Labour in the Cotton Mills in India, by S.R. Deshpande (Delhi 1946).

Legislative Assembly Debates, UP, 1937–39 (Allahabad annual).

Montgomery, R., *Statistical Report of the District of Cawnpore* (Calcutta 1849).

Narrative of Events in the North West Provinces in 1857–58 (Calcutta n.d.).

Nevill, H.R., *Cawnpore: A Gazetteer* (Allahabad 1909).

Playne, S. and A.Wright, *The Bombay Presidency: The UP and the Punjab: Their History, People, Commerce and Natural Resources* (London 1920).

Prices and Wages in India (Calcutta annual).

Provincial Banking Enquiry Committee: UP, vol. 1, Report and vols ii–iv, Evidence (Allahabad 1930–1).

Report of the Cawnpore Textile Labour Enquiry Committee (Allahabad 1938).

Report of the Committee Appointed by the Cawnpore Harijan Sevak Sangh, 1933–34 (Kanpur 1934).

'Report of the Citizen's Committee for Inquiry into the Kanpur Massacre', 23.2.1978.

Report of the Fact Finding Committee (Handloom and Mills) (Delhi 1942).

Report of the Fifth Quinquennial Wage Census of the United Provinces (Allahabad 1936).

Report of the Indian Factory Commission, 1890 with Proceedings and Appendices (Calcutta 1890).

Report of the Indian Factory Labour Commission, 1908, 2 vols (Simla 1908).

Report of the Kanpur Textile Mills Rationalization Enquiry Committee, 1955–56 (Lucknow 1956).

Report of the National Commission on Labour (Delhi 1969).

Report of the Study Team on Prohibition, vol. II (New Delhi 1964).

Report of the United Provinces Labour Enquiry Committee, vol. i, Part i and ii (Allahabad 1946).

Report on the Administration of the United Provinces of Agra and Awadh (Allahabad annual).

Reports of the Merchant's Chamber of Commerce, UP (Kanpur annual).

Reports on Native Newspapers of UP.

Reports of the United Provinces Chamber of Commerce (Kanpur annual).

Reports of the Upper India Chamber of Commerce 1889–1946 (Kanpur annual).

Reports on the Working of the Factories Act in Uttar Pradesh (Allahabad annual).

Reports on the Working of the Workmen's Compensation Act (Allahabad annual).

Review of the Trade of India (Calcutta annual).

Rose, H.A., *A Glossary of the Tribes and Castes of Punjab and North-West Frontier Provinces* (Delhi 1970).

Royal Commission on Labour: Evidence, vol. III: Parts i and ii (London 1931).

Royal Commission on Labour: Supplementary, vol. xi (London 1934).

Royal Commission on Labour: Report (London 1931).

Rural and Urban Wages in the United Provinces (Lucknow 1956).

Settlement of the Cawnpore Labour Dispute (Lucknow n.d.).

Silberrad, C.A., *A Monograph on Cotton Fabrics Produced in N.W.P. and Awadh* (Allahabad 1898).

Silver Jubilee Souvenir, 1914–31, UP Chamber of Commerce (Kanpur n.d.).

Statistical Abstracts for British India (Calcutta annual).

Statistics of Large Industrial Establishments (Calcutta annual).

UP Chamber of Commerce: Silver Jubilee Souvenir, 1914–39 (Kanpur 1939).

Upper India Chamber of Commerce: Golden Jubilee, 1888–1938 (Kanpur 1938).

Vatal, J.S., *Report on the Industrial Survey of Cawnpore District* (Allahabad 1924).

Wright, F.N., *Final Report on the Settlement of the Cawnpore District* (Allahabad 1878).

12. Local Language Publications

Alekhakar, Babu Ramcharan, *Anyaya se Achut* (Kanpur n.d.).

Arora, A., 'Kanpur ka Mazdur Andolan Jo Yad Raha', in A. Arora, *Shri Suraj Prasad Awasthi Hirak Jayanti Abhinandan Granth* (Kanpur 1973).

Arora, N.P. and Lakshmi Kant Tripathi, *Pratap Narayan Misra* (Kanpur 1947).

Arora, N.P., *Kanpur ke Prasidh Purush* (Kanpur 1947).

———, *Narayan Nibandhavali* (Kanpur 1945).

Chakr, Sudarshan, *Communist Katha* (Kanpur 1961).

———, *Communism Kavitavali* (Kanpur 1958).

———, *Jay Janta* (Kanpur 1965).

———, *Jit ke Geet* (Kanpur 1965).

———, *Kanpur Mazdur Andolan ka Itihas* (Kanpur 1986).

———, *Pita Putra* (Kanpur n.d.).

———, *Sachi Kavitayen*(Poems written between 1935 and 1955) (Kanpur n.d.).

———, *Shahidon ki Katar* (Kanpur 1953).

———, *Vishvamahabharata* (Kanpur 1977).

Chakr, 'Sudarshan Misra' , ' Jhansi ki Rani', proscribed pub., nos 612–14 (NAI).

Chaturvedi, B., et al., eds, *Ganesh Smarak Granth: Amar Shahid Ganesh Shankar Vidyarthi* (Kanpur 1960).

Chaturvedi, B., J.D. Sharma, O.S. Vidyarthi and S.N. Saxena, eds,

Narmada: Amar Shahid Ganesh Shankar Vidyarthi Smiriti Ank (Gwalior 1961).

Chaturvedi, N.C., *Narayan Prasad Arora: Sankshipt Jeevni* (Kanpur n.d.).

Chaube, Ganga Sahai, 'Ganeshji ki Sharan Mein', in B. Chaturvedi, J. Sharma and P. Verma, eds, *Ganesh Smarak Granth: Amar Shahid Ganesh Shankar Vidyarthi Granth* (Kalpi 1960).

Chauhan, Sudha, *Subhadra Kumari Chauhan* (New Delhi 1981).

Chowdhari, K.N., *Sarvahara Comrade Shriram* (Kanpur n.d.).

Dixit, J.C., 'Kanpur Mazdur Sabha ka Shaishav Kal', Ramesh Mishra, et al., eds, *Sri Surya Prasad Awasthi Heerak Jayanti Abhinandan Granth* (Kanpur 1973).

Dubey, Uma Shankar, 'Kushti Premi Aroraji', in Naresh Chandra Chaturvedi, eds, *Narayan Prasad Arora: Jeevanvrit* (Kanpur 1950).

Duniya ke Mazduron Ek Ho Jao, A bulletin of the UP Communist party (Kanpur 1937).

Ham Bhooke Nangen Kyon Hain (Kanpur 1935), proscribed pub., no. 89 (NAI).

Kailash Mil Mein Sangharsh ka Elan: Sabhi Mazdur Bhaiyon ke Nam Ek Apil (n.d.), leaflet issued by workers of the J.K. Manufacturers, Ltd.

Kant, Krishna, *Harihar Nath Shastri Smarak Granth* (Lucknow 1969).

Kranti ka Udgosh: Ganesh Shankar Vidyarthi ki Kalam Se, ed. Radhakrishna Awasthi (Kanpur 1978).

Kureel, Ramcharan, *Holi ka Premuphar* (Kanpur 1938).

————, *Kureel Bhaiyon ki Seva Men Khuli Chitthi* (Danakhori, Kanpur 1934).

Mazdur Jhande ka Awahan, proscribed pub., no. 552 (NAI).

Mazdur Jhande Ki Prarthana (Kanpur 1930), proscribed pub., no. 552 (NAI) published by S.P. Awasthi for the Mazdur Sabha.

Mishra, Ramesh and K.K. Sharma, eds, *Sri Surya Prasad Awasthi Hirak Jayanti Abhinandan Granth* (Kanpur 1973).

Misra, S.P., 'Mazdur Andolan ka Itihas', in Krishna Kant, ed., *Harihar Nath Shastri Smarak Granth* (Lucknow 1969).

Narayan Prasad Arora: Jeevanvrit (Kanpur 1951)

Nizami, Hazan, *Kanpur ki Khuni Dastan* (Meerath 1913), proscribed pub., no. 41, IOL.

Sat Karor Ki Pukar, sd. Jiya Lal Chowdhary (Kanpur 1923).

Prasad, Bhavani, *Achut Bhaiyon ke Liye Shubh Sandesh* (Sitapur n.d.)

Ram, Bhushan, *Kusambhi ke Charmkar Bhaiyon Ki Panchayat* (Kanpur n.d.).

Rathor, Maggulal, 'Mitr', *Chu Chu ka Murabba,* proscribed pub., HIN B177 (IOL).

Sharma, Surendra, 'Nirbhik Lekhni ki Kahani' in B Chaturvedi, et al., eds, *Ganesh Smarak Granth: Amar Shahid Ganesh Shankar Vidyarthi* (Kanpur 1960).

Shastri, Devrata, *Ganesh Shankar Vidyarthi* (Delhi n.d.).

Shastri, Harihar Nath, *Amar Shahidon ke Sansmaran* (Kanpur 1981).

Shriram, *Ek Sarvahara ka Jivan Vritanta* (Kanpur n.d.),

Tandon, Shivnarain, *Bolshevik Russia* (Kanpur 1932), proscribed pub., no. 320–2 (NAI).

Tripathi, Surya Kant and Narayan Prasad Arora, *Kanpur kaa Itihaas* (1940).

Tripathi, Surya Prakash, *Vishvakavi Shri Sudarshan Chakr* (Kanpur 1973).

Vidyalankar, S., *Arya Samaj ka Itihas,* vol. 2 (New Delhi 1987).

Vidyarthi, G.S., *Chuni Huyi Rachnaye* (Delhi 1991).

13. Books and Articles

Adhikari, G., *Documents of the History of the Communist Party of India* (New Delhi 1971).

Agnihotri, V., *Housing Condition of Factory Workers in Kanpur* (Lucknow 1954).

Amin, Shahid, *Sugarcane and Sugar in Gorakhpur: An Inquiry into Peasant Production for Capitalist Enterprise in Colonial India* (Delhi 1984).

———, *Event, Metaphor, Memory: Chauri Chaura, 1922–1992* (California 1995).

Aminzade, Ronald, 'Reinterpreting Capitalist Industrialisation: A Study of Nineteenth-Century France', in Stephen Kaplan and Cynthia J. Koepp, eds, *Work in France: Representation, Meaning, Organisation and Practice* (Cornell 1986).

Anderson, Michael, 'Household Structure and the Industrial Revolution: Mid-Nineteenth Century Preston in Comparative Perspective', in Peter Laslett, ed., *Household and Family in Past Time* (Cambridge 1972).

———, *Family Structure in Nineteenth-century Lancashire* (Cambridge 1971).

Arnold, D., *Colonizing the Body: State Medicine and Epidemic Disease in Nineteenth-Century India* (California 1993).

Bagchi, Amiya Kumar, *Private Investment in India: 1900–1939* (Cambridge 1972, Madras 1975).

———, *The Evolution of the State Bank of India, vol. 2, The Era of Presidency Banks, 1876–1920* (Delhi 1997).

Bahl, V., *The Making of the Indian Working Class: The Case of the Tata Iron and Steel Industry* (Delhi 1995).

Ball, Charles, *The History of the Indian Mutiny* (London n.d.).

Ballhatchet, Kenneth, *Race, Sex and Class under the Raj: Imperial Attitudes and Policies and their Critics, 1793–1905* (London 1980).

Banerji, D., 'Measurement of Poverty and Undernutrition', *EPW*, 16:39, Sep. 1981.

Barrier, N.G., ed., *Roots of Communal Politics* (Delhi 1976).

Bayly, C.A., *Rulers, Townsmen and Bazaars: North Indian Society in the Age of British Expansion, 1770–1870* (Cambridge 1988).

Behal, R.P., 'Forms of Labour Protest in the Assam Valley', *EPW*, 20:4, Jan. 1985.

Behal, R.P. and P. Mohapatra, 'Tea and Money versus Human Life: The Rise and Fall of the Indenture System in the Assam Tea Plantations 1840–1908', *Journal of Peasant Studies*, 19: 34, 1992.

Bellwinkel, Maren, *Die Kasen-Klassenproblematik im Stadtisch-Inustriellen Bereich Historisch-Empirische Fallstudie uber die Industriestadt Kanpur in Uttar Pradesh, Indien* (Wiesbaden 1980).

Berg, Maxine, *The Age of Manufactures, 1700–1820* (London 1985).

Bhabha, Homi, 'Dissemi Nation: Time, Narrative, and the Margins of the Modern Nation, in H. Bhabha, ed., *Nation and Narration* (London 1990).

Bhattacharya, S., 'The Outsiders: A Historical Note', in Ashok Mitra, ed., *The Truth Unites: Essays in Tribute to Samar Sen* (Calcutta 1985).

———, 'The Colonial State Capital and Labour: Bombay 1919–31', in S. Bhattacharya and R. Thapar, eds, *Situating Indian History* (Delhi 1986).

———, 'Capital and Labour in Bombay City, 1928–29', *EPW*, 16:42 and 43, Oct. 1981.

———, 'Swaraj and the Kamgar: The Indian National Congress and the Bombay Working Class, 1919–1931', in R. Sisson and S. Wolpert, eds, *Congress and Indian Nationalism: The Pre-Independence Phase* (Berkeley 1988).

Bourdieu, Pierre, *Outline of a Theory of Practice* (Cambridge 1977).

Bozon, Michel and Anne-Marie Thiesse, 'The Collapse of Memory: The Case of Farm Workers', *History and Anthropology*, 2, 1986.

Brass, Paul, *Language, Religion and Politics in North India* (Cambridge 1974).

———, *Theft of an Idol: Text and Context in the Representation of Collective Violence* (Calcutta 1997).

Breman, Jan, 'A Dualistic Labour System: A Critique of the "Informal Sector" Concept', *EPW*, 11: 48,49 and 50, Nov. and Dec. 1976.

————, *Footloose Labour: Working in India's Informal Economy* (Cambridge 1995).

Broughton, G.N., *Labour in Indian Industries* (London 1924).

Catanach, I.J., 'Plague and the Tensions of Empire, 1896–1918', in D. Arnold, ed., *Imperial Medicine and Indigenous Societies* (Manchester 1988).

Chakrabarty, Dipesh and Ranajit Das Gupta, 'Some Aspects of Labour History of Bengal in the Nineteenth Century: Two Views', Occasional Paper No. 40, Calcutta Centre for Studies in Social Sciences, Oct. 1981.

Chakrabarty, Dipesh, 'Sasipada Banerjee: A Study in the Nature of the First Contact of Bengali Bhadralok with Working Classes of Bengal', *Indian Historical Review*, 2:2, Jan. 1976.

————, 'Invitation to Dialogue', *Subaltern Studies, vol. IV* (New Delhi 1985).

————, *Rethinking Working Class History* (New Delhi 1989).

————, *Provincializing Europe: Postcolonial Thought and Historical Difference* (Princeton 2000).

————, 'Class Consciousness and the Indian Working Class: Dilemmas of a Marxist Historiography', *Journal of African and Asian Studies*, 23:1–2,1988.

Chakravarty, Lalitha, 'Emergence of an Industrial Labour-Force in a Dual Economy—British India, 1880–1920', *IESHR*, 15:3, July 1978.

Chandavarkar, Rajnarayan, *Imperial Power and Popular Politics: Class, Resistance and the State in India, 1850–1950* (Cambridge 1998).

————, *The Origins of Industrial Capitalism in India: Business Strategies and the Working Classes in Bombay, 1900–1940* (Cambridge 1994).

Chandra, Bipan, ed., *The Indian Left: Critical Appraisals* (New Delhi 1983).

————, 'Jawaharlal Nehru and the Capitalist Class, 1936', in Bipan Chandra, *Nationalism and Colonialism in Modern India* (New Delhi 1979).

Chandrashekar, C.P., 'Growth and Technical Change in Indian Cotton-Mill Industry', *EPW*, 19:4, PE 22–39, 1984.

Chartier, Roger, *Cultural History: Between Practice and Representation* (Polity 1988).

Chatterjee, Basudev, 'The Political Economy of "Discriminating Protection": The Case of Textiles in the 1920s', *IESHR*, 20:3, 1983.

————, *Towards Freedom:Documents on the Movement for Independence in India, 1938, Part III* (Delhi 1997).

Chatterjee, Partha, *The Nation and Its Fragments* (Princeton 1993).

Chevalier, Louis, *Laboring Classes and Dangerous Classes in Paris During the First Half of the Nineteenth Century* (Princeton 1973).

Chowdhury-Sengupta, Indira, 'The Effeminate and the Masculine: Nationalism and the Concept of Race in Colonial Bengal', in Peter Robb, ed., *The Concept of Race in South Asia* (Delhi 1995).

Clifford, J. and G.E. Marcus, *Writing Culture: The Poetics and Politics of Ethnography* (California 1986).

Cohn, Bernard, 'Cloth, Clothes and Colonialism: India in the Nineteenth Century', in Cohn, *Colonialism and Its Forms of Knowledge: The British in India* (Princeton 1996).

———, 'Chamar Family in a North Indian Village', in *An Anthropologist Among the Historians and Other Essays* (Delhi 1987).

Cooper, Frederick, 'Back to Work: Categories, Boundaries and Connections in the Study of Labour', in P. Alexander and R. Halpern, eds, *Racializing Class, Classifying Race: Labour and Difference in Britain, the USA and Africa* (London 2000).

Corbin, Alain, *The Foul and the Fragrant: Odor and the French Social Imagination* (Harvard 1986).

Creighton, Colin, 'The Rise of the Male Breadwinner Family: A Reappraisal', in *Comparative Studies in Society and History*, 38:2, 1996.

Crooke, W., *Tribes and Castes of North Western India,* vol. III (Calcutta 1896, Delhi 1975).

Dandekar, V.M., 'Economics of Nutrition', *EPW*, 16:30, July 1981.

Das Gupta, Ranajit, 'Poverty and Protest: A Study of Calcutta's Industrial Workers and Labouring Poor, 1875–1899', in Das Gupta, *Labour and Working Class in Eastern India: Studies in Colonial History* (Calcutta 1994).

———, 'Factory Labour in Eastern India: Sources of Supply, 1855–1946: Some Preliminary Findings', *IESHR*, 13:3,1976.

Das, R.K., *History of Indian Labour Legislation* (Calcutta 1941).

Das, Veena, ed., *Mirrors of Violence: Communities, Riots and Survivors in South Asia* (Delhi 1990).

Datar, B.N., ed., *Harihar Nath Shastri: Life and Work* (Bombay 1968).

Dayal, H.H., 'Agricultural Labourers in Unnao', in Radhakamal Mukerjee, ed., *Fields and Farms in Awadh* (London 1929).

Deliege, Robert, 'The Myths of Origin of the Indian Untouchables', *Man* (new series) 18, 1993.

De Haan, Arjaan, *Unsettled Settlers: Migrant Workers and Industrial Capitalism in Calcutta* (Rotterdam 1994).

Douglas, Dave, '"Worms of the Earth": The Miners' Own Story', in R. Samuel, ed., *People's History and Socialist Theory* (London 1981).

Dube, Saurabh, *Untouchable Pasts: Religion, Identity, and Power among a Central Indian Community, 1780–1950* (New York 1998).

Dunbar, Janet, *Tigers, Durbars and Kings: Fanny Eden's Indian Journals 1837–38* (London 1938).

Eden, Emily, *Up the Country: Letters Written to her Sister from the Upper Provinces of India* (Oxford 1930, rpt. London 1983).

Fisher, Michael A., *Clash of Cultures: Awadh, the British and the Mughals* (Delhi 1987).

Forrest, G.W., *Cities of India* (London 1905).

Foster, John, *Class Struggle and the Industrial Revolution: Early Industrial Capitalism in Three English Towns* (London 1974).

Freitag, Sandria, ed., *Culture and Power in Benaras: Commuity, Performance, and Environment, 1800–1980* (Delhi 1989).

———, *Collective Action and Community: Public Arenas and the Emergence of Communalism in North India* (California 1989).

Genovese, Eugene, D., *Roll Jordon Roll: The World the Slaves Made* (New York 1974).

Ghosh, Parimal, 'Communalism and Colonial Labour, Experience of Calcutta Jute Mill Workers 1880–1930', *EPW*, 25:30, July 1990.

Gooptu, Nandini, 'Caste and Labour: Untouchable Social Movements in Urban Uttar Pradesh in the Early Twentieth Century', in Peter Robb, ed., *Dalit Movements and the Meanings of Labour in India* (Delhi 1993).

———, *The Politics of the Urban Poor in Early Twentiety-Century India* (Cambridge 2000).

Gopal, S., ed., *Selected Works of Jawaharlal Nehru*, vol. 8 (New Delhi 1975).

———, 'The Formative Ideology of Jawaharlal Nehru', in K.N. Panikkar, ed., *National and Left Movements in India* (New Delhi 1980).

Goswami, Omkar, ' State-owned Enterprises in India', mimeo for OECD Paris.

———, 'Sickness and Growth of India's Textile Industry: Analysis and Policy Options', *EPW*, 25:44 and 45, Oct. and Nov. 1990.

Graff, Violette, ed., *Lucknow: Memories of a City* (Delhi 1997).

Guha, Ranajit, 'The Career of an Anti-God in Heaven and on Earth', in Sugata Bose, ed., *Credit, Markets, and the Agrarian Economy of Colonial India* (Delhi 1994).

———, *Elementary Aspects of Peasant Insurgency in Colonial India* (Delhi 1983).

Gupta, P.S., 'Notes on the Origin and Structuring of the Industrial Labour Force in India, 1880–1920', in R.S. Sharma, ed., *Indian Society: Historical Probings* (New Delhi 1974).

Gutman, H.G., *Work, Culture, and Society in Industrialising America* (New York 1977).

Hall, Catherine, *White, Male and Middle-Class: Explorations in Feminism and History* (Oxford 1992).

Hall, S., 'Introduction: Who needs Identity?', in S. Hall and Paul du Gay, eds, *Questions of Cultural Identity* (Sage 1996).

———, 'Notes on Deconstructing "the Popular" ', in R. Samuel, ed., *People's History and Socialist Theory* (London 1981).

Hardgrave, Robert, 'The Breast Cloth Controversy: Caste Consciousness and Social Change in Southern Travancore', *IESHR*, 5, 1968.

Hareven, Tamara K., *Family Time and Industrial Time: The Relationship between the Family and Work in a New England Industrial Community* (Cambridge 1982).

Harrison, Mark, *Climates and Constitutions: Health, Race, Environment and British Imperialism in India, 1600–1850* (New Delhi 1999).

Hasan, Mushirul, *Nationalism and Communal Politics in India, 1916–28* (Delhi 1979).

Haynes, D. and G. Prakash, eds, *Contesting Power: Resistance and Everyday Relations in South Asia* (Delhi 1991).

Hobsbawm, E.J., *Worlds of Labour: Further Studies in the History of Labour* (London 1984).

———, *Labouring Men: Studies in the History of Labour* (London 1986).

Hodges, William, *Travels in India, 1780–83* (London 1793, Delhi 1999).

Hoey, W., *Trade and Manufactures in North India* (Lucknow 1880).

Holmstrom, Mark, *Industry and Inequality: The Social Anthropology of Indian Labour* (Cambridge 1984).

Hone, Angus, 'High Absenteeism and High Commitment', *EPW*, 3: 21–2, May 1968.

Hudson, Pat, *Regions and Industries* (Cambridge 1981).

Jagga, Lajpat, 'Colonial Railwaymen and British Rule—A Probe into Railway Labour Agitation in India, 1919–22'. *Studies in History*, 3: 1 & 2, Jan.–Dec. 1981.

Jahoda, Marie, Paul F. Lazarfeld and Hans Zeisel, eds, *Marienthal: The Sociography of an Unemployed Community* (London 1972).

James, R.C., 'The Casual Labour Problem in Indian Manufacturing', *Quarterly Journal of Economics*, 74:1, Feb. 1960.

Jones, Gareth Stedman, *Languages of Class: Studies in English Working Class History, 1832–1982* (Cambridge 1983).

———, *Outcast London: A Study in the Relationship between Classes in Victorian Society* (Harmondsworth 1971).

Josh, Bhagwan, *Struggle for Hegemony in India, 1920–4: Colonial State, the Left and the National Movement, vol. II, 1934–41* (New Delhi 1992).

Joshi, C., Kanpur Textile Labour: Some Structural Features of Formative Years', *EPW*, 16:44–6, Nov. 1981.

———, 'The Formation of Work Culture: Industrial Labour in a North Indian City (1890s–1940s)', *Purusartha* 14, 1992, special issue on 'Travailler en Inde', ed. Gerard Heuze.

———, 'Making Spaces: Questions of Gender and Domesticity', paper presented at the Second International Conference of the Association of Indian Labour Historians, V.V. Giri Institute of Labour, March 2000.

———, 'Bonds of Community, Ties of Religion: Kanpur Textile Workers in the Early Twentieth Century', *IESHR*, 22:3, 1985.

Joshi, P.C., 'The Decline of Indigenous Handicrafts in Uttar Pradesh', *IESHR*, 1:1, 1963–4.

Joyce, Patrick, ed., *The Historical Meanings of Work* (Cambridge 1987).

———, *Visions of the People: Industrial England and the Question of Class, 1840–1914* (Cambridge 1991).

Juergensmeyer, Mark, *Religion as Social Vision: The Movement against Untouchability in 20th Century Punjab* (California 1982).

Kannapan, Subbiah, 'Labour Force Commitment in the Early Stages of Industrialization', *Indian Journal of Industrial Relations*, 5:3, 1970.

Kaplan, Steven L. and C.J. Koepp, eds, *Work in France: Representations, Meanings, Organization and Practice* (Conell 1986).

Karnik, V.B., *Indian Trade Unions: A Survey* (Bombay 1966).

Katznelson, Ira, *City Trenches: Urban Politics and the Patterning of Class in the United States* (Chicago 1981).

Katznelson, Ira and A. Zolberg, eds, *Working Class Formation: Nineteenth Century Patterns in Western Europe and the United States* (Princeton 1986).

Kaye, H. and K. McClelland, eds, *E.P. Thompson: Critical Perspectives* (Cambridge 1990).

Kelman, J.H., *Labour in India: A Study of Conditions of Indian Women in Modern Industry* (London 1923).

Kerr, Clark, F.H. Harbison, J. Dunlop and C.A. Myers, eds, *Industrialism and Industrial Man* (London 1973).

Kerr, Clark, J. Dunlop, et al., eds, *Industrialism and Industrial Man* (London 1973).

Kerr, Ian, *Building the Railways of the Raj: 1850–1900* (Delhi 1995).

Khare, R.S., *The Untouchable as Himself: Ideology, Identity and Pragmatism Among the Lucknow Chamars* (Cambridge 1986).

Kidambi, Prashant, 'Housing the Poor in Colonial Bombay: The City Improvement Trust, 1898–1918', *Studies in History*, 17:1, Jan.–June 2001.

King, Antony, D., *Colonial Urban Development* (London 1976).

Knorriga, Peter, 'Artisan Labour in the Agra Footwear Industry: Continued Informality and Changing Threats', in Jonathan P. Parry, Jan Breman and Karin Kapadia, eds, *The Worlds of Indian Industrial Labour* (New Delhi 1999).

Kocka, Jurgen, 'Craft Traditions and the Labour Movement in Nineteenth-Century Germany', in Pat Thane et al., eds, *The Power of the Past: Essays for Eric Hobsbawm* (Cambridge 1984).

Kooiman, Dick, *Bombay Textile Labour: Managers, Trade Unionists and Officials 1918–1939* (Delhi 1989).

———, 'Jobbers and the Emergence of Trade Unions in Bombay City', *IRSH*, 22:3, 1977.

Krishnaji, N., 'On Measuring Incidence of Undernutrition: What is a Consumer Unit?', *EPW*, 16:37, Sep. 1981.

———, 'On Measuring Increase of Undernutrition: A Note on Sukhatme's Procedure', *EPW*, 16:22, May 1981.

Kumar, Nita, *The Artisans of Benaras: Popular Culture and Identity, 1880–1986* (Princeton 1988).

Kumar, R., 'From Swaraj to Purna Swaraj: Nationalist Politics in the City of Bombay, 1920–32', in D.A. Low, ed., *Congress and the Raj: Facets of the Indian Struggle* (New Delhi 1977).

———, 'The Bombay Textile Strike, 1919', *IESHR*, 8:1, 1971.

Kumar, Radha, 'Family and Factory: Women in the Bombay Cotton Textile Industry, 1919–1939', *IESHR*, 20:1, 1983.

Kumar, Uday, 'Self, Body and Inner Sense: Some Reflections on Sree Narayana Guru and Kumaran Asan', *Studies in History*, 13:2, July 1997.

Lakshman, P.P., *Congress and the Labour Movement in India* (Allahabad 1947).

Linebaugh, Peter, *The London Hanged: Crime and Civil Society in the Eighteenth Century* (Cambridge 1992).

Llewellyn-Jones, Rosie, *A Fatal Friendship: The Nawabs, the British and the City of Lucknow* (Delhi 1985).

———, *A Very Ingenious Man: Claude Martin in Early Colonial India* (Delhi 1992).

Ludtke, A., 'What Happened to the "Fiery Red Glow"? Workers' Experiences and German Fascism', in Ludtke, ed., *The History of Everyday Life: Reconstructing Historical Experiences and Ways of Life* (New Jersey 1995).

————, 'The Historiography of Everyday Life: The Personal and the Political', in Raphael Samuel and Gareth Stedman Jones, eds, *Culture Ideology and Politics* (London 1982).

————, 'Cash, Coffee-Breaks, Horseplay: *Eigensinn* and Politics among Factory Workers in Germany *circa* 1900', in M. Hanagan, ed., *Class Confrontation and the Labour Process* (New York 1986).

Linden Marcel van der, ed., *Editorial, International Review of Social History*, 38, Supplement 1, 1993.

Lynch, Owen, *The Politics of Untouchability: Social Movements and Social Change in a City of India* (Columbia 1969).

Masselos, Jim, 'Power in the Bombay "Mohalla", 1904–1915: An Initial Exploration into the World of the Indian Urban Muslim', *South Asia*, 6, Dec. 1976.

Mathur, A.S. and J.S. Mathur, *Trade Union Movement in India* (Allahabad 1957).

Mazumdar, D., 'Labour Supply in Early Industrialization: The Case of the Bombay Textile Industry', *Economic History Review*, 26:3, 1973.

Mazumdar, D.N., *Social Contours of an Industrial City: Social Survey of Kanpur* (Bombay 1960).

Medick, Hans, 'Plebeian Culture in the Transition to Capitalism', in Raphael Samuel and Gareth Stedman Jones, eds, *Culture, Ideology and Politics* (London 1982).

Mehra, S.P., *Cawnpore Civic Problems* (Kanpur 1952).

Mehta, M.M., *Structure of the Cotton Mill Industry in India* (Allahabad 1949).

Mehta, S.D., *Structure of Indian Industries* (Bombay 1955).

————, *The Indian Cotton Textile Industry: An Economic Analysis* (Bombay 1953).

Menon, Visalakshi, 'The Indian National Congress and Mass Mobilization—A Study of UP, 1937–39, *Studies in History*, 2:2, 1980.

Misra, Baniprasanna, 'Factory Labour during the Early Years of Industrialization: An Appraisal in the Light of the Indian Factory Commission, 1890', *IESHR*, July–Sep. 1975.

Mohapatra, Prabhu, 'Immobilising Labour: Indenture Laws and Enforcement in Assam and the West Indies 1860–1920', paper presented at the First Annual Conference of AILH, New Delhi 1998.

————, 'Coolies and Colliers: A Study of the Agrarian Context of Labour Migration from Chotanagpur, 1880–1920', *Studies in History*, 1:2, 1985.

————, 'Situating the Renewal: Reflections on Labour Studies in India', *Labor and Development*, 5:1,1999.

Molund, Stefan, *First We are People: The Koris of Kanpur between Caste and Class* (Stockholm 1988).

Moore, W.E., *The Impact of Industry* (New Delhi 1969).

Morris, Morris David, *The Emergence of an Industrial Labour Force in India: A Study of the Bombay Cotton Mills, 1854–1947* (Oxford 1965).

————, 'The Recruitment of an Industrial Labour Force in India, with British and American Comparisons', *Comparative Studies in Society and History*, 2:3, 1959–60.

Mukerjee, Radhakamal, ed., *Fields and Farms in Awadh* (Calcutta 1929).

————, *The Indian Working Class* (Bombay 1948).

Mukherjee, Rudrangshu, *Spectre of Violence: The 1857 Kanpur Massacres* (New Delhi 1998).

Munshi, S., 'Industrial Labour in Developing Economies: A Critique of the Labour Commitment Theory', *EPW*, 12:35, Aug. 1977.

Murphy, E.D., *Unions in Conflict: A Comparative Study of Four South Indian Textile Centres, 1918–1939* (New Delhi 1981).

Myers, Charles A., *Labour Problems in the Industrialisation of India* (Cambridge 1958).

Nair, Janaki, *Miners and Millhands: Work, Culture and Politics in Princely Mysore* (New Delhi 1998).

Newman, R. K., 'Social Factors in the Recruitment of Bombay Millhands', in K.N. Chaudhuri and C.J. Dewey, eds, *Economy and Society: Essays in Indian Economic and Social History* (Delhi 1979).

Newman, R., *Workers and Unions in Bombay, 1918–1929: A Study of Organization in the Cotton Mills* (Canberra 1981).

Niehoff, A., *Factory Workers in India* (Milwaukee 1959).

O' Hanlon, Rosalind, *Caste, Conflict and Ideology: Mahatma Jotirao Phule and Low Caste Protest in Nineteenth-Century Western India* (Cambridge 1985).

Oldenberg, Veena T., *The Making of Colonial Lucknow: 1856–1877* (Princeton 1984).

Omvedt, G., *Dalits and the Democratic Revolution: Dr Ambedkar and the Dalit Movement in Colonial India* (Delhi 1994).

————, *Dalit Visions* (Delhi 1995).

Pakulski, Jan, 'The Dying of Class or of Marxist Theory?' *International Sociology*, 8, 1993.

Pandey, Gyanendra, 'Economic Dislocation in Nineteenth Century Eastern Uttar Pradesh: Some Implications of the Decline of Artisanal

Industry in Colonial India', in Peter Robb, ed., *Rural South Asia: Linkages, Change and Development* (London 1983).

————, *The Ascendancy of the Congress in Uttar Pradesh, 1926–34: A Study in Imperfect Mobilization* (Delhi 1978).

————, 'The Bigoted Julaha', in *The Construction of Communalism in Colonial North India* (Delhi 1990).

Pandey, S.M., *As Labour Organises: A Study of Unionism in the Kanpur Cotton Textile Industry* (New Delhi 1970).

Parks, Fanny, *Wanderings of a Pilgrim in Search of the Picturesque* (Karachi 1975, first pub. London 1850).

Parry, Jonathan P., 'Lords of Labour: Working and Shirking in Bhilai', in Parry, J. Breman and Karin Kapadia, eds, *The Worlds of Indian Industrial Labour* (New Delhi 1999).

Passerini, Luisa, *Fascism in Popular Memory: The Cultural Experience of the Turin Working Class* (Cambridge 1987).

Patel, S., *The Making of Industrial Relations: The Ahmedabad Textile Industry, 1918–1939* (Delhi 1987).

Pearse, Arno, *The Cotton Industry of India* (Manchester 1930).

Pecheux, Michel, *Language, Semantics and Ideology* (Macmillan 1982).

Perks, Robert and Alistair Thomson, eds, *The Oral History Reader* (London 1998).

Perrot, Michel, *Workers on Strike: France, 1871–1890* (Paris 1984, Leamington Spa 1987).

Prashad, Vijay, *Untouchable Freedom: A Social History of the Dalit Community* (Oxford 2000).

Price, Richard, 'Structures of Subordination in Nineteenth-Century British Industry', in P. Thane, et al. eds, *The Power of the Past: Essays for Eric Hobsbawm* (Cambridge 1984).

Punekar, S.D., *Trade Unionism in India: A Study of Industrial Democracy* (Bombay 1948).

Radhakrishna, Meena, 'Colonial Construction of a "Criminal Tribe": The Itinerant Trading Communities of Madras Presidency', in Neera Chandoke, ed., *Mapping Histories: Essays Presented to Ravinder Kumar* (New Delhi 2000).

Rajadhyaksha, Ashish and Paul Willemen, *Encyclopaedia of Indian Cinema* (New Delhi 1999).

Ranciere, Jacques, 'The Myth of the Artisan: Critical Reflections on a Category of Social History', in Cynthia K. Koepp and Steven L. Kaplan, eds, *Work in France* (New York 1987).

Read, M,, *The Indian Peasant Uprooted* (London 1931).

————, *From Field to Factory: An Introductory Study of the Indian Peasant Turned Factory Hand* (London 1927).

Reddy, William, *Rise of Market Culture: The Textile Trade and French Society, 1750–1900* (Cambridge 1984).

Roberts, Emma, *Hindostan: The Shores of the Red Sea and the Mountains*, vol. 2 (London n.d.).

Rohini P.H., Sujata, S.V. and Neelam, C., eds, *My Life is One Long Struggle: Women, Work, Organization and Struggle* (Madras n.d.).

Rose, Sonya, 'Gender at Work: Sex, Class and Industrial Capitalism', *History Workshop*, 21,1986.

Roy, Tirthankar, 'Economic Reforms and Textile Industry in India', *EPW*, 33, 32, 1998.

Sarkar, Sumit, *The Swadeshi Movement in Bengal: 1903–1908* (New Delhi 1977).

————, 'The Logic of Gandhian Nationalism: Civil Disobedience and the Gandhi–Irwin Pact (1930–31), *IHR*, 3:1, 1976.

————, *Writing Social History* (Delhi 1998).

Sarkar, Tanika, 'The First Phase of Civil Disobedience in Bengal, 1929–31', *IHR*, 4:1, July 1977.

————, *Hindu Wife and Hindu Nation: Community, Religion and Cultural Nationalism* (Delhi 2001).

Scott, James C., *Weapons of the Weak: Everyday Forms of Peasant Resistance* (Yale 1985).

————, *Domination and the Arts of Resistance: Hidden Transcripts* (Yale 1990).

Secombe, Wally, 'Patriarchy Stabilized: The Construction of the Male Breadwinner Wage Norm in Nineteenth Century Britain', *Social History*, 11:1, 1986.

Segalen, Martine, 'The Industrial Revolution: From Proletariat to Bourgeoisie', in Andre Burguiere and Christiane Klapisch-Zuber, eds, *A History of the Family, Vol. II: The Impact of Modernity* (Paris 1986, Oxford 1996).

Sen, Samita, *Women and Labour in Late Colonial India: The Bengal Jute Industry* (Cambridge 1999).

————, 'Gendered Exclusion: Domesticity and Dependence in Bengal', *International Review of Social History, Supplement*, 5:42, 1997.

Sen, Sukomal, *Working Class of India: History of Emergence and Movement, 1830–1970* (Calcutta 1979).

Sewell, William, *Work and Revolution in France: The Language of Labour from the Old Regime to 1848* (Cambridge 1980).

Sharma, Baldev R., 'The Industrial Worker: Some Myths and Realities', *EPW*, 5: 22, May 1970.

Sharma, G.K., *Labour Movement in India* (Delhi 1963).

Sharma, Sadhna, 'The Organisation, Development and Working of Kanpur Mazdur Sabha', Unpublished Masters Dissertation in Economics, Agra University, 1952.

Sharma, Sanjay, *Famine, Philanthropy and the Colonial State: North India in the Early Nineteenth Century* (New Delhi 2001).

Sharpe, Jenny, *Allegories of Empire: The Figure of Woman in the Colonial Text* (Minneapolis 1993).

Shepherd, W.J., *A Personal Narrative of the Outbreak and Massacre at Cawnpore during the Sepoy Revolt* (Lucknow 1879, New Delhi 1980).

Shiva Rao, B., *The Industrial Worker in India* (London 1939).

Siddiqi, Asiya, *Agrarian Change in a North Indian State* (Oxford 1973).

Simeon, Dilip, *The Politics of Labour Under Late Colonialism: Workers, Unions and the State in Chota Nagpur, 1928–29* (Delhi 1995).

————, 'Work and Resistance in the Jharia Coalfield', in J. Parry, ed., *The Worlds of Indian Industrial Labour.*

Simmons, C.P., 'Recruiting and Organizing an Industrial Labour Force in Colonial India: The Case of the Coal Mining Industry, 1880–1939', *IESHR,* 13:4, 1976.

Singh, V.B., *Climate for Industrial Relations: A Study of Kanpur Cotton Mills* (Bombay 1968).

————, *Wage Patterns, Mobility and Savings of Workers in India* (Bombay 1973).

Somers, Margaret R., 'Deconstructing and Reconstructing Class Formation Theory: Narrativity, Relational Analysis, and Social Theory', in John R. Hall, ed., *Reworking Class* (Cornell 1997).

Srivastava, G.N., *When Congress Ruled* (Lucknow n.d.)

Sukhatme, P.V., 'Assessement of Adequacy of Diets at Different Income Levels', *EPW,* 12:31, 32, 33, Aug. 1978.

————, 'Measurement of Undernutrition, *EPW,* 17:50, Dec. 1982.

————, 'Measuring Increase of Undernutrition: A Comment', *EPW,* 16:23, June 1981.

————, 'On Measurement of Poverty', *EPW,* 16:32, Aug. 1981.

Tajbaksh, Kian, 'History of a Subject or the Subjects of a History? Or Is a Labour History Possible?' *Studies in History,* 11:1, 1995.

Thomas, D.A., 'Lucknow and Kanpur,1880–1920: Stagnation and Development under the Raj', *South Asia,* 5:2, New Series, 1982.

Thompson, E.P., *The Making of the English Working Class* (Harmondsworth 1968).

————, 'Time, Work-Discipline and Industrial Capitalism', *Past and Present,* 38, Dec. 1967.

————, 'The Moral Economy of the English Crowd in the Eighteenth Century', *Past and Present*, 50, 1971.

————, 'Eighteenth-Century English Society: Class Struggle Without Class?' *Social History*, 3: 2, May 1978.

Tilly, Louise A., 'Individual Lives and Family Strategies in the French Proletariat', *Journal of Family History*, 4:1979.

Trevelyan, G.O., *Cawnpore* (London 1865).

Upadhyaya, Shashi Bhushan, 'Cotton Mill Workers in Bombay, 1875–1918: Conditions of Life and Work', *EPW*, 25:30, July 1990.

Vaid, K.N., *Papers on Absenteeism* (New Delhi 1967).

Varady, R.G., 'The Diary of Road: A Sequential Narration of the Origins of the Lucknow–Kanpur Road (1825–1856)', *IESHR*, 15:2, 1978.

Vigarello, Georges, *Concepts of Cleanliness: Changing Attitudes in France since the Middle Ages* (Cambridge 1988).

Walby, Sylvia, *Patriarchy at Work: Patriarchal and Capitalist Relations in Employment* (Polity 1986).

Ward, Andrew, *Our Bones are Scattered: The Cawnpore Massacres and the Indian Mutiny of 1857* (London 1996).

Wersch, H. van, *The Bombay Textile Strike, 1982–83* (Bombay 1982).

Whitehead, Judy, 'Bodies Clean and Unclean: Prostitution, Sanitary Legislation and Respectable Feminity in Colonial India', *Gender and History*, 7:1, 1995.

Whipp, R., ' "A Time to Every Purpose": An Essay on Time and Work', in Patrick Joyce, ed., *The Historical Meanings of Work* (Cambridge 1987).

Willis, Paul, *Learning to Labour: How Working Class Kids Get Working Class Jobs* (Guildford 1977).

Yalland, Z., *A Guide to the Kacheri Cemetery and the Early History of Kanpur* (London 1983).

————, *Boxwallahs: The British in Cawnpore, 1857–1901* (Norwich 1994).

————, *Traders and Nabobs: The British in Cawnpore, 1765–1857* (Salisbury 1987).

Yeo, Eileen and Stephen Yeo, *Popular Culture and Class Conflict* (Sussex 1981).

Index

absenteeism, 91–3; and managers, 172; in trade union discourse, 174; and weaving, 162
accidents, 163–4
Achutanand, 248
akharas, 117, 118–19, 222; and nationalists, 279–80
Allen, G., 35, 42
Arora, Arjun, 207, 218, 224, 244n
Arora, Narayan Prasad, 279, 303
Artisans and service groups, 15–16, 17, 21, 72
Arya Samaj, and communal politics, 269–70, 272–3; and KMS, 188–90, 243; and lower-caste mobilisation, 245–8; see also Vidyarthi
authority, of managers, 154–5; of mistris, 133, 146–54; opposition to, 168–9; see also work discipline
Azizan, 310–11

badlis, 67–8, 116, 132, 140, 164, 172, 208
Brahmans, in the labour force, 81–3
Breach of Contract (Act xii, 1859), 77–8

cantonment, boundaries of, 23, 27–9; and place names 33–4; and prostitutes, 28–9; and sanitation, 57–9; see also space
caste, and KMS, 190, 253–4; and mistris, 83–4; organisations, 248–53; and housing, 237–9, 106–7; and women, 85–6, 241; and the workplace, 79–84, 239–42
casual labour, 21, 72, 115–16, 140
Chakr, Sudarshan, and Communists, 282; on KMS, 180,186–8, 190; on lower castes, 255–6; on nationalism, 307–11; and religious idiom, 180, 243–4
Chakrabarty, D., 6–8, 107, 302n
Chamars, and family strategy, 106; in the labour force, 79–81; and origin myths, 250–1; and pollution taboos, 169, 239–42; see also rural links
Chandavarkar, R., 7–8
child workers, in managerial discourse, 88–9, 156–7; numbers of, 68–9, 88; and work discipline, 145
city, commerce and Kanpur, 21–3; in workers' accounts, 108–11, 121; women and the, 111–14
class, 7–11, and community, 237–76; nationalist rhetoric and, 288–92
colonial state, and labour recruitment, 78; and strikes, 191–8, 300–1; workers' images of, 196–9, 304–5
community, and segregation, 237–9; and workplace, 239–43; see also class
communal conflict, and Depression, 207, 208–9; and riots, 261–5; and workers, 211, 263–5; see also Arya Samaj
Communists, and dadas, 118; and KMS, 290–1; and lower castes, 254–6; and mill committees, 222–5, 281; and radical rhetoric, 225–36
Congress, and election campaigns, 209–10; and labour, 292–301, 311–12; and strikes, 216, 218
consumption, and calorie intake, 139–40; and Depression, 142; and income levels, 140–2
coolies, 21, 72; see also casual labour

discourse, 174–5; and worker collectivities, 190

work discipline, and fines, 144–5; and managers, 169–73; *see also* everyday resistance, mistris, trade unions, War period

work, and its representations, 316–18

working-class neighbourhoods, and communal riots, 262–5; and strikes, 210

workload, rationalisation and; 67, 161–2, 209; women and, 163n; *see also* shift system, War period

Yusuf, Sant Singh, 280–1

www.ingramcontent.com/pod-product-compliance
Lightning Source LLC
Chambersburg PA
CBHW061000280326
41935CB00009B/771